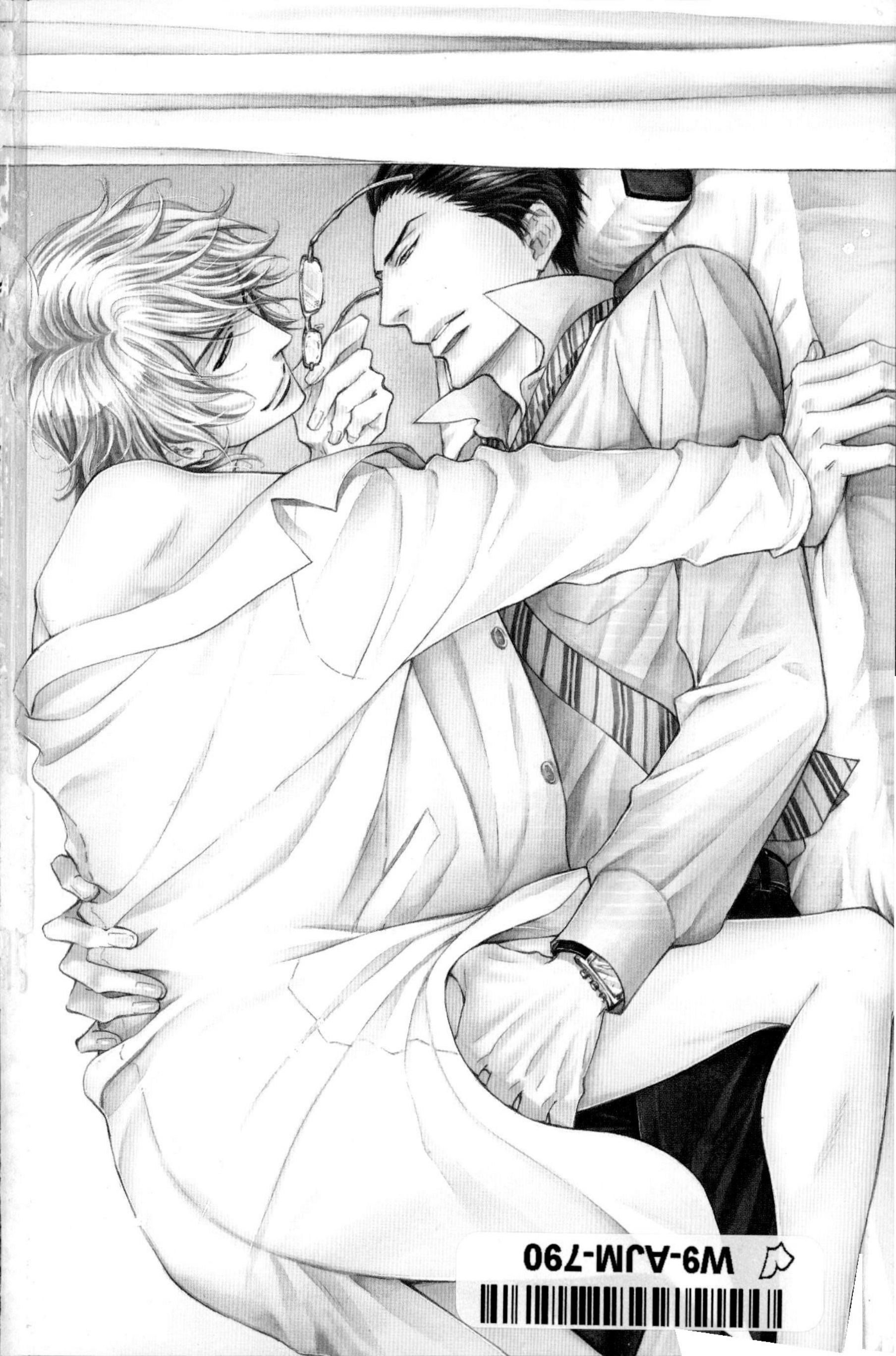

Story and Art by Yaya Sakuragi

volume 2

CONTENTS

SuBLime Manga Edition

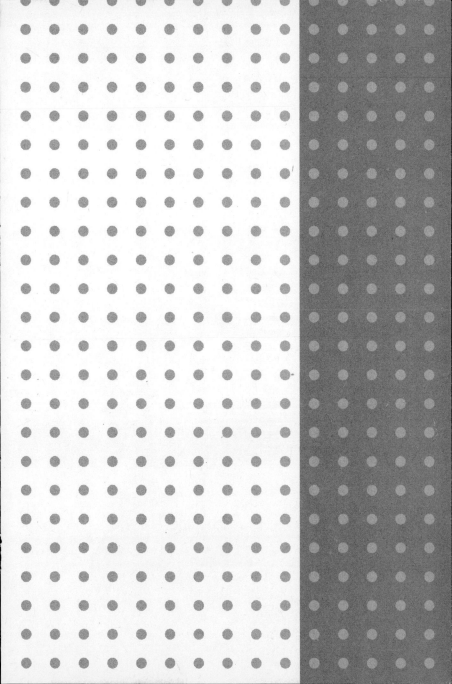

ASUKA COMICS CL-DX

秘めごとあそび

2

桜城やや
YAYA SAKURAGI

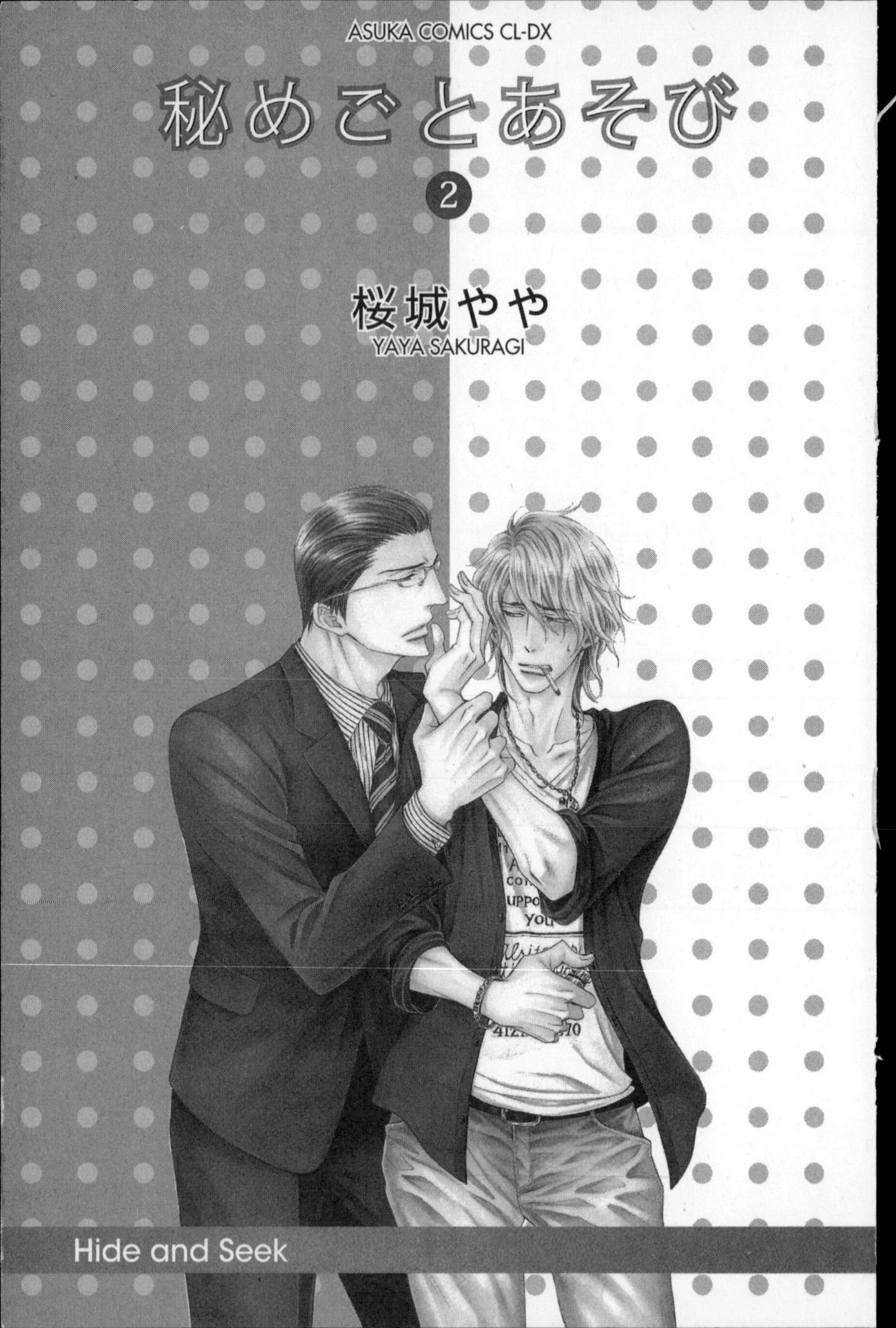

Hide and Seek

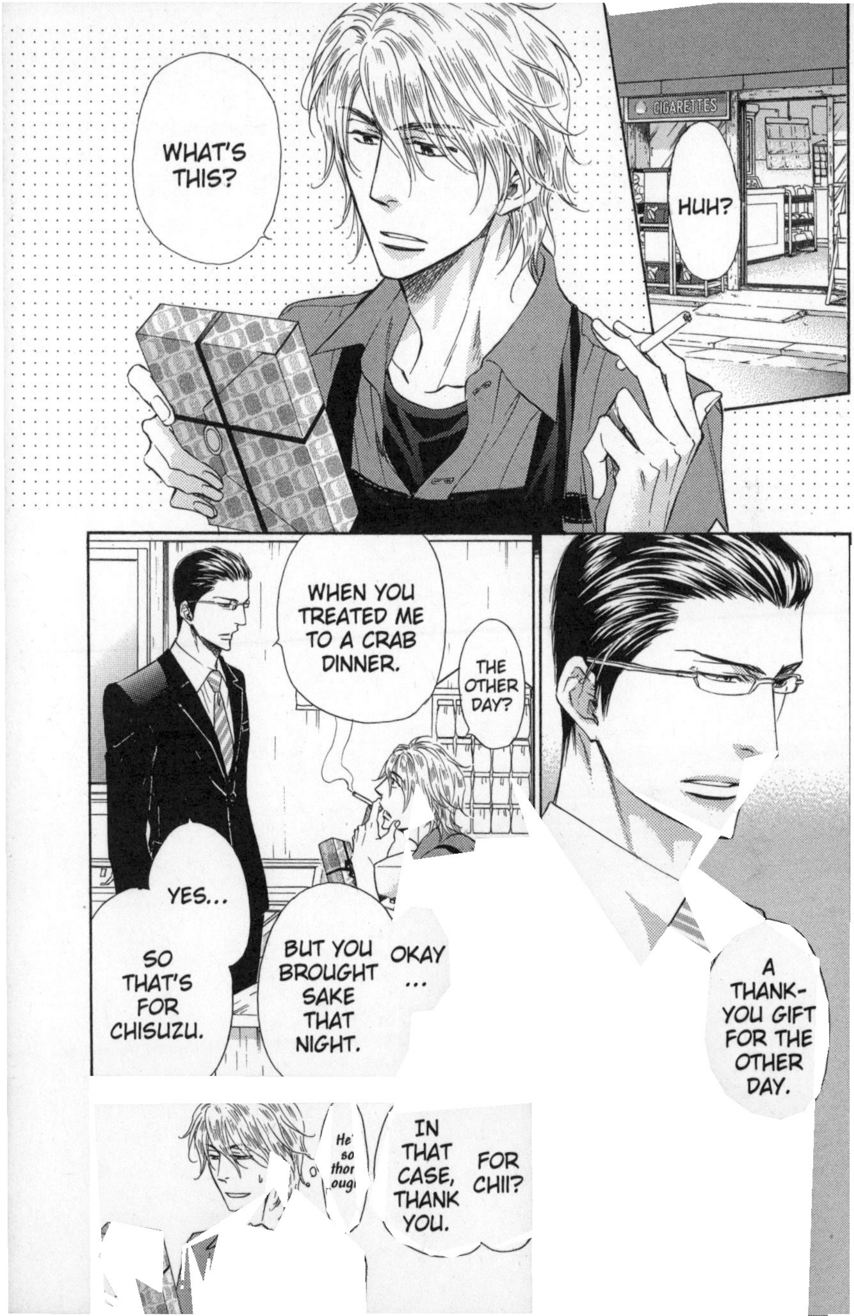
CIGARETTES
HUH?
WHAT'S THIS?
A THANK-YOU GIFT FOR THE OTHER DAY.
THE OTHER DAY?
WHEN YOU TREATED ME TO A CRAB DINNER.
OKAY...
BUT YOU BROUGHT SAKE THAT NIGHT.
YES...
SO THAT'S FOR CHISUZU.
FOR CHII?
IN THAT CASE, THANK YOU.

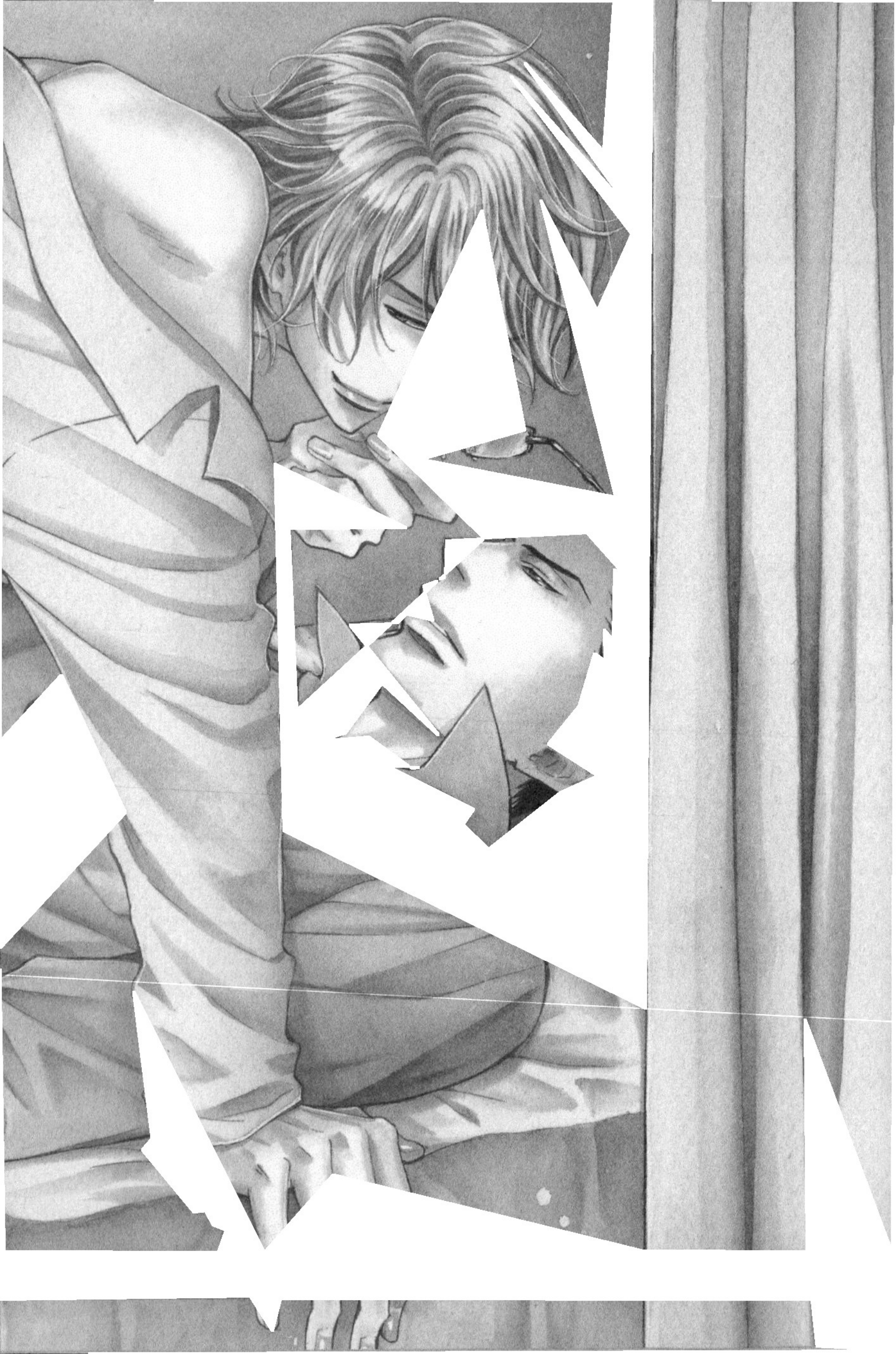

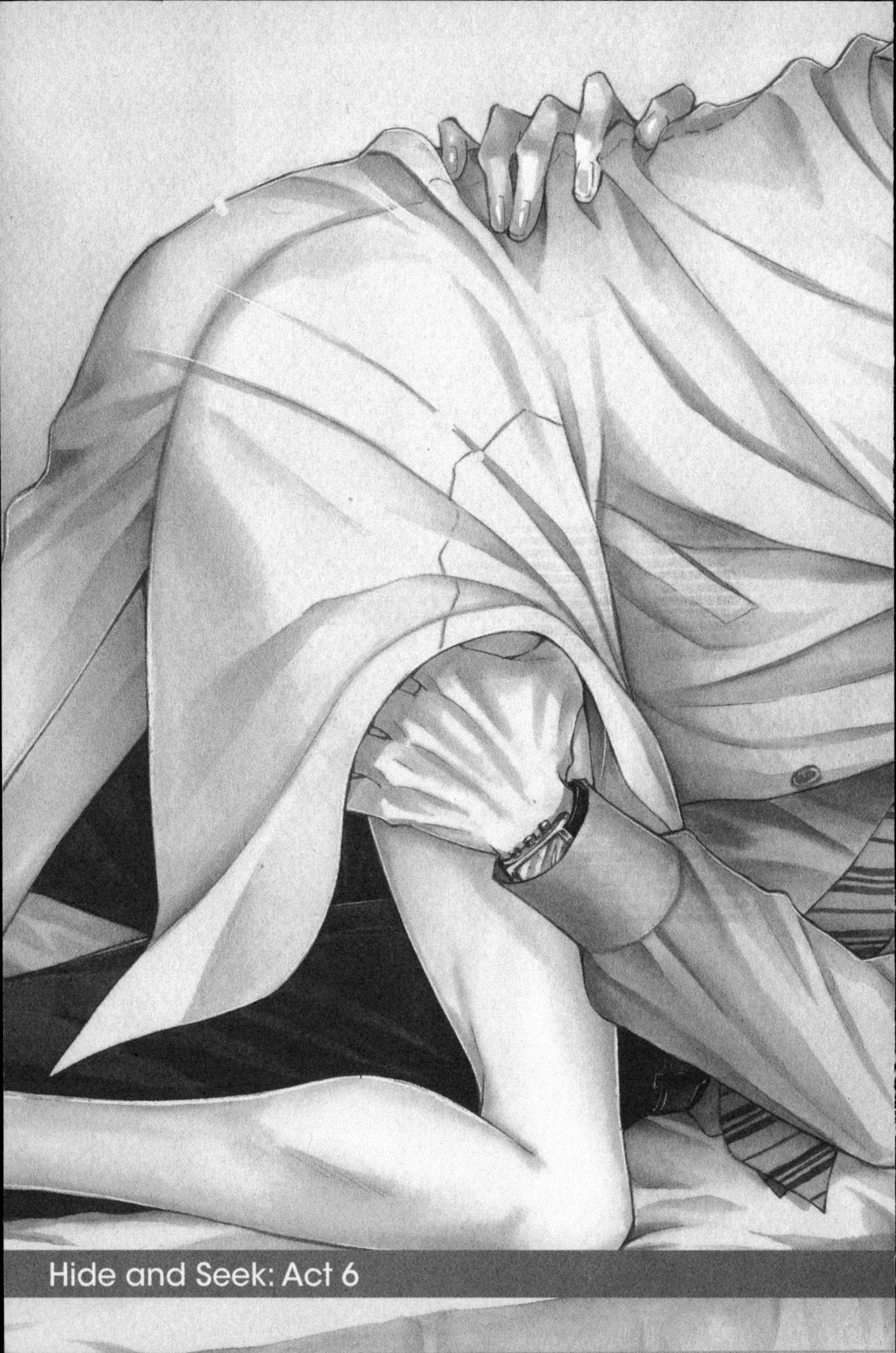
Hide and Seek: Act 6

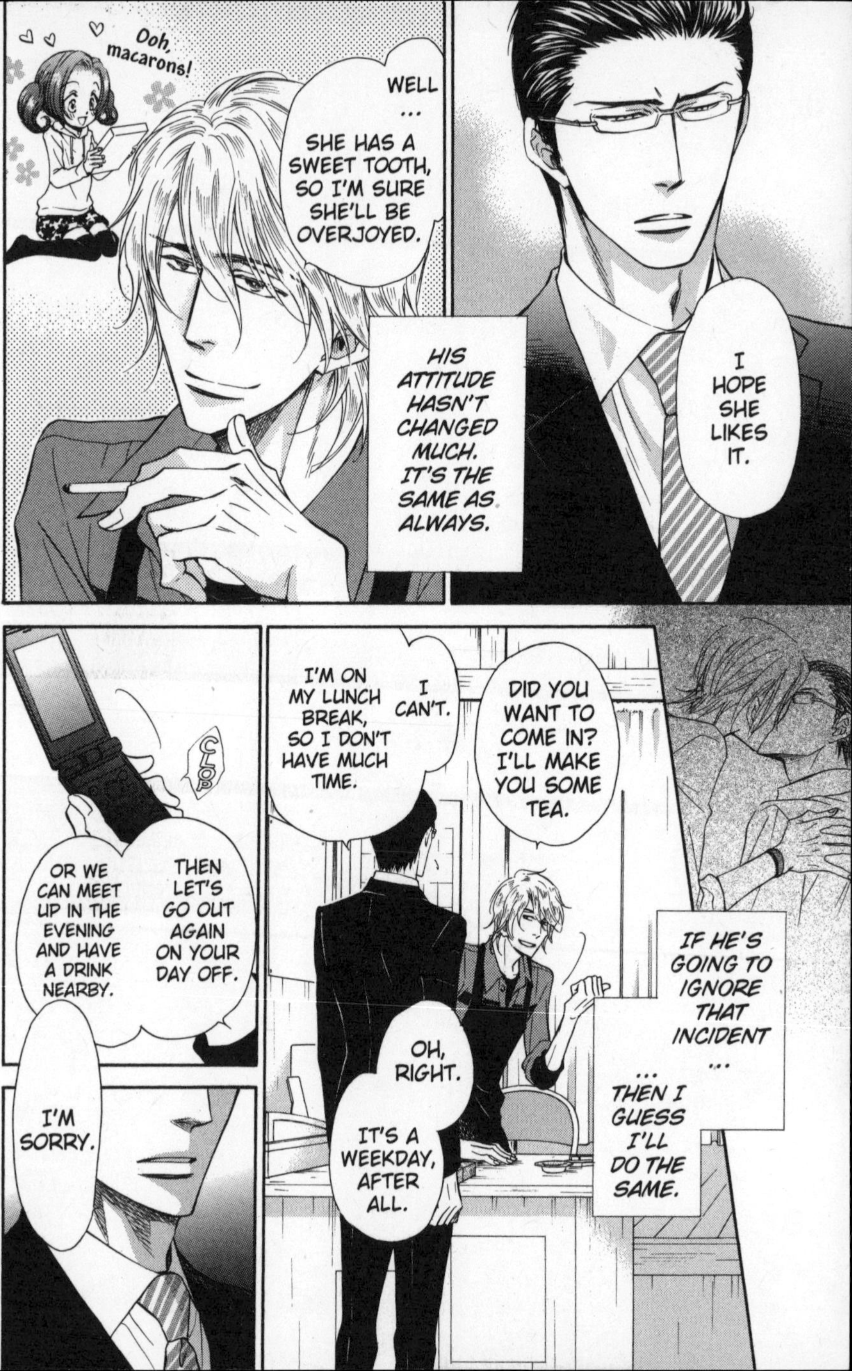
I HOPE SHE LIKES IT.
WELL ...
SHE HAS A SWEET TOOTH, SO I'M SURE SHE'LL BE OVERJOYED.
Ooh, macarons!
HIS ATTITUDE HASN'T CHANGED MUCH. IT'S THE SAME AS ALWAYS.
IF HE'S GOING TO IGNORE THAT INCIDENT ...
... THEN I GUESS I'LL DO THE SAME.
DID YOU WANT TO COME IN? I'LL MAKE YOU SOME TEA.
I CAN'T.
I'M ON MY LUNCH BREAK, SO I DON'T HAVE MUCH TIME.
OH, RIGHT.
IT'S A WEEKDAY, AFTER ALL.
CLOP
THEN LET'S GO OUT AGAIN ON YOUR DAY OFF.
OR WE CAN MEET UP IN THE EVENING AND HAVE A DRINK NEARBY.
I'M SORRY.

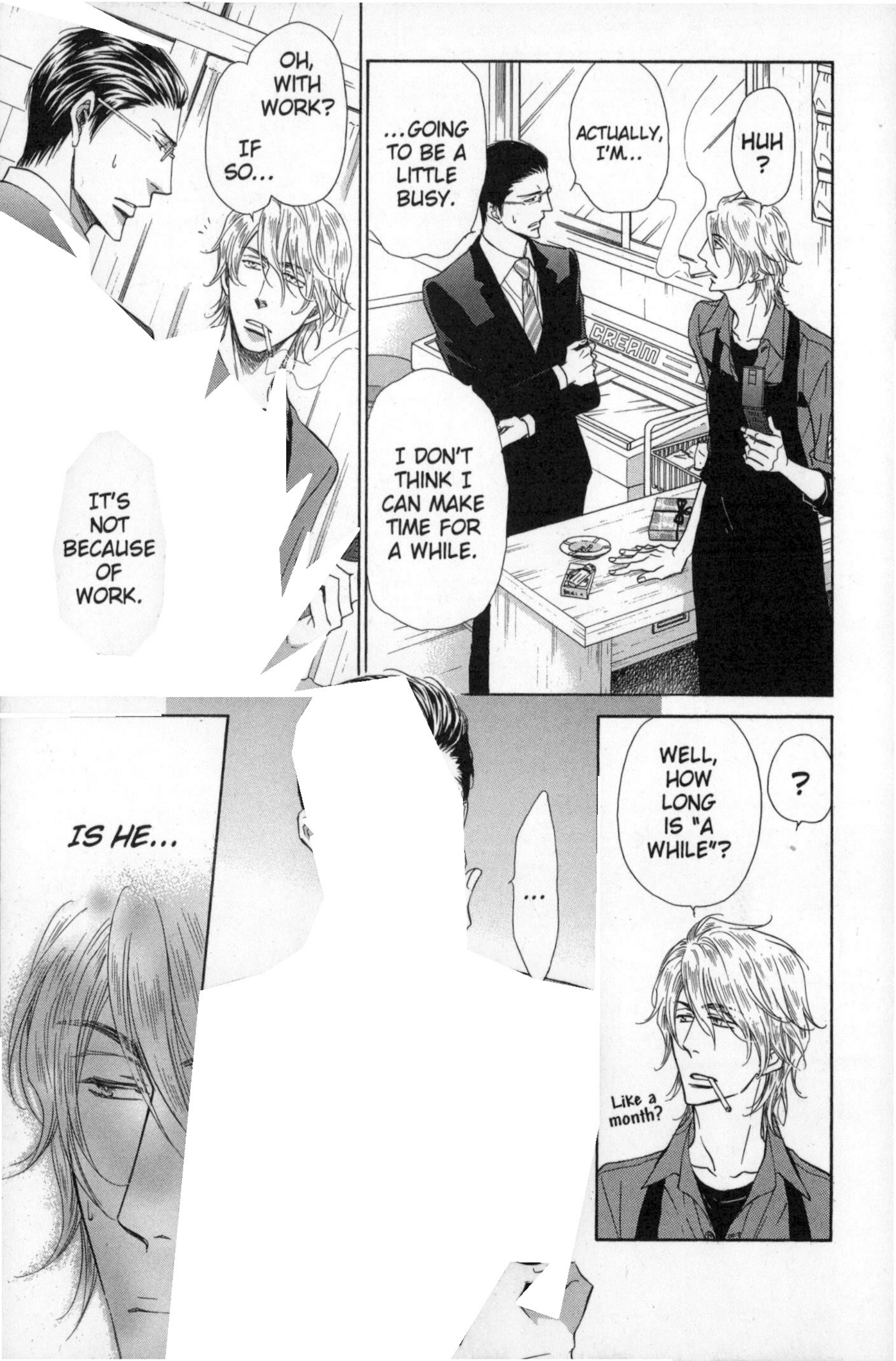
HUH?
ACTUALLY, I'M...
...GOING TO BE A LITTLE BUSY.
I DON'T THINK I CAN MAKE TIME FOR A WHILE.
OH, WITH WORK? IF SO...
IT'S NOT BECAUSE OF WORK.
?
WELL, HOW LONG IS "A WHILE"?
Like a month?
...
IS HE...

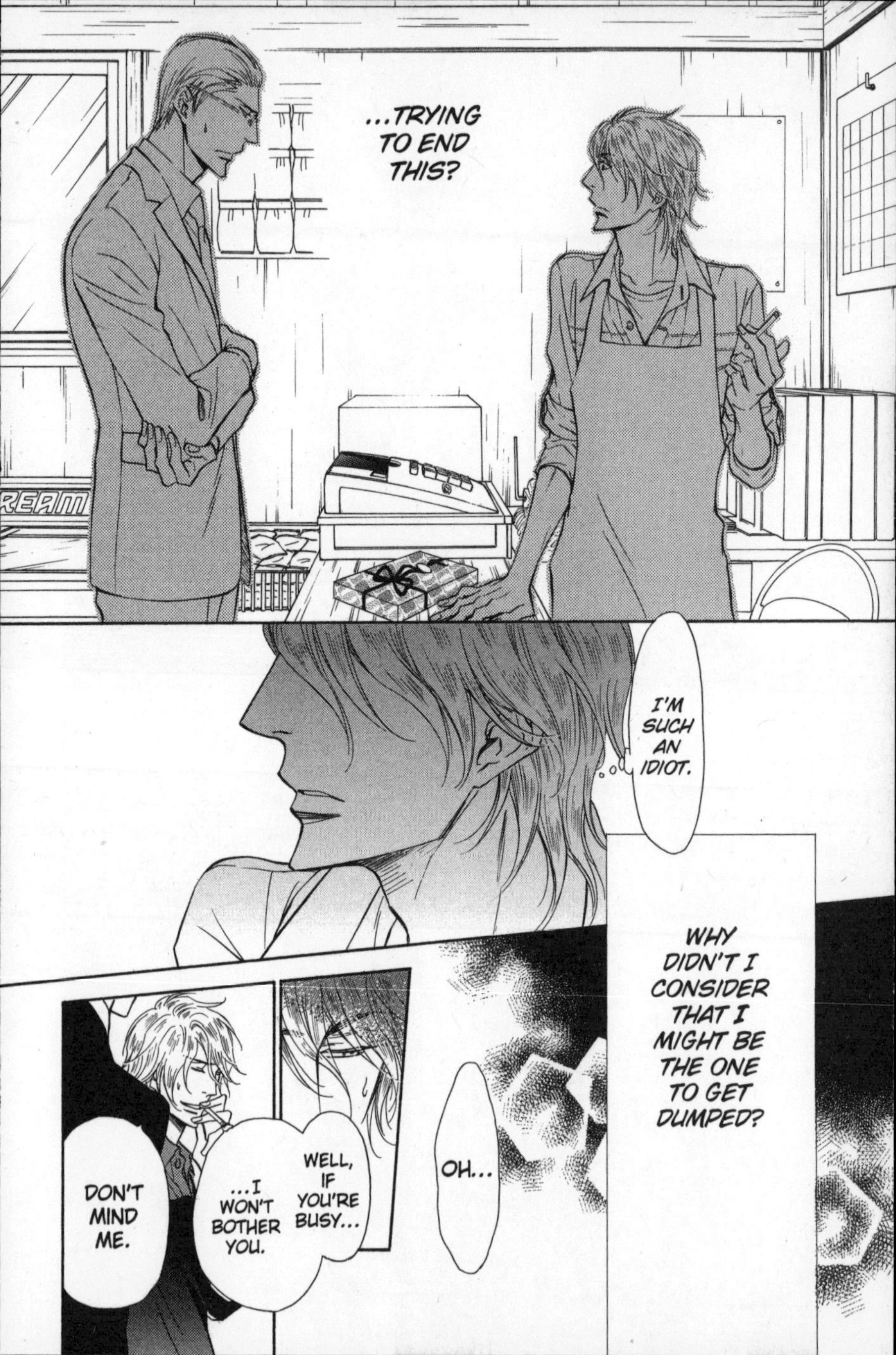
...TRYING TO END THIS?
I'M SUCH AN IDIOT.
WHY DIDN'T I CONSIDER THAT I MIGHT BE THE ONE TO GET DUMPED?
OH...
WELL, IF YOU'RE BUSY...
...I WON'T BOTHER YOU.
DON'T MIND ME.

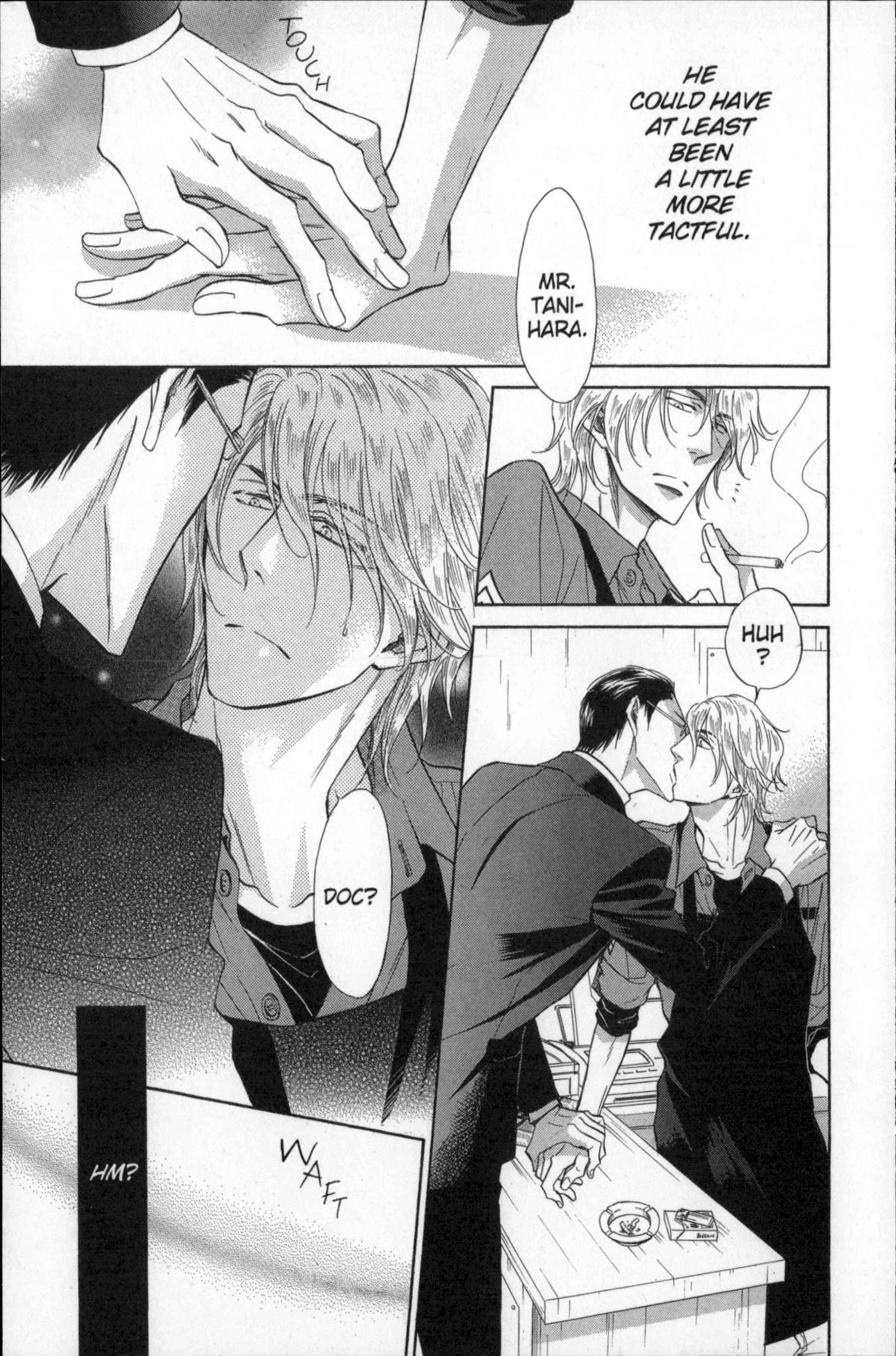
HE COULD HAVE AT LEAST BEEN A LITTLE MORE TACTFUL.
TOUCH
MR. TANI-HARA.
HUH ?
DOC?
WAFT
HM?

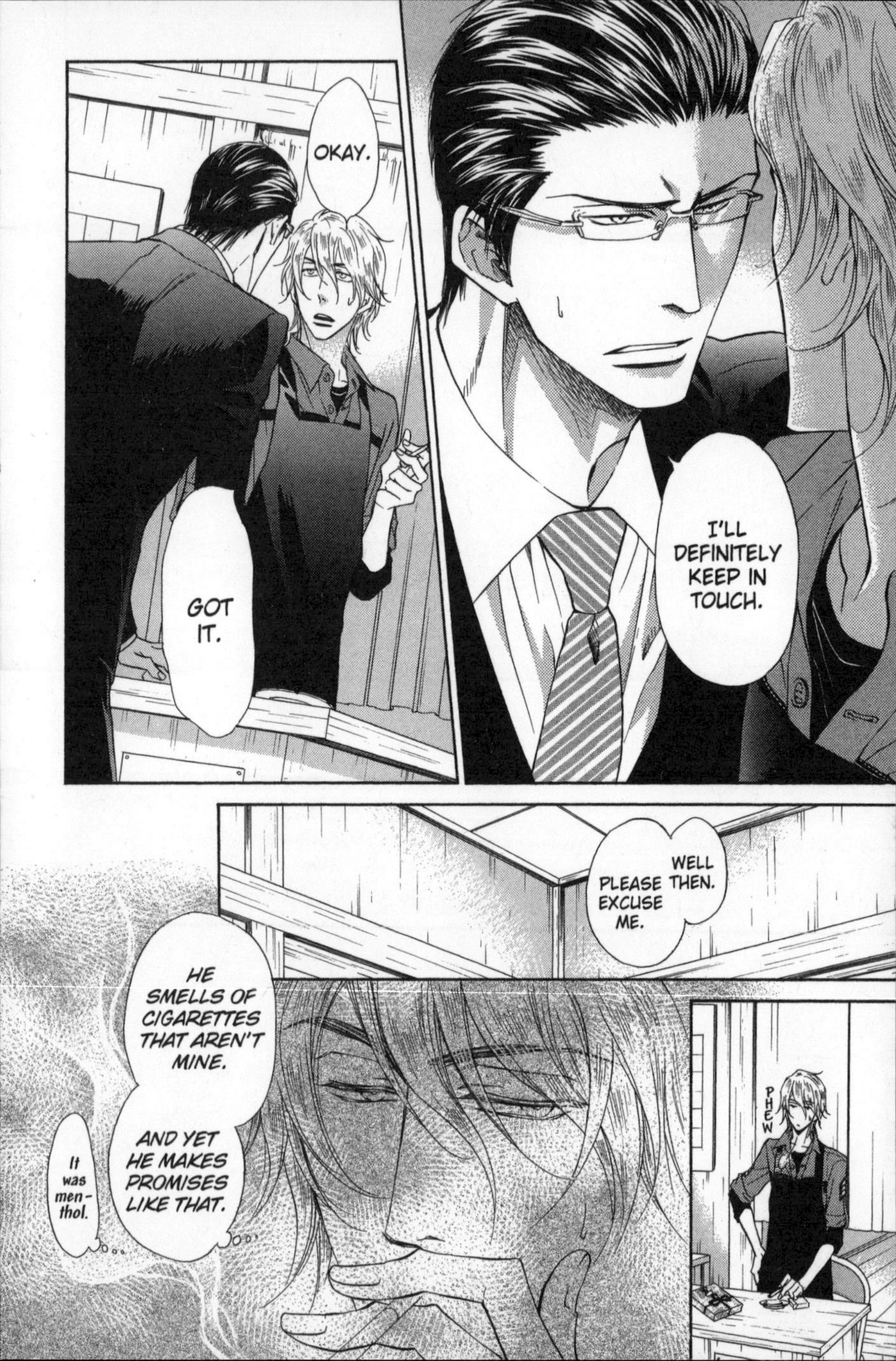
I'LL DEFINITELY KEEP IN TOUCH.
OKAY.
GOT IT.
WELL THEN. PLEASE EXCUSE ME.
PHEW
HE SMELLS OF CIGARETTES THAT AREN'T MINE.
AND YET HE MAKES PROMISES LIKE THAT.
It was men-thol.

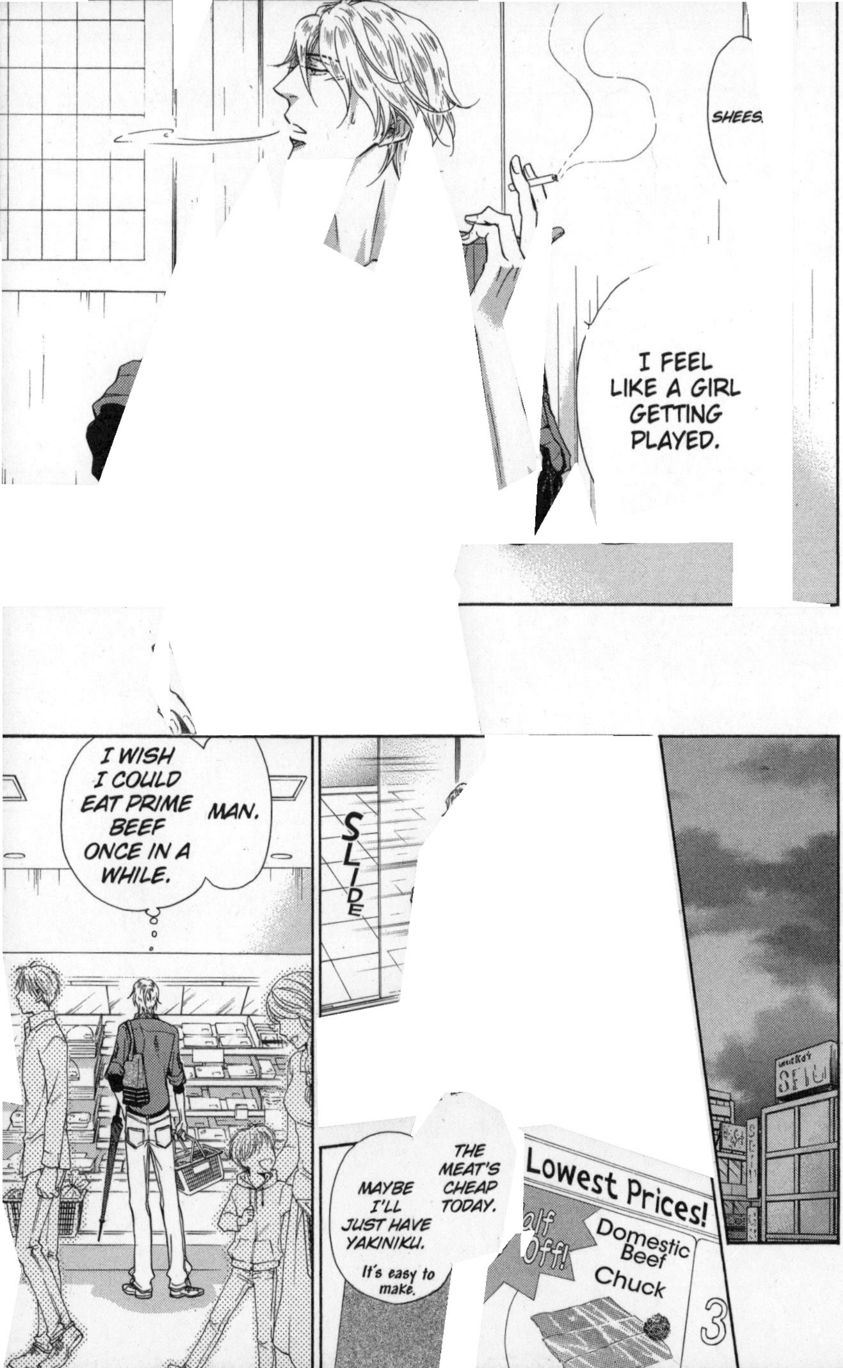
SHEES
I FEEL LIKE A GIRL GETTING PLAYED.
SLIDE
Lowest Prices!
alf Off!
Domestic Beef Chuck
3
THE MEAT'S CHEAP TODAY.
MAYBE I'LL JUST HAVE YAKINIKU.
It's easy to make.
MAN.
I WISH I COULD EAT PRIME BEEF ONCE IN A WHILE.

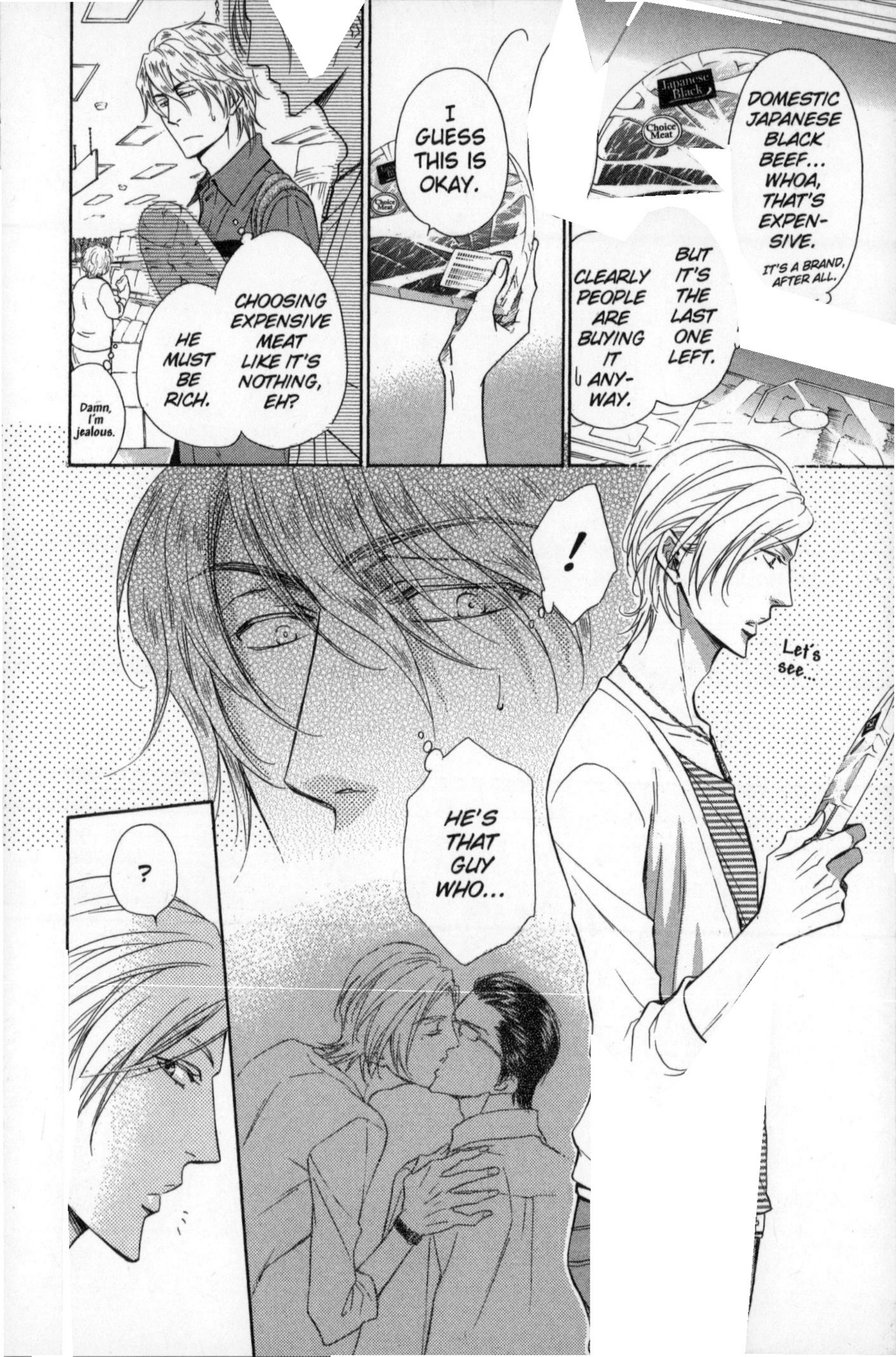
Japanese Black
Choice Meat
DOMESTIC JAPANESE BLACK BEEF... WHOA, THAT'S EXPEN-SIVE.
IT'S A BRAND, AFTER ALL.
BUT IT'S THE LAST ONE LEFT.
CLEARLY PEOPLE ARE BUYING IT ANY-WAY.
I GUESS THIS IS OKAY.
Choice Meat
CHOOSING EXPENSIVE MEAT LIKE IT'S NOTHING, EH?
HE MUST BE RICH.
Damn, I'm jealous.
Let's see...
!
HE'S THAT GUY WHO...
?

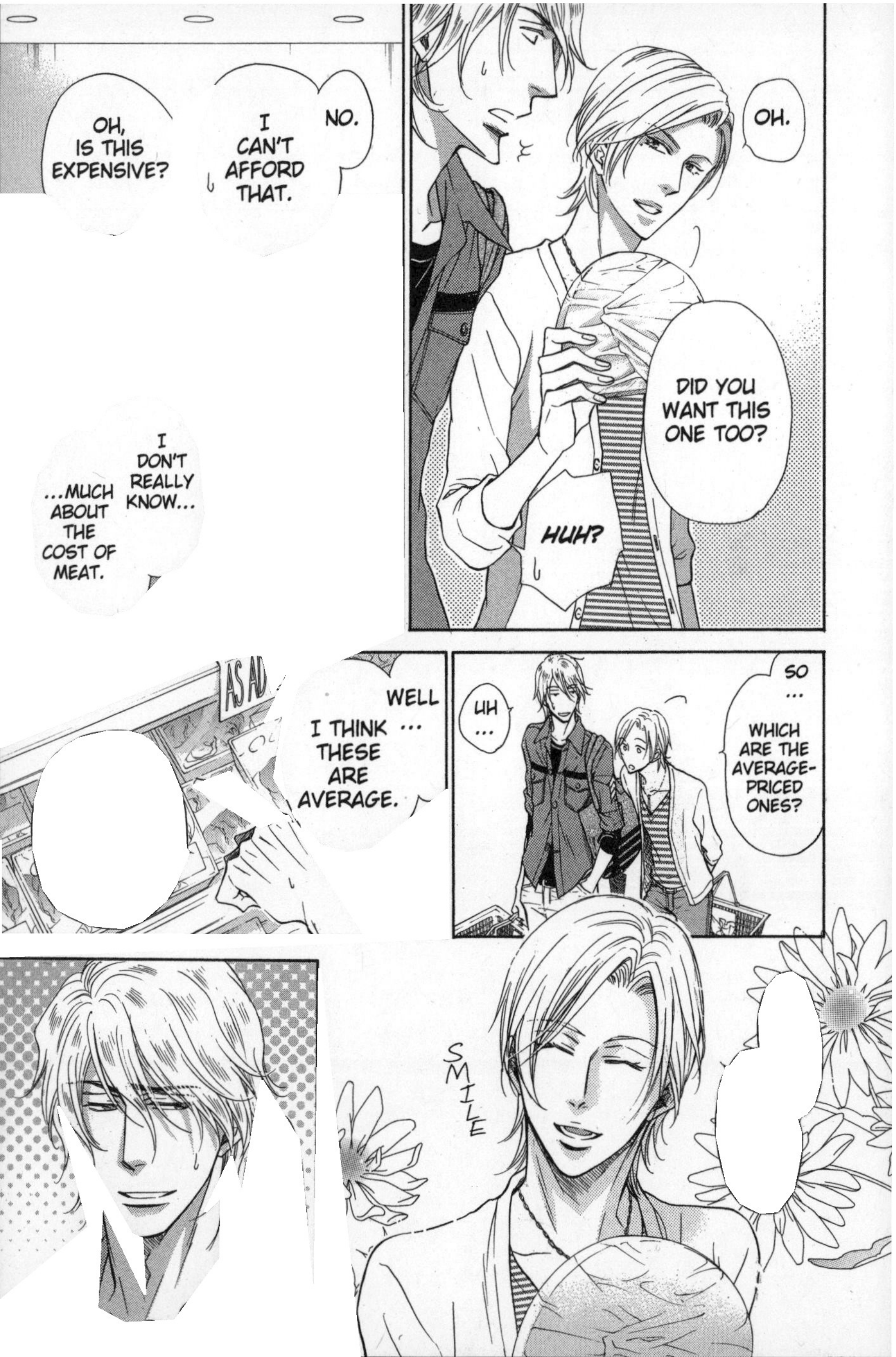
OH.
DID YOU WANT THIS ONE TOO?
HUH?
NO.
I CAN'T AFFORD THAT.
OH, IS THIS EXPENSIVE?
I DON'T REALLY KNOW...
...MUCH ABOUT THE COST OF MEAT.
SO ... WHICH ARE THE AVERAGE-PRICED ONES?
UH ...
WELL ...
I THINK THESE ARE AVERAGE.
SMILE

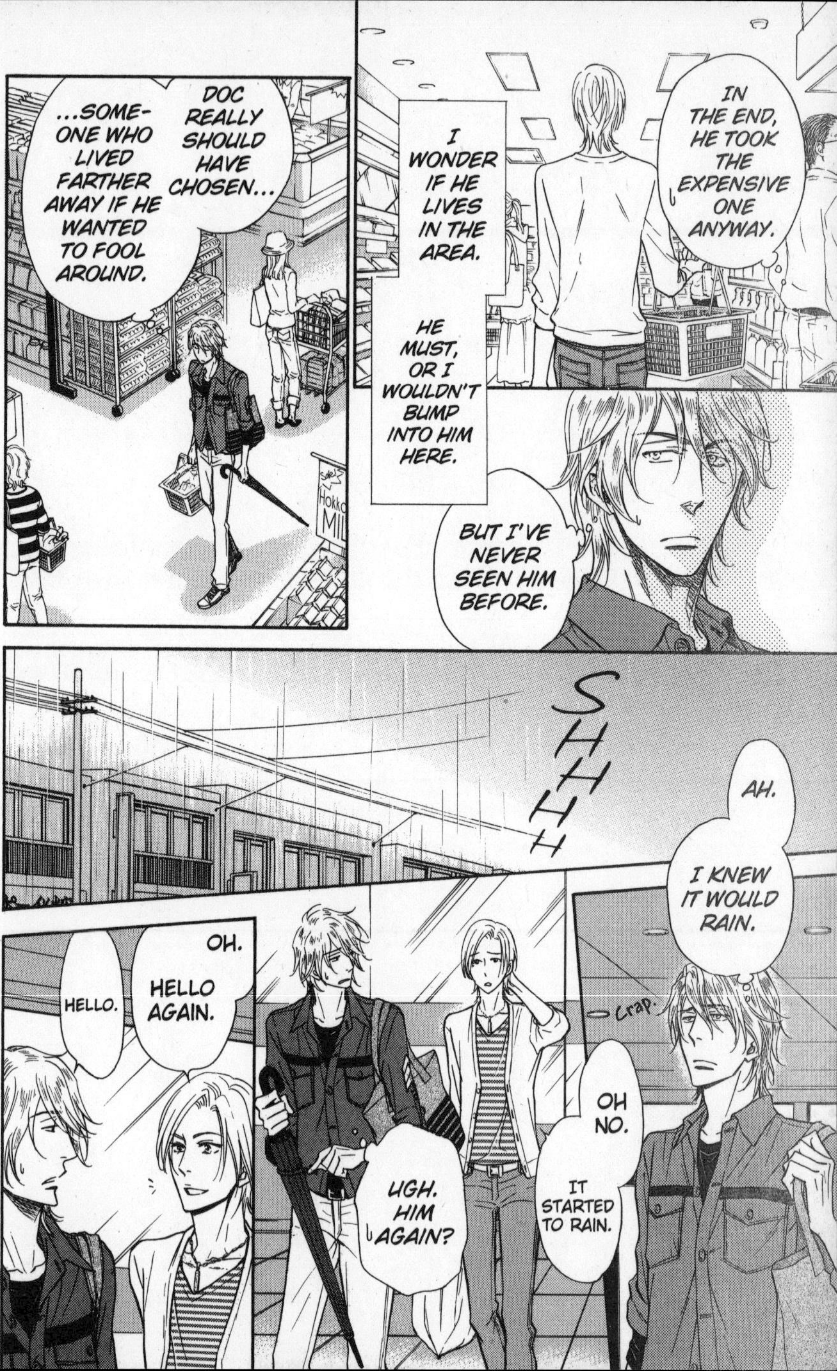
IN THE END, HE TOOK THE EXPENSIVE ONE ANYWAY.
I WONDER IF HE LIVES IN THE AREA.
HE MUST, OR I WOULDN'T BUMP INTO HIM HERE.
BUT I'VE NEVER SEEN HIM BEFORE.
DOC REALLY SHOULD HAVE CHOSEN...
...SOME-ONE WHO LIVED FARTHER AWAY IF HE WANTED TO FOOL AROUND.
SHHHH
AH.
I KNEW IT WOULD RAIN.
Crap.
OH NO.
IT STARTED TO RAIN.
UGH. HIM AGAIN?
OH.
HELLO AGAIN.
HELLO.

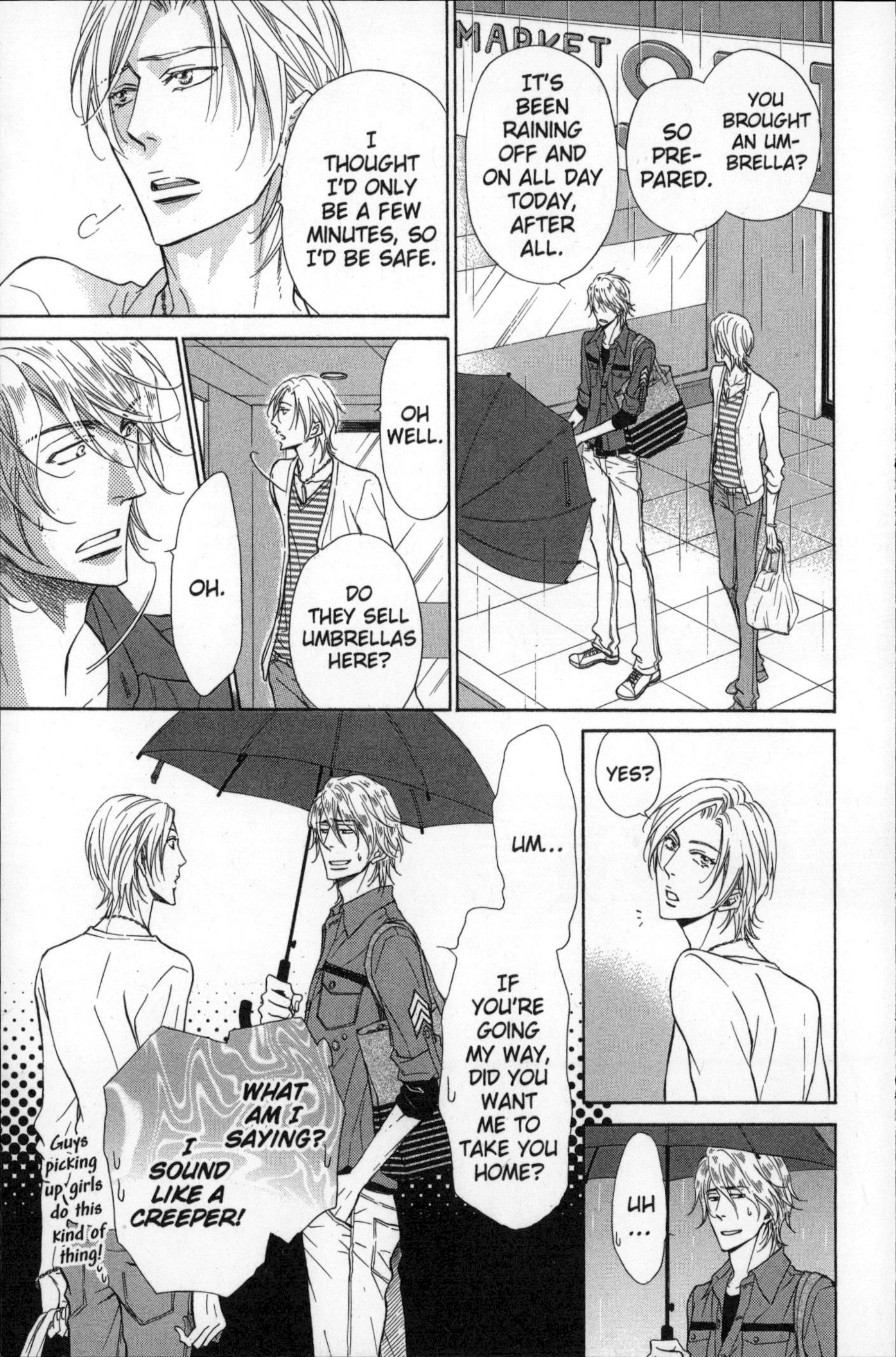
MARKET
YOU BROUGHT AN UM-BRELLA?
SO PRE-PARED.
IT'S BEEN RAINING OFF AND ON ALL DAY TODAY, AFTER ALL.
I THOUGHT I'D ONLY BE A FEW MINUTES, SO I'D BE SAFE.
OH WELL.
DO THEY SELL UMBRELLAS HERE?
OH.
YES?
UH ...
UM..
IF YOU'RE GOING MY WAY, DID YOU WANT ME TO TAKE YOU HOME?
WHAT AM I SAYING?
I SOUND LIKE A CREEPER!
Guys picking up girls do this kind of thing!

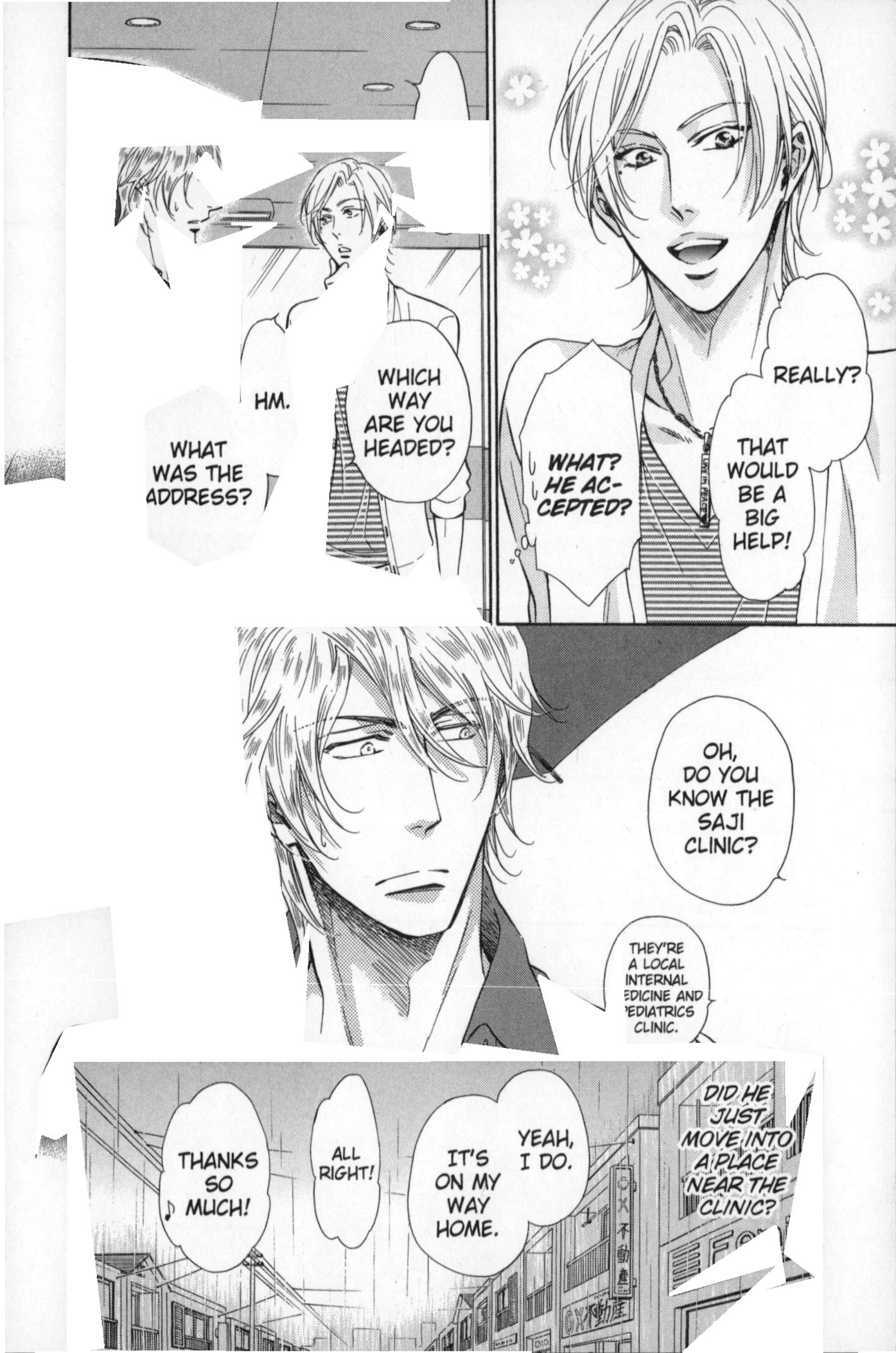
REALLY? THAT WOULD BE A BIG HELP!
WHAT? HE ACCEPTED?
WHICH WAY ARE YOU HEADED?
HM.
WHAT WAS THE ADDRESS?
OH, DO YOU KNOW THE SAJI CLINIC?
THEY'RE A LOCAL INTERNAL EDICINE AND EDIATRICS CLINIC.
DID HE JUST MOVE INTO A PLACE NEAR THE CLINIC?
YEAH, I DO.
IT'S ON MY WAY HOME.
ALL RIGHT!
THANKS SO MUCH! ♪
不動産

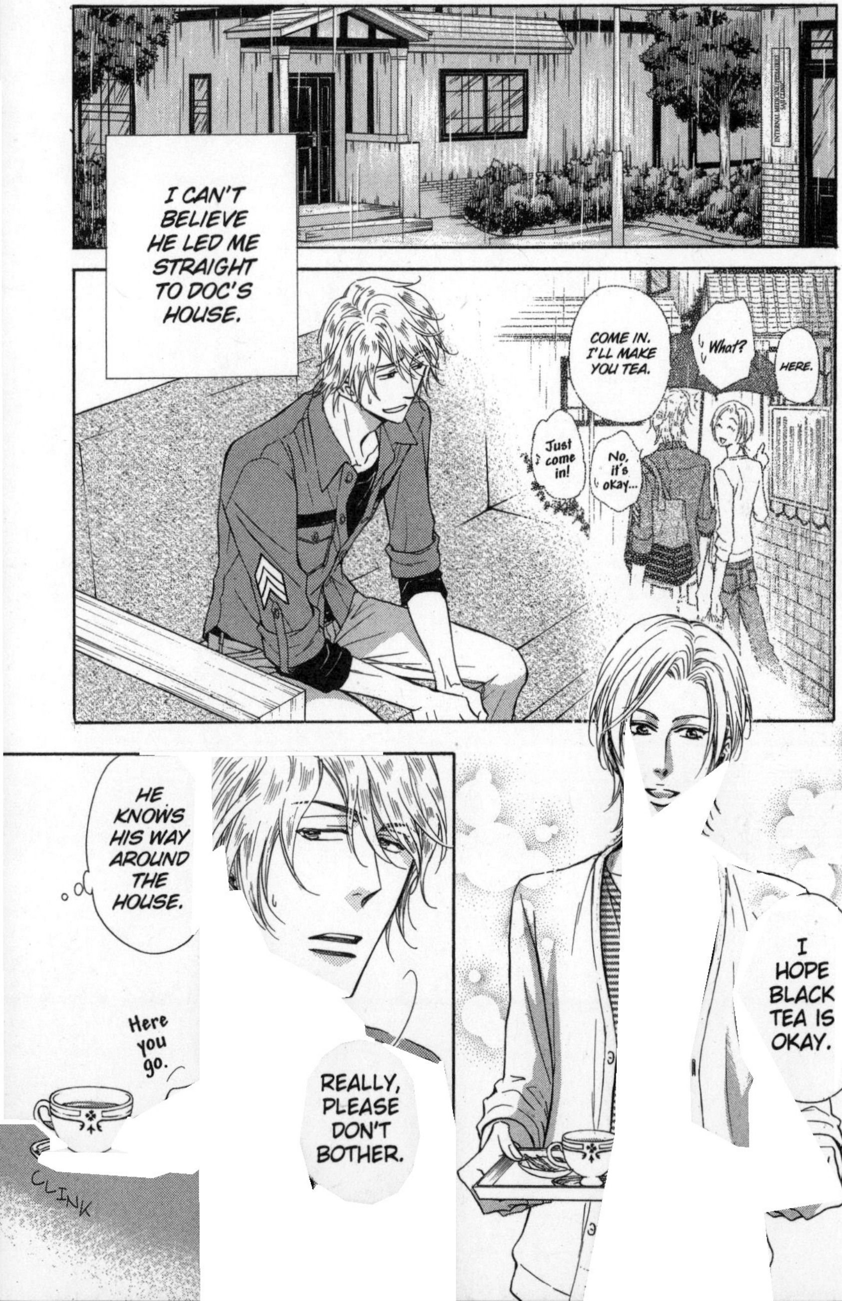
I CAN'T BELIEVE HE LED ME STRAIGHT TO DOC'S HOUSE.
HERE.
What?
COME IN. I'LL MAKE YOU TEA.
No, it's okay...
Just come in!
I HOPE BLACK TEA IS OKAY.
REALLY, PLEASE DON'T BOTHER.
HE KNOWS HIS WAY AROUND THE HOUSE.
Here you go.
CLINK

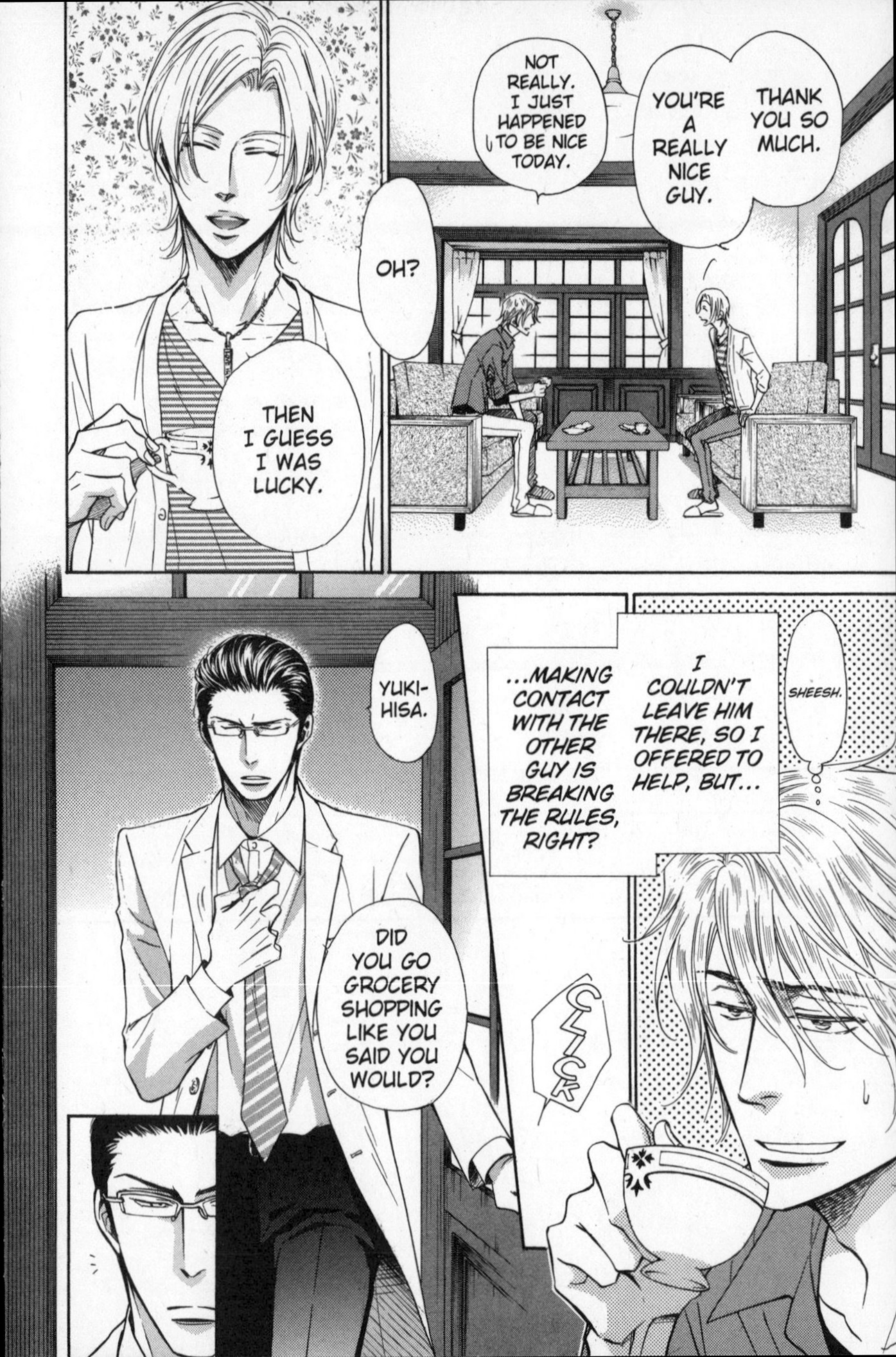
THANK YOU SO MUCH.
YOU'RE A REALLY NICE GUY.
NOT REALLY. I JUST HAPPENED TO BE NICE TODAY.
OH?
THEN I GUESS I WAS LUCKY.
SHEESH.
I COULDN'T LEAVE HIM THERE, SO I OFFERED TO HELP, BUT...
...MAKING CONTACT WITH THE OTHER GUY IS BREAKING THE RULES, RIGHT?
CLICK
YUKI-HISA.
DID YOU GO GROCERY SHOPPING LIKE YOU SAID YOU WOULD?

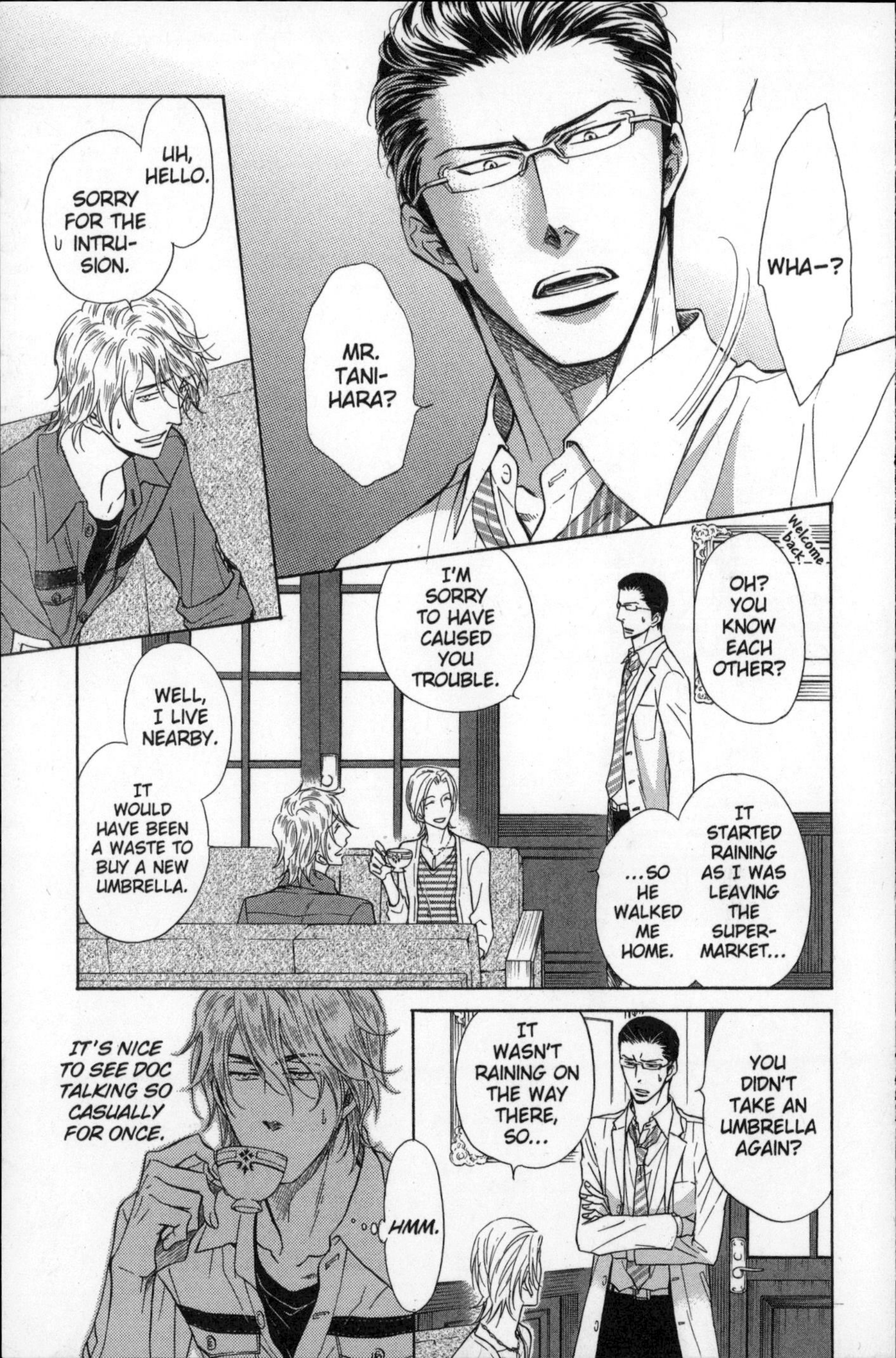
WHA-?
MR. TANI-HARA?
UH, HELLO. SORRY FOR THE INTRU-SION.
Welcome back
OH? YOU KNOW EACH OTHER?
I'M SORRY TO HAVE CAUSED YOU TROUBLE.
IT STARTED RAINING AS I WAS LEAVING THE SUPER-MARKET...
...SO HE WALKED ME HOME.
WELL, I LIVE NEARBY.
IT WOULD HAVE BEEN A WASTE TO BUY A NEW UMBRELLA.
YOU DIDN'T TAKE AN UMBRELLA AGAIN?
IT WASN'T RAINING ON THE WAY THERE, SO...
HMM.
IT'S NICE TO SEE DOC TALKING SO CASUALLY FOR ONCE.

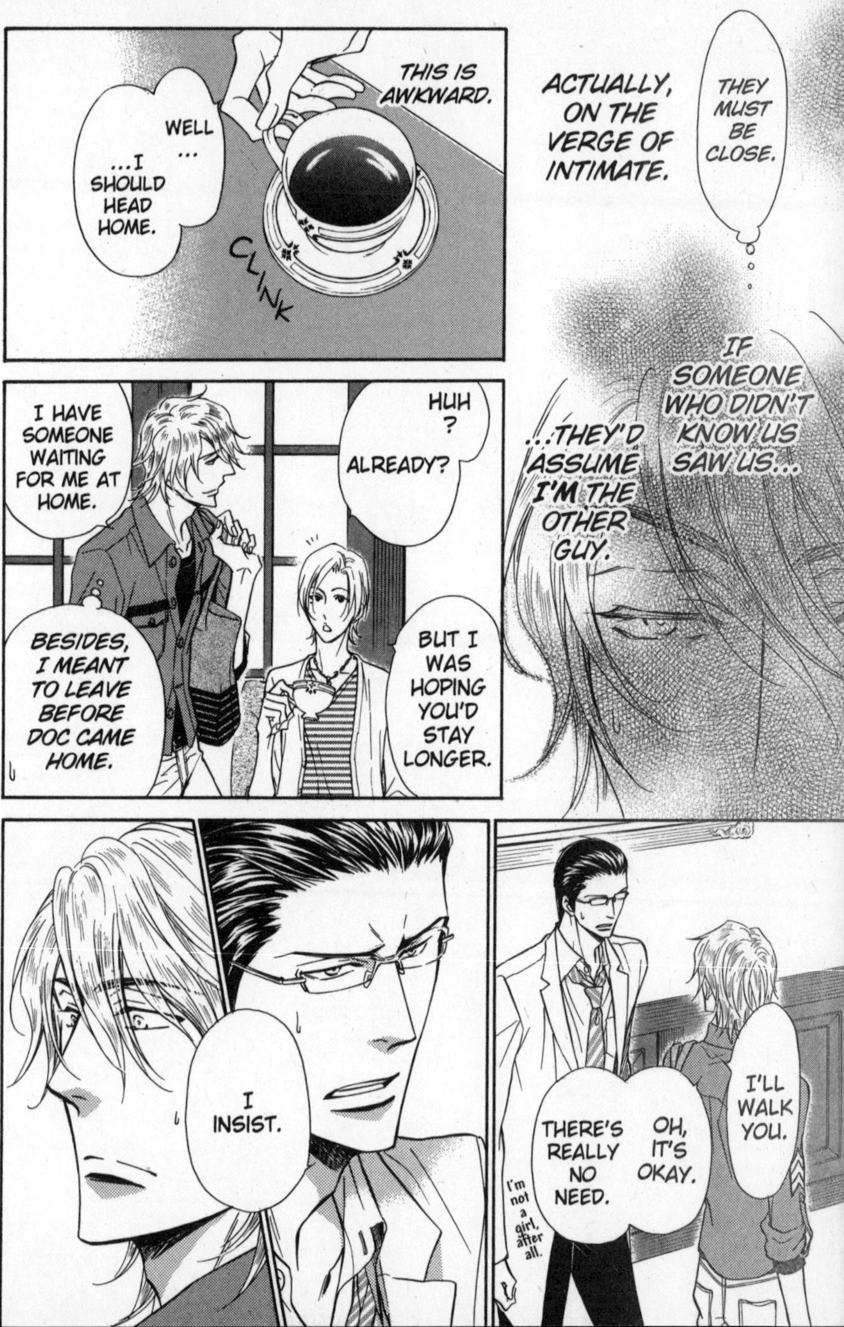
THEY MUST BE CLOSE.
ACTUALLY, ON THE VERGE OF INTIMATE.
IF SOMEONE WHO DIDN'T KNOW US SAW US...
...THEY'D ASSUME I'M THE OTHER GUY.
THIS IS AWKWARD.
WELL... ...I SHOULD HEAD HOME.
CLINK
HUH? ALREADY?
I HAVE SOMEONE WAITING FOR ME AT HOME.
BUT I WAS HOPING YOU'D STAY LONGER.
BESIDES, I MEANT TO LEAVE BEFORE DOC CAME HOME.
I'LL WALK YOU.
OH, IT'S OKAY.
THERE'S REALLY NO NEED.
I'm not a girl, after all.
I INSIST.

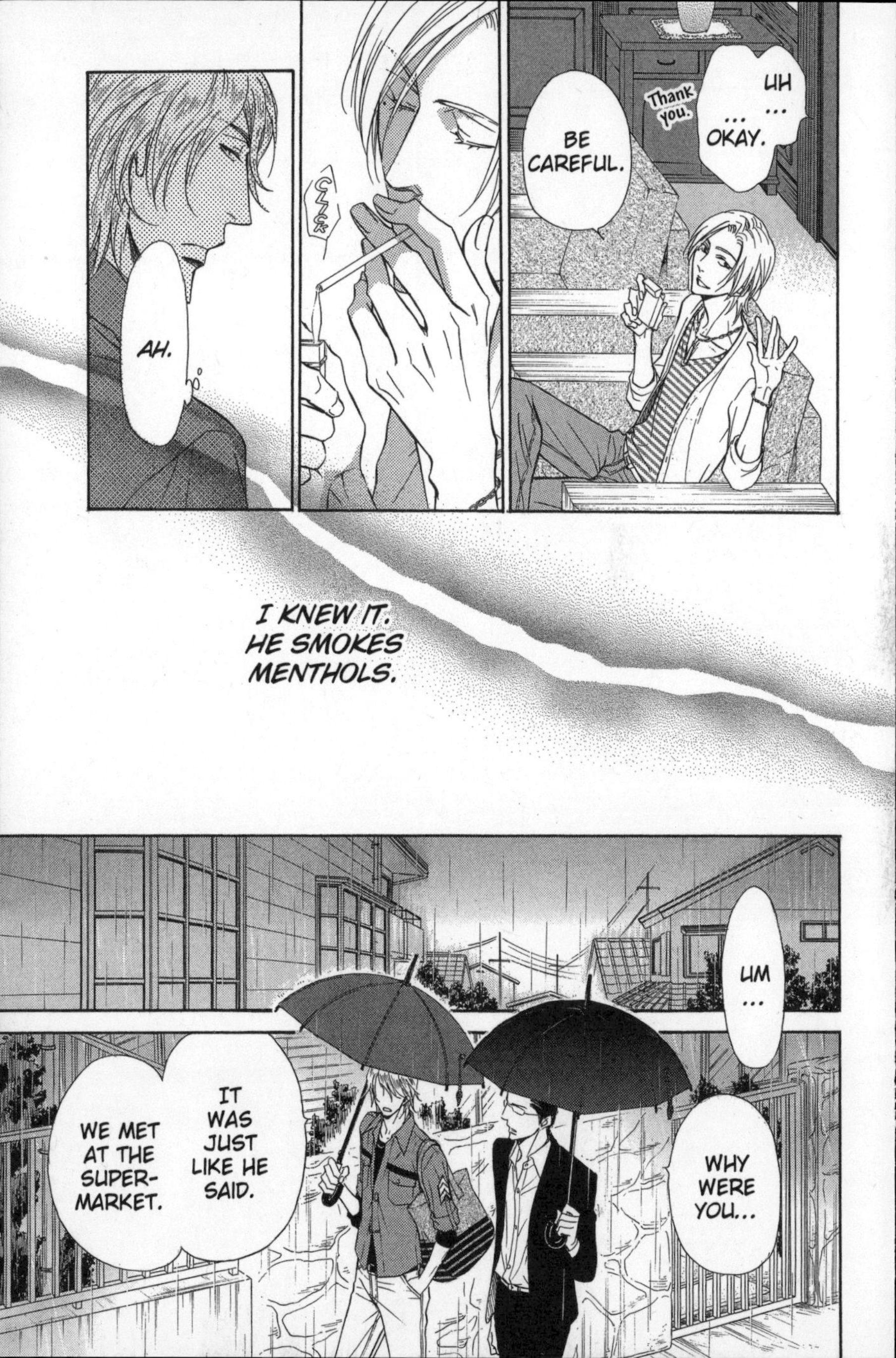
UH ... ... OKAY.
Thank you.
BE CAREFUL.
CLICK
AH.
I KNEW IT. HE SMOKES MENTHOLS.
UM ...
WHY WERE YOU...
IT WAS JUST LIKE HE SAID.
WE MET AT THE SUPER-MARKET.

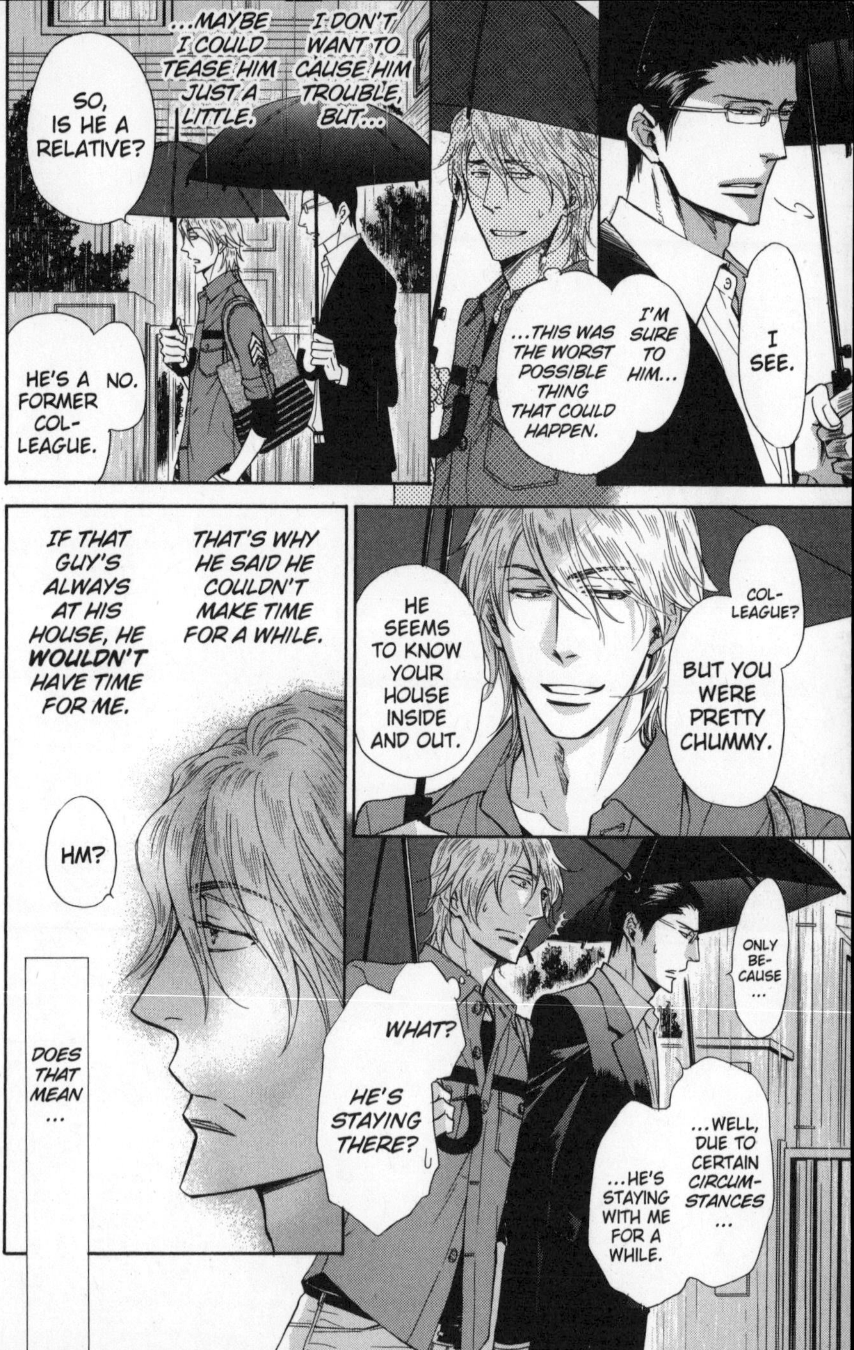
I SEE.
I'M SURE TO HIM...
...THIS WAS THE WORST POSSIBLE THING THAT COULD HAPPEN.
I DON'T WANT TO CAUSE HIM TROUBLE, BUT...
...MAYBE I COULD TEASE HIM JUST A LITTLE.
SO, IS HE A RELATIVE?
NO. HE'S A FORMER COL-LEAGUE.
COL-LEAGUE?
BUT YOU WERE PRETTY CHUMMY.
HE SEEMS TO KNOW YOUR HOUSE INSIDE AND OUT.
ONLY BE-CAUSE...
...WELL, DUE TO CERTAIN CIRCUM-STANCES...
...HE'S STAYING WITH ME FOR A WHILE.
WHAT?
HE'S STAYING THERE?
THAT'S WHY HE SAID HE COULDN'T MAKE TIME FOR A WHILE.
IF THAT GUY'S ALWAYS AT HIS HOUSE, HE WOULDN'T HAVE TIME FOR ME.
HM?
DOES THAT MEAN...

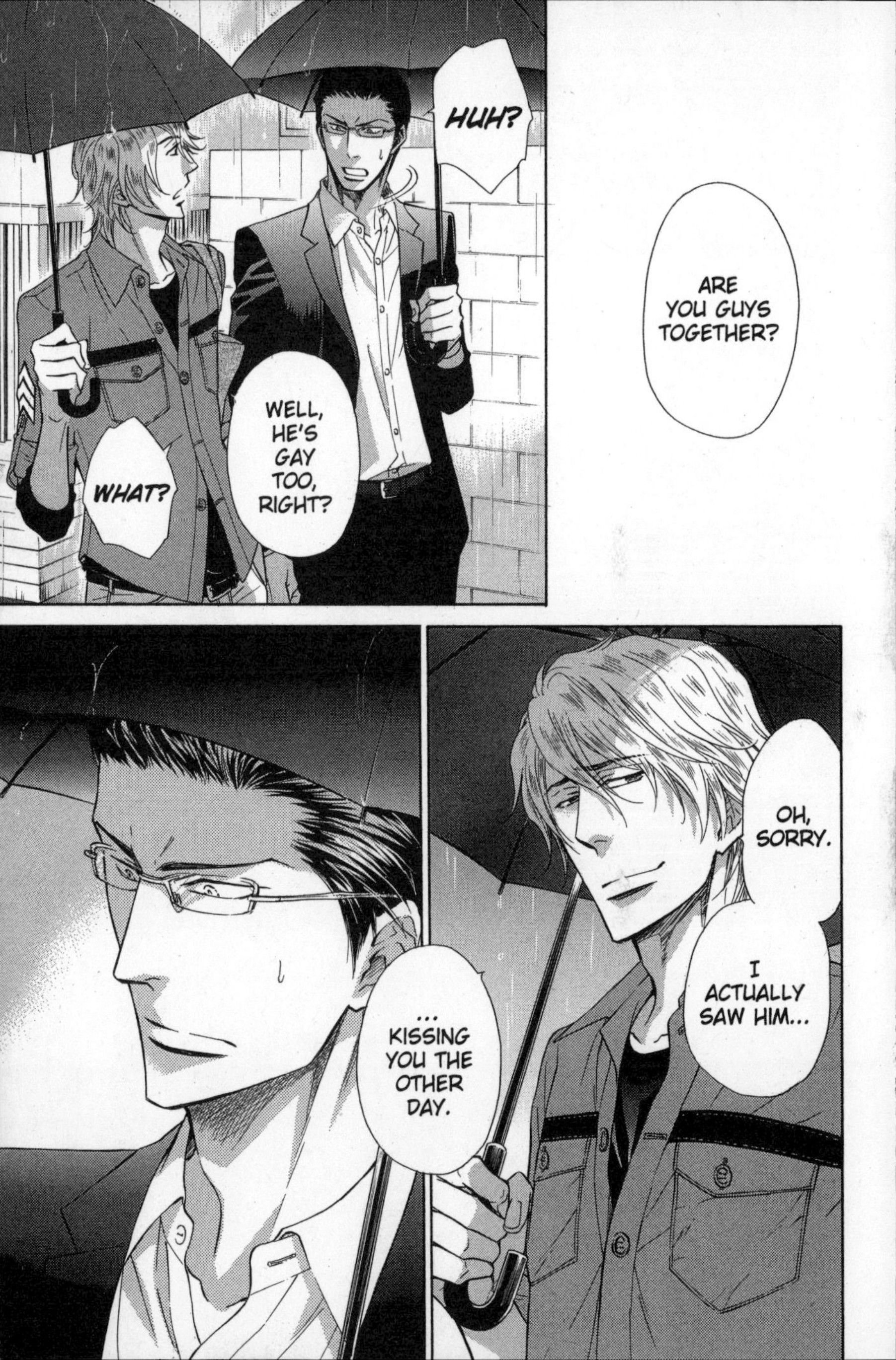
ARE YOU GUYS TOGETHER?
HUH?
WELL, HE'S GAY TOO, RIGHT?
WHAT?
OH, SORRY.
I ACTUALLY SAW HIM...
...KISSING YOU THE OTHER DAY.

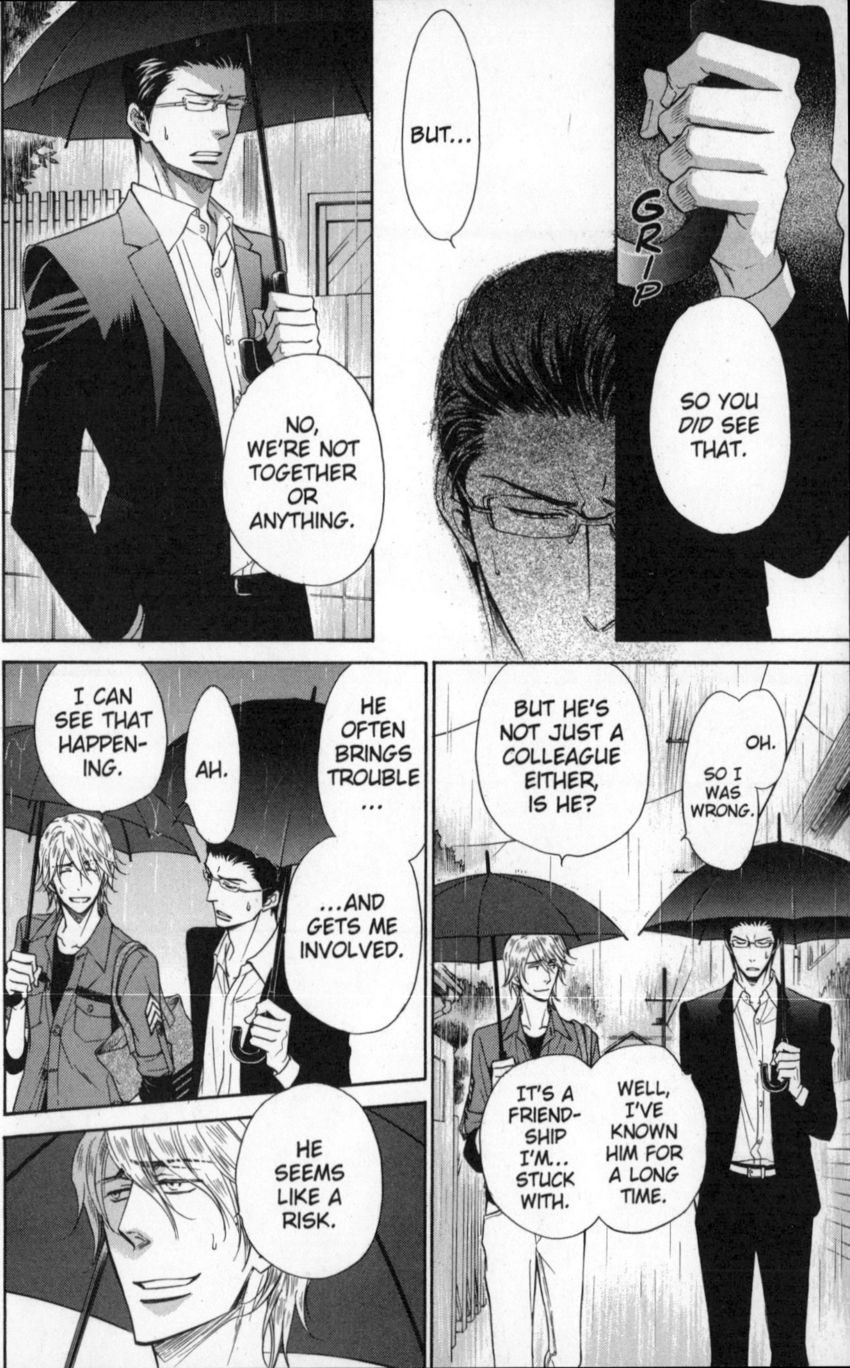
GRIP
SO YOU DID SEE THAT.
BUT...
NO, WE'RE NOT TOGETHER OR ANYTHING.
OH. SO I WAS WRONG.
BUT HE'S NOT JUST A COLLEAGUE EITHER, IS HE?
WELL, I'VE KNOWN HIM FOR A LONG TIME.
IT'S A FRIEND-SHIP I'M... STUCK WITH.
HE OFTEN BRINGS TROUBLE ...
...AND GETS ME INVOLVED.
AH.
I CAN SEE THAT HAPPEN-ING.
HE SEEMS LIKE A RISK.

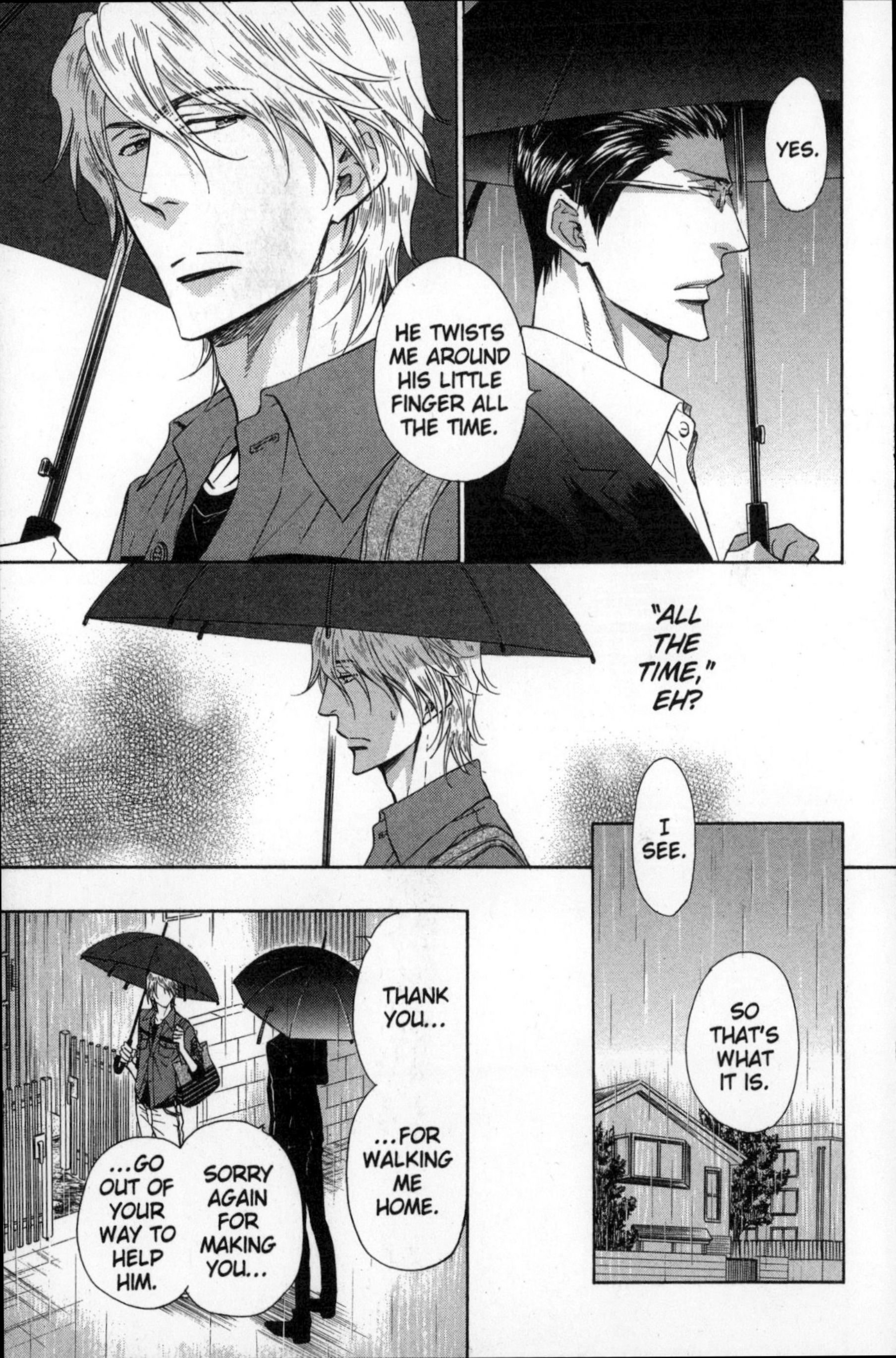
YES.
HE TWISTS ME AROUND HIS LITTLE FINGER ALL THE TIME.
"ALL THE TIME," EH?
I SEE.
SO THAT'S WHAT IT IS.
THANK YOU...
...FOR WALKING ME HOME.
SORRY AGAIN FOR MAKING YOU...
...GO OUT OF YOUR WAY TO HELP HIM.

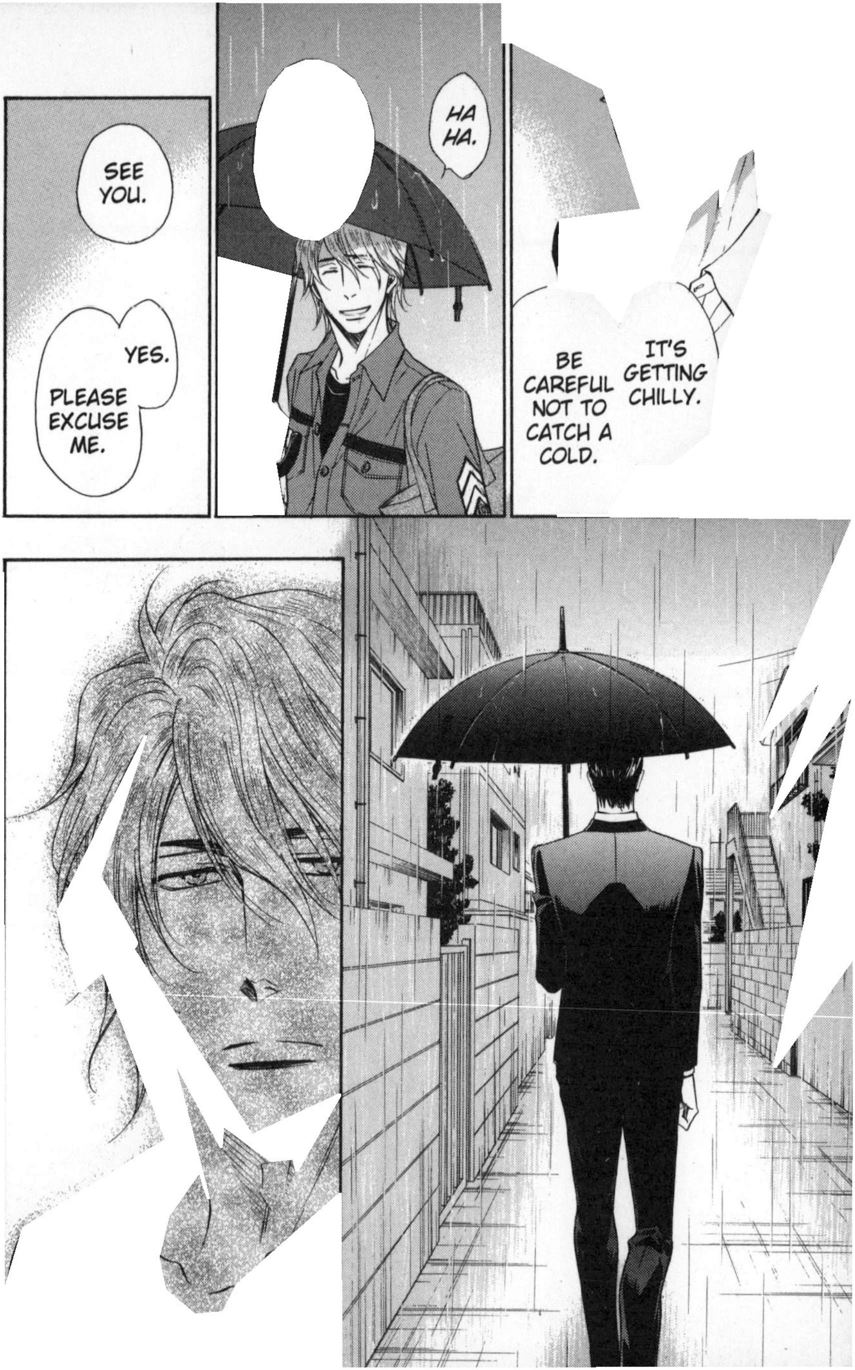
IT'S GETTING CHILLY.
BE CAREFUL NOT TO CATCH A COLD.
HA HA.
SEE YOU.
YES.
PLEASE EXCUSE ME.

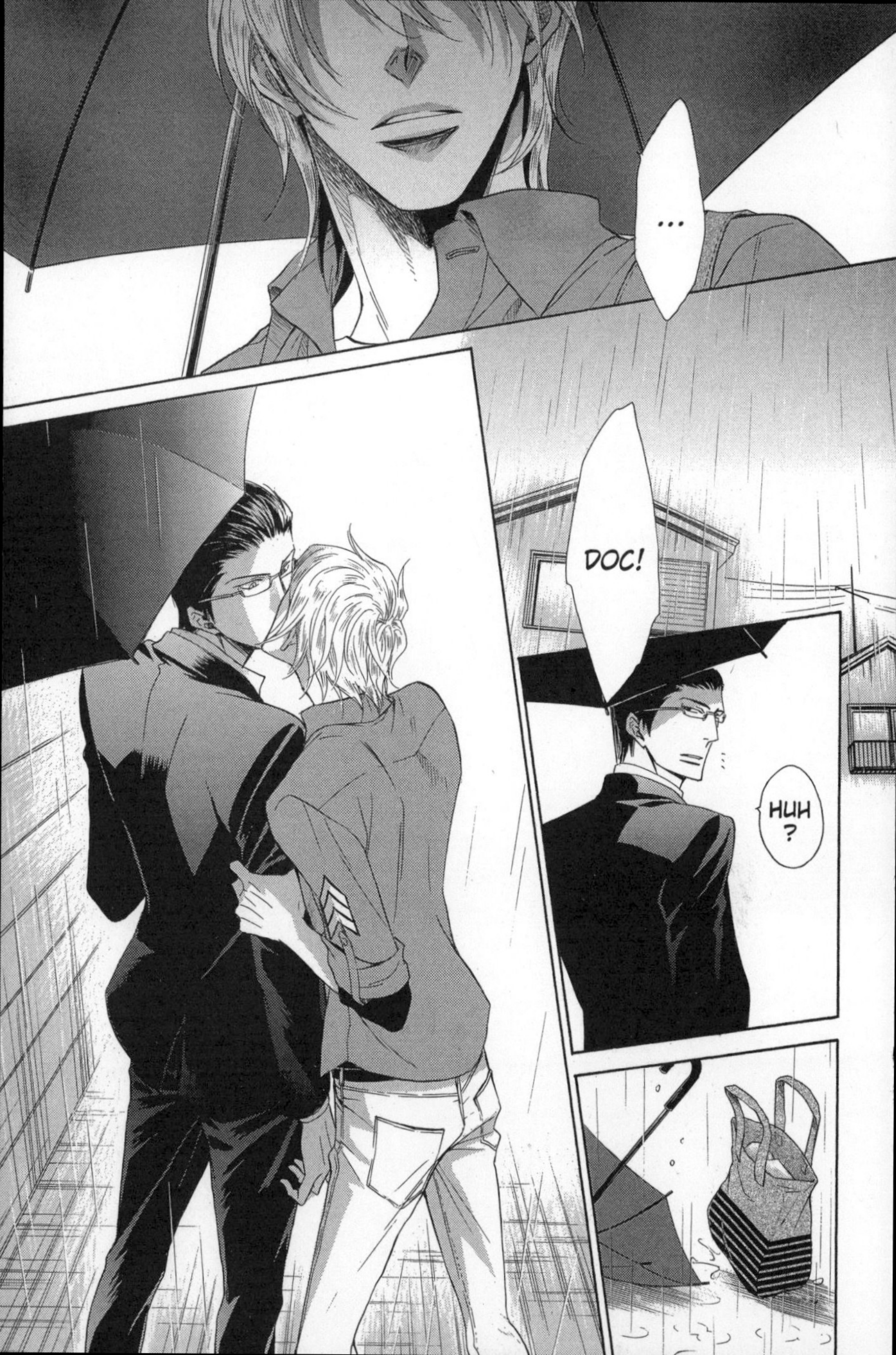
...
DOC!
HUH?

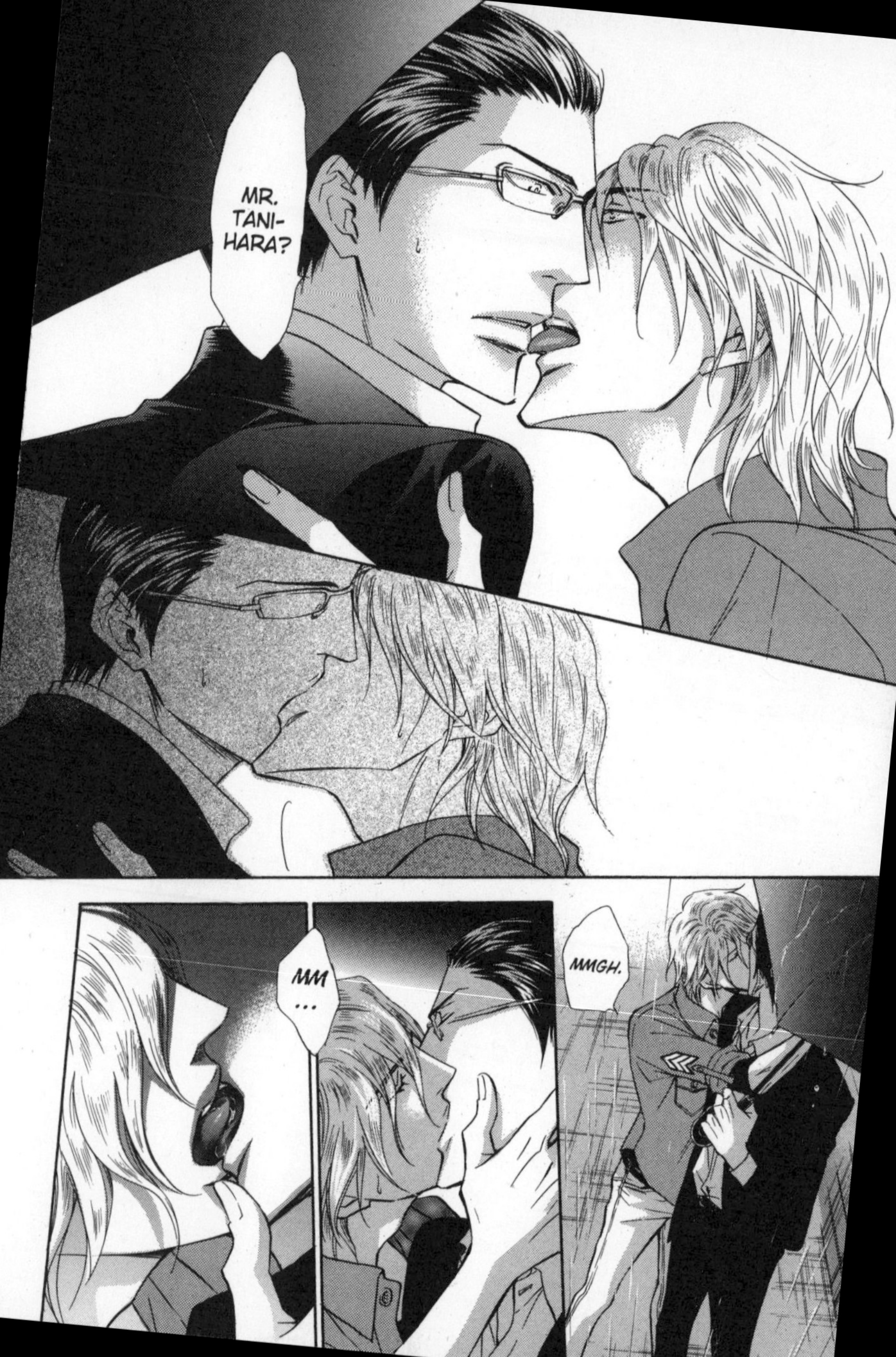
MR. TANI-HARA?
MMGH.
MM ...

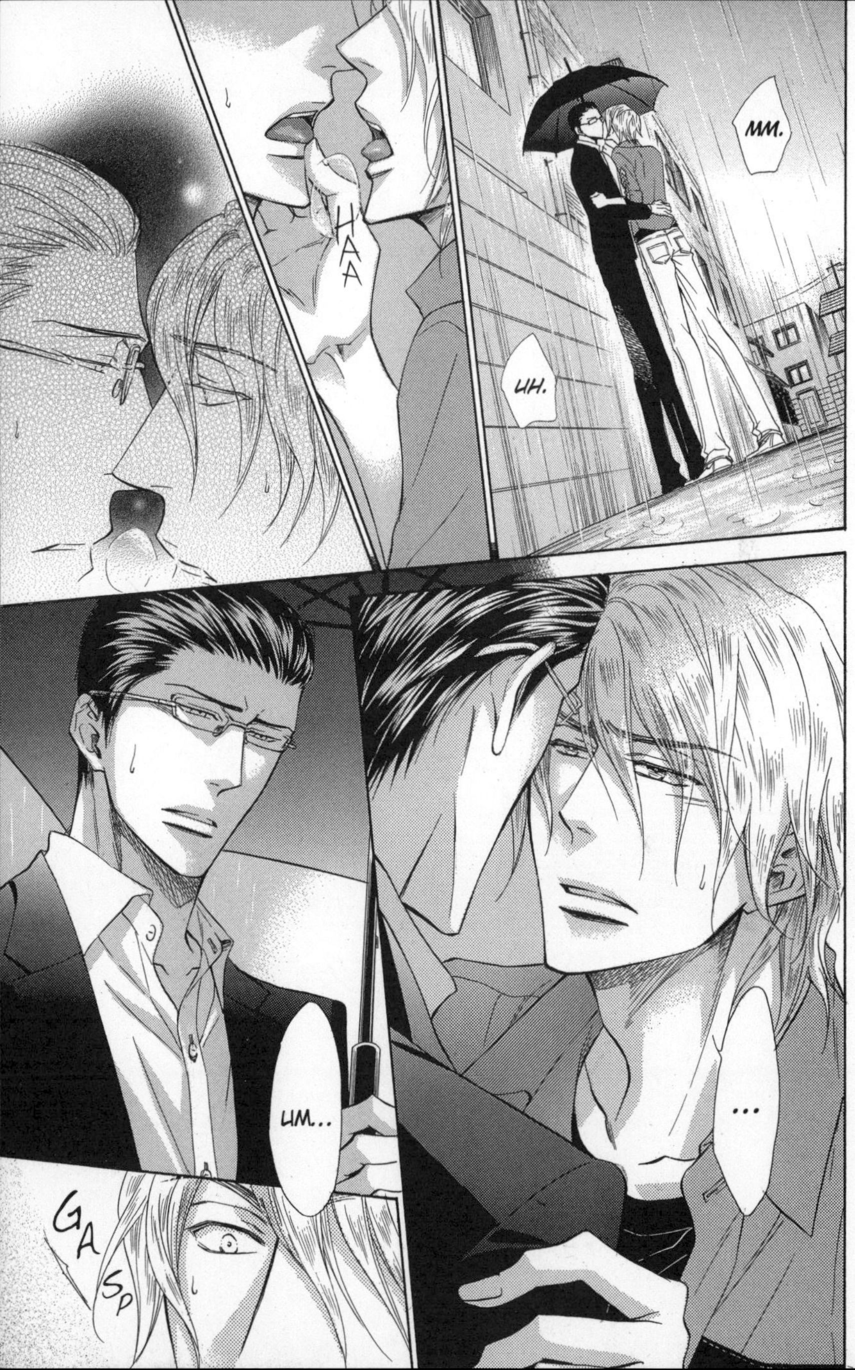
MM.
UH.
HAA
...
UM...
GASP

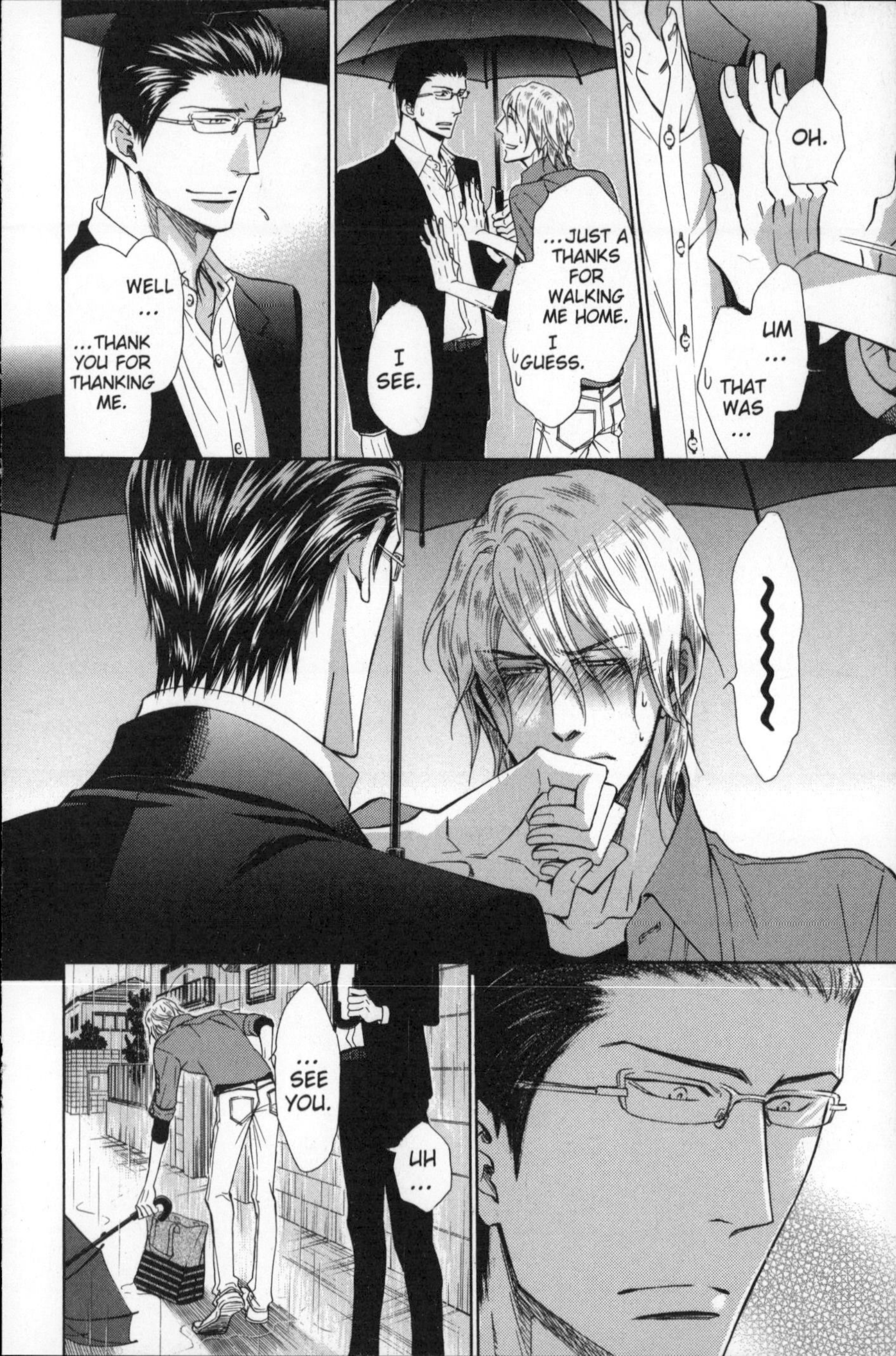
OH.
UM ... THAT WAS ...
...JUST A THANKS FOR WALKING ME HOME. I GUESS.
I SEE.
WELL ... ...THANK YOU FOR THANKING ME.
...SEE YOU.
UH ...

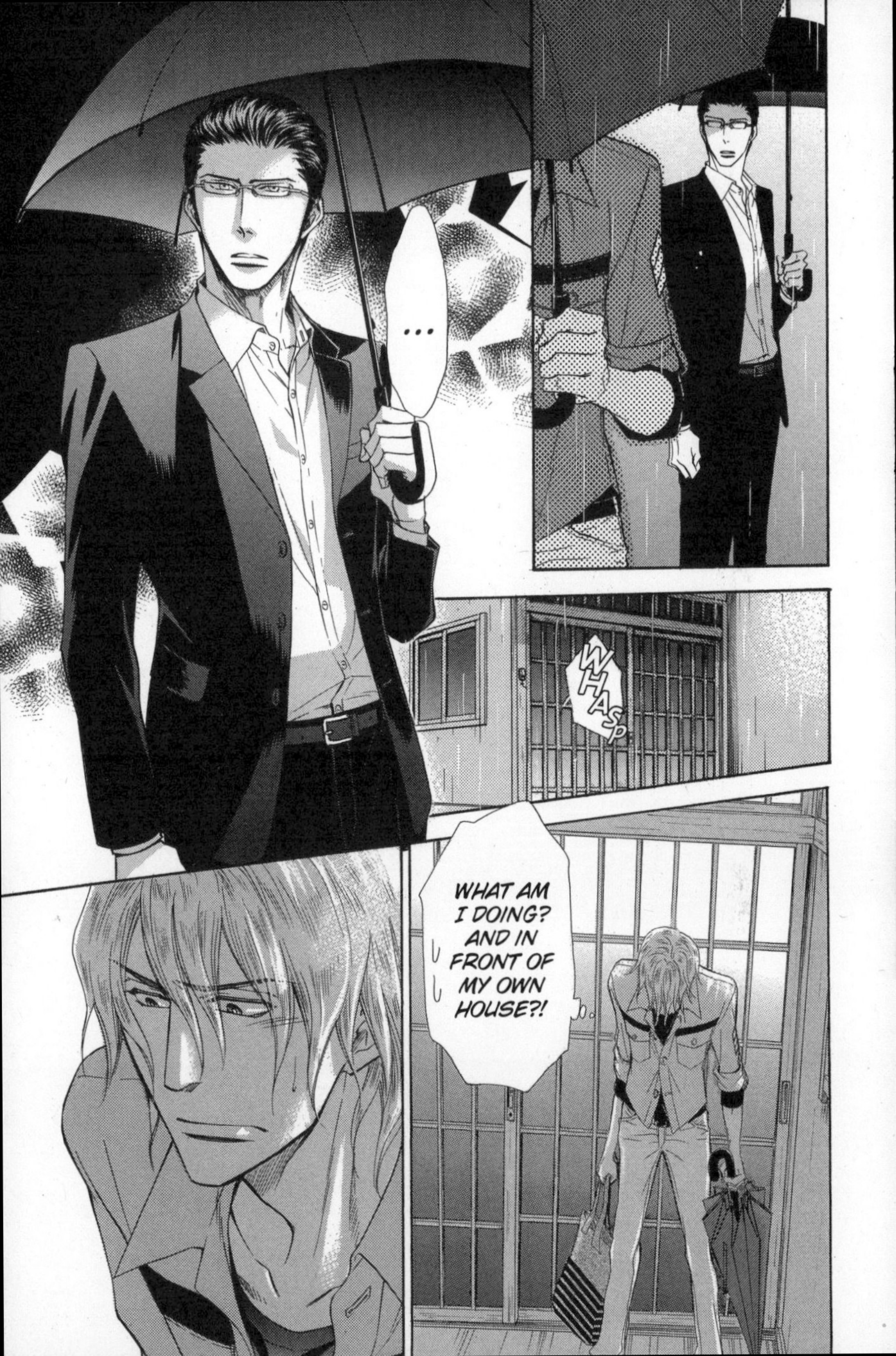
WHASP
...
WHAT AM I DOING? AND IN FRONT OF MY OWN HOUSE?!

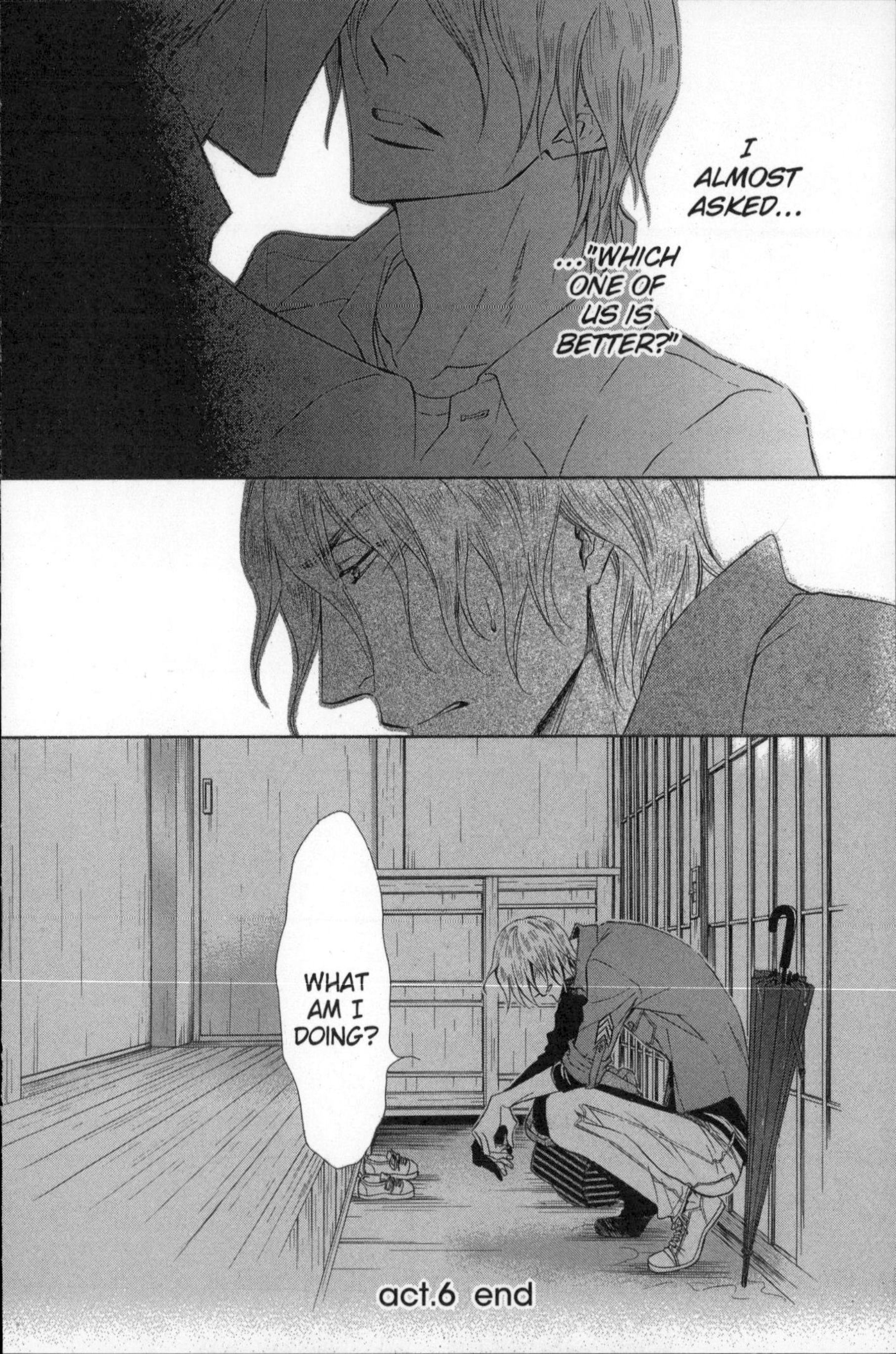
I ALMOST ASKED...
..."WHICH ONE OF US IS BETTER?"
WHAT AM I DOING?
act.6 end

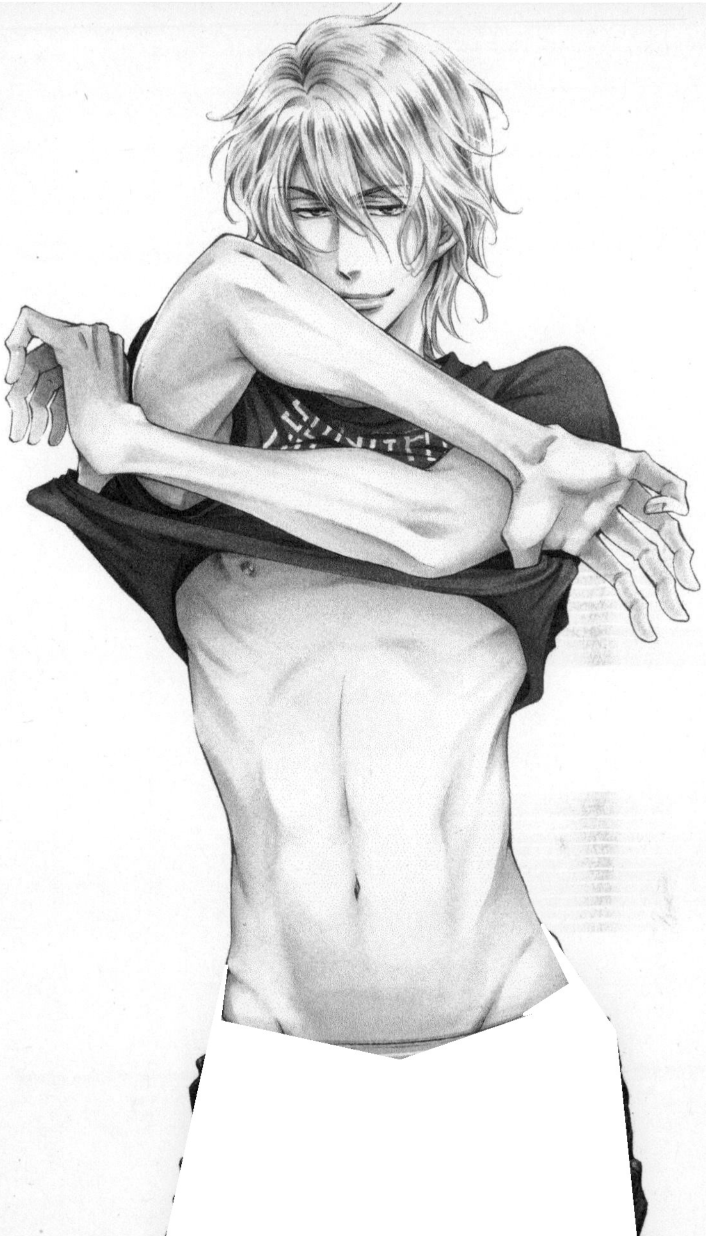

秘めごとあそび

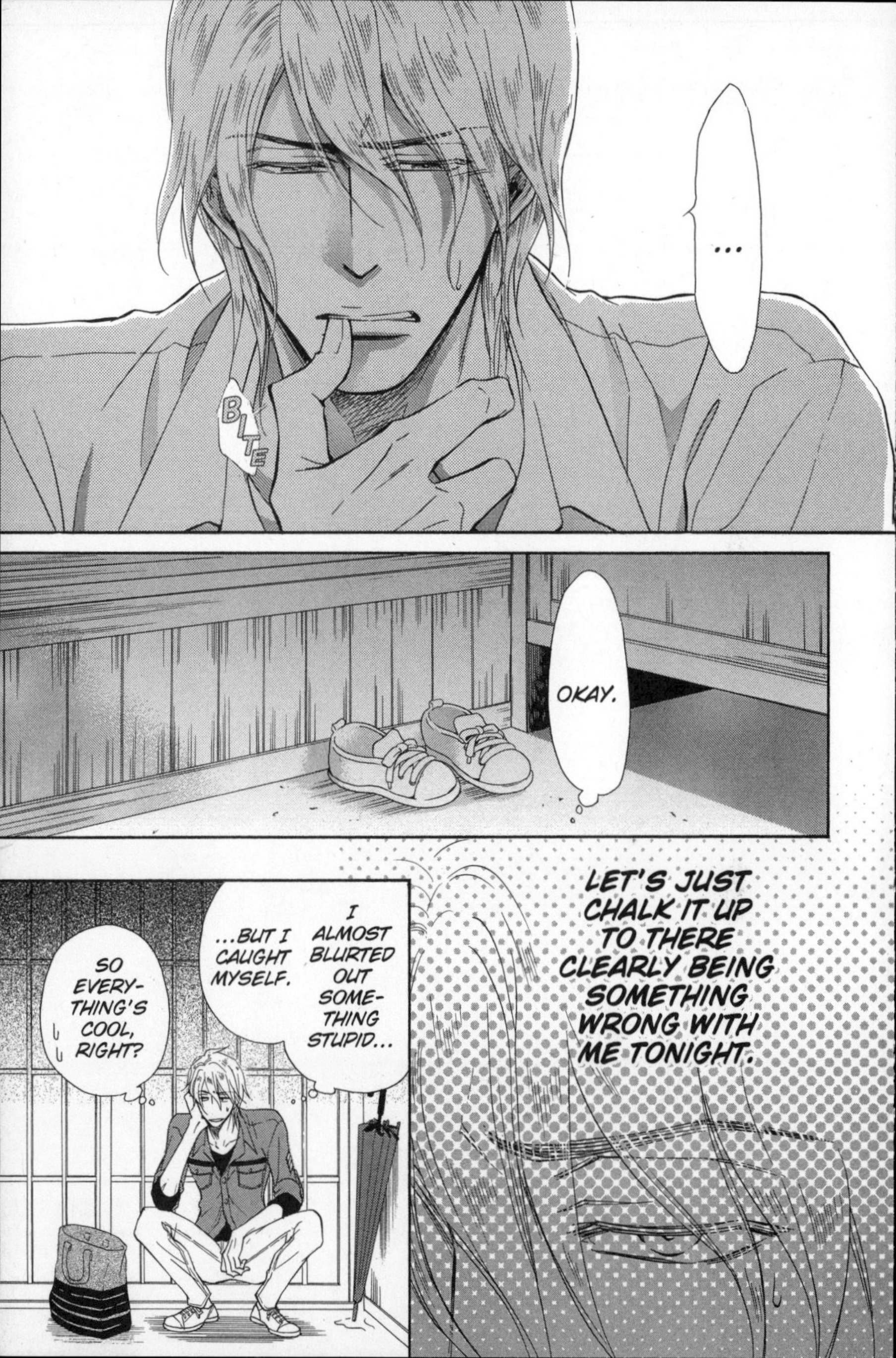
...
BITE
OKAY.
LET'S JUST CHALK IT UP TO THERE CLEARLY BEING SOMETHING WRONG WITH ME TONIGHT.
I ALMOST BLURTED OUT SOMETHING STUPID...
...BUT I CAUGHT MYSELF.
SO EVERYTHING'S COOL, RIGHT?

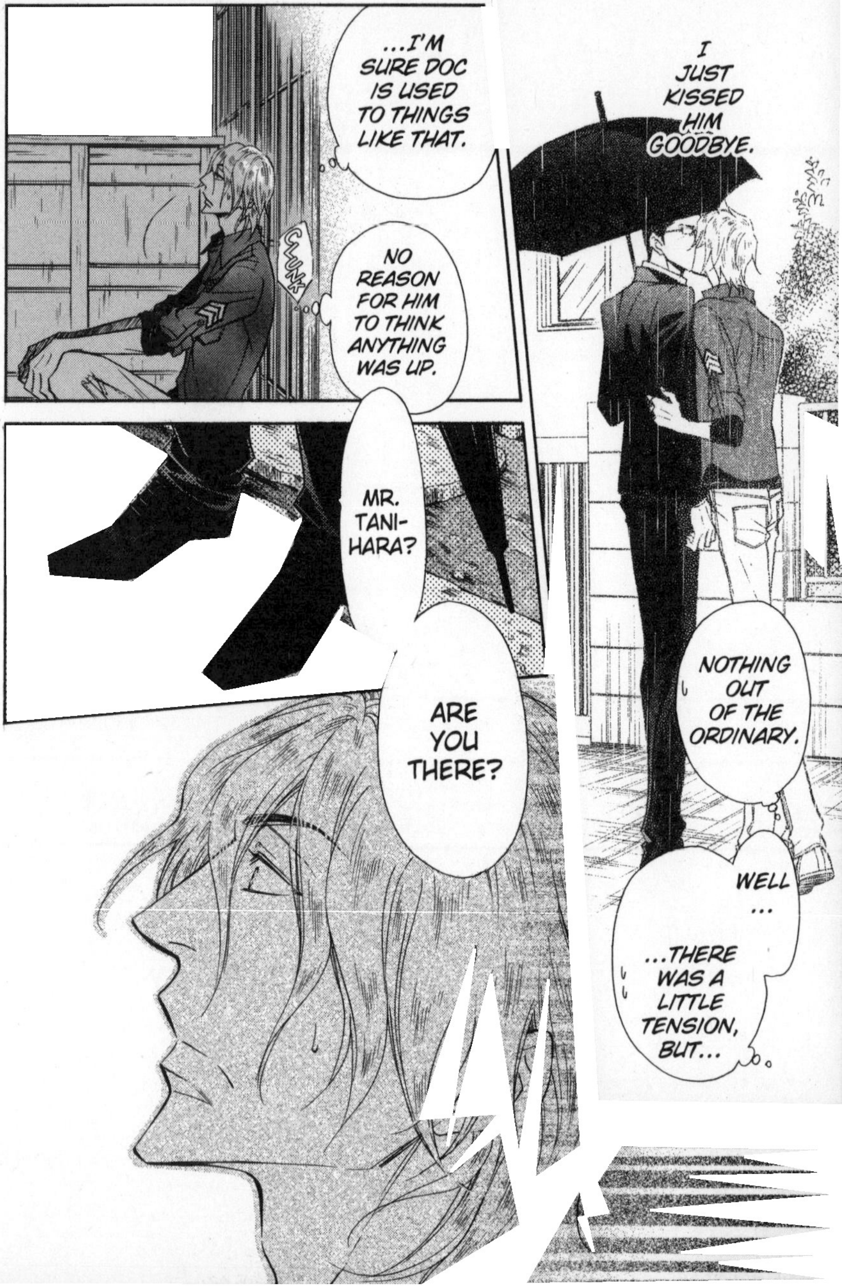
I JUST KISSED HIM GOODBYE.
NOTHING OUT OF THE ORDINARY.
WELL...
...THERE WAS A LITTLE TENSION, BUT...
...I'M SURE DOC IS USED TO THINGS LIKE THAT.
CLUNK
NO REASON FOR HIM TO THINK ANYTHING WAS UP.
MR. TANI-HARA?
ARE YOU THERE?

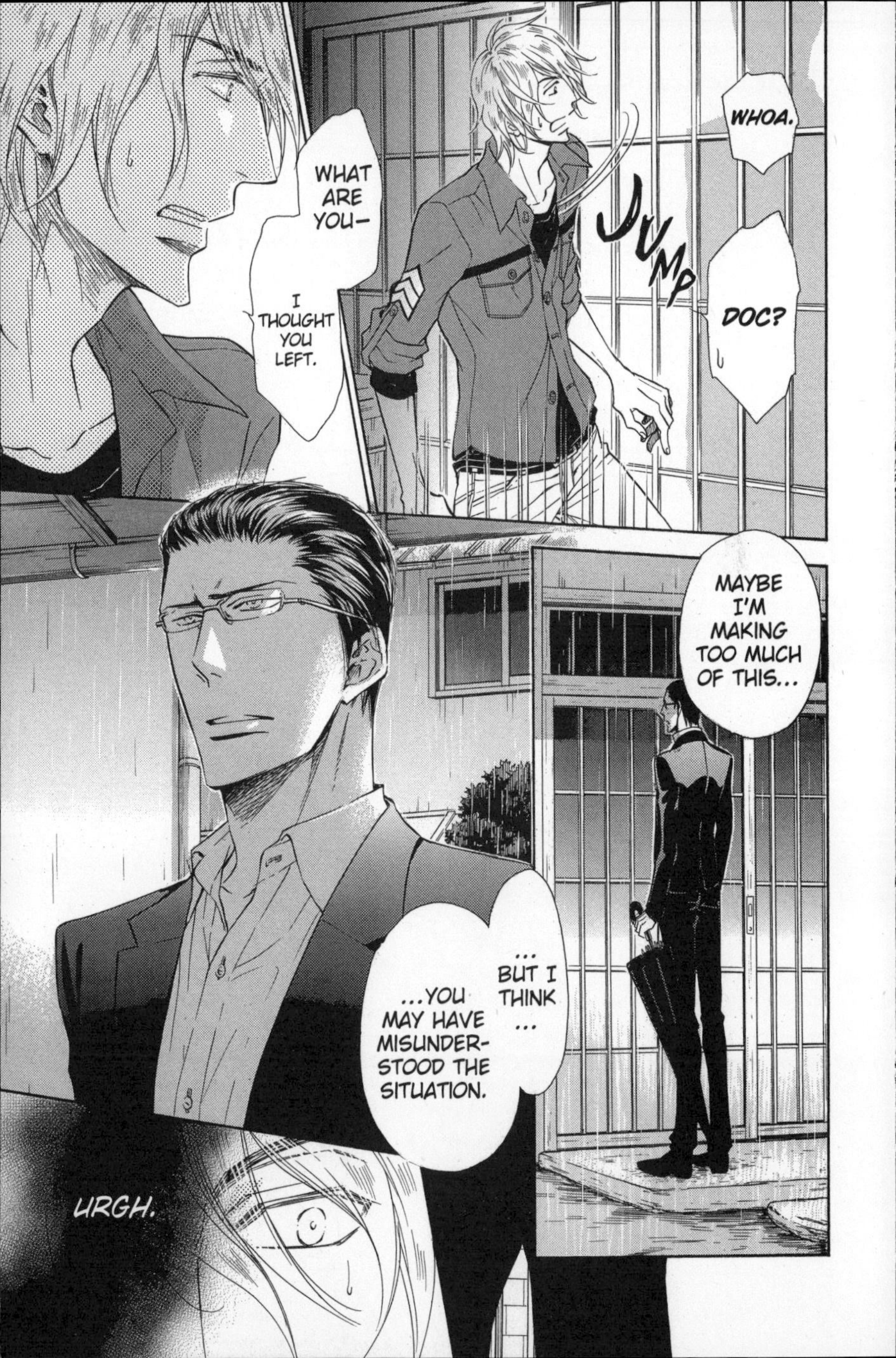
WHOA.
JUMP
DOC?
WHAT ARE YOU—
I THOUGHT YOU LEFT.
MAYBE I'M MAKING TOO MUCH OF THIS...
...BUT I THINK...
...YOU MAY HAVE MISUNDER-STOOD THE SITUATION.
URGH.

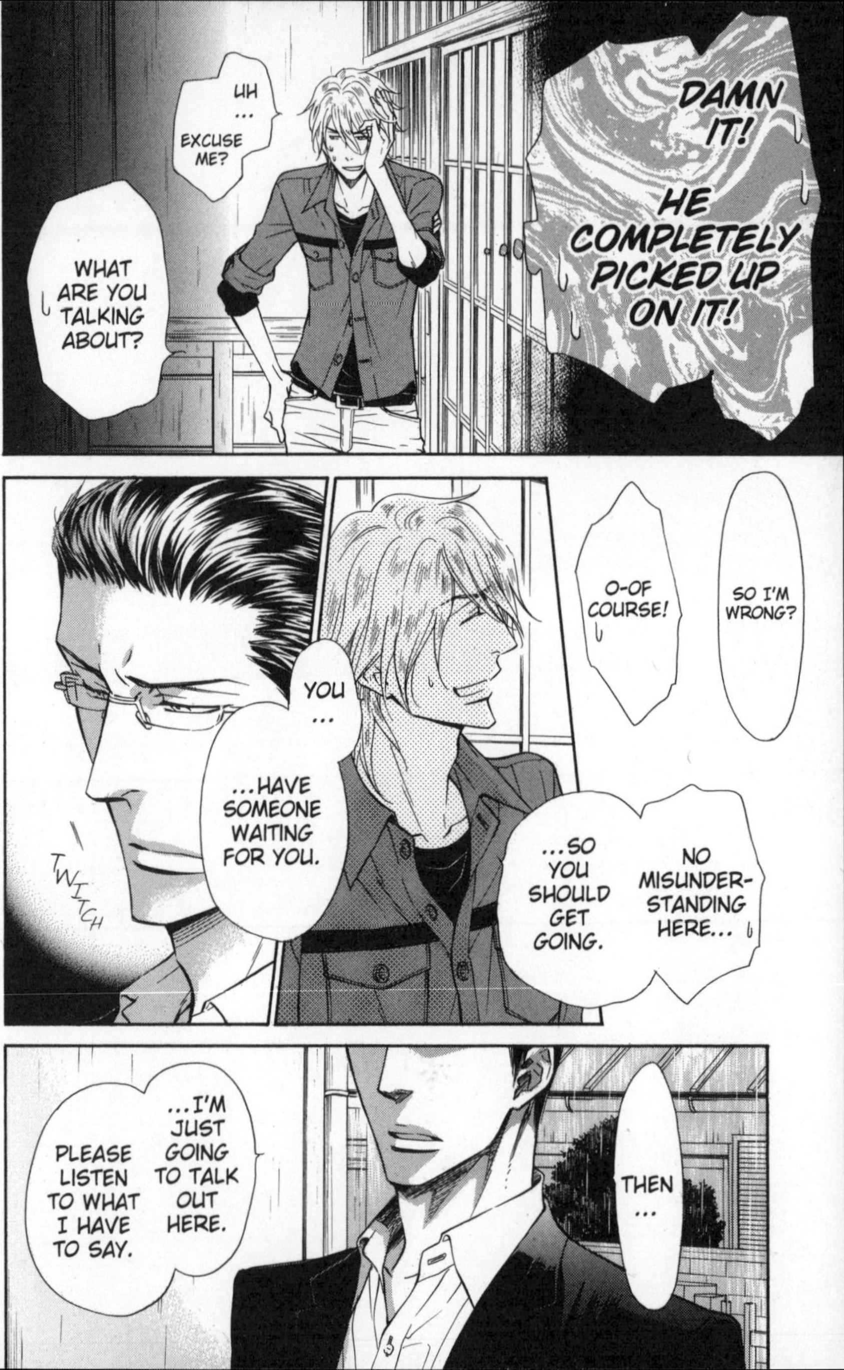
DAMN IT! HE COMPLETELY PICKED UP ON IT!
UH ... EXCUSE ME?
WHAT ARE YOU TALKING ABOUT?
SO I'M WRONG?
O-OF COURSE!
NO MISUNDER-STANDING HERE...
...SO YOU SHOULD GET GOING.
YOU ...
...HAVE SOMEONE WAITING FOR YOU.
TWITCH
THEN ...
...I'M JUST GOING TO TALK OUT HERE.
PLEASE LISTEN TO WHAT I HAVE TO SAY.

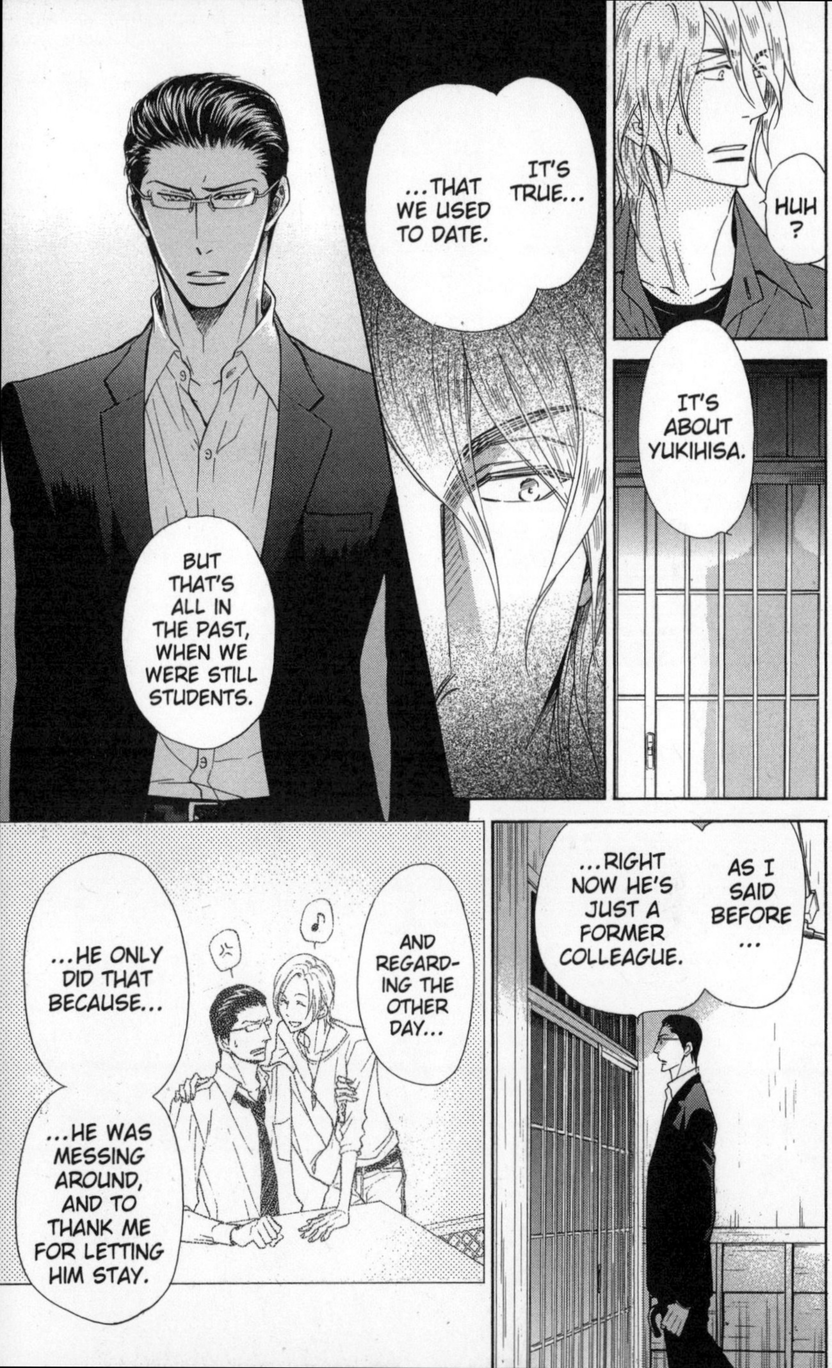
HUH?
IT'S ABOUT YUKIHISA.
IT'S TRUE...
...THAT WE USED TO DATE.
BUT THAT'S ALL IN THE PAST, WHEN WE WERE STILL STUDENTS.
AS I SAID BEFORE...
...RIGHT NOW HE'S JUST A FORMER COLLEAGUE.
AND REGARDING THE OTHER DAY...
...HE ONLY DID THAT BECAUSE...
...HE WAS MESSING AROUND, AND TO THANK ME FOR LETTING HIM STAY.

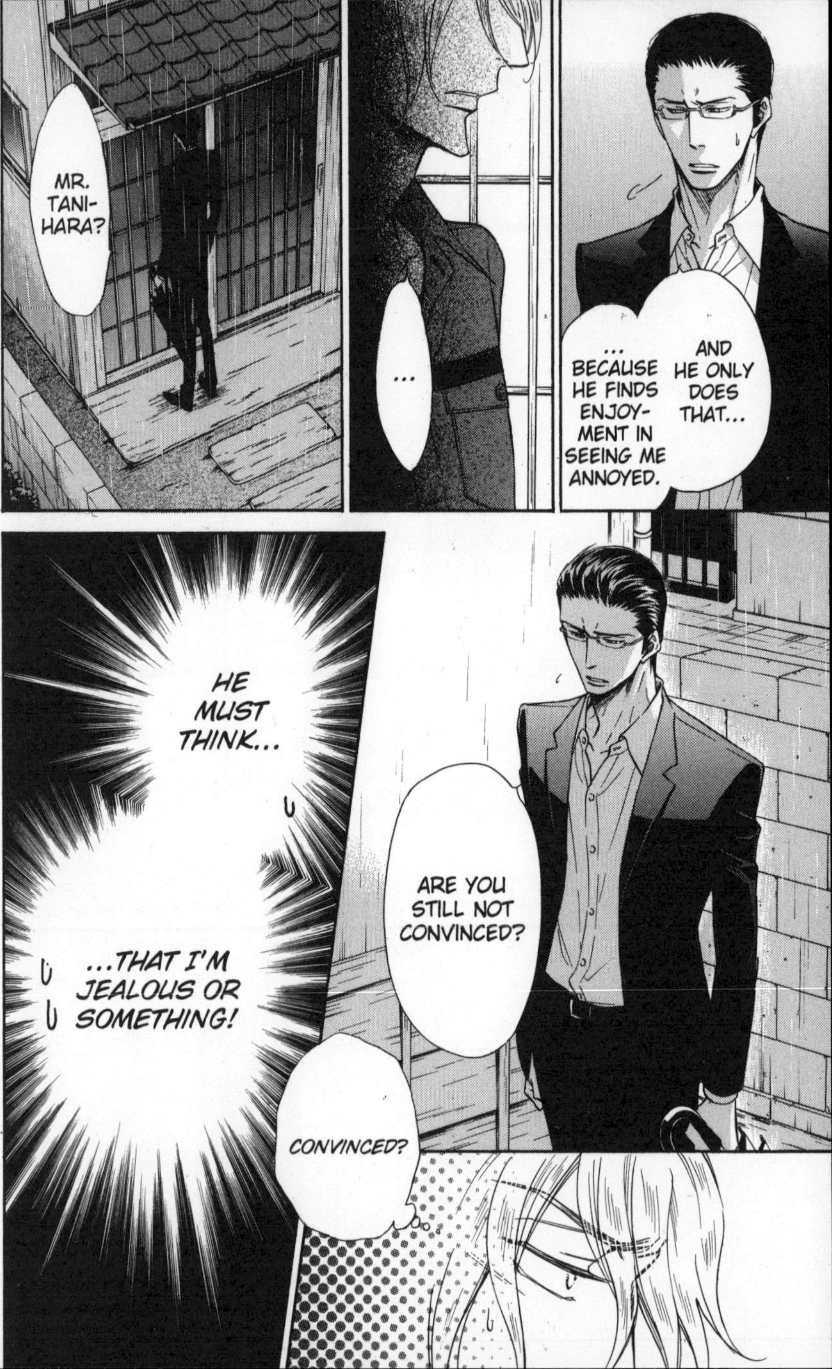
AND HE ONLY DOES THAT...
...BECAUSE HE FINDS ENJOYMENT IN SEEING ME ANNOYED.
...
MR. TANI-HARA?
ARE YOU STILL NOT CONVINCED?
CONVINCED?
HE MUST THINK...
...THAT I'M JEALOUS OR SOMETHING!

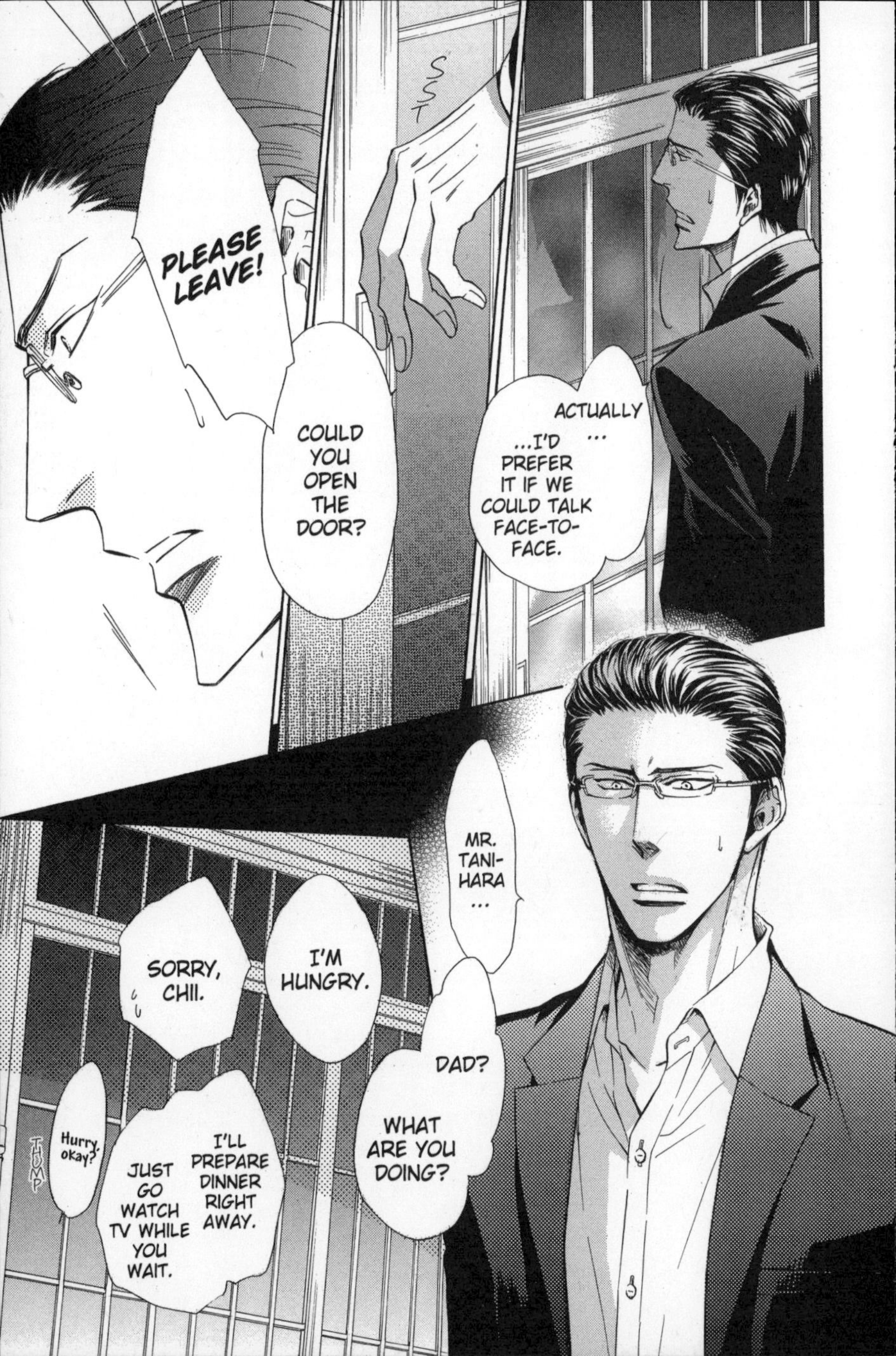
ACTUALLY ... ...I'D PREFER IT IF WE COULD TALK FACE-TO-FACE.
SST
COULD YOU OPEN THE DOOR?
PLEASE LEAVE!
MR. TANI-HARA ...
DAD?
WHAT ARE YOU DOING?
I'M HUNGRY.
SORRY, CHII.
I'LL PREPARE DINNER RIGHT AWAY.
JUST GO WATCH TV WHILE YOU WAIT.
Hurry, okay?
THUMP

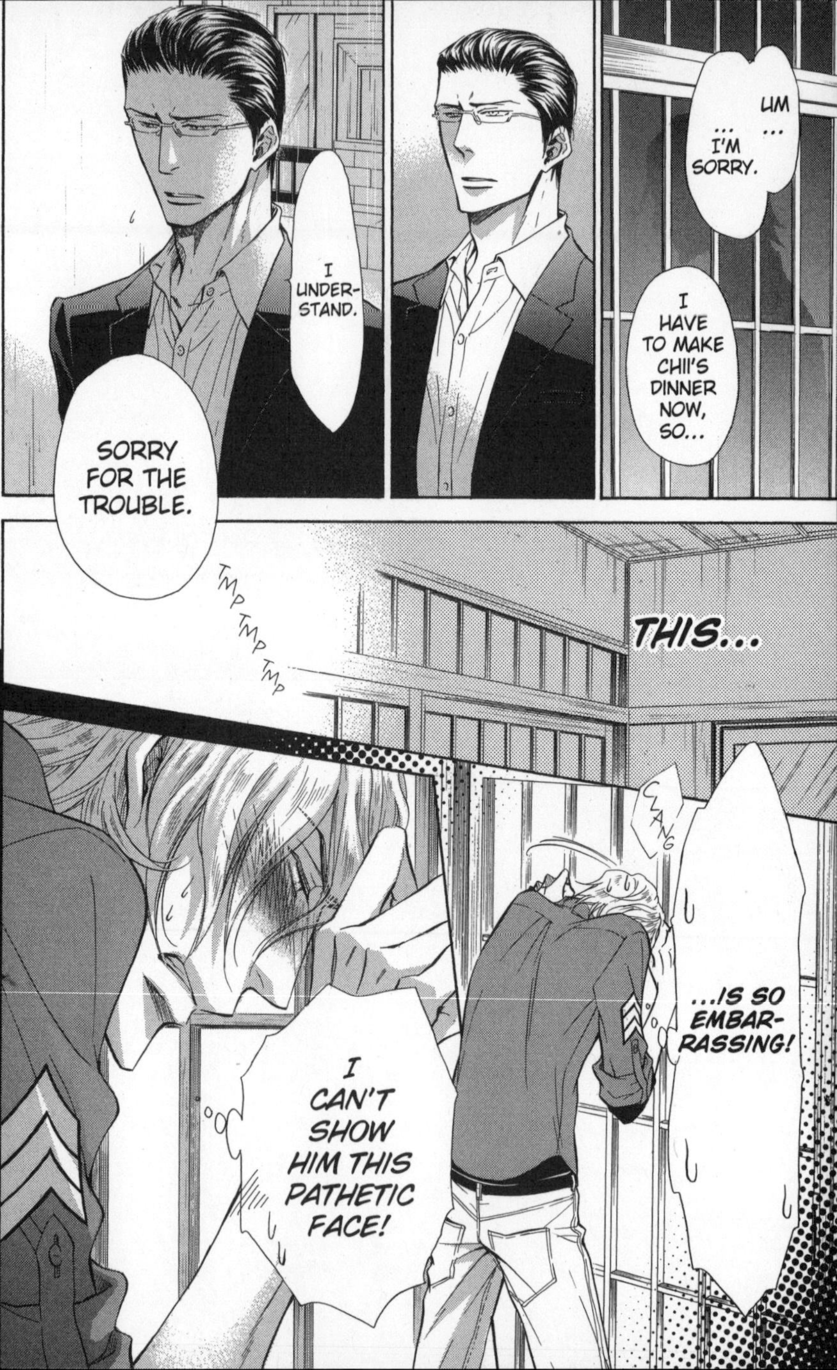
UM... I'M SORRY.
I HAVE TO MAKE CHII'S DINNER NOW, SO...
I UNDERSTAND.
SORRY FOR THE TROUBLE.
TMP TMP TMP TMP
THIS...
CLANG
...IS SO EMBARRASSING!
I CAN'T SHOW HIM THIS PATHETIC FACE!

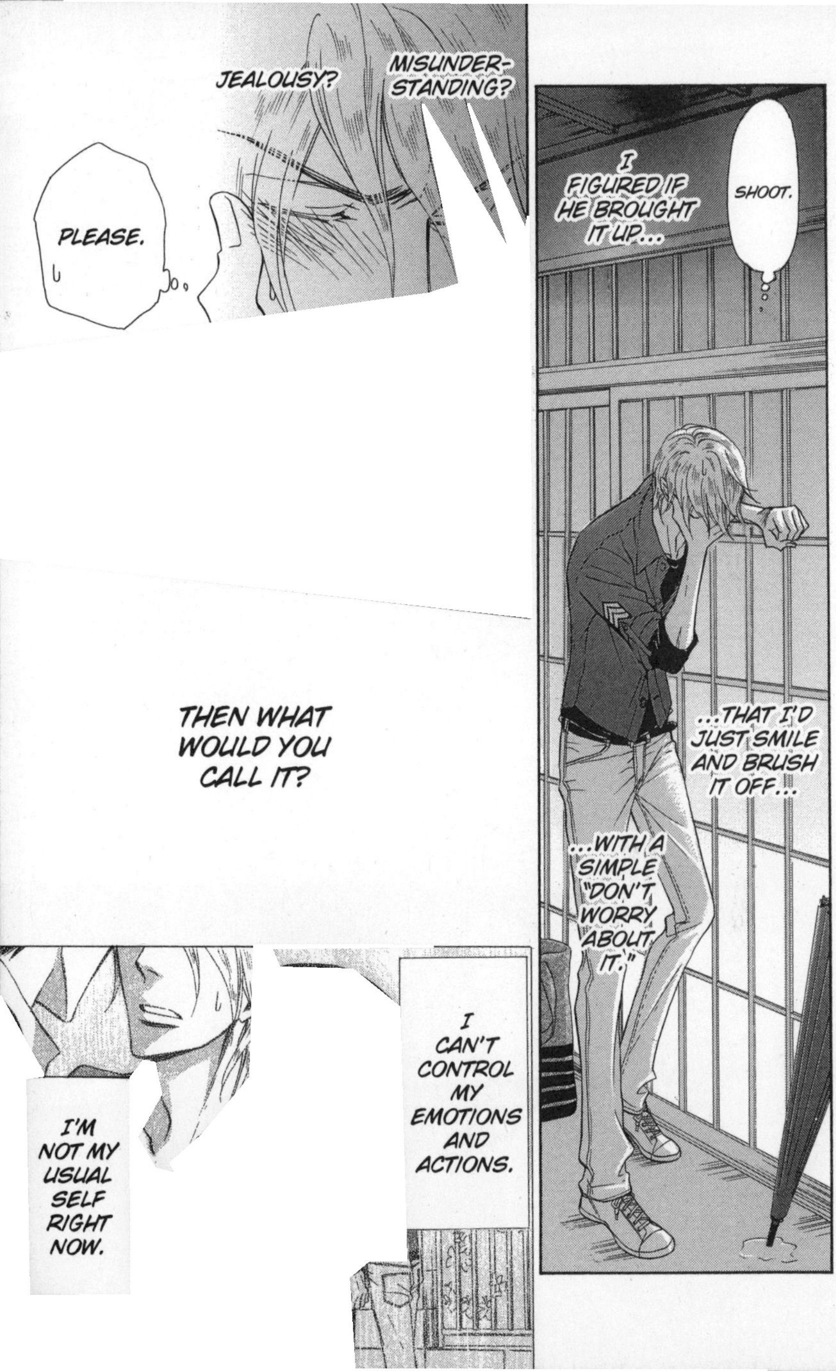
MISUNDER-STANDING?
JEALOUSY?
PLEASE.
THEN WHAT WOULD YOU CALL IT?
SHOOT.
I FIGURED IF HE BROUGHT IT UP...
...THAT I'D JUST SMILE AND BRUSH IT OFF...
...WITH A SIMPLE "DON'T WORRY ABOUT IT."
I CAN'T CONTROL MY EMOTIONS AND ACTIONS.
I'M NOT MY USUAL SELF RIGHT NOW.

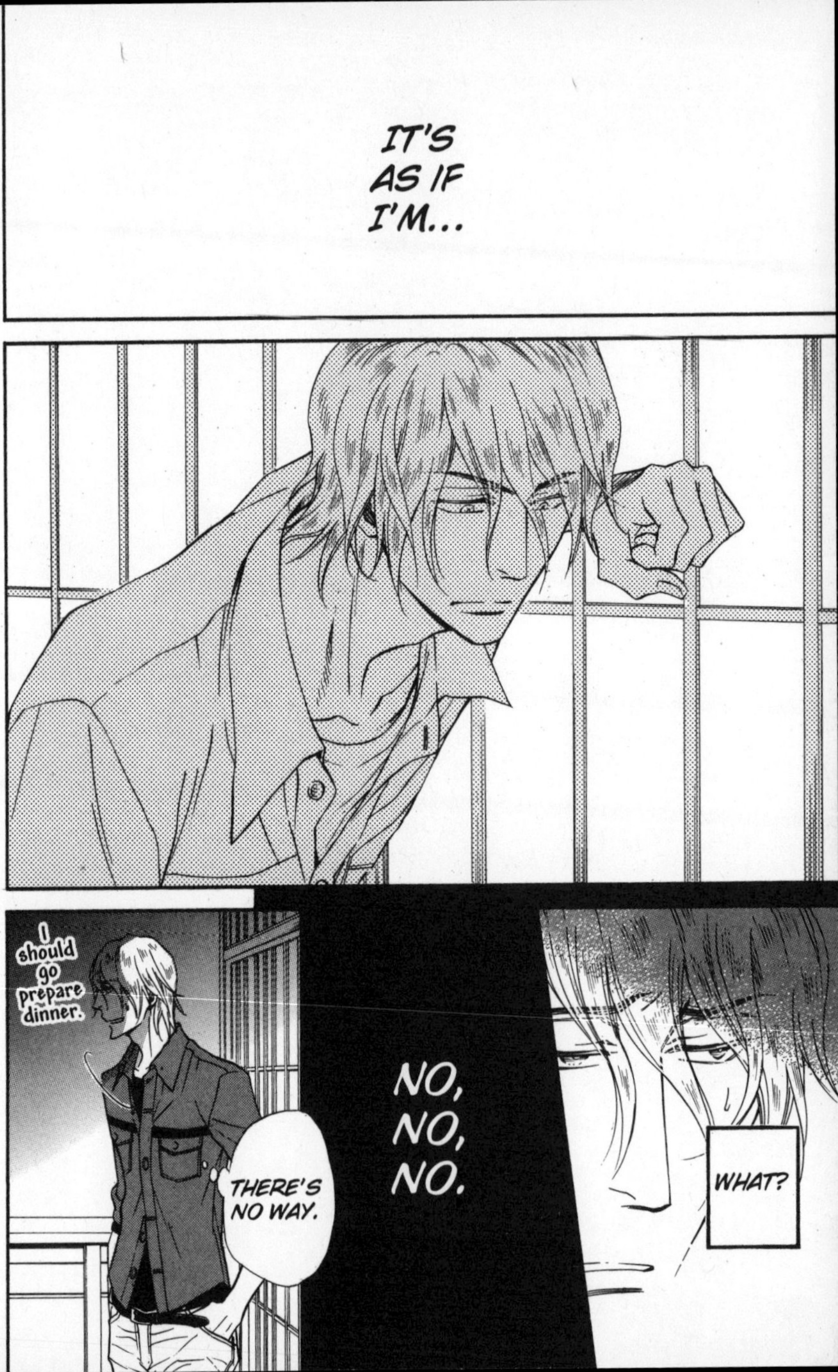
IT'S AS IF I'M...
WHAT?
NO, NO, NO.
THERE'S NO WAY.
I should go prepare dinner.

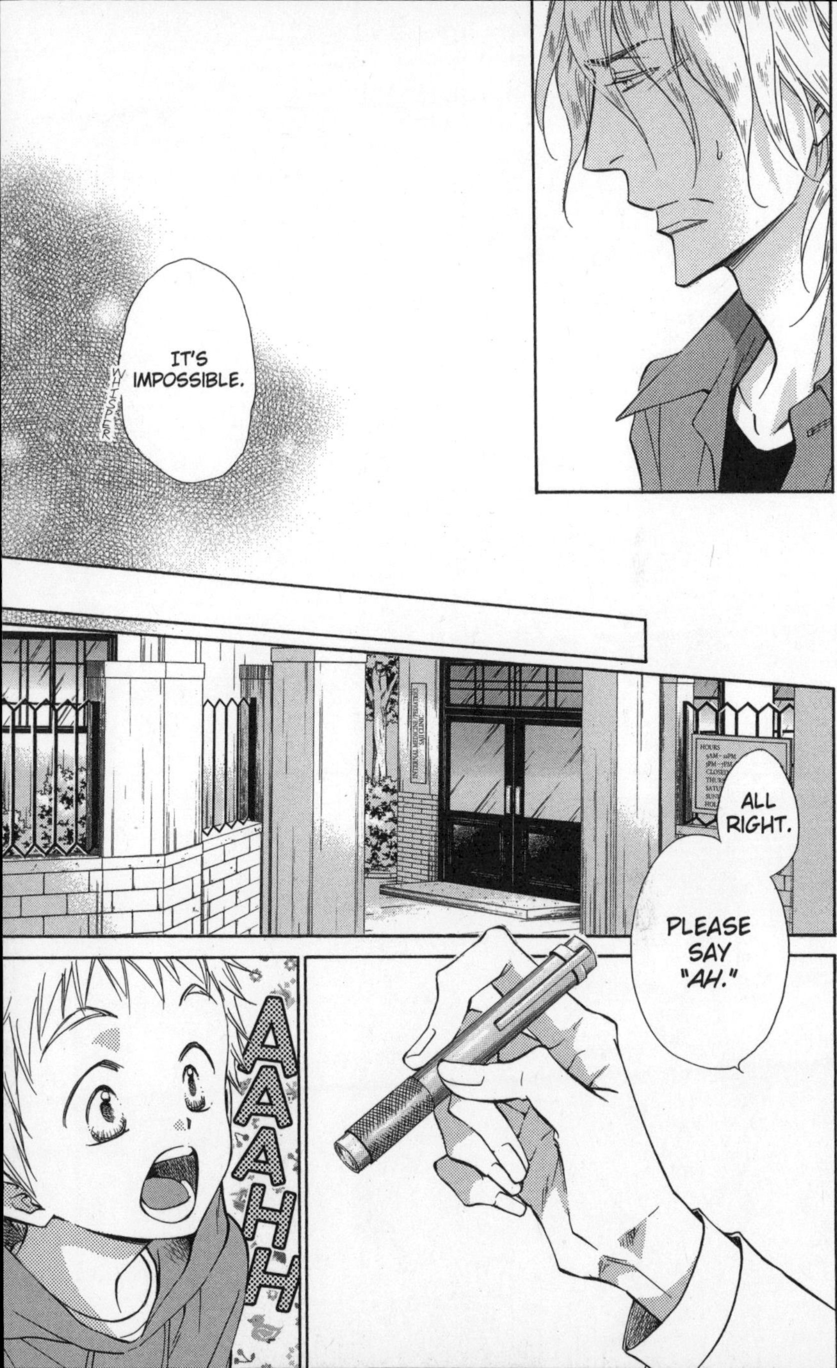
WHISPER
IT'S IMPOSSIBLE.
INTERNAL MEDICINE PEDIATRICS SAJI CLINIC
HOURS
ALL RIGHT.
PLEASE SAY "AH."
AAAHH

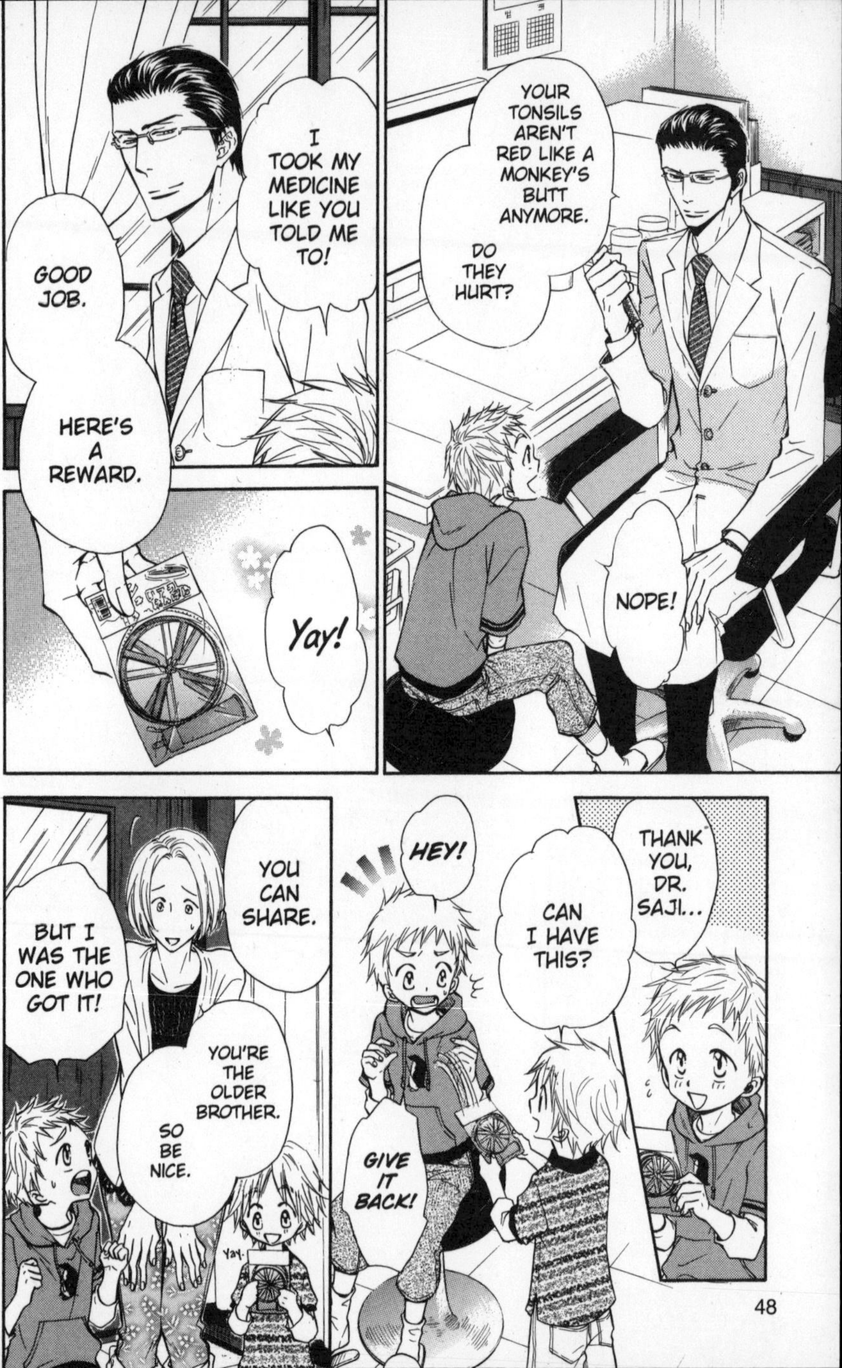
YOUR TONSILS AREN'T RED LIKE A MONKEY'S BUTT ANYMORE.
DO THEY HURT?
NOPE!
I TOOK MY MEDICINE LIKE YOU TOLD ME TO!
GOOD JOB.
HERE'S A REWARD.
Yay!
THANK YOU, DR. SAJI...
CAN I HAVE THIS?
HEY!
GIVE IT BACK!
YOU CAN SHARE.
BUT I WAS THE ONE WHO GOT IT!
YOU'RE THE OLDER BROTHER.
SO BE NICE.
Yay.

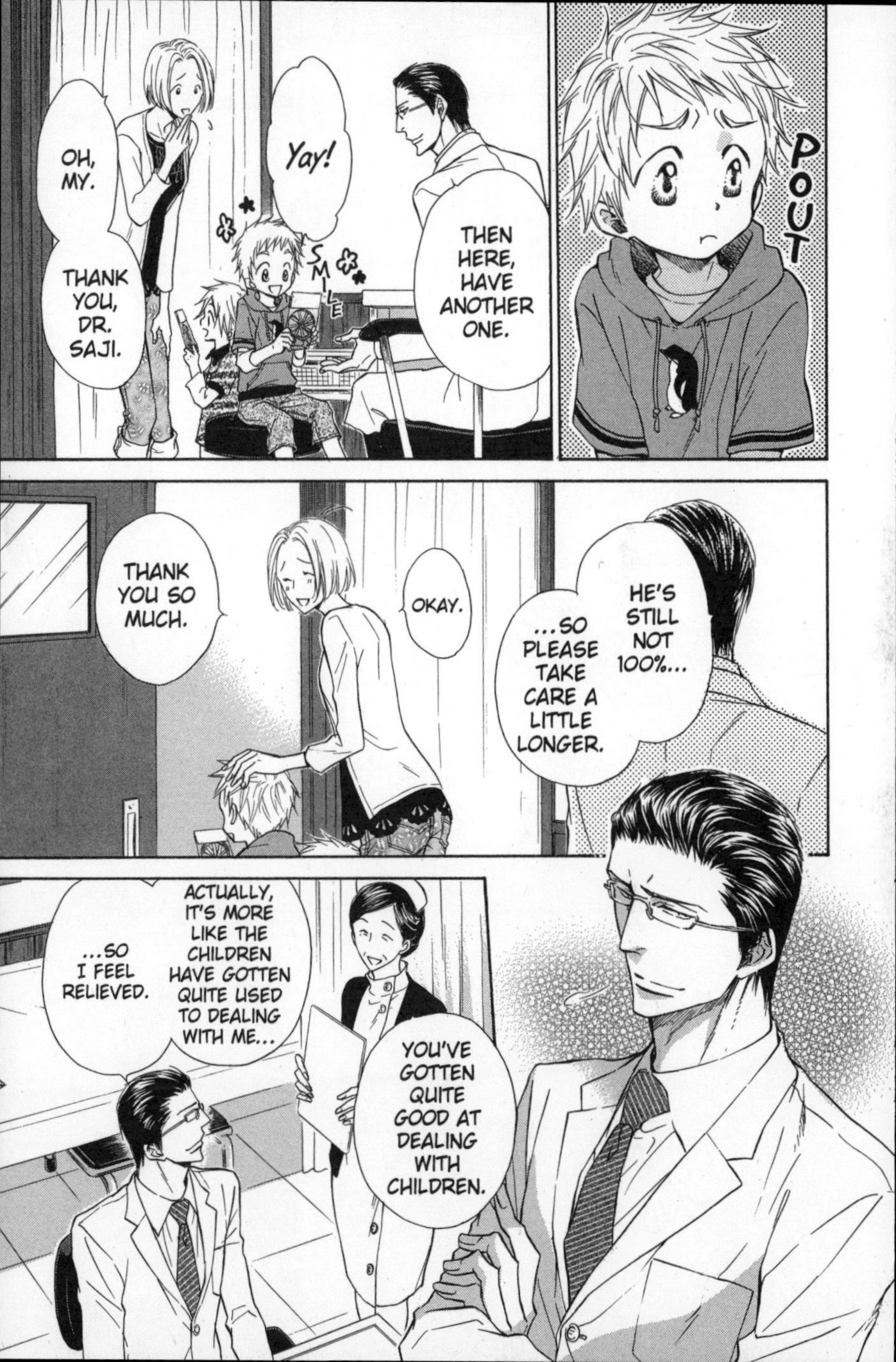
POUT
THEN HERE, HAVE ANOTHER ONE.
Yay!
SMILE
OH, MY.
THANK YOU, DR. SAJI.
HE'S STILL NOT 100%...
...SO PLEASE TAKE CARE A LITTLE LONGER.
OKAY.
THANK YOU SO MUCH.
YOU'VE GOTTEN QUITE GOOD AT DEALING WITH CHILDREN.
ACTUALLY, IT'S MORE LIKE THE CHILDREN HAVE GOTTEN QUITE USED TO DEALING WITH ME...
...SO I FEEL RELIEVED.

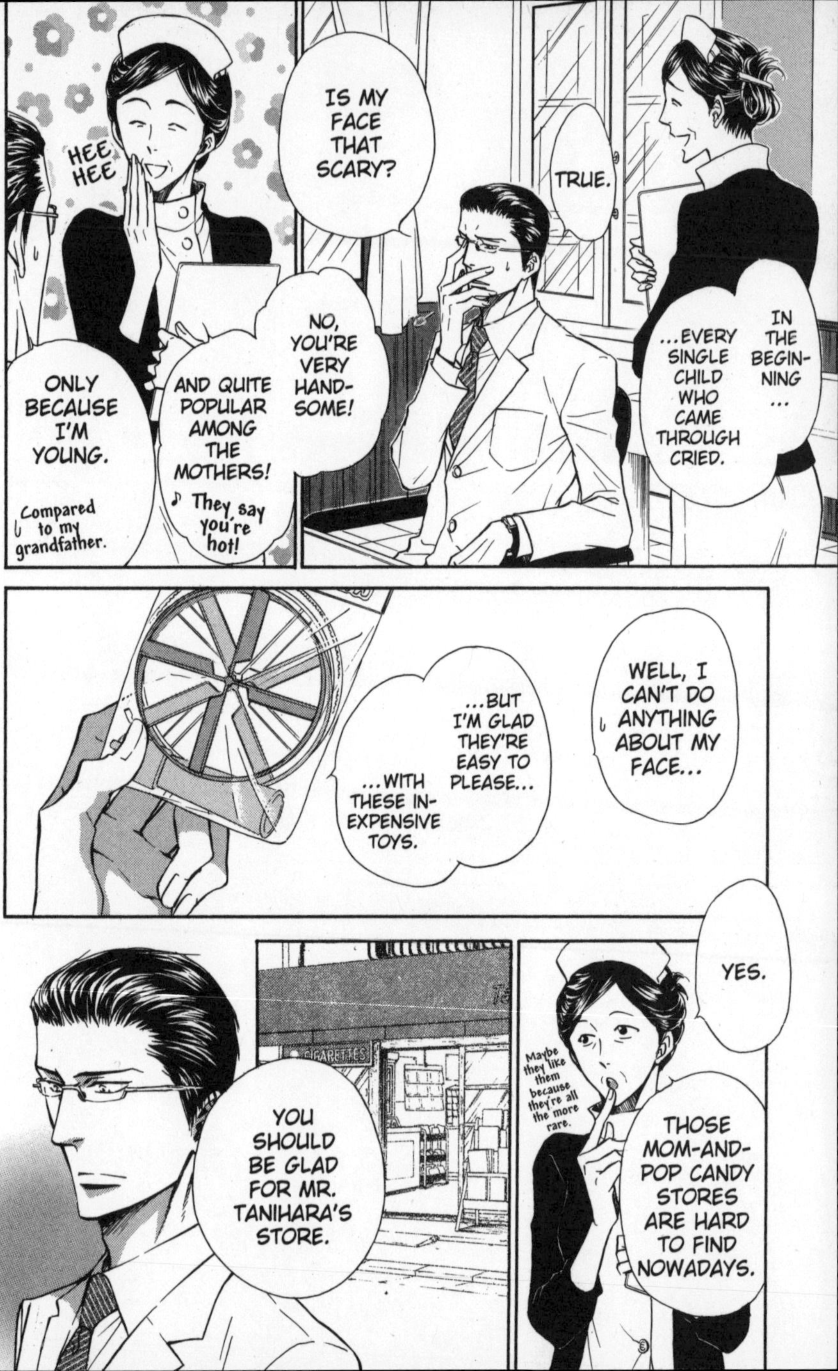
IN THE BEGIN-NING...
...EVERY SINGLE CHILD WHO CAME THROUGH CRIED.
TRUE.
IS MY FACE THAT SCARY?
NO, YOU'RE VERY HAND-SOME!
AND QUITE POPULAR AMONG THE MOTHERS!
♪ They say you're hot!
HEE HEE
ONLY BECAUSE I'M YOUNG.
Compared to my grandfather.
WELL, I CAN'T DO ANYTHING ABOUT MY FACE...
...BUT I'M GLAD THEY'RE EASY TO PLEASE...
...WITH THESE IN-EXPENSIVE TOYS.
YES.
THOSE MOM-AND-POP CANDY STORES ARE HARD TO FIND NOWADAYS.
Maybe they like them because they're all the more rare.
CIGARETTES
YOU SHOULD BE GLAD FOR MR. TANIHARA'S STORE.

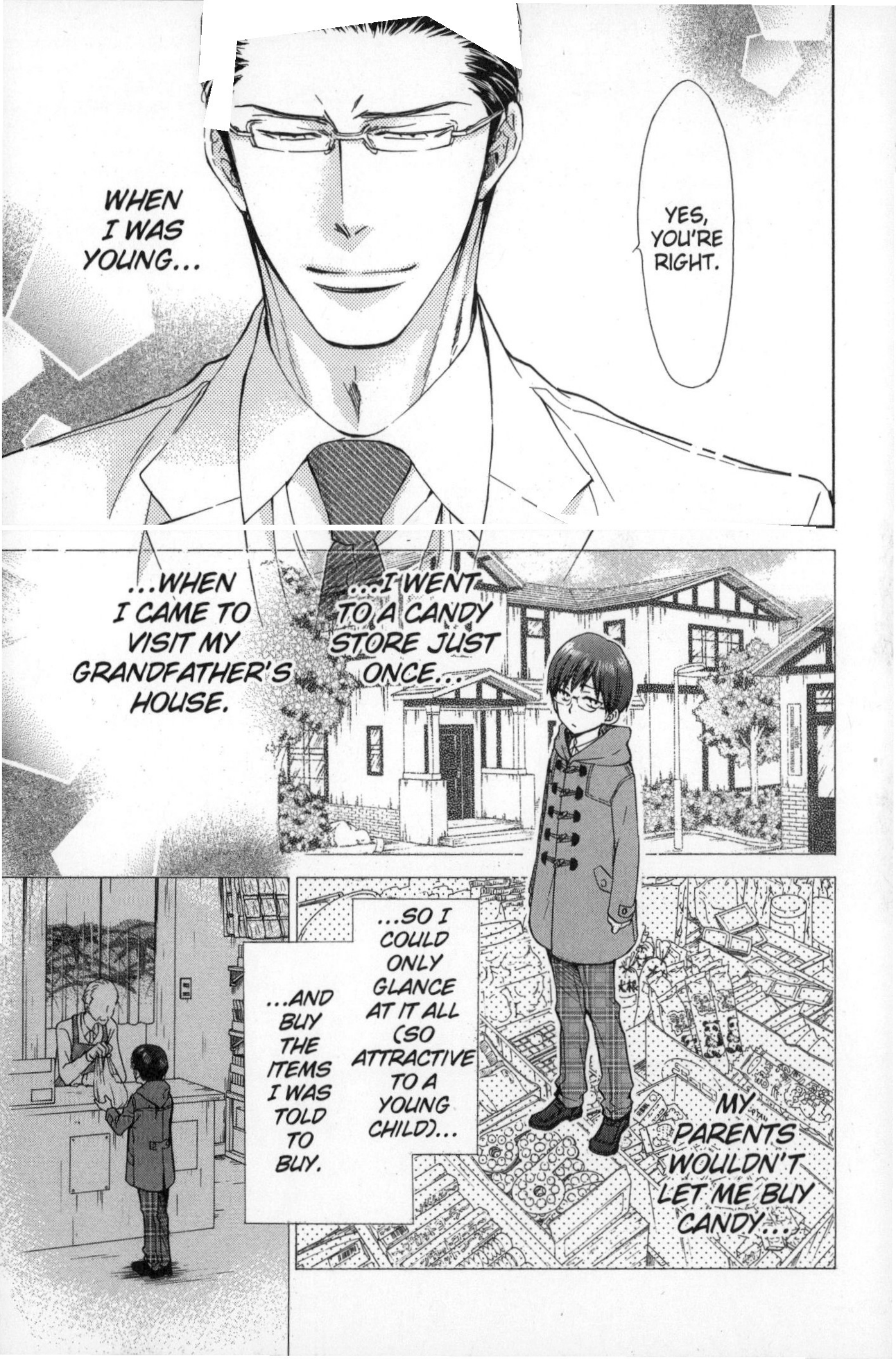
YES, YOU'RE RIGHT.
WHEN I WAS YOUNG...
...WHEN I CAME TO VISIT MY GRANDFATHER'S HOUSE.
...I WENT TO A CANDY STORE JUST ONCE...
MY PARENTS WOULDN'T LET ME BUY CANDY...
...SO I COULD ONLY GLANCE AT IT ALL (SO ATTRACTIVE TO A YOUNG CHILD)...
...AND BUY THE ITEMS I WAS TOLD TO BUY.

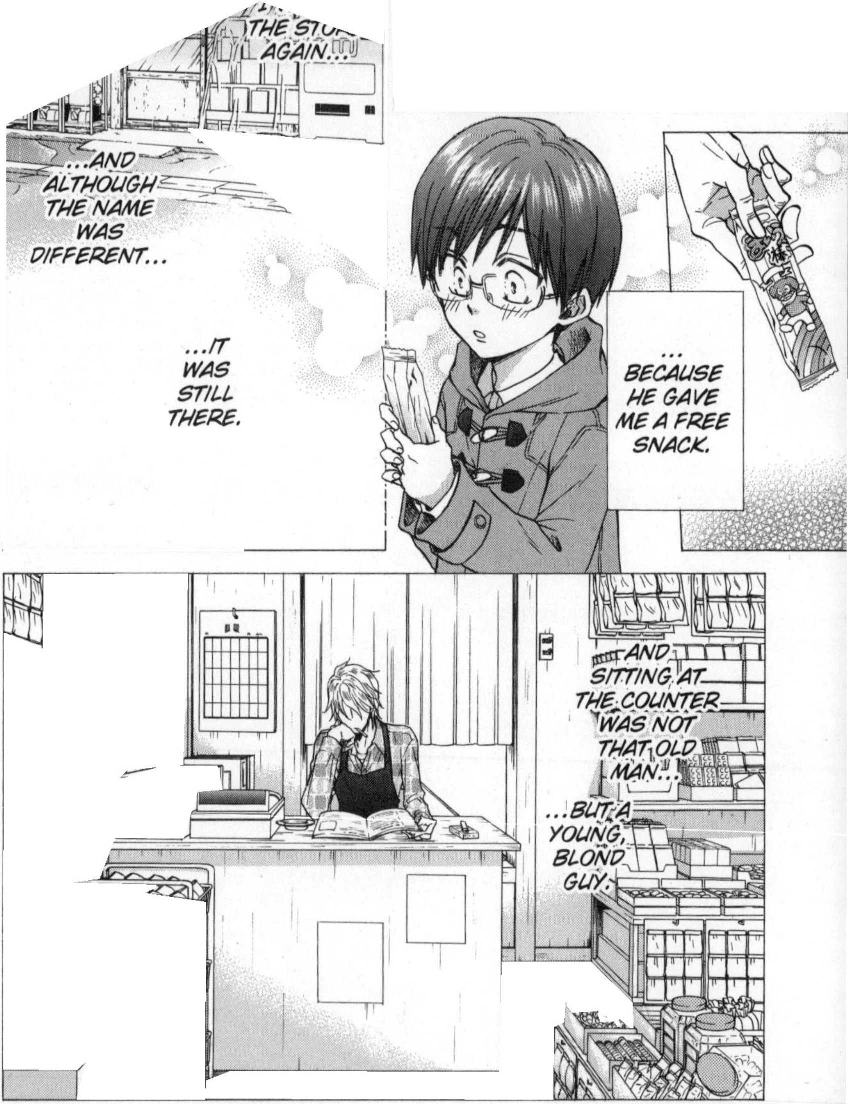
THE STO AGAIN...
...AND ALTHOUGH THE NAME WAS DIFFERENT...
...IT WAS STILL THERE.
...BECAUSE HE GAVE ME A FREE SNACK.
AND SITTING AT THE COUNTER WAS NOT THAT OLD MAN...
...BUT A YOUNG, BLOND GUY.

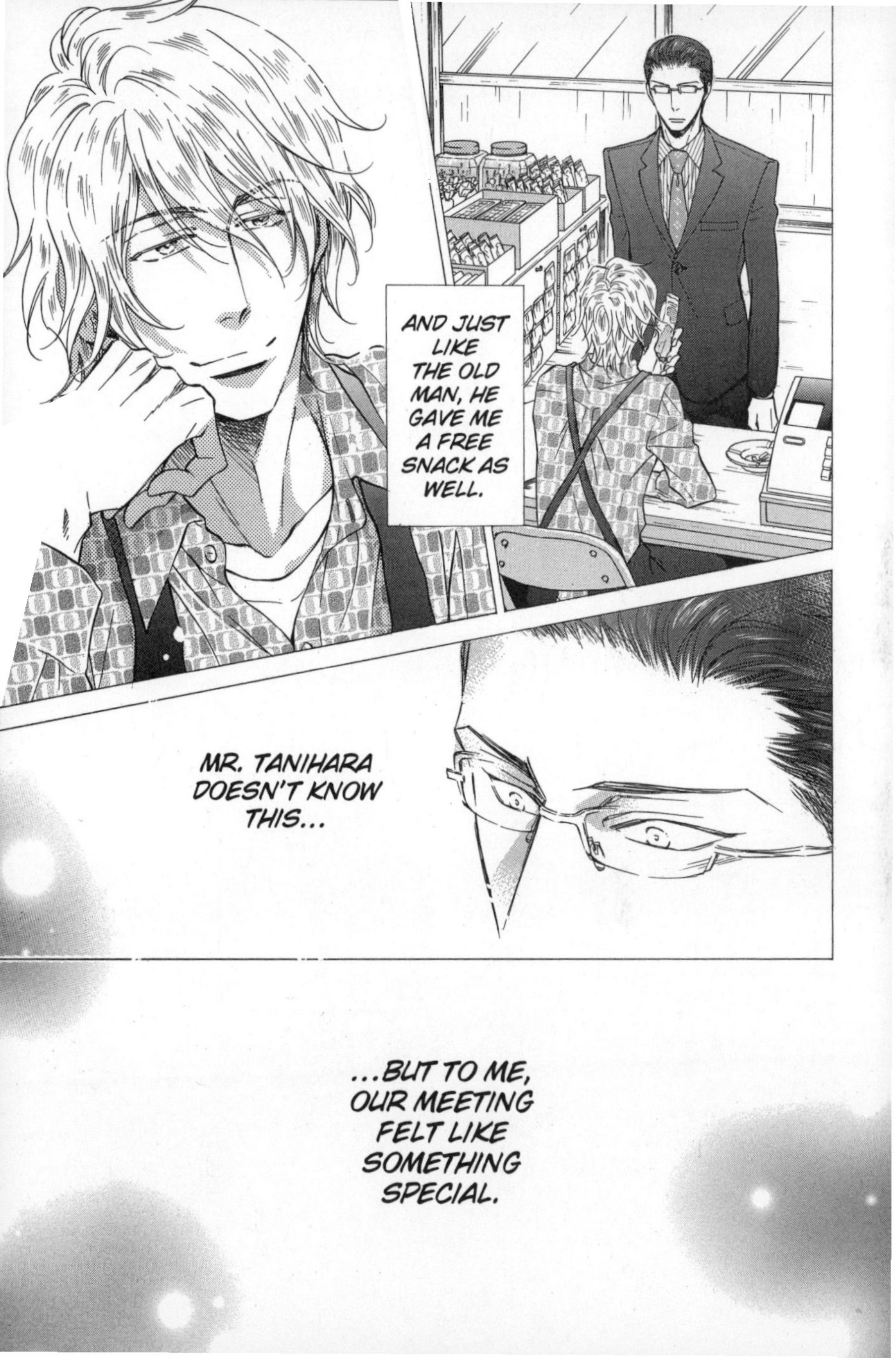
AND JUST LIKE THE OLD MAN, HE GAVE ME A FREE SNACK AS WELL.
MR. TANIHARA DOESN'T KNOW THIS...
...BUT TO ME, OUR MEETING FELT LIKE SOMETHING SPECIAL.

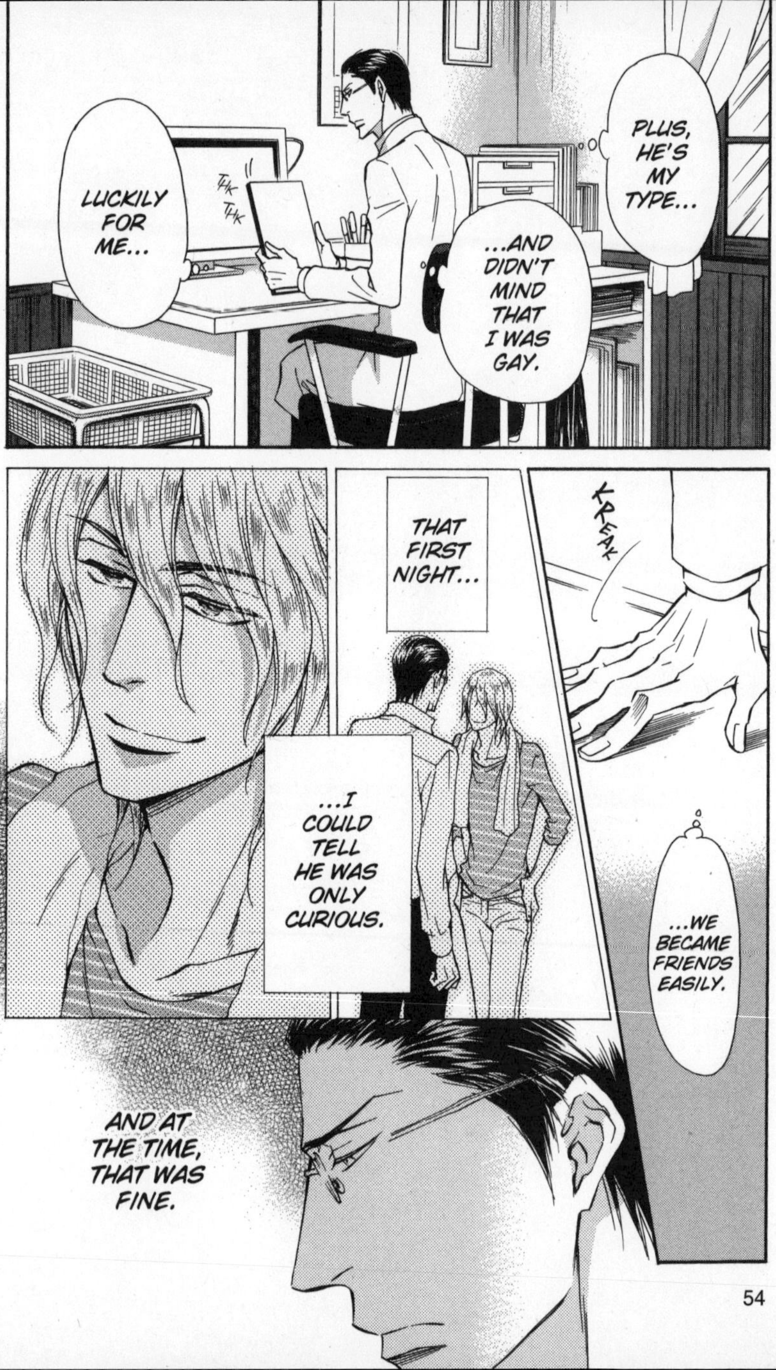
PLUS, HE'S MY TYPE...
...AND DIDN'T MIND THAT I WAS GAY.
LUCKILY FOR ME...
THK THK
KREAK
...WE BECAME FRIENDS EASILY.
THAT FIRST NIGHT...
...I COULD TELL HE WAS ONLY CURIOUS.
AND AT THE TIME, THAT WAS FINE.

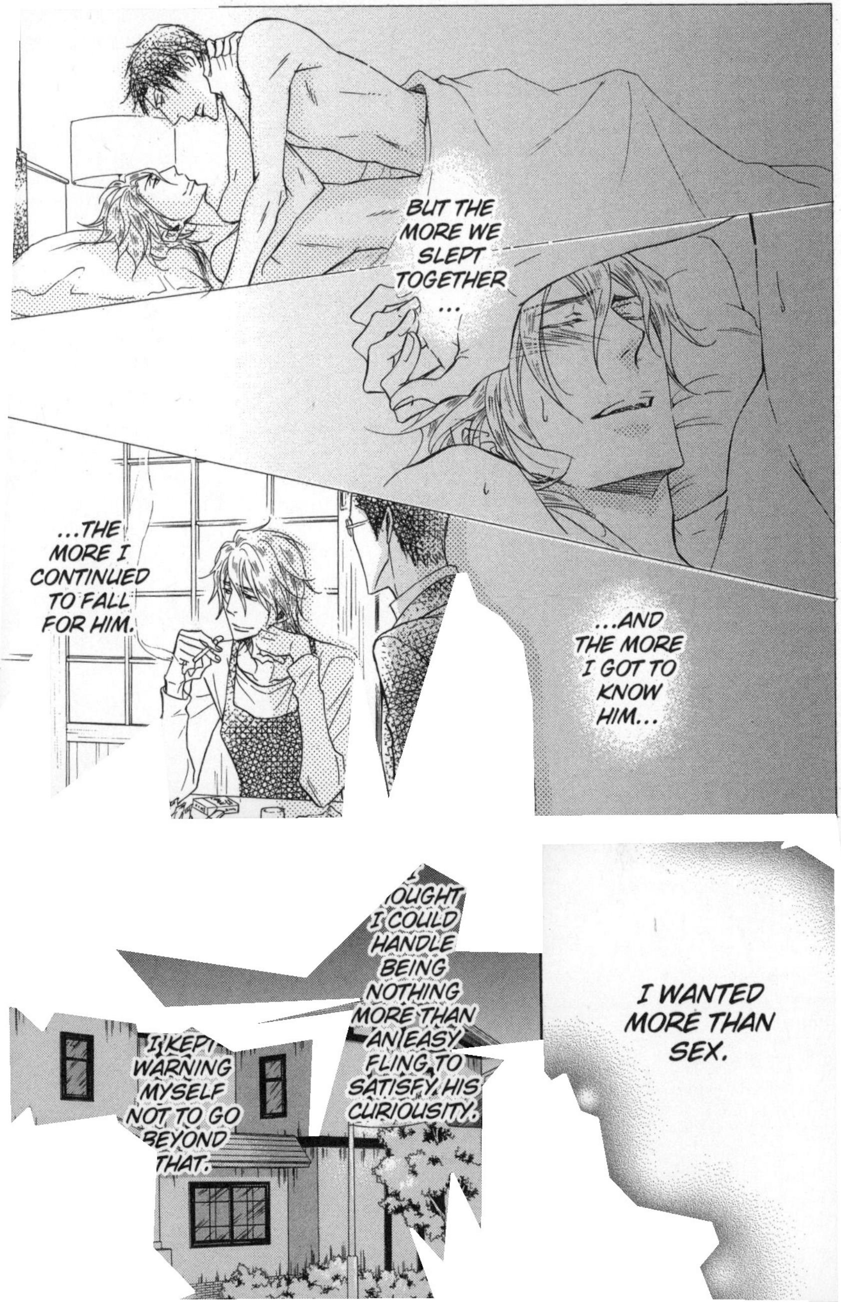
BUT THE MORE WE SLEPT TOGETHER ...
...AND THE MORE I GOT TO KNOW HIM...
...THE MORE I CONTINUED TO FALL FOR HIM.
I WANTED MORE THAN SEX.
I COULD HANDLE BEING NOTHING MORE THAN AN EASY FLING TO SATISFY HIS CURIOUSITY.
I KEPT WARNING MYSELF NOT TO GO BEYOND THAT.

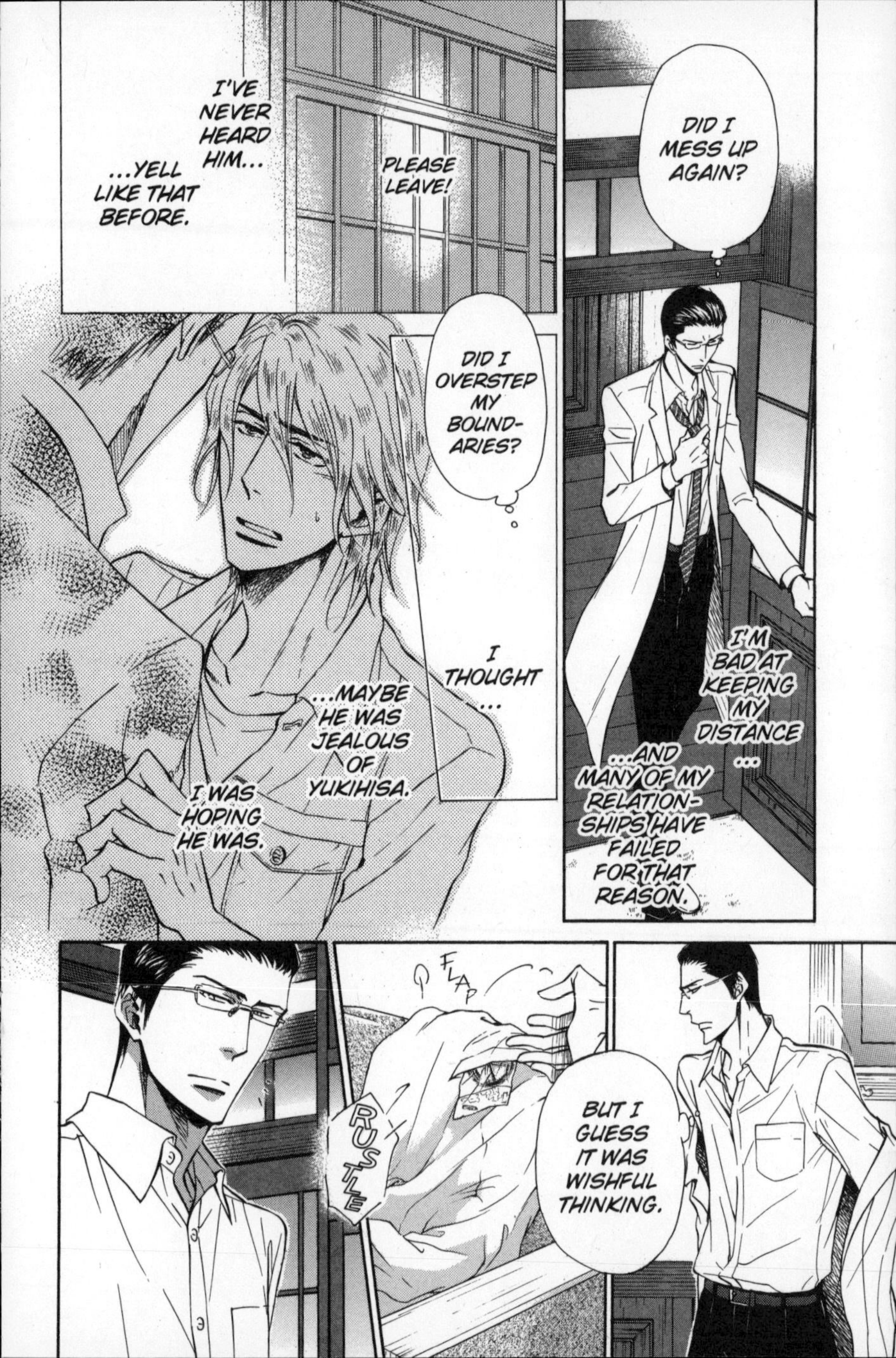
DID I MESS UP AGAIN?
I'M BAD AT KEEPING MY DISTANCE...
...AND MANY OF MY RELATIONSHIPS HAVE FAILED FOR THAT REASON.
PLEASE LEAVE!
I'VE NEVER HEARD HIM...
...YELL LIKE THAT BEFORE.
DID I OVERSTEP MY BOUNDARIES?
I THOUGHT...
...MAYBE HE WAS JEALOUS OF YUKIHISA.
I WAS HOPING HE WAS.
BUT I GUESS IT WAS WISHFUL THINKING.
FLAP
RUSTLE

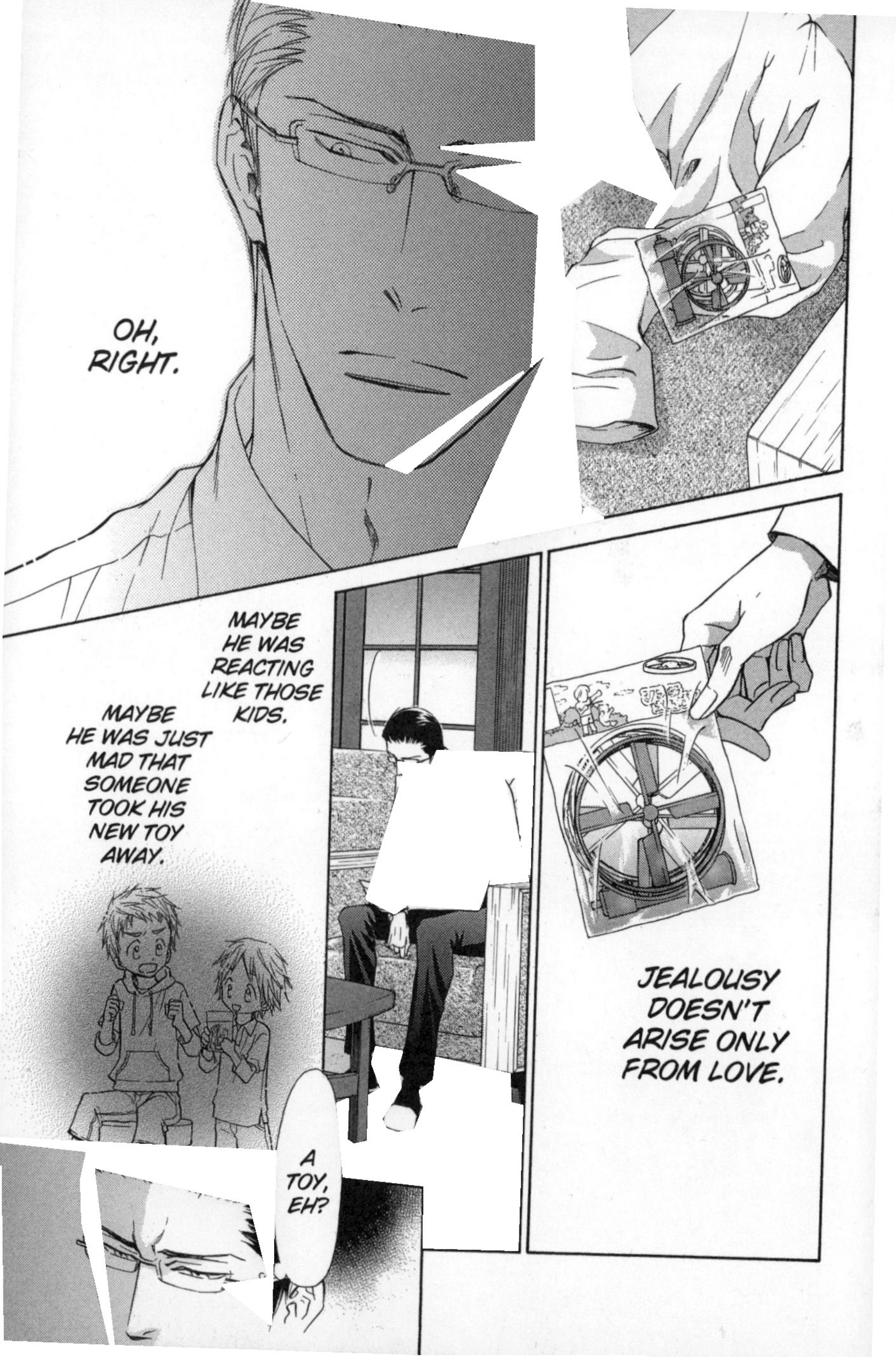
OH, RIGHT.
JEALOUSY DOESN'T ARISE ONLY FROM LOVE.
MAYBE HE WAS REACTING LIKE THOSE KIDS.
MAYBE HE WAS JUST MAD THAT SOMEONE TOOK HIS NEW TOY AWAY.
A TOY, EH?

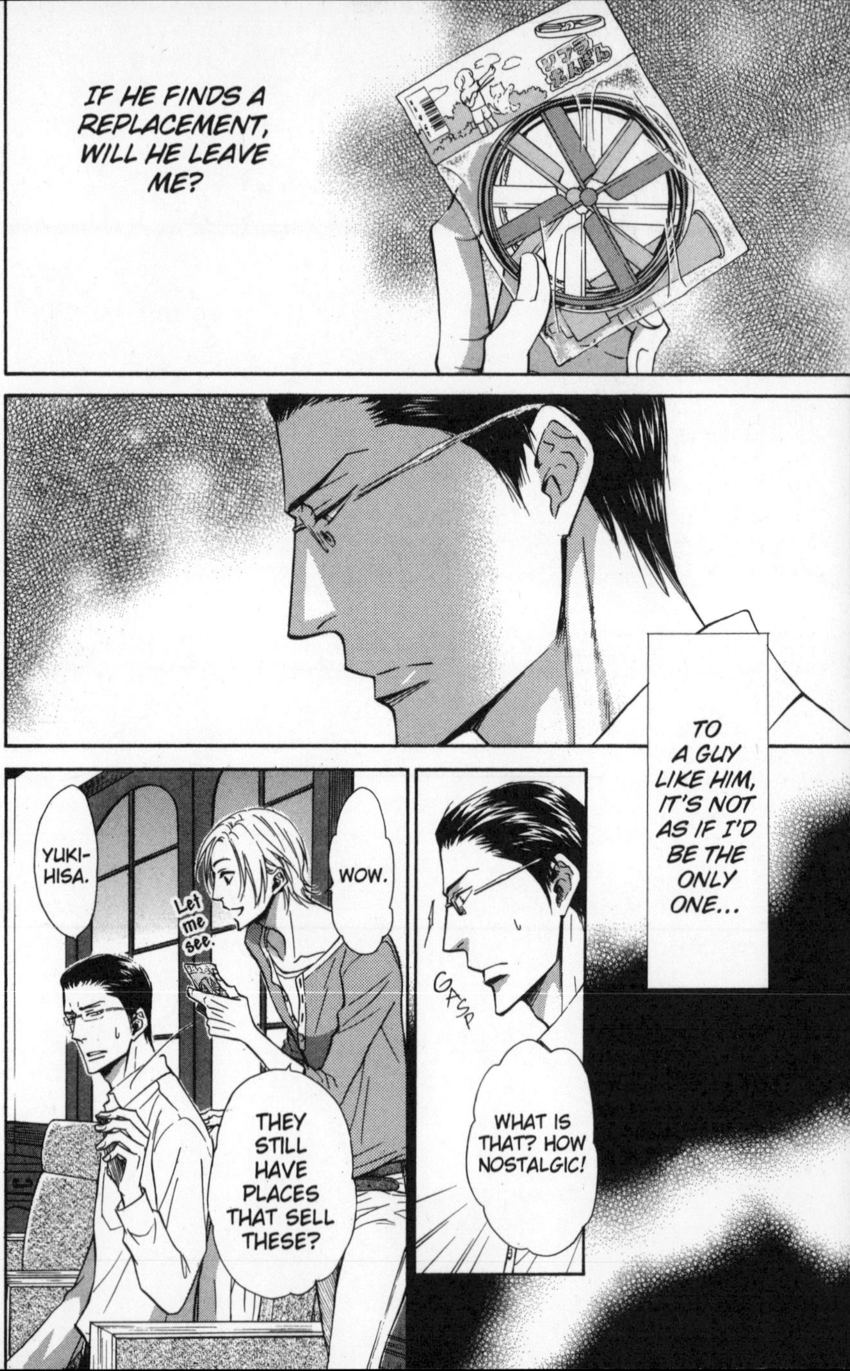
IF HE FINDS A REPLACEMENT, WILL HE LEAVE ME?
TO A GUY LIKE HIM, IT'S NOT AS IF I'D BE THE ONLY ONE...
GASP
WHAT IS THAT? HOW NOSTALGIC!
WOW.
Let me see.
YUKI-HISA.
THEY STILL HAVE PLACES THAT SELL THESE?

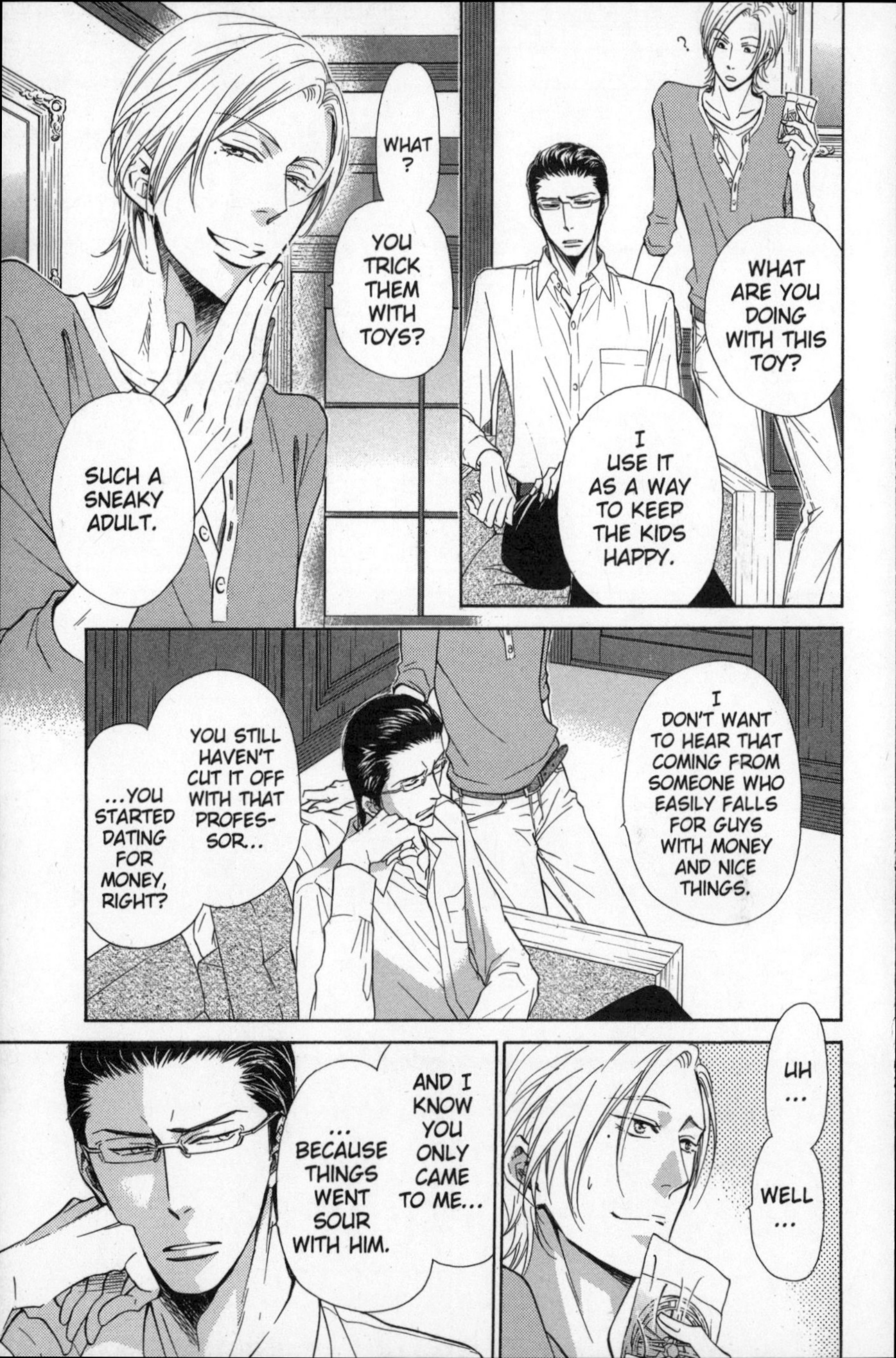
?
WHAT ARE YOU DOING WITH THIS TOY?
I USE IT AS A WAY TO KEEP THE KIDS HAPPY.
WHAT?
YOU TRICK THEM WITH TOYS?
SUCH A SNEAKY ADULT.
I DON'T WANT TO HEAR THAT COMING FROM SOMEONE WHO EASILY FALLS FOR GUYS WITH MONEY AND NICE THINGS.
YOU STILL HAVEN'T CUT IT OFF WITH THAT PROFES-SOR...
...YOU STARTED DATING FOR MONEY, RIGHT?
UH...
WELL...
AND I KNOW YOU ONLY CAME TO ME...
...BECAUSE THINGS WENT SOUR WITH HIM.

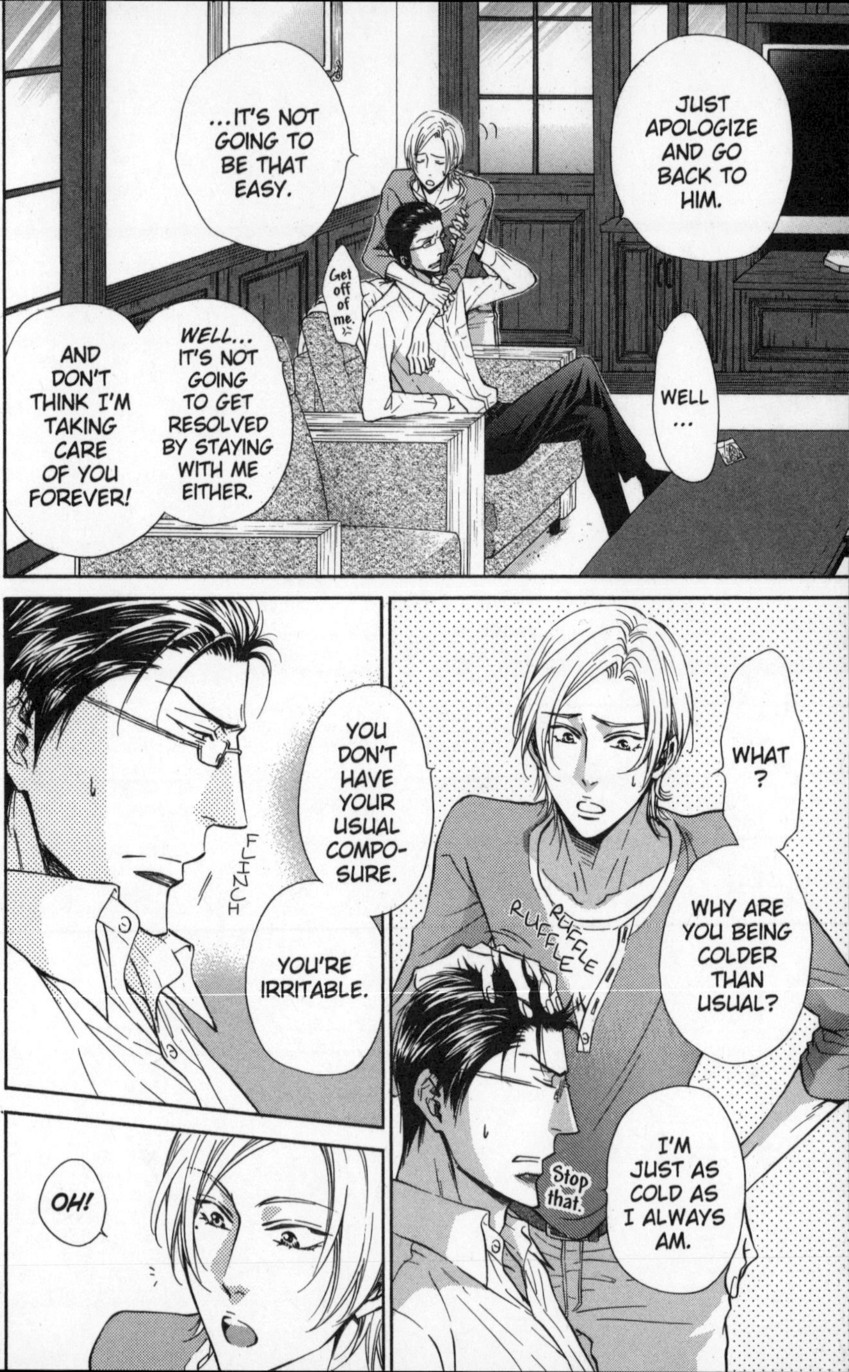
JUST APOLOGIZE AND GO BACK TO HIM.
...IT'S NOT GOING TO BE THAT EASY.
Get off of me.
WELL...
WELL... IT'S NOT GOING TO GET RESOLVED BY STAYING WITH ME EITHER.
AND DON'T THINK I'M TAKING CARE OF YOU FOREVER!
WHAT?
WHY ARE YOU BEING COLDER THAN USUAL?
RUFFLE RUFFLE
I'M JUST AS COLD AS I ALWAYS AM.
Stop that.
YOU DON'T HAVE YOUR USUAL COMPOSURE.
FLINCH
YOU'RE IRRITABLE.
OH!

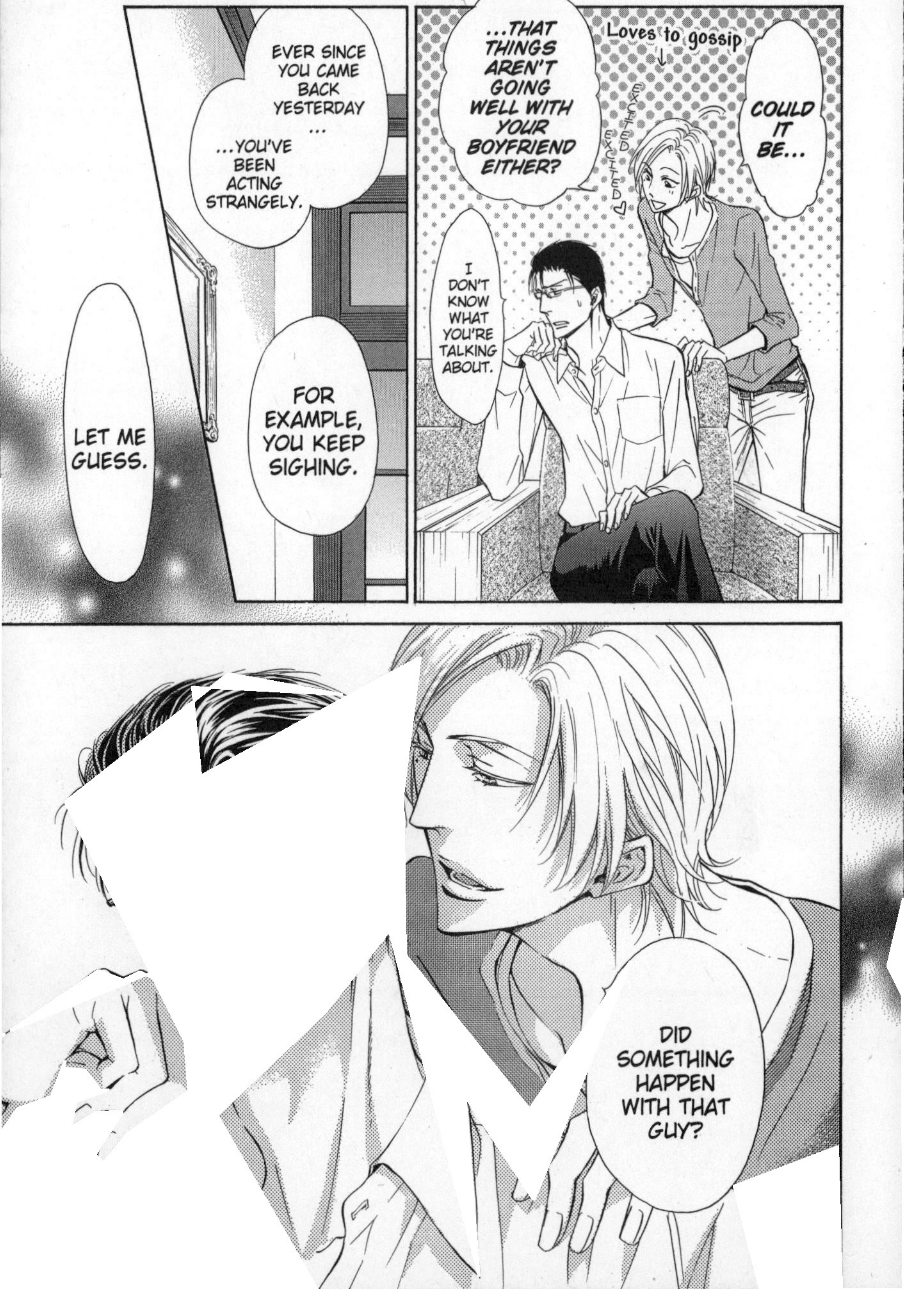
COULD IT BE...
Loves to gossip
EXCITED EXCITED
...THAT THINGS AREN'T GOING WELL WITH YOUR BOYFRIEND EITHER?
I DON'T KNOW WHAT YOU'RE TALKING ABOUT.
EVER SINCE YOU CAME BACK YESTERDAY... ...YOU'VE BEEN ACTING STRANGELY.
FOR EXAMPLE, YOU KEEP SIGHING.
LET ME GUESS.
DID SOMETHING HAPPEN WITH THAT GUY?

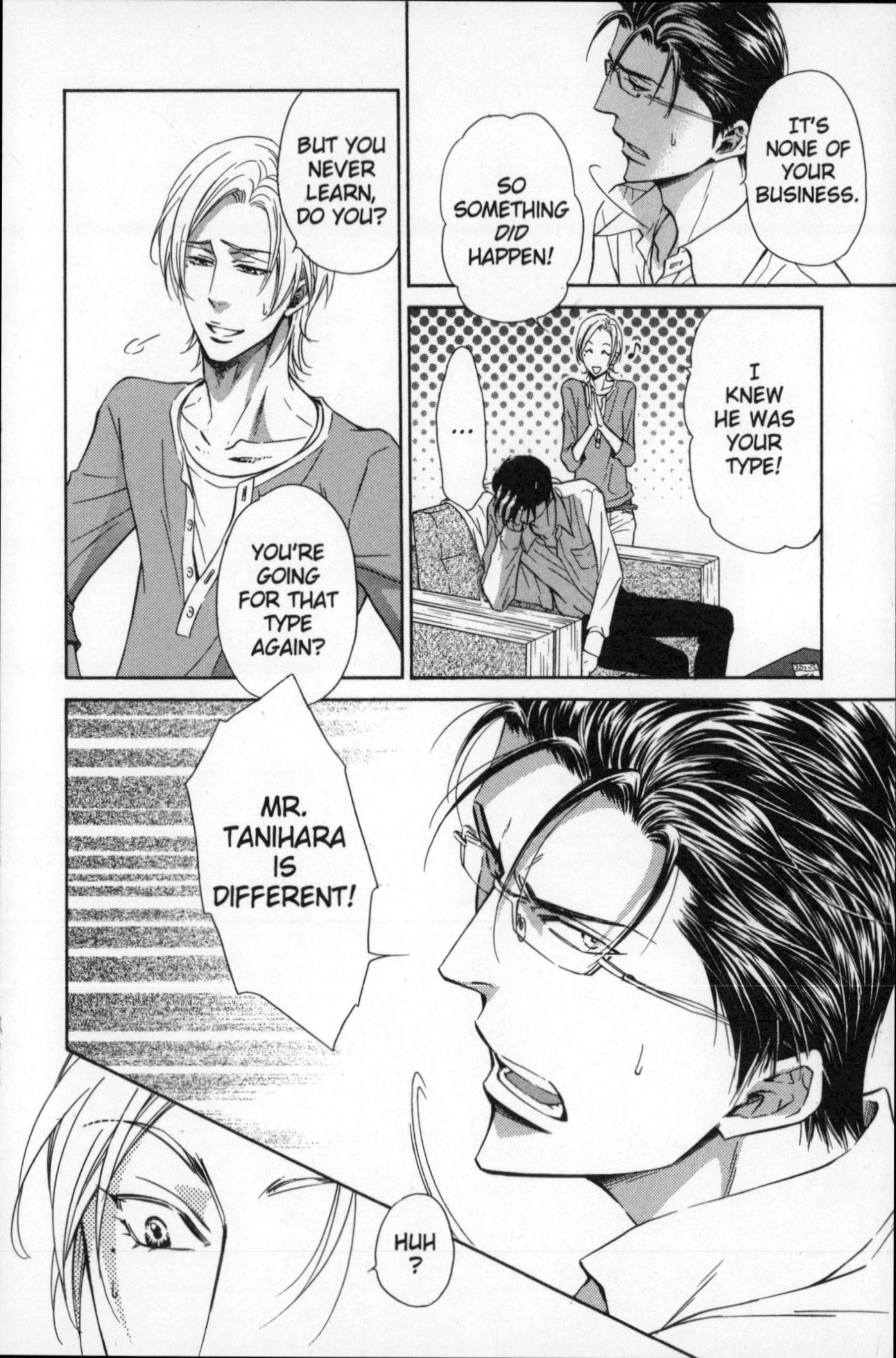
IT'S NONE OF YOUR BUSINESS.
SO SOMETHING *DID* HAPPEN!
I KNEW HE WAS YOUR TYPE!
...
BUT YOU NEVER LEARN, DO YOU?
YOU'RE GOING FOR THAT TYPE AGAIN?
MR. TANIHARA IS DIFFERENT!
HUH?

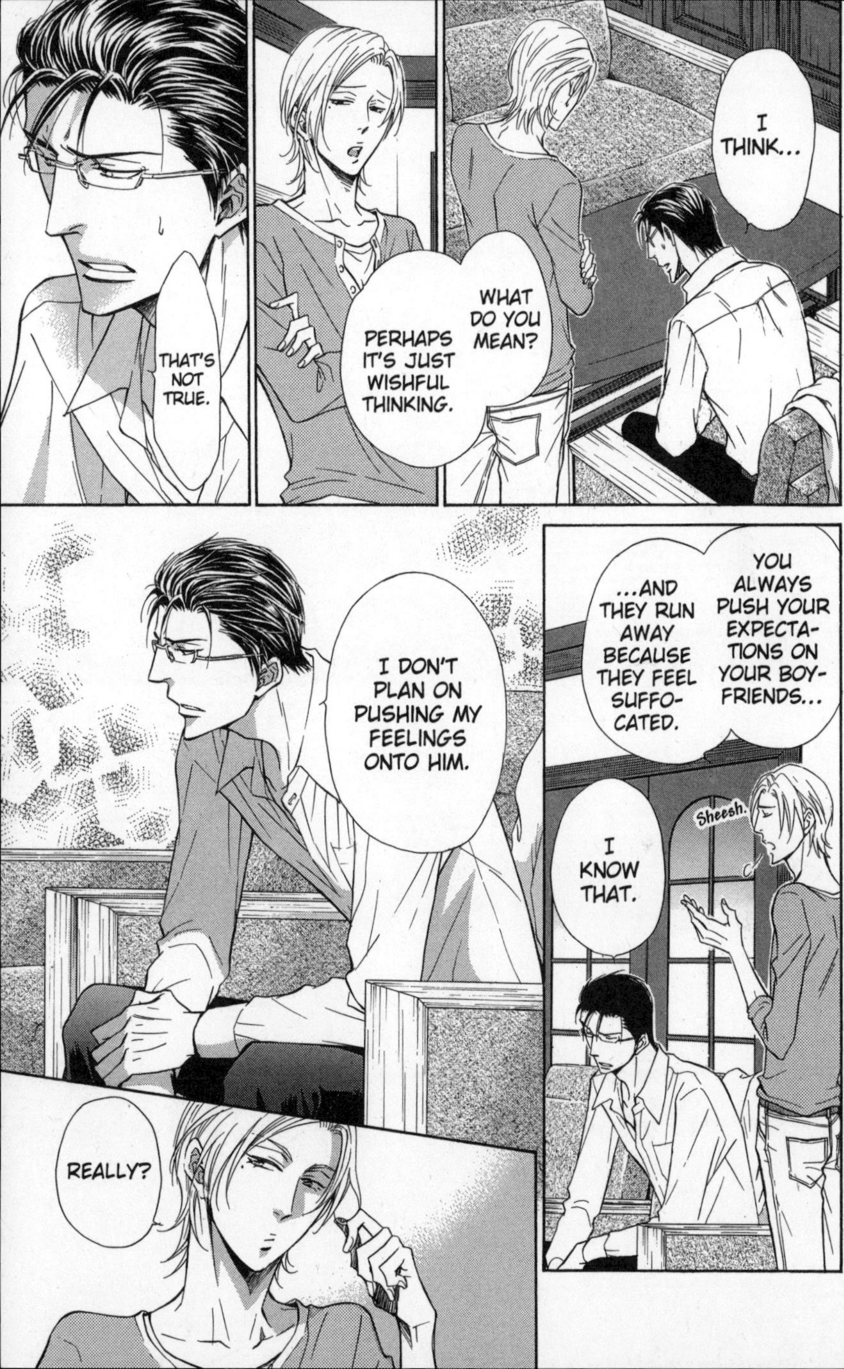
I THINK...
WHAT DO YOU MEAN?
PERHAPS IT'S JUST WISHFUL THINKING.
THAT'S NOT TRUE.
YOU ALWAYS PUSH YOUR EXPECTA-TIONS ON YOUR BOY-FRIENDS...
...AND THEY RUN AWAY BECAUSE THEY FEEL SUFFO-CATED.
Sheesh.
I KNOW THAT.
I DON'T PLAN ON PUSHING MY FEELINGS ONTO HIM.
REALLY?

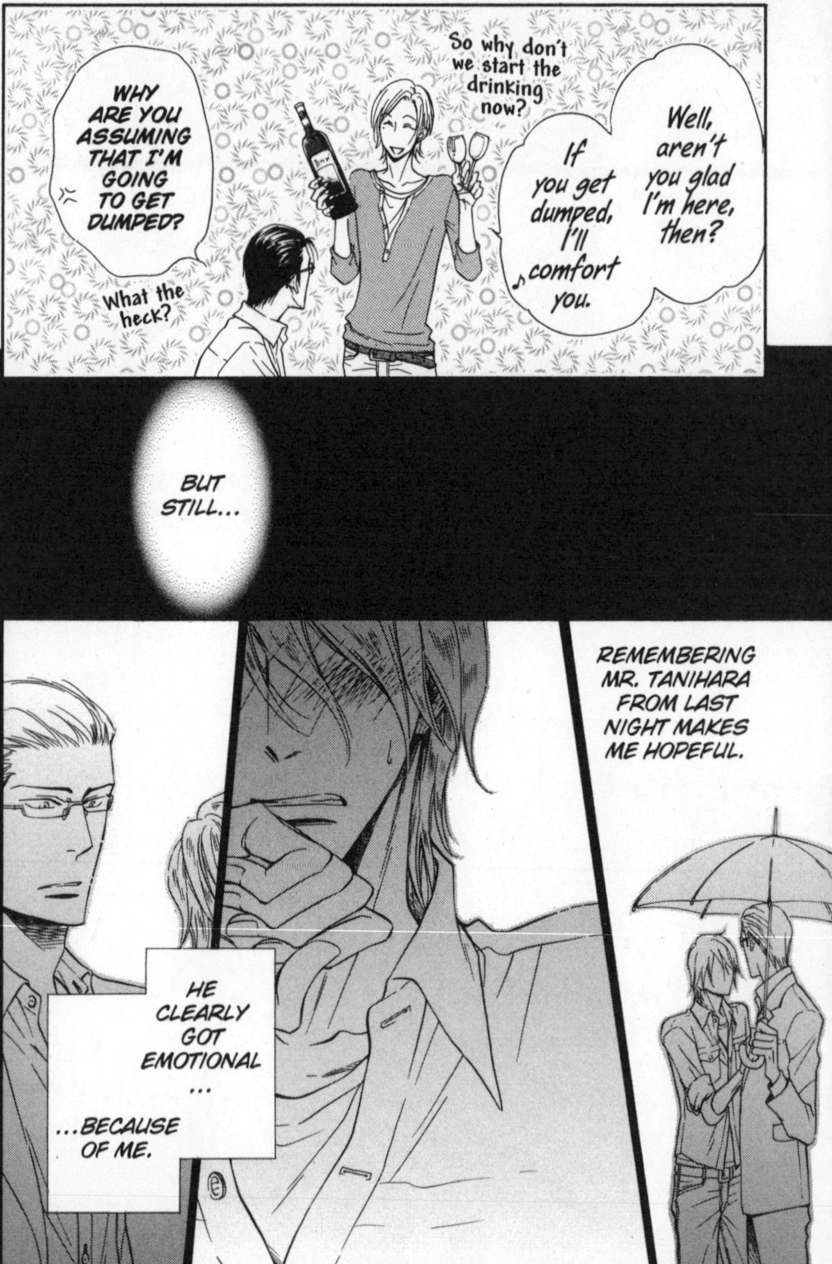
Well, aren't you glad I'm here, then?
If you get dumped, I'll comfort you.
So why don't we start the drinking now?
WHY ARE YOU ASSUMING THAT I'M GOING TO GET DUMPED?
What the heck?
BUT STILL...
REMEMBERING MR. TANIHARA FROM LAST NIGHT MAKES ME HOPEFUL.
HE CLEARLY GOT EMOTIONAL...
...BECAUSE OF ME.

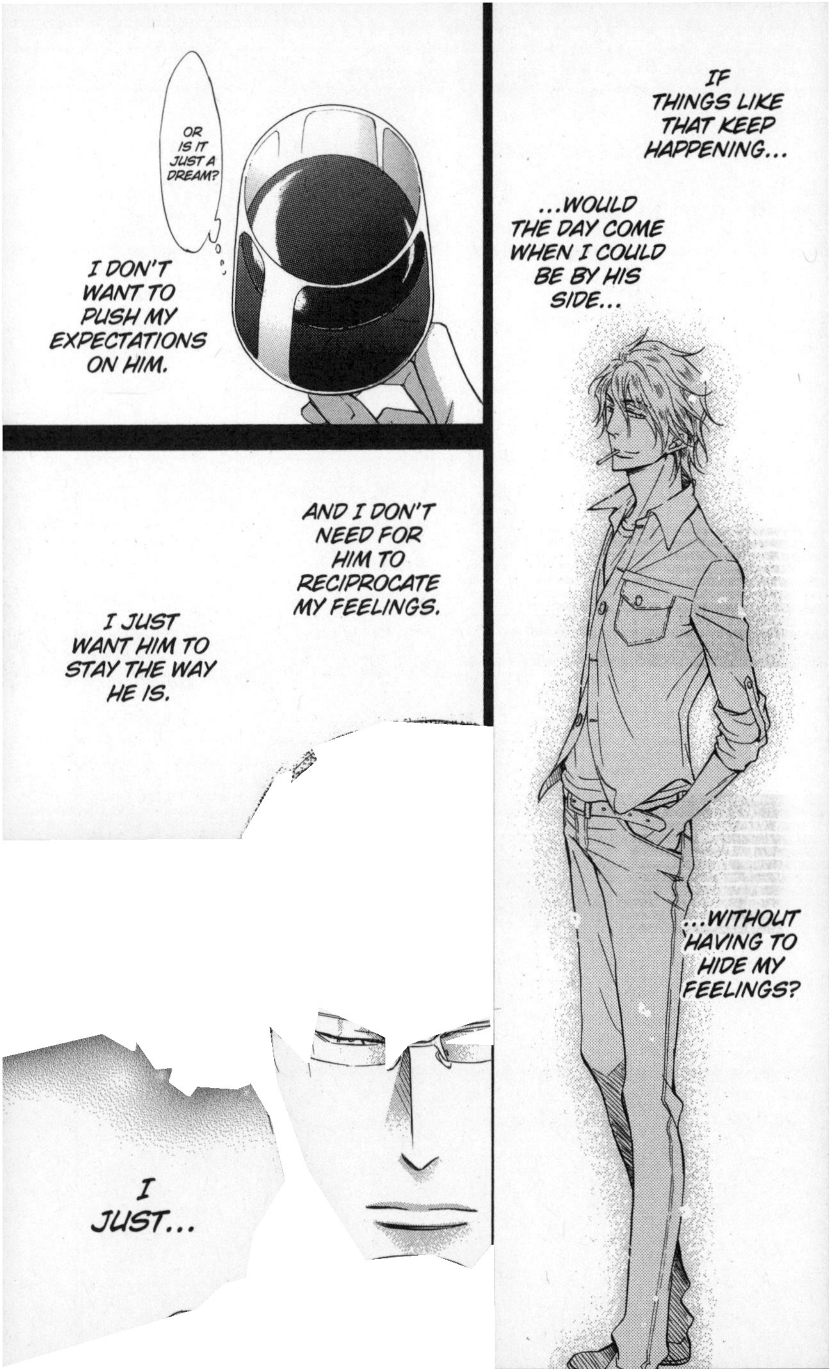
IF THINGS LIKE THAT KEEP HAPPENING...
...WOULD THE DAY COME WHEN I COULD BE BY HIS SIDE...
...WITHOUT HAVING TO HIDE MY FEELINGS?
OR IS IT JUST A DREAM?
I DON'T WANT TO PUSH MY EXPECTATIONS ON HIM.
AND I DON'T NEED FOR HIM TO RECIPROCATE MY FEELINGS.
I JUST WANT HIM TO STAY THE WAY HE IS.
I JUST...

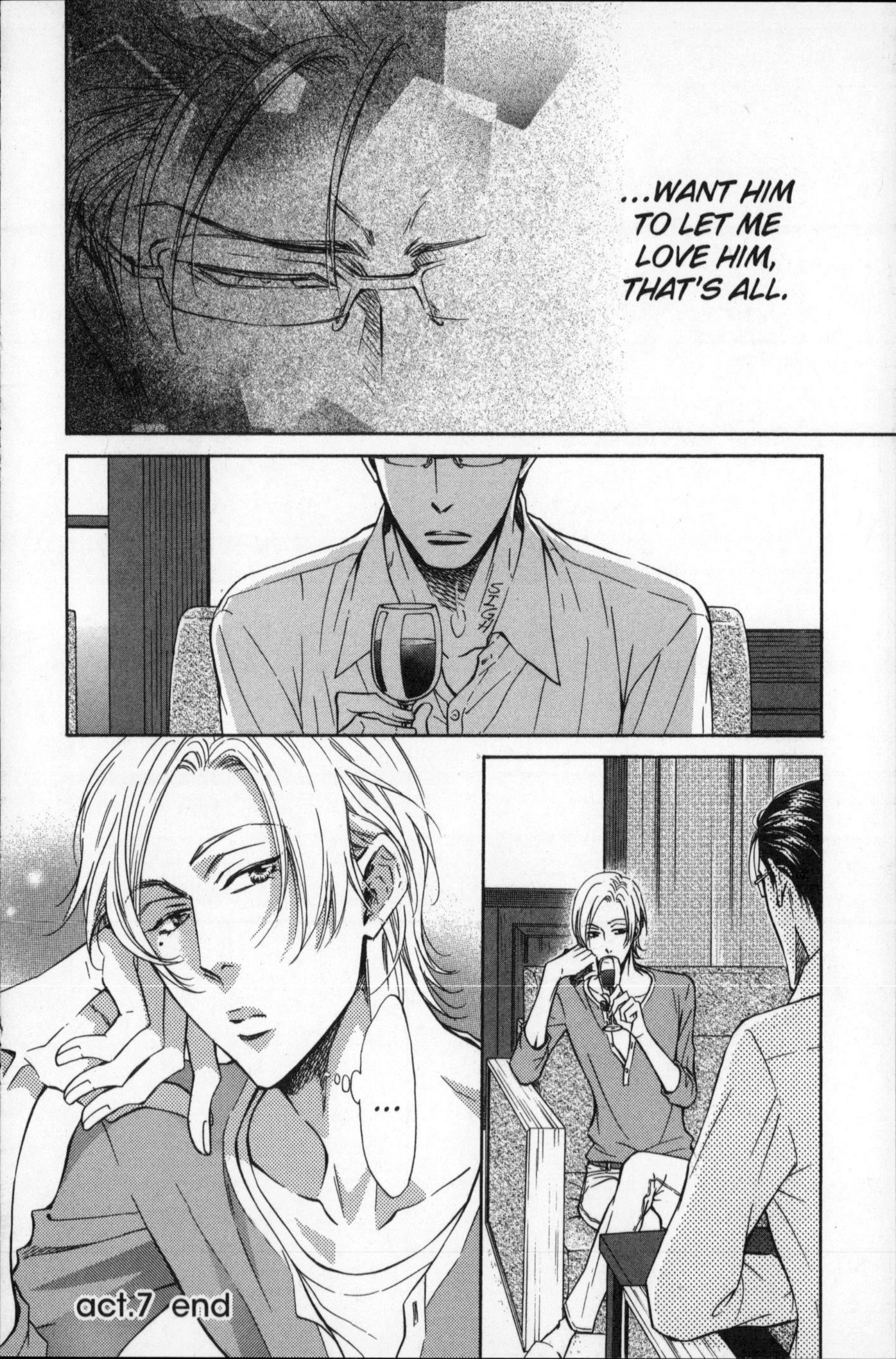
...WANT HIM TO LET ME LOVE HIM, THAT'S ALL.
SIGH
...
act.7 end

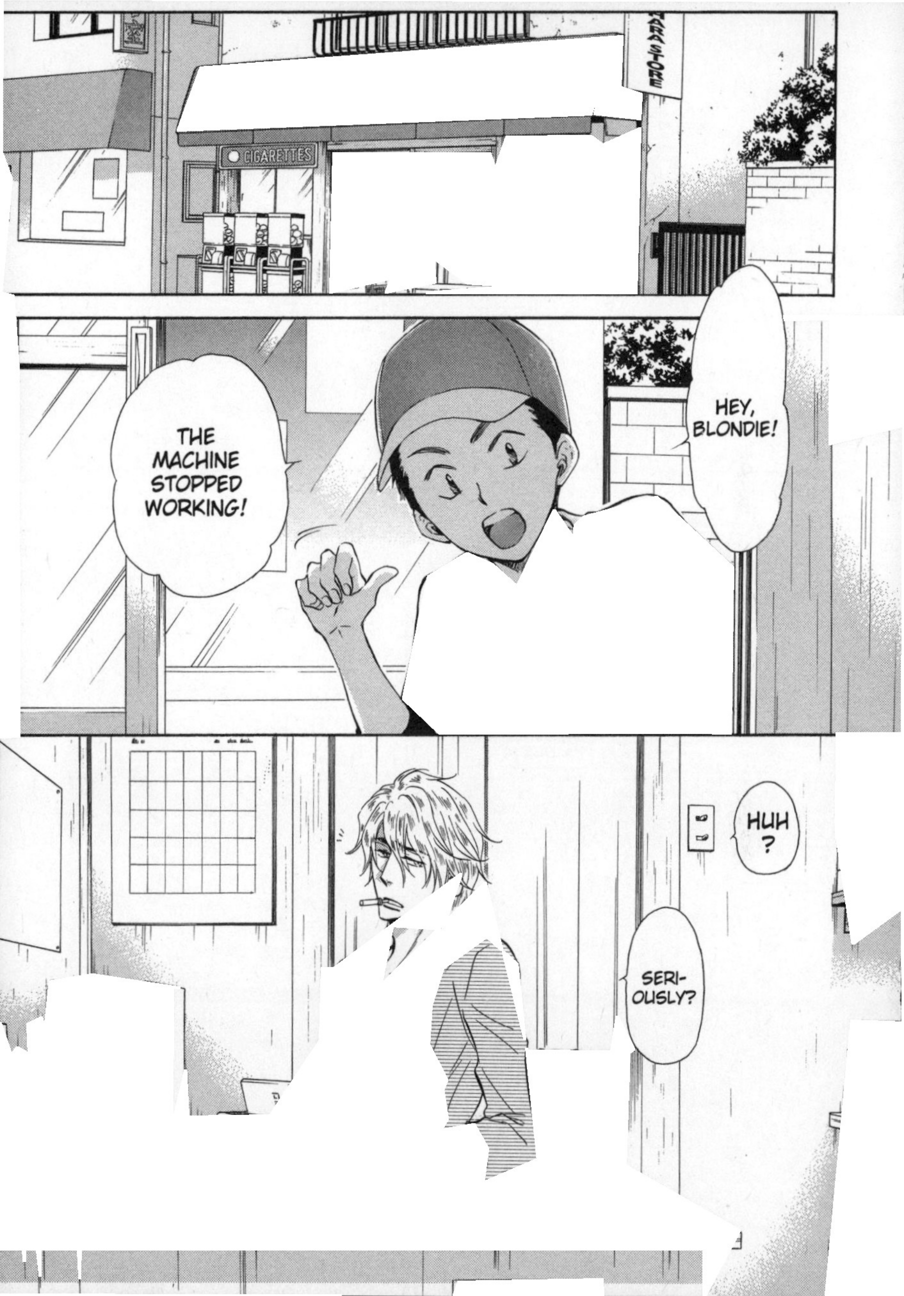
HARA STORE
CIGARETTES
HEY, BLONDIE!
THE MACHINE STOPPED WORKING!
HUH?
SERI-OUSLY?

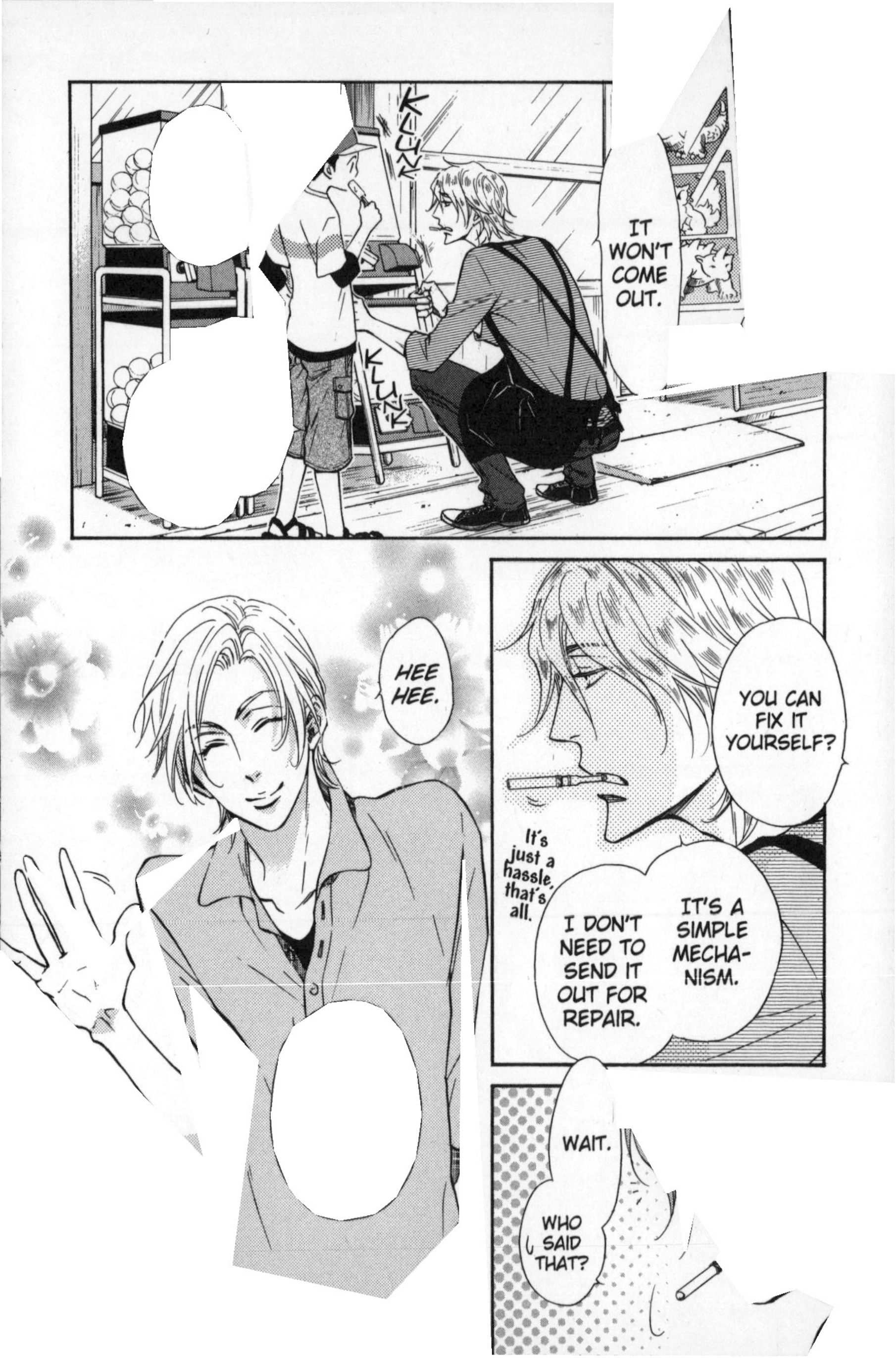
IT WON'T COME OUT.
KLUNK
KLUNK
YOU CAN FIX IT YOURSELF?
IT'S A SIMPLE MECHANISM.
I DON'T NEED TO SEND IT OUT FOR REPAIR.
It's just a hassle, that's all.
WAIT.
WHO SAID THAT?
HEE HEE.

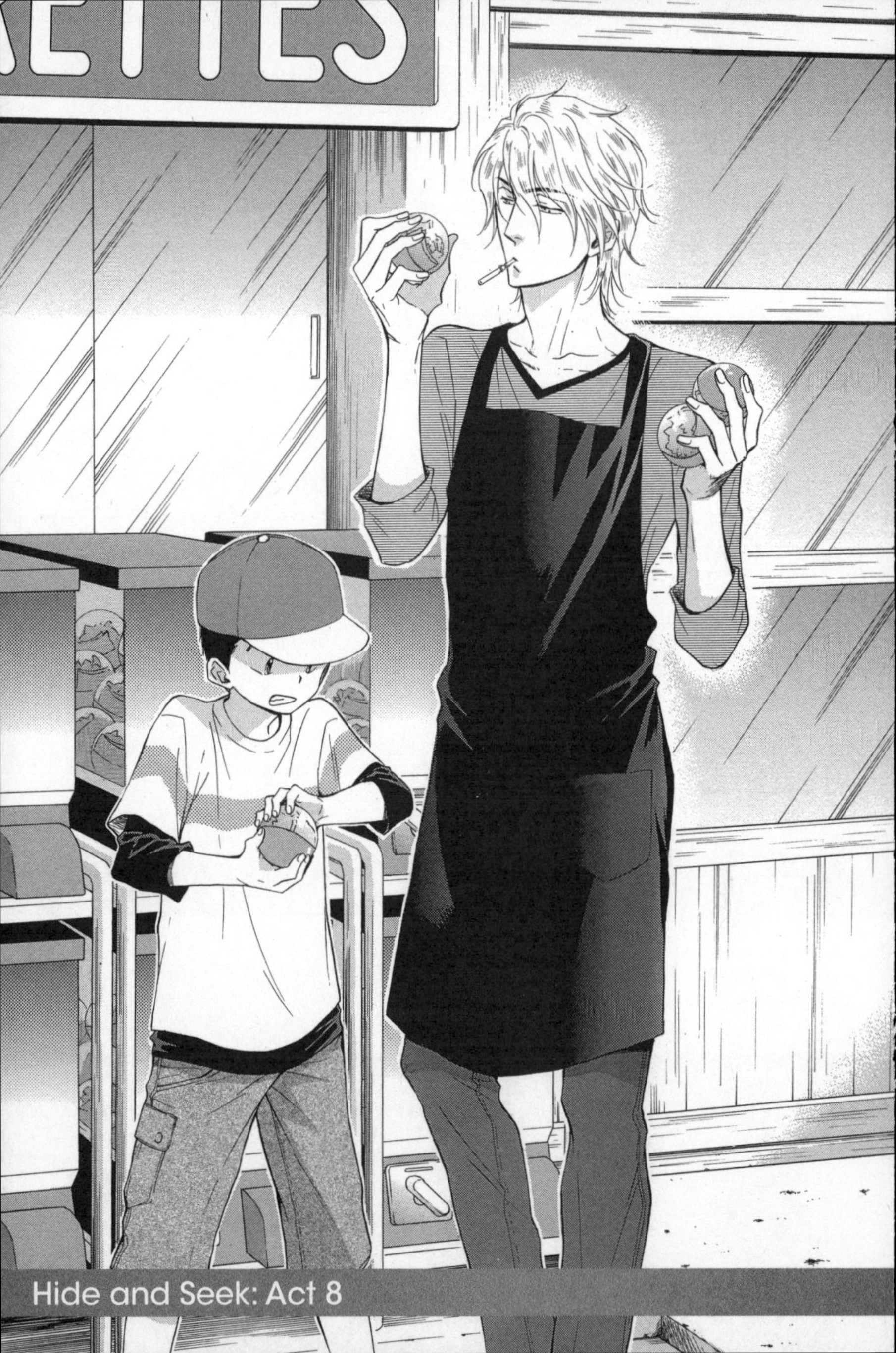

Hide and Seek: Act 8

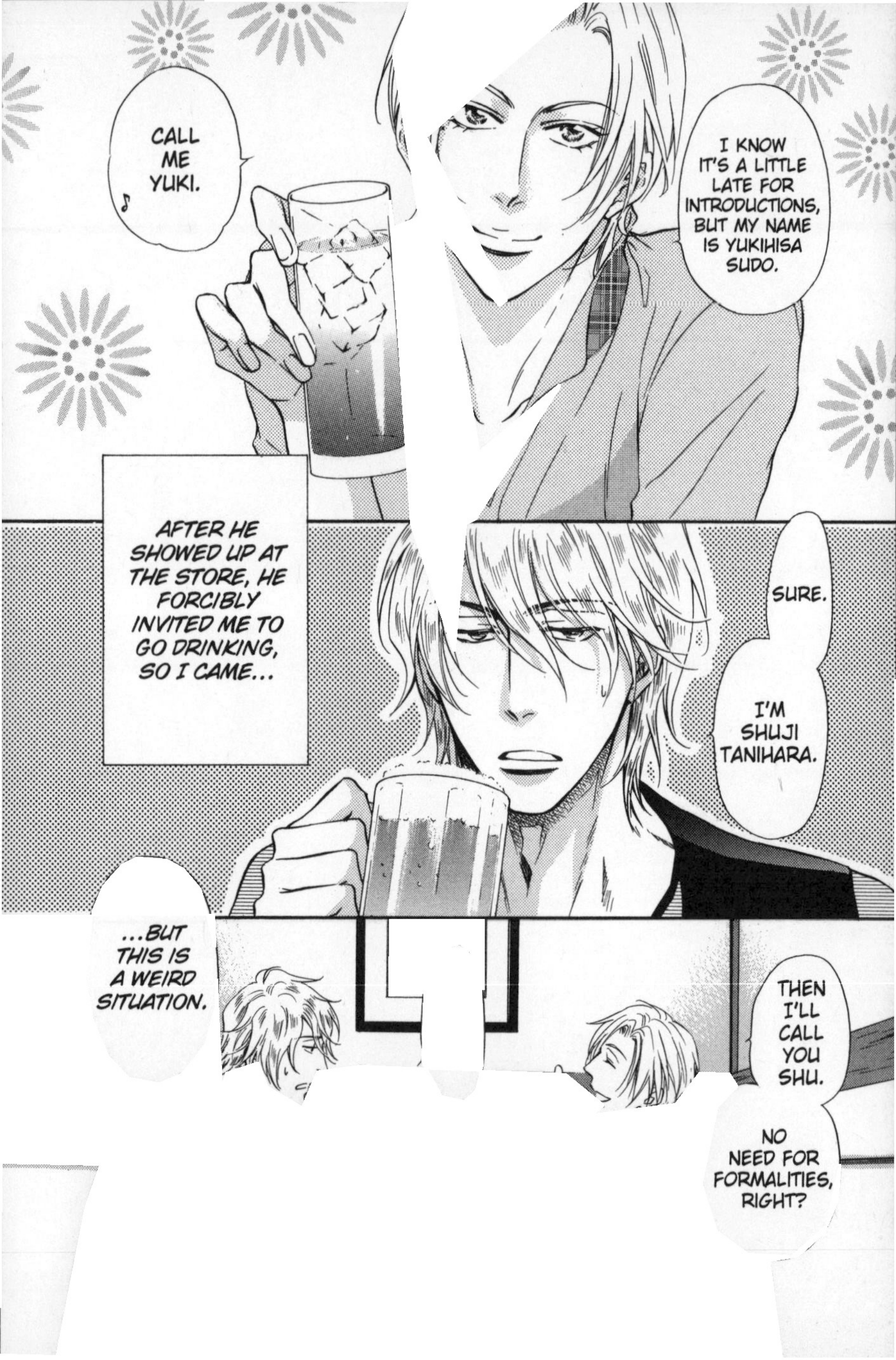
I KNOW IT'S A LITTLE LATE FOR INTRODUCTIONS, BUT MY NAME IS YUKIHISA SUDO.
CALL ME YUKI. ♪
SURE.
I'M SHUJI TANIHARA.
AFTER HE SHOWED UP AT THE STORE, HE FORCIBLY INVITED ME TO GO DRINKING, SO I CAME...
THEN I'LL CALL YOU SHU.
NO NEED FOR FORMALITIES, RIGHT?
...BUT THIS IS A WEIRD SITUATION.

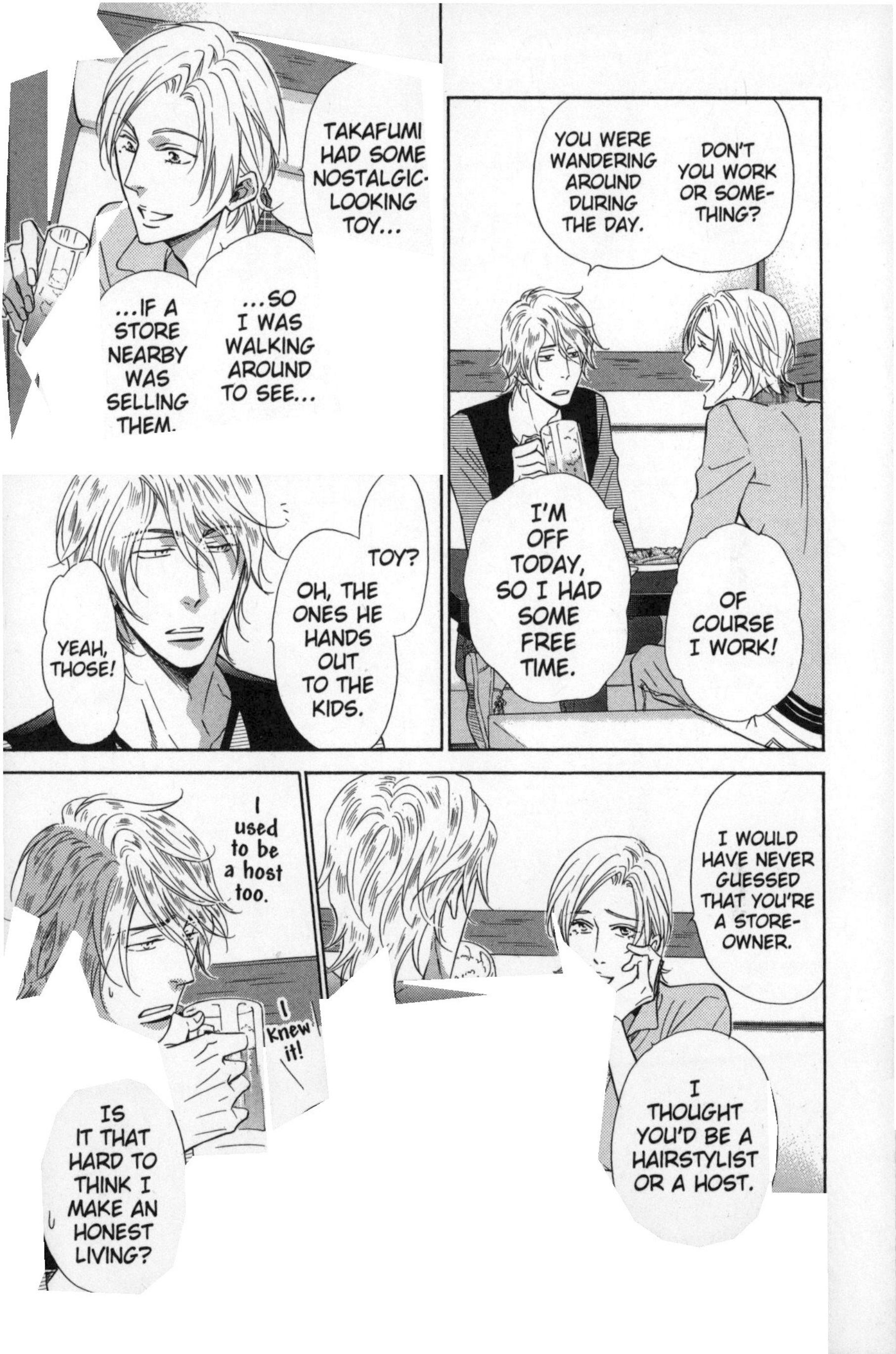
TAKAFUMI HAD SOME NOSTALGIC-LOOKING TOY...
...SO I WAS WALKING AROUND TO SEE...
...IF A STORE NEARBY WAS SELLING THEM.
TOY?
OH, THE ONES HE HANDS OUT TO THE KIDS.
YEAH, THOSE!
DON'T YOU WORK OR SOME-THING?
YOU WERE WANDERING AROUND DURING THE DAY.
OF COURSE I WORK!
I'M OFF TODAY, SO I HAD SOME FREE TIME.
I WOULD HAVE NEVER GUESSED THAT YOU'RE A STORE-OWNER.
I THOUGHT YOU'D BE A HAIRSTYLIST OR A HOST.
I used to be a host too.
I knew it!
IS IT THAT HARD TO THINK I MAKE AN HONEST LIVING?

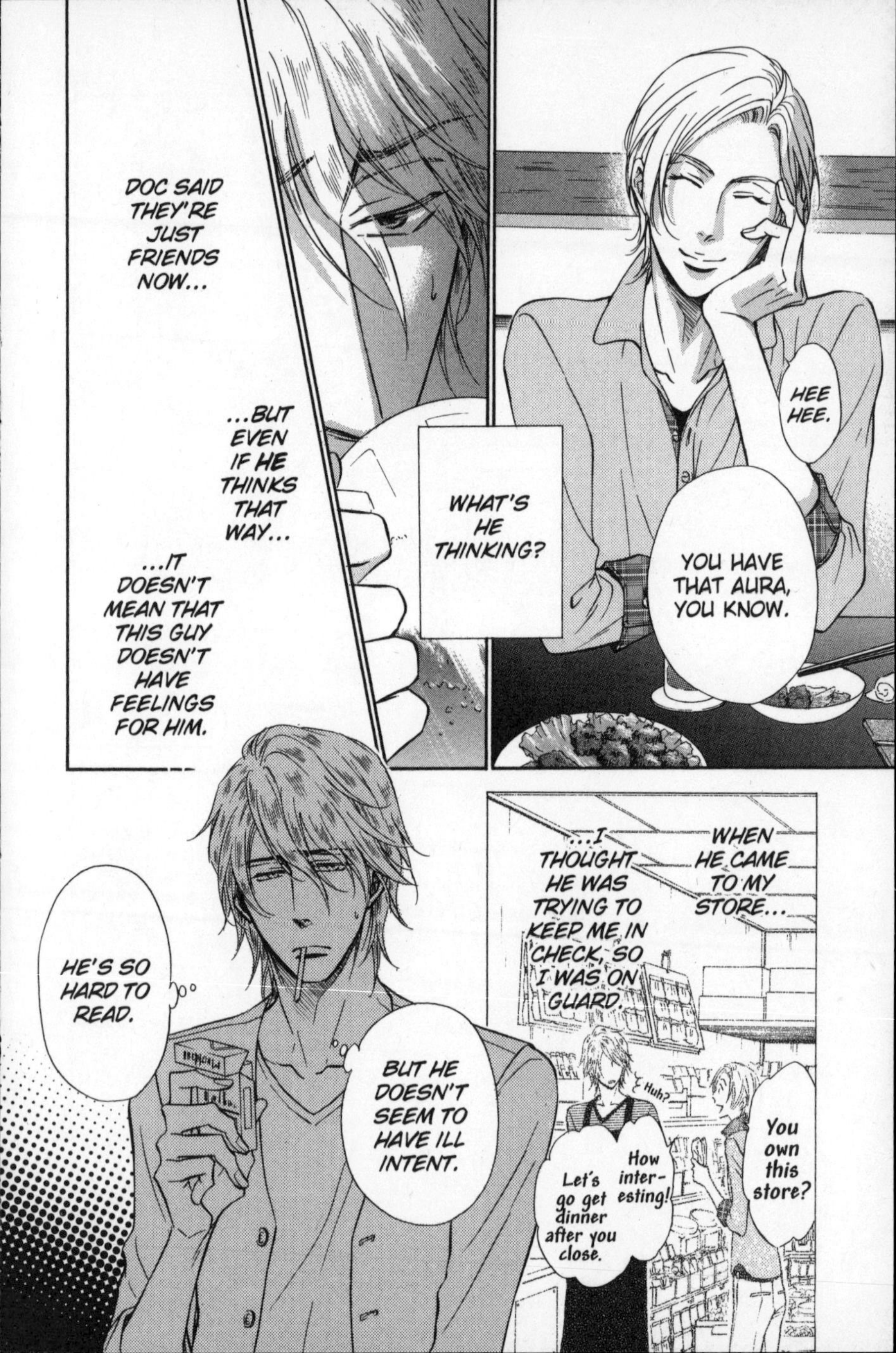
HEE HEE.
YOU HAVE THAT AURA, YOU KNOW.
WHAT'S HE THINKING?
DOC SAID THEY'RE JUST FRIENDS NOW...
...BUT EVEN IF HE THINKS THAT WAY...
...IT DOESN'T MEAN THAT THIS GUY DOESN'T HAVE FEELINGS FOR HIM.
WHEN HE CAME TO MY STORE...
...I THOUGHT HE WAS TRYING TO KEEP ME IN CHECK, SO I WAS ON GUARD.
You own this store?
Huh?
How inter-esting!
Let's go get dinner after you close.
HE'S SO HARD TO READ.
BUT HE DOESN'T SEEM TO HAVE ILL INTENT.

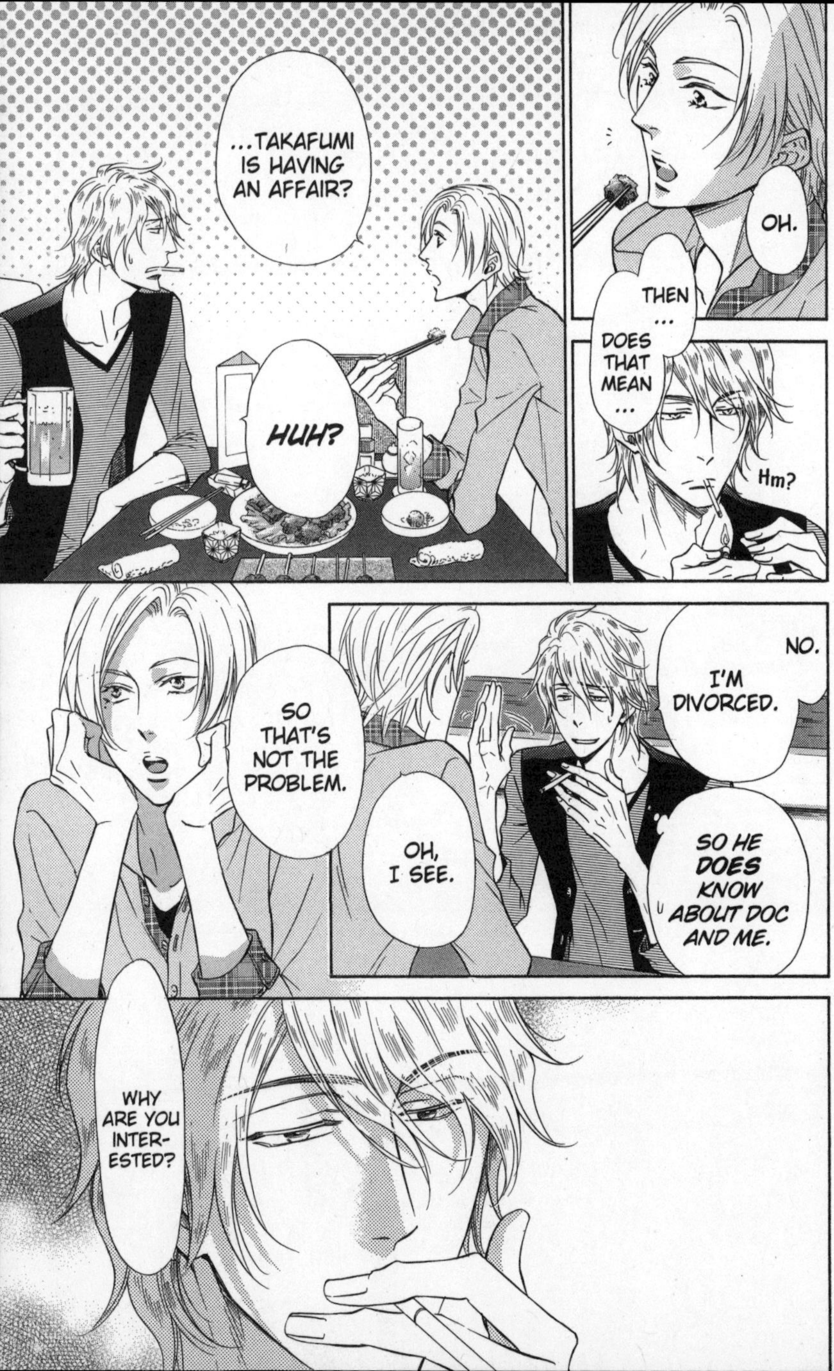
OH.
THEN ... DOES THAT MEAN ...
Hm?
...TAKAFUMI IS HAVING AN AFFAIR?
HUH?
NO. I'M DIVORCED.
SO HE DOES KNOW ABOUT DOC AND ME.
OH, I SEE.
SO THAT'S NOT THE PROBLEM.
WHY ARE YOU INTER-ESTED?

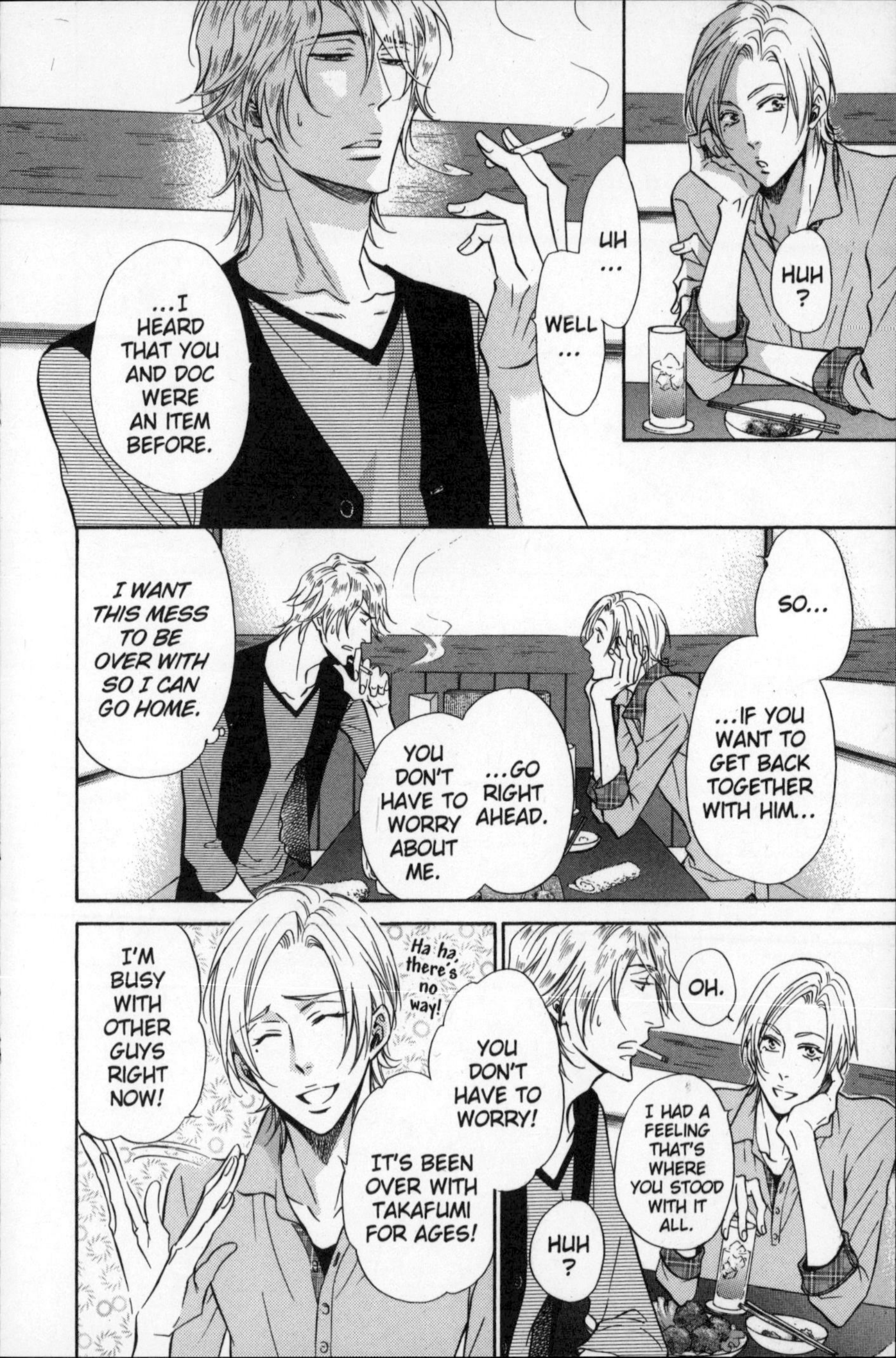
HUH?
UH... WELL...
...I HEARD THAT YOU AND DOC WERE AN ITEM BEFORE.
SO...
...IF YOU WANT TO GET BACK TOGETHER WITH HIM...
...GO RIGHT AHEAD.
YOU DON'T HAVE TO WORRY ABOUT ME.
I WANT THIS MESS TO BE OVER WITH SO I CAN GO HOME.
OH.
I HAD A FEELING THAT'S WHERE YOU STOOD WITH IT ALL.
HUH?
YOU DON'T HAVE TO WORRY!
IT'S BEEN OVER WITH TAKAFUMI FOR AGES!
Ha ha, there's no way!
I'M BUSY WITH OTHER GUYS RIGHT NOW!

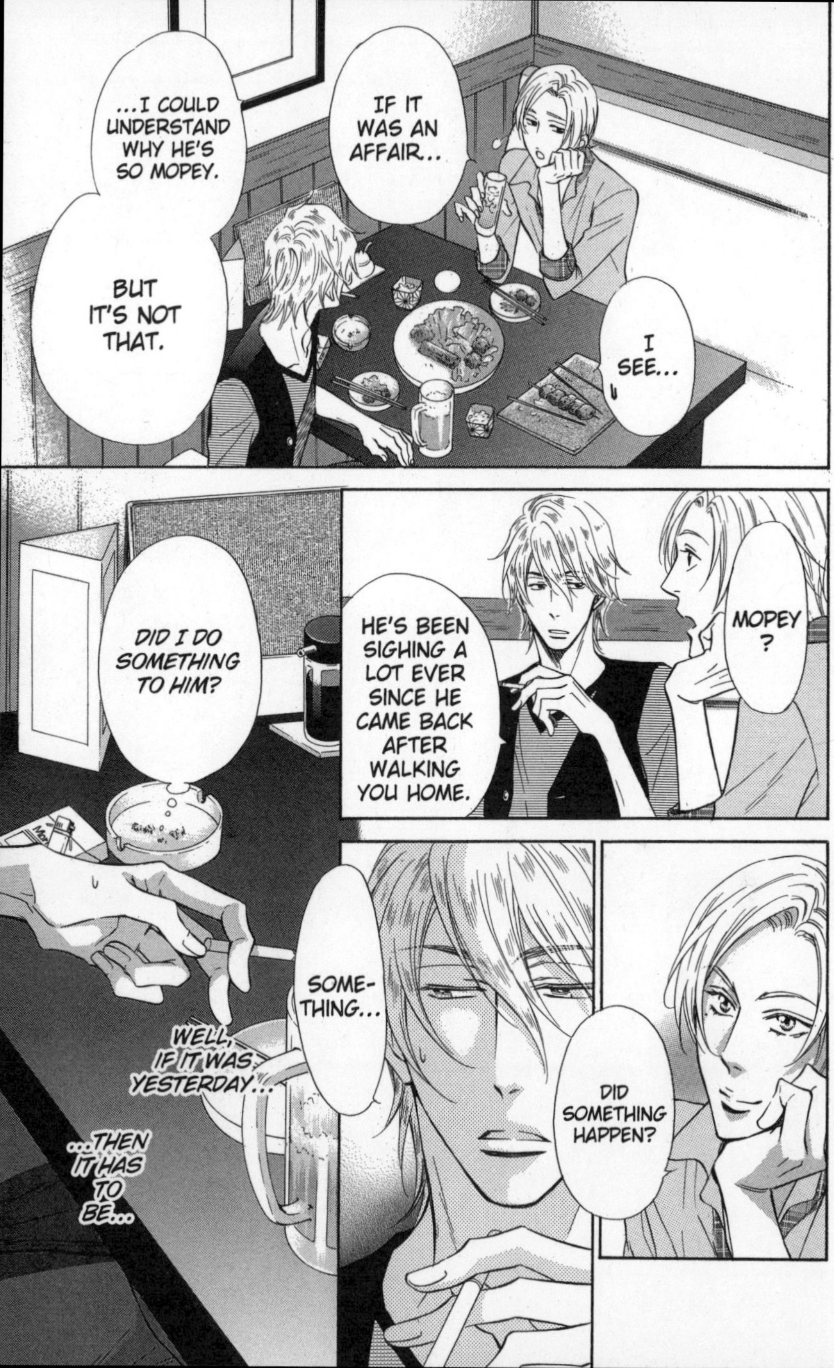

I SEE...
IF IT WAS AN AFFAIR...
...I COULD UNDERSTAND WHY HE'S SO MOPEY.
BUT IT'S NOT THAT.
MOPEY?
HE'S BEEN SIGHING A LOT EVER SINCE HE CAME BACK AFTER WALKING YOU HOME.
DID SOMETHING HAPPEN?
SOMETHING...
DID I DO SOMETHING TO HIM?
WELL, IF IT WAS YESTERDAY...
...THEN IT HAS TO BE...

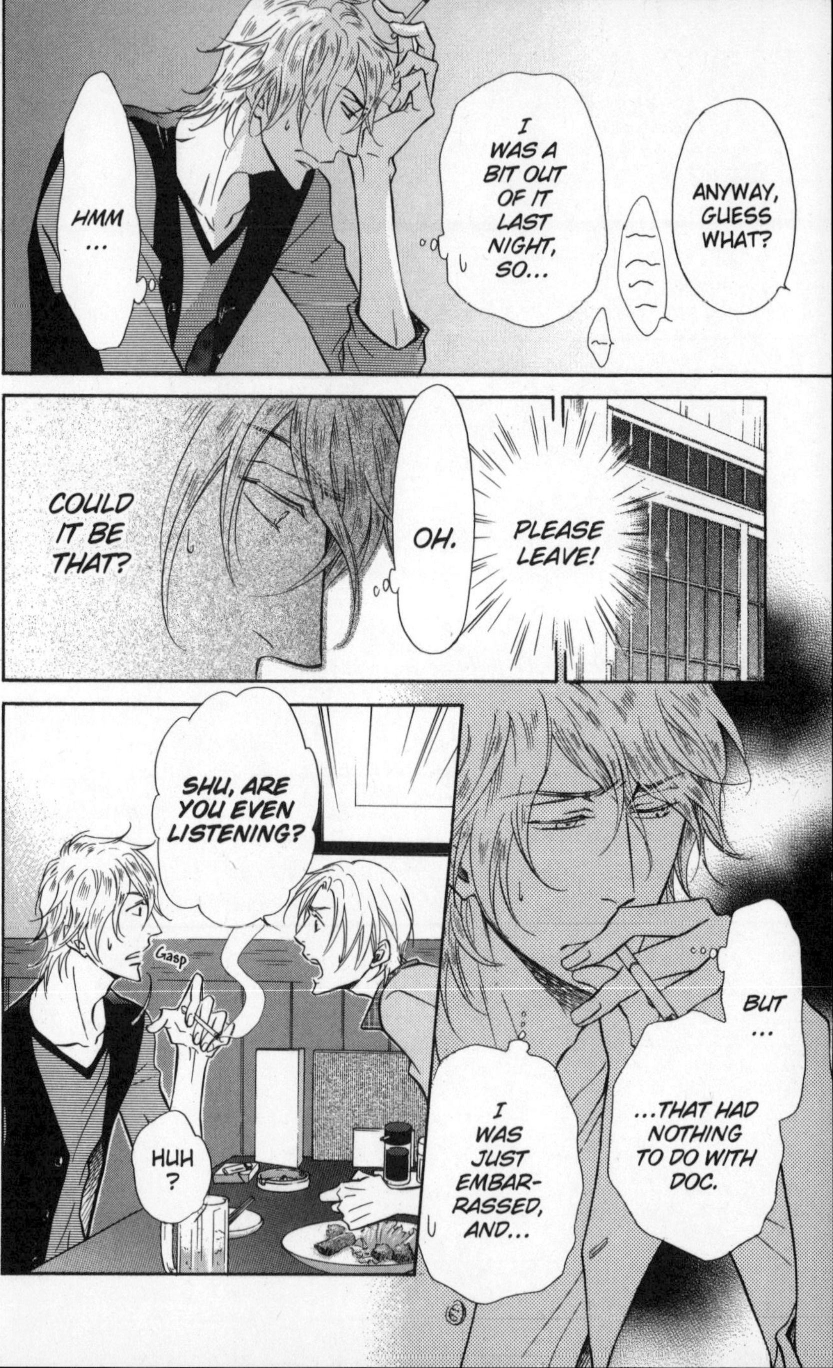
ANYWAY, GUESS WHAT?
I WAS A BIT OUT OF IT LAST NIGHT, SO...
HMM ...
PLEASE LEAVE!
OH.
COULD IT BE THAT?
I WAS JUST EMBARRASSED, AND...
BUT ...
...THAT HAD NOTHING TO DO WITH DOC.
SHU, ARE YOU EVEN LISTENING?
Gasp
HUH ?

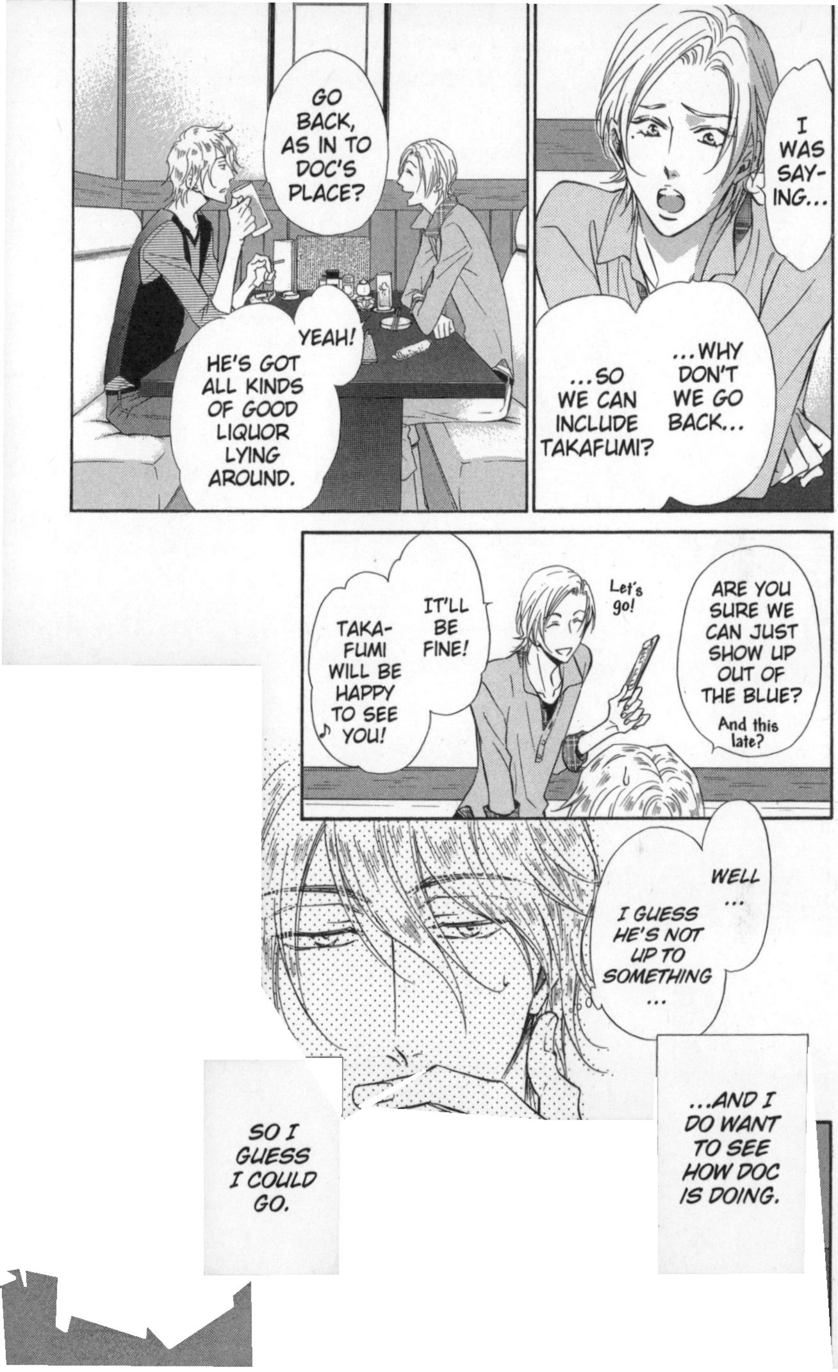
I WAS SAYING...
...WHY DON'T WE GO BACK...
...SO WE CAN INCLUDE TAKAFUMI?
GO BACK, AS IN TO DOC'S PLACE?
YEAH!
HE'S GOT ALL KINDS OF GOOD LIQUOR LYING AROUND.
ARE YOU SURE WE CAN JUST SHOW UP OUT OF THE BLUE?
And this late?
Let's go!
IT'LL BE FINE!
TAKAFUMI WILL BE HAPPY TO SEE YOU! ♪
WELL...
I GUESS HE'S NOT UP TO SOMETHING...
...AND I DO WANT TO SEE HOW DOC IS DOING.
SO I GUESS I COULD GO.

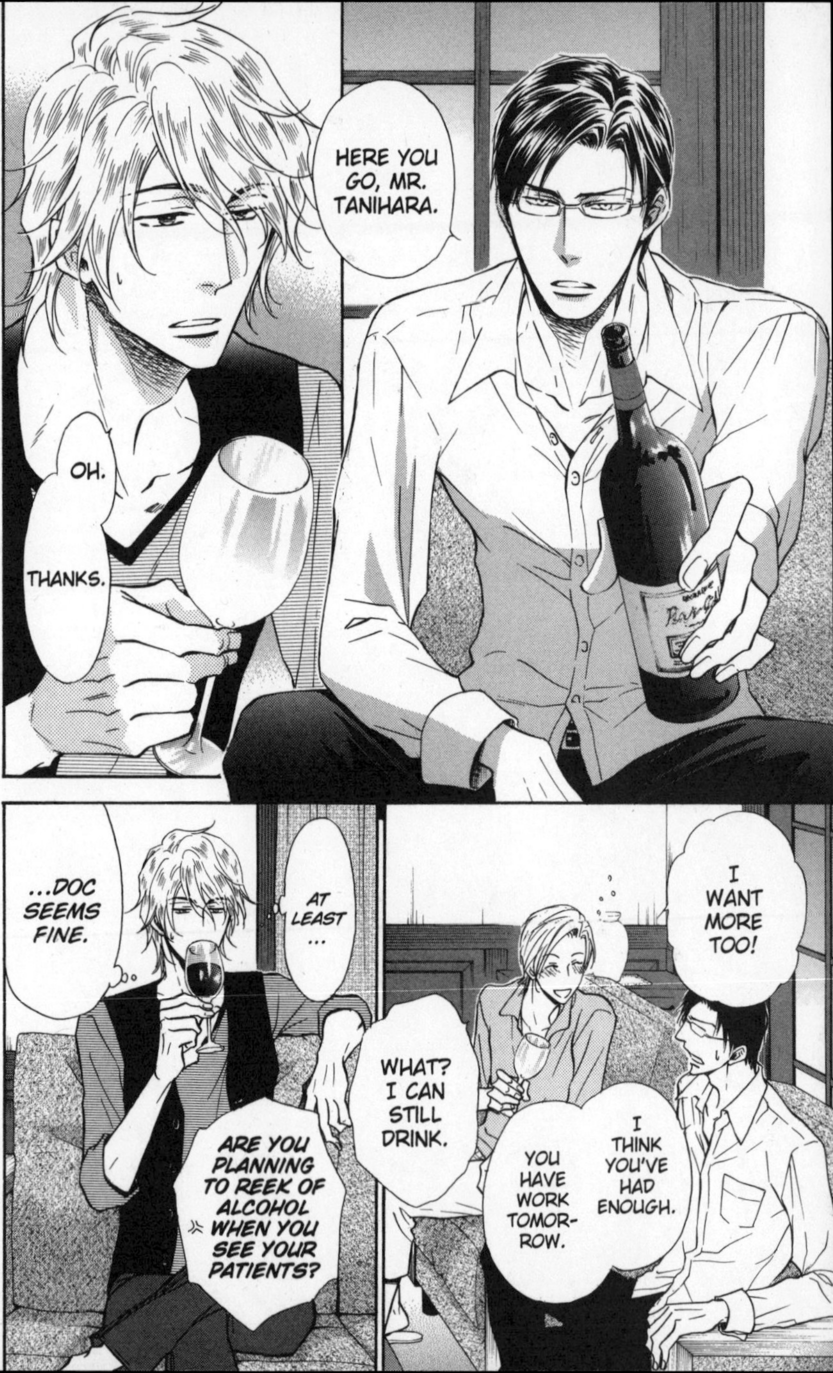
HERE YOU GO, MR. TANIHARA.
OH.
THANKS.
I WANT MORE TOO!
I THINK YOU'VE HAD ENOUGH.
WHAT? I CAN STILL DRINK.
YOU HAVE WORK TOMOR-ROW.
AT LEAST...
...DOC SEEMS FINE.
ARE YOU PLANNING TO REEK OF ALCOHOL WHEN YOU SEE YOUR PATIENTS?

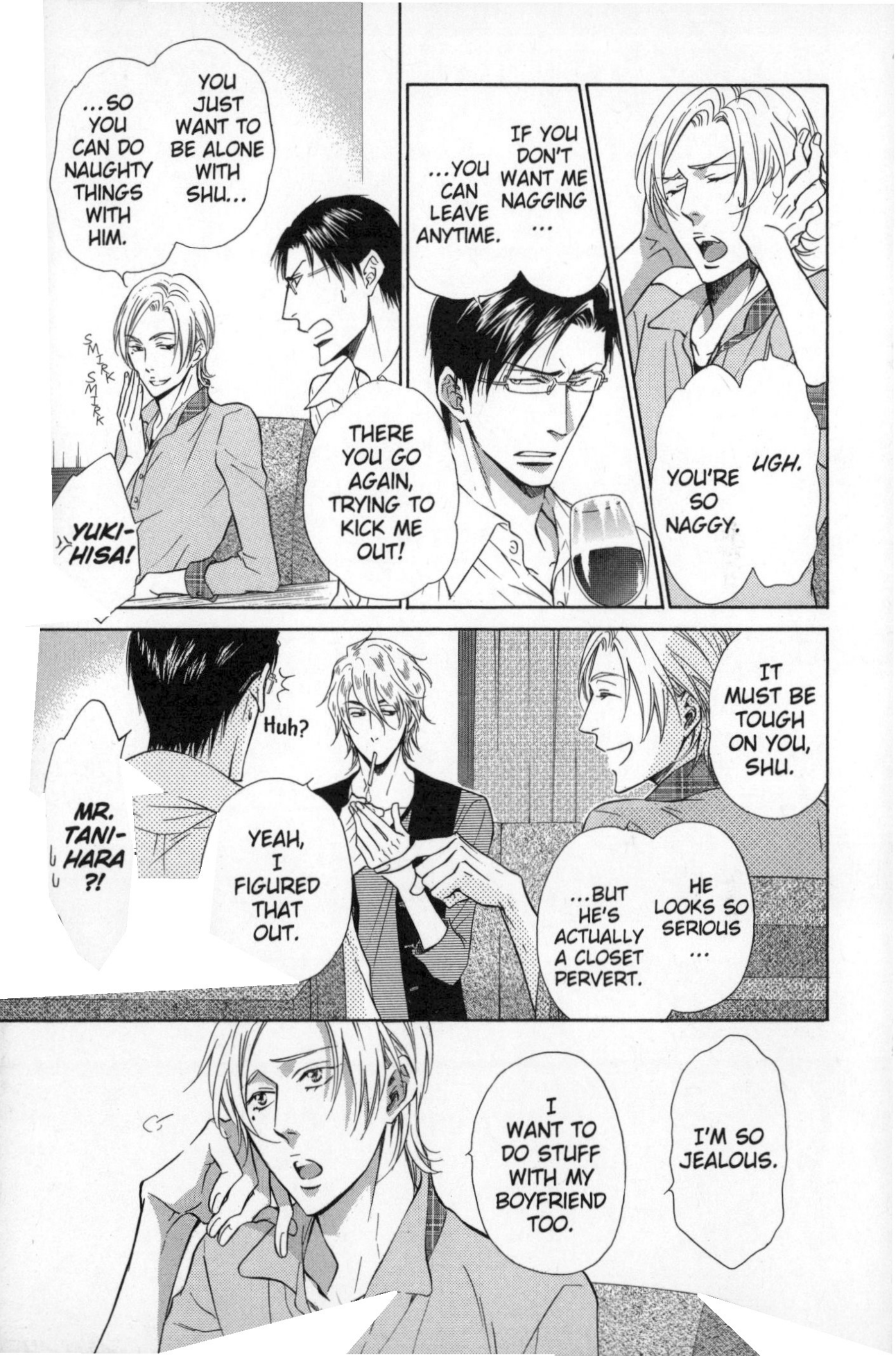
UGH.
YOU'RE SO NAGGY.
IF YOU DON'T WANT ME NAGGING...
...YOU CAN LEAVE ANYTIME.
THERE YOU GO AGAIN, TRYING TO KICK ME OUT!
YOU JUST WANT TO BE ALONE WITH SHU...
...SO YOU CAN DO NAUGHTY THINGS WITH HIM.
SMIRK SMIRK
YUKI-HISA!
IT MUST BE TOUGH ON YOU, SHU.
HE LOOKS SO SERIOUS...
...BUT HE'S ACTUALLY A CLOSET PERVERT.
YEAH, I FIGURED THAT OUT.
Huh?
MR. TANI-HARA?!
I'M SO JEALOUS.
I WANT TO DO STUFF WITH MY BOYFRIEND TOO.

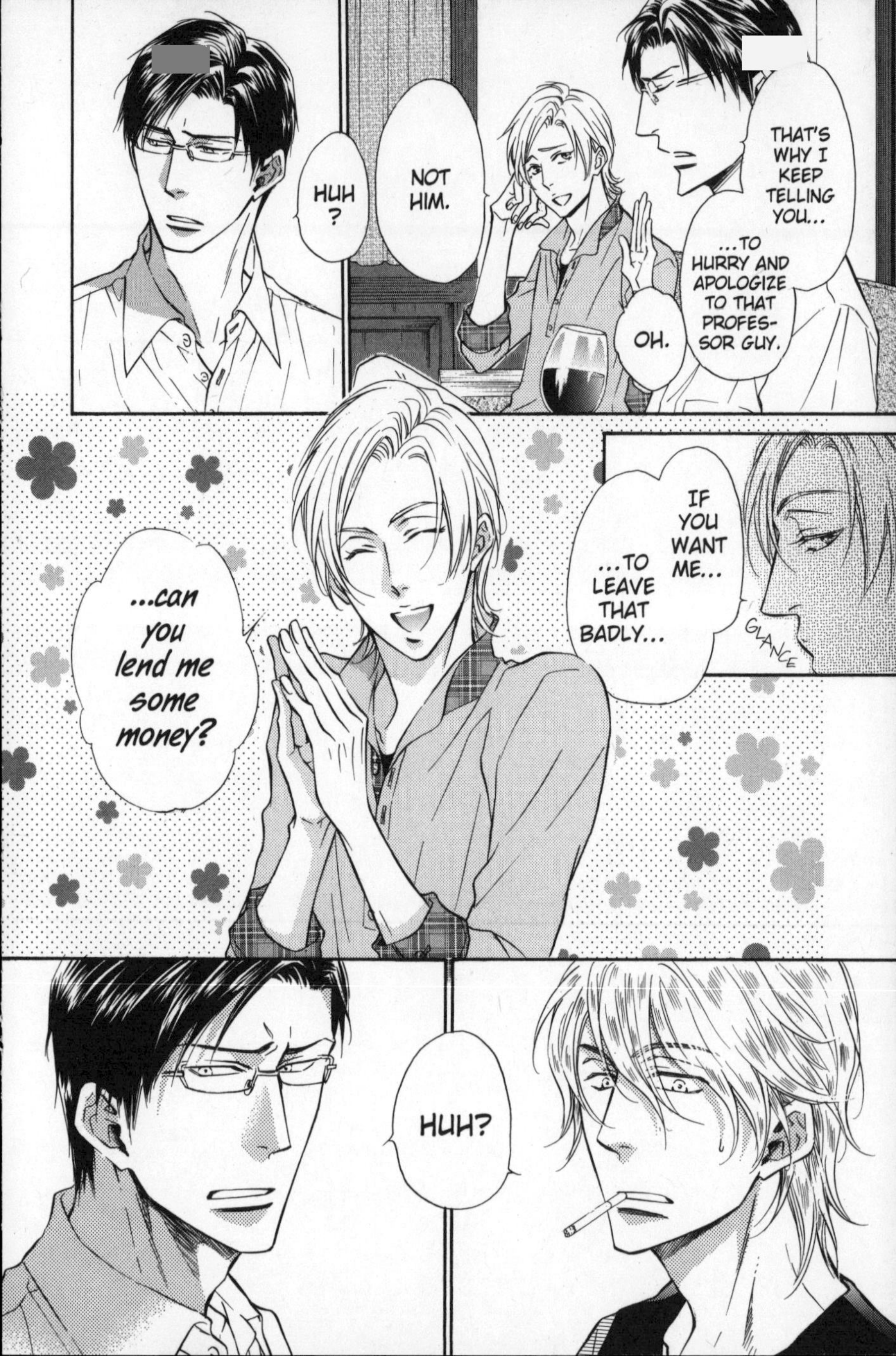
THAT'S WHY I KEEP TELLING YOU...
...TO HURRY AND APOLOGIZE TO THAT PROFES-SOR GUY.
OH.
NOT HIM.
HUH?
IF YOU WANT ME...
...TO LEAVE THAT BADLY...
GLANCE
...can you lend me some money?
HUH?

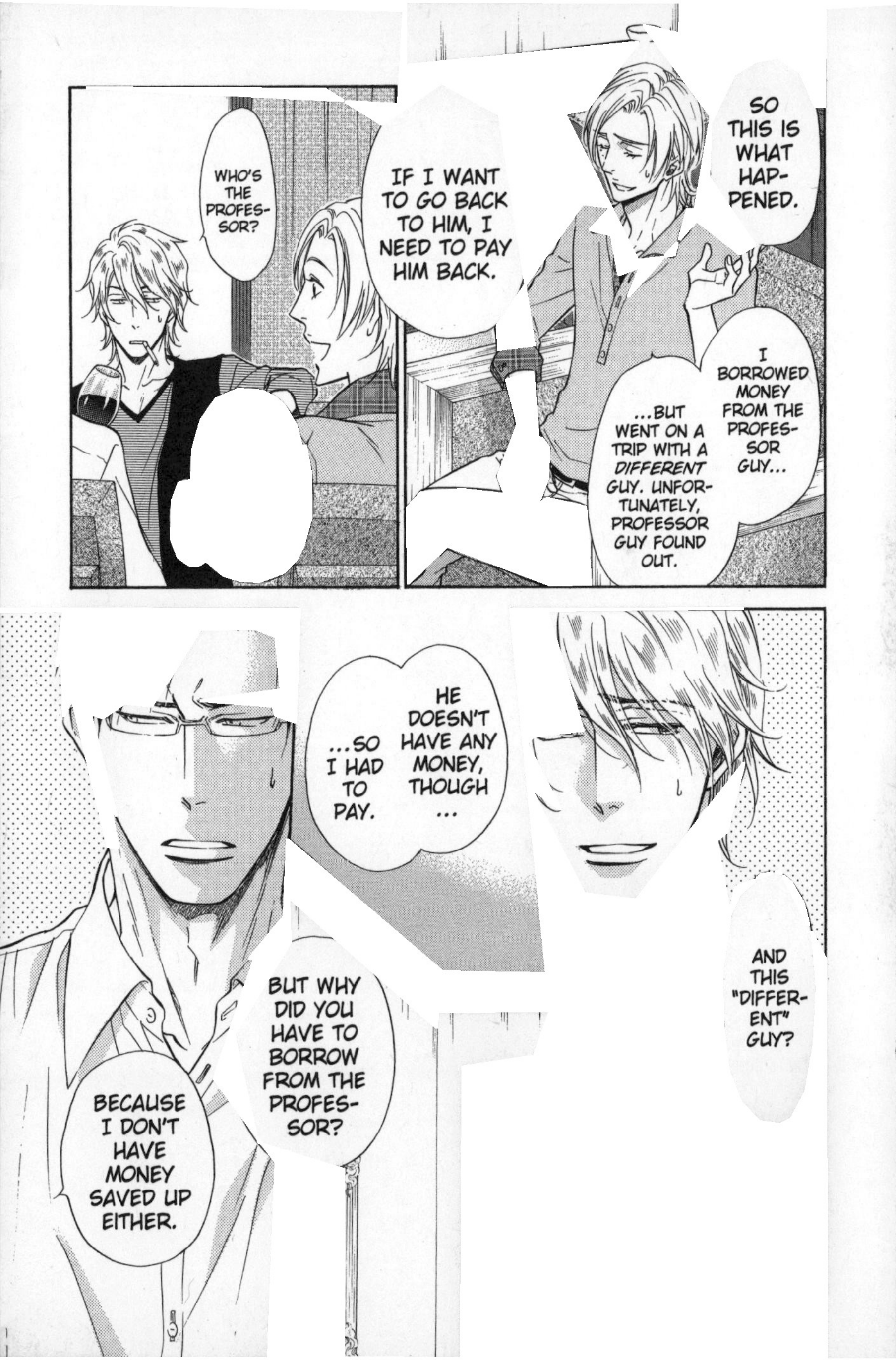
SO THIS IS WHAT HAP-PENED.
I BORROWED MONEY FROM THE PROFES-SOR GUY...
...BUT WENT ON A TRIP WITH A *DIFFERENT* GUY. UNFOR-TUNATELY, PROFESSOR GUY FOUND OUT.
IF I WANT TO GO BACK TO HIM, I NEED TO PAY HIM BACK.
WHO'S THE PROFES-SOR?
AND THIS "DIFFER-ENT" GUY?
HE DOESN'T HAVE ANY MONEY, THOUGH...
...SO I HAD TO PAY.
BUT WHY DID YOU HAVE TO BORROW FROM THE PROFES-SOR?
BECAUSE I DON'T HAVE MONEY SAVED UP EITHER.

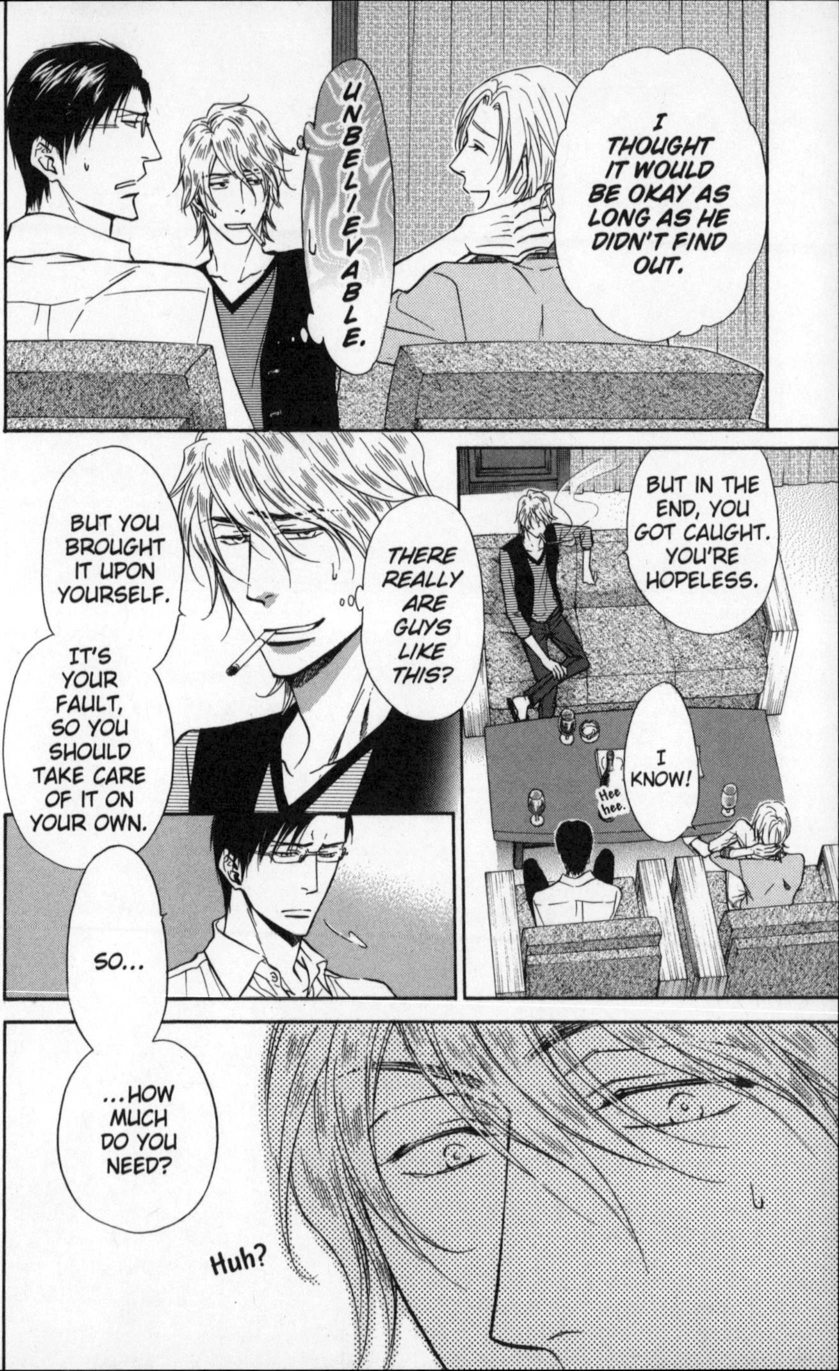
I THOUGHT IT WOULD BE OKAY AS LONG AS HE DIDN'T FIND OUT.
UNBELIEVABLE.
BUT IN THE END, YOU GOT CAUGHT. YOU'RE HOPELESS.
I KNOW!
Hee hee.
THERE REALLY ARE GUYS LIKE THIS?
BUT YOU BROUGHT IT UPON YOURSELF.
IT'S YOUR FAULT, SO YOU SHOULD TAKE CARE OF IT ON YOUR OWN.
SO...
...HOW MUCH DO YOU NEED?
Huh?

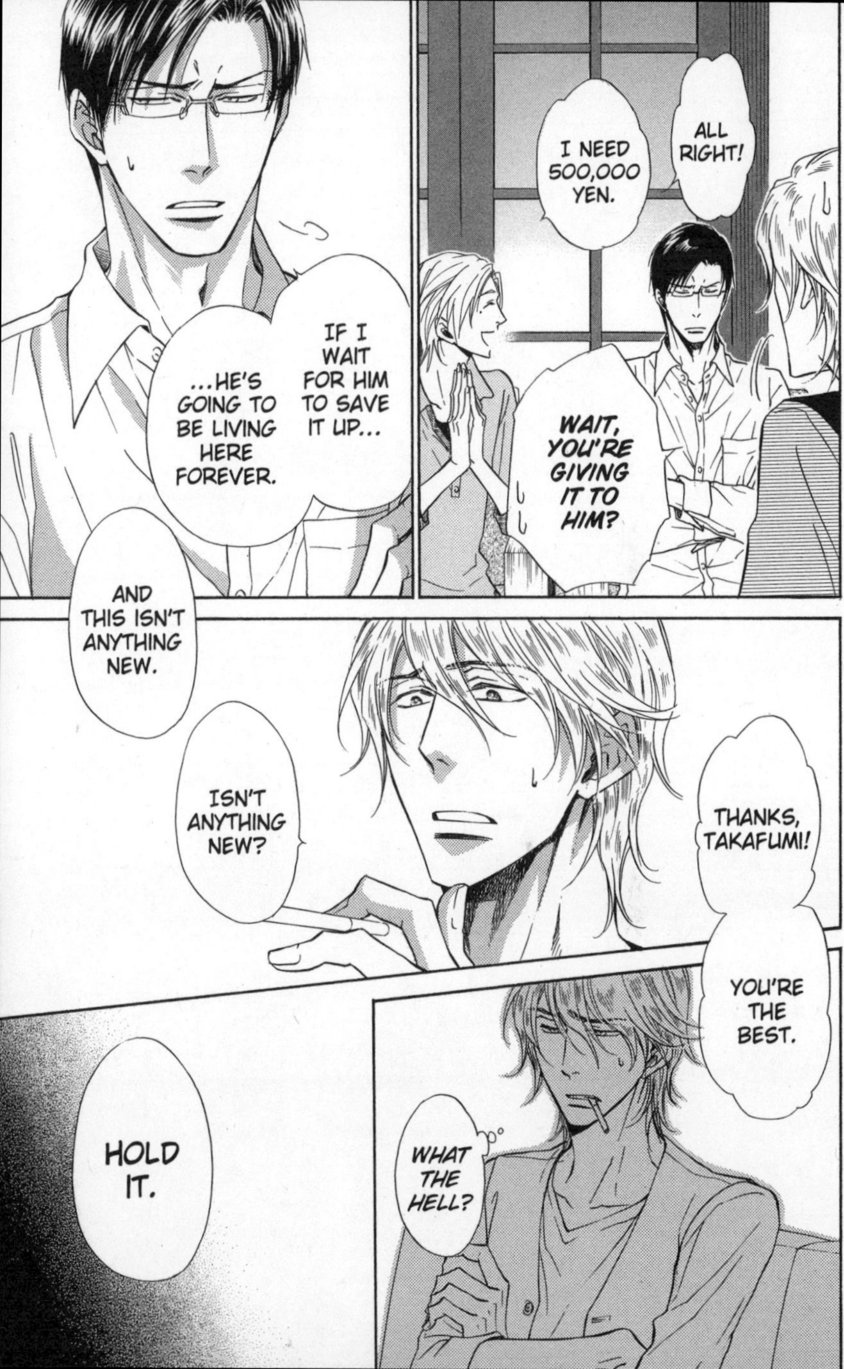
ALL RIGHT!
I NEED 500,000 YEN.
WAIT, YOU'RE GIVING IT TO HIM?
IF I WAIT FOR HIM TO SAVE IT UP...
...HE'S GOING TO BE LIVING HERE FOREVER.
AND THIS ISN'T ANYTHING NEW.
THANKS, TAKAFUMI!
ISN'T ANYTHING NEW?
YOU'RE THE BEST.
WHAT THE HELL?
HOLD IT.

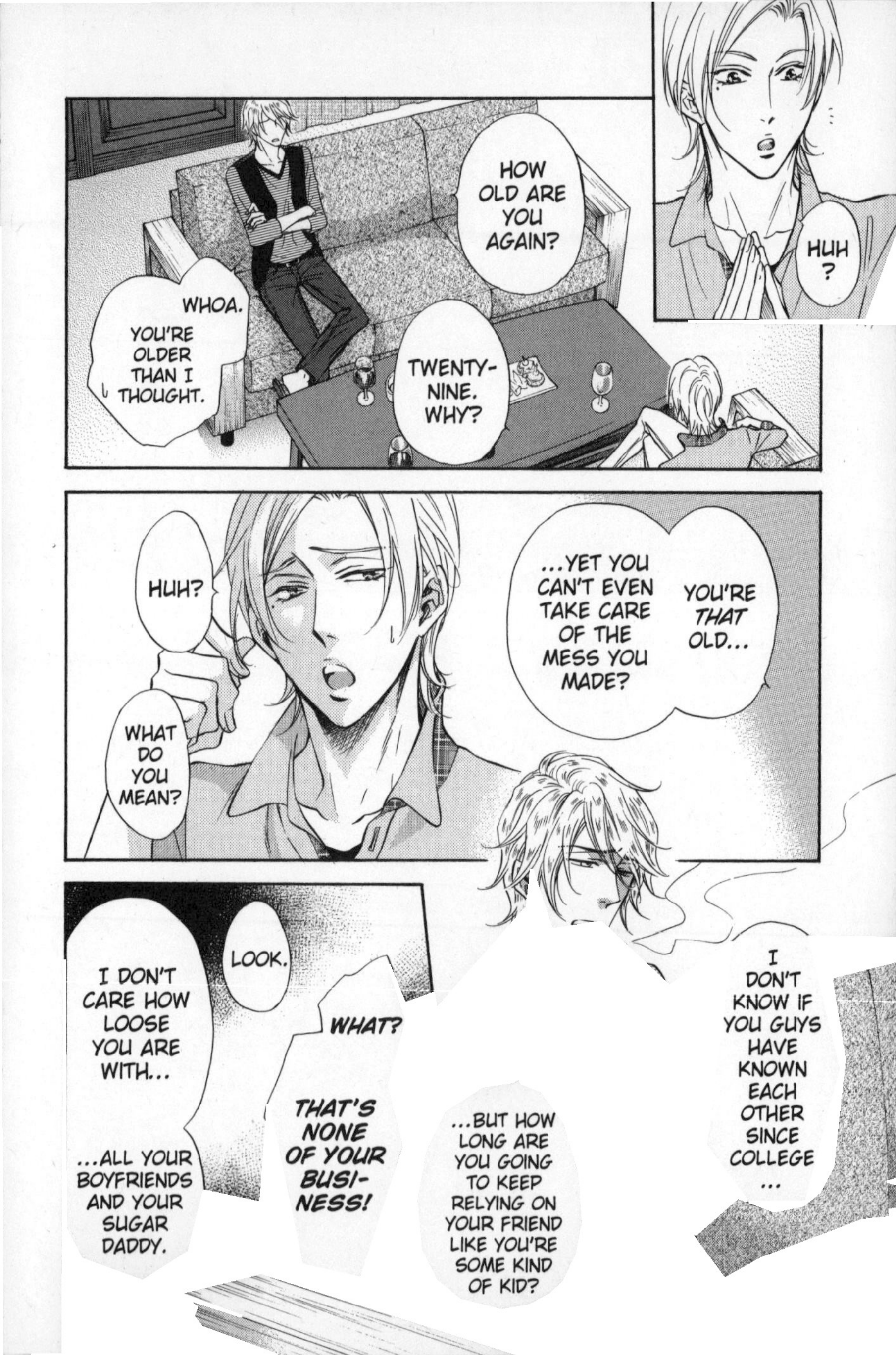
HUH?
HOW OLD ARE YOU AGAIN?
TWENTY-NINE. WHY?
WHOA. YOU'RE OLDER THAN I THOUGHT.
YOU'RE *THAT* OLD...
...YET YOU CAN'T EVEN TAKE CARE OF THE MESS YOU MADE?
HUH?
WHAT DO YOU MEAN?
I DON'T KNOW IF YOU GUYS HAVE KNOWN EACH OTHER SINCE COLLEGE...
...BUT HOW LONG ARE YOU GOING TO KEEP RELYING ON YOUR FRIEND LIKE YOU'RE SOME KIND OF KID?
WHAT?
THAT'S NONE OF YOUR BUSI-NESS!
LOOK.
I DON'T CARE HOW LOOSE YOU ARE WITH...
...ALL YOUR BOYFRIENDS AND YOUR SUGAR DADDY.

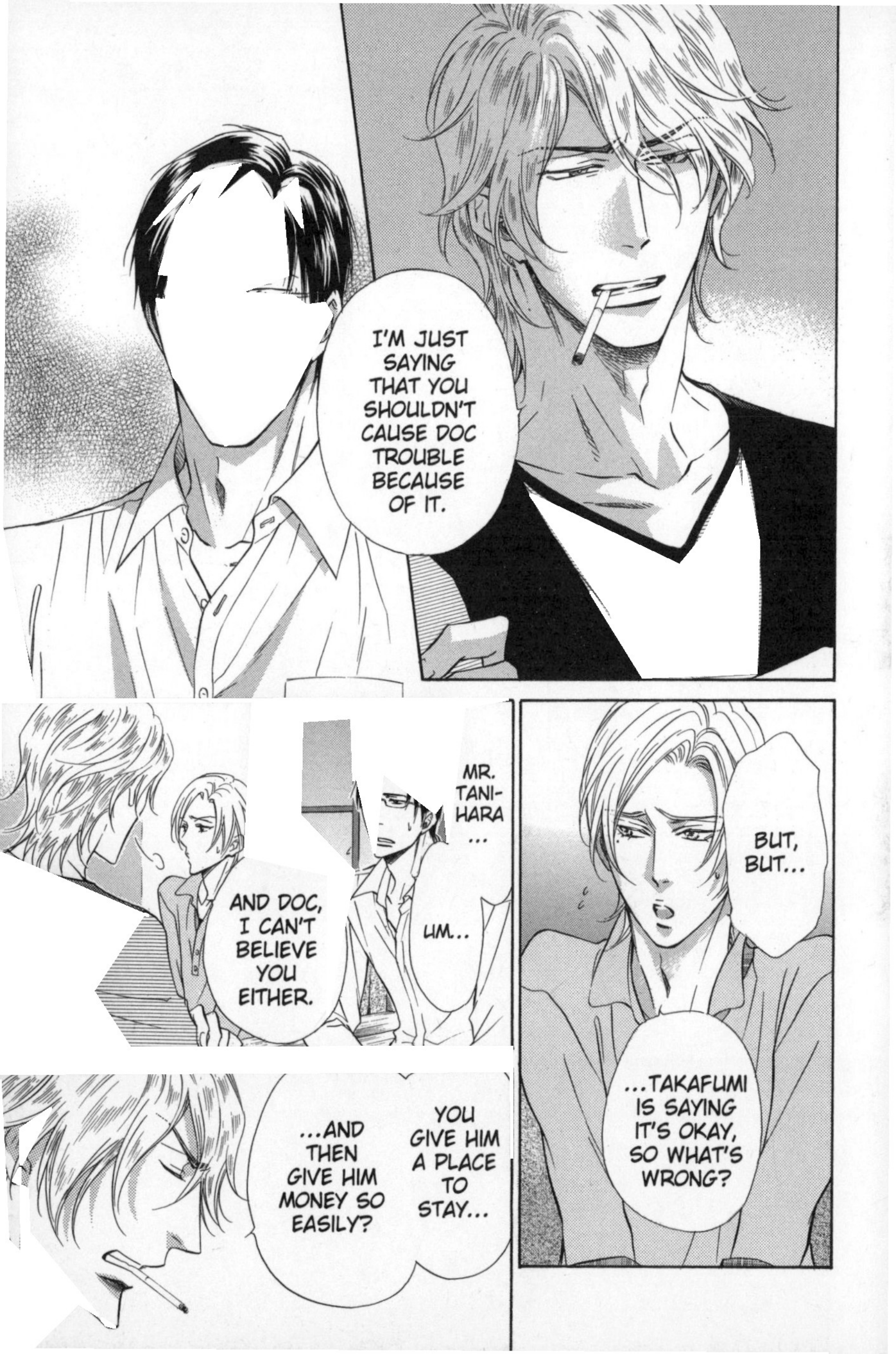
I'M JUST SAYING THAT YOU SHOULDN'T CAUSE DOC TROUBLE BECAUSE OF IT.
BUT, BUT...
...TAKAFUMI IS SAYING IT'S OKAY, SO WHAT'S WRONG?
MR. TANI-HARA...
UM...
AND DOC, I CAN'T BELIEVE YOU EITHER.
YOU GIVE HIM A PLACE TO STAY...
...AND THEN GIVE HIM MONEY SO EASILY?

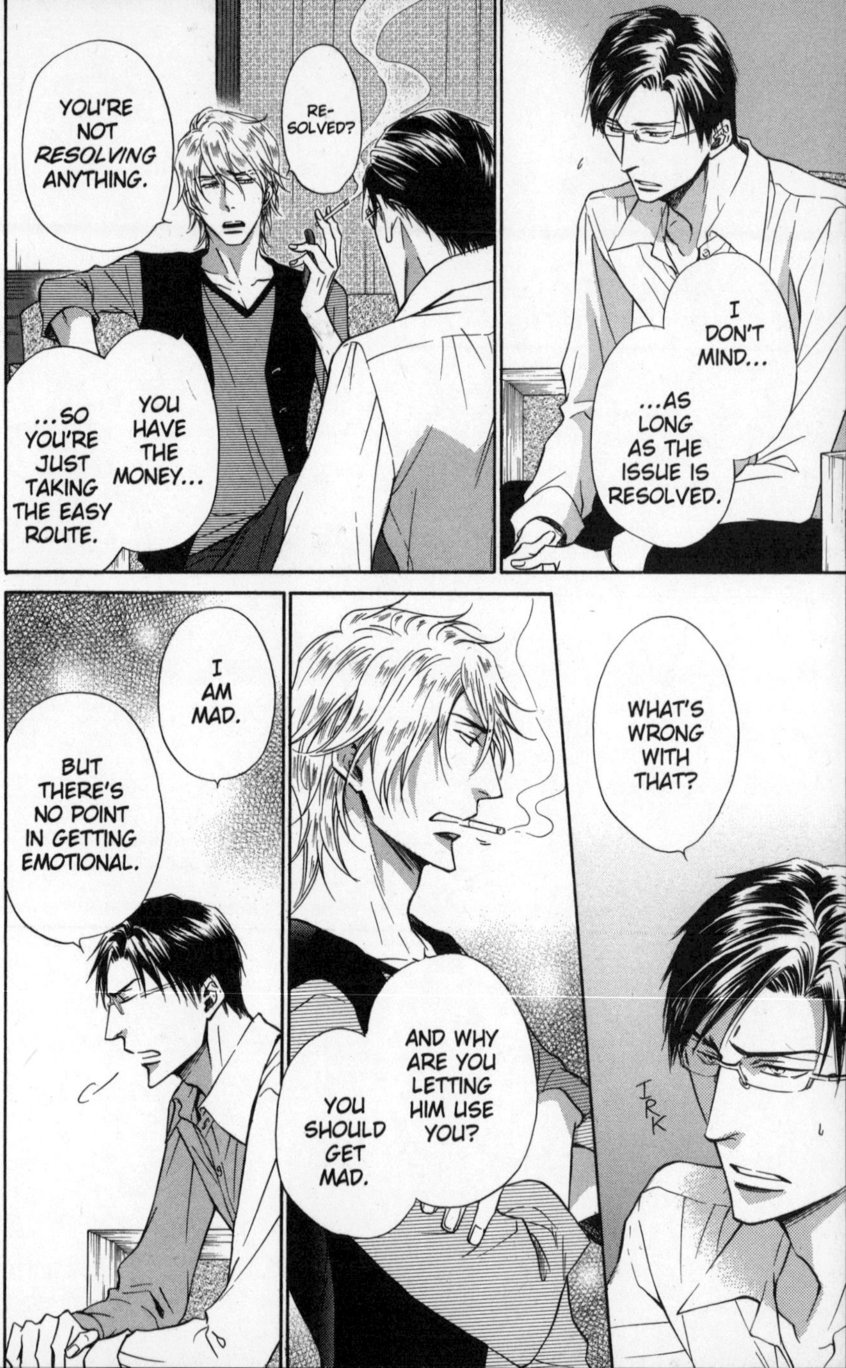
I DON'T MIND...
...AS LONG AS THE ISSUE IS RESOLVED.
RE-SOLVED?
YOU'RE NOT *RESOLVING* ANYTHING.
YOU HAVE THE MONEY...
...SO YOU'RE JUST TAKING THE EASY ROUTE.
WHAT'S WRONG WITH THAT?
AND WHY ARE YOU LETTING HIM USE YOU?
YOU SHOULD GET MAD.
IRK
I AM MAD.
BUT THERE'S NO POINT IN GETTING EMOTIONAL.

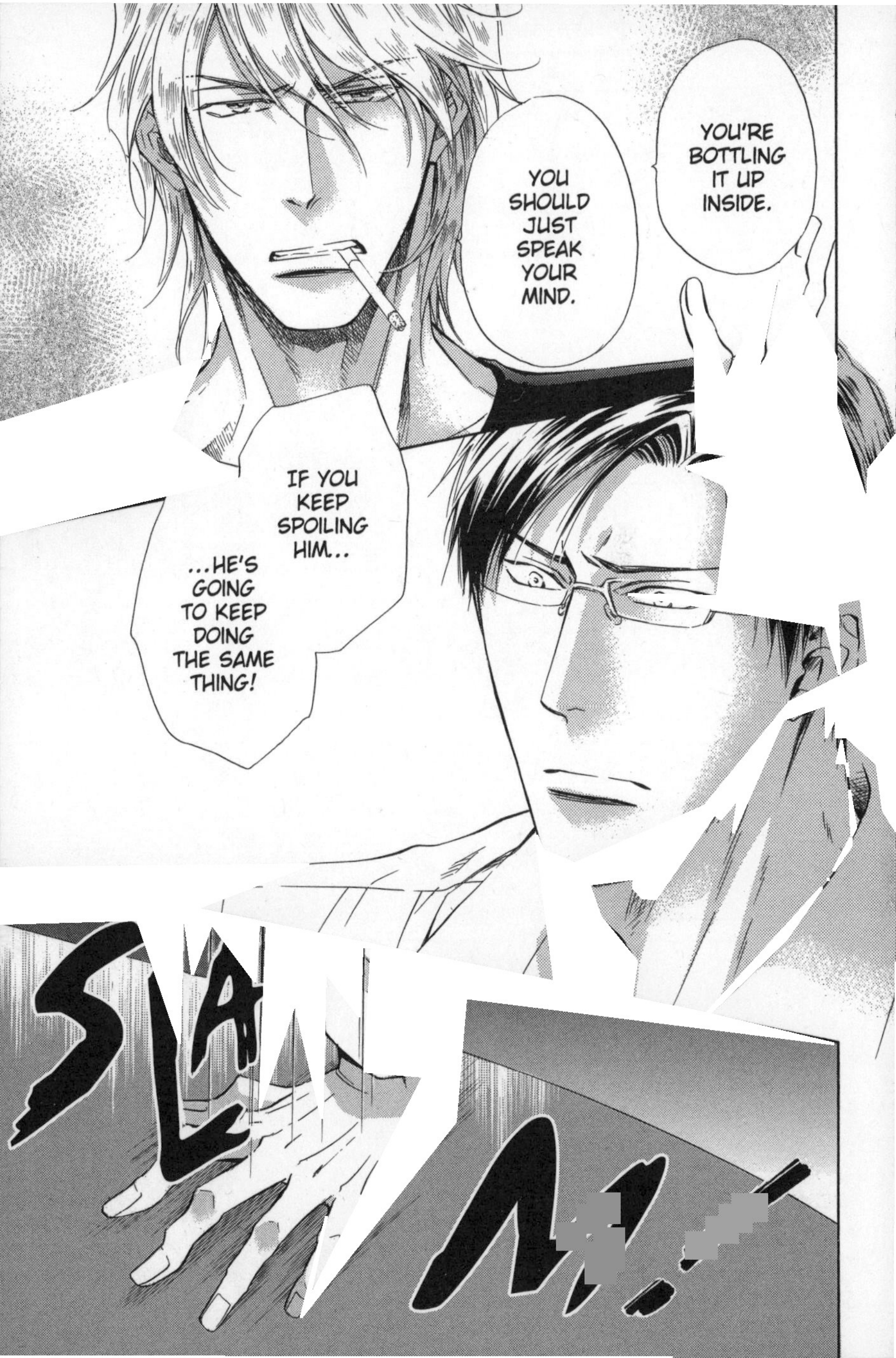
YOU'RE BOTTLING IT UP INSIDE.
YOU SHOULD JUST SPEAK YOUR MIND.
IF YOU KEEP SPOILING HIM...
...HE'S GOING TO KEEP DOING THE SAME THING!
SLAM!!

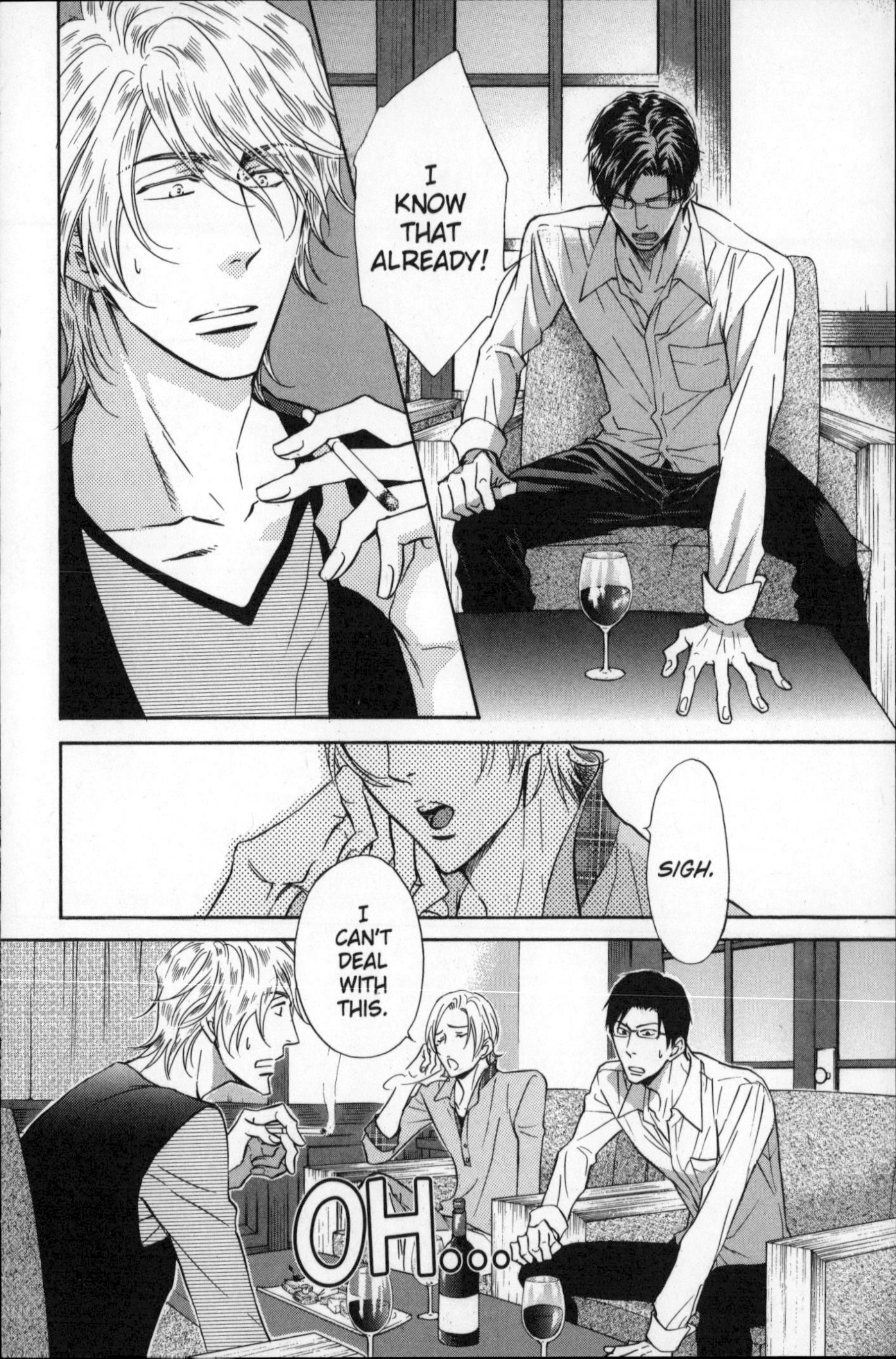
I KNOW THAT ALREADY!
SIGH.
I CAN'T DEAL WITH THIS.
OH...

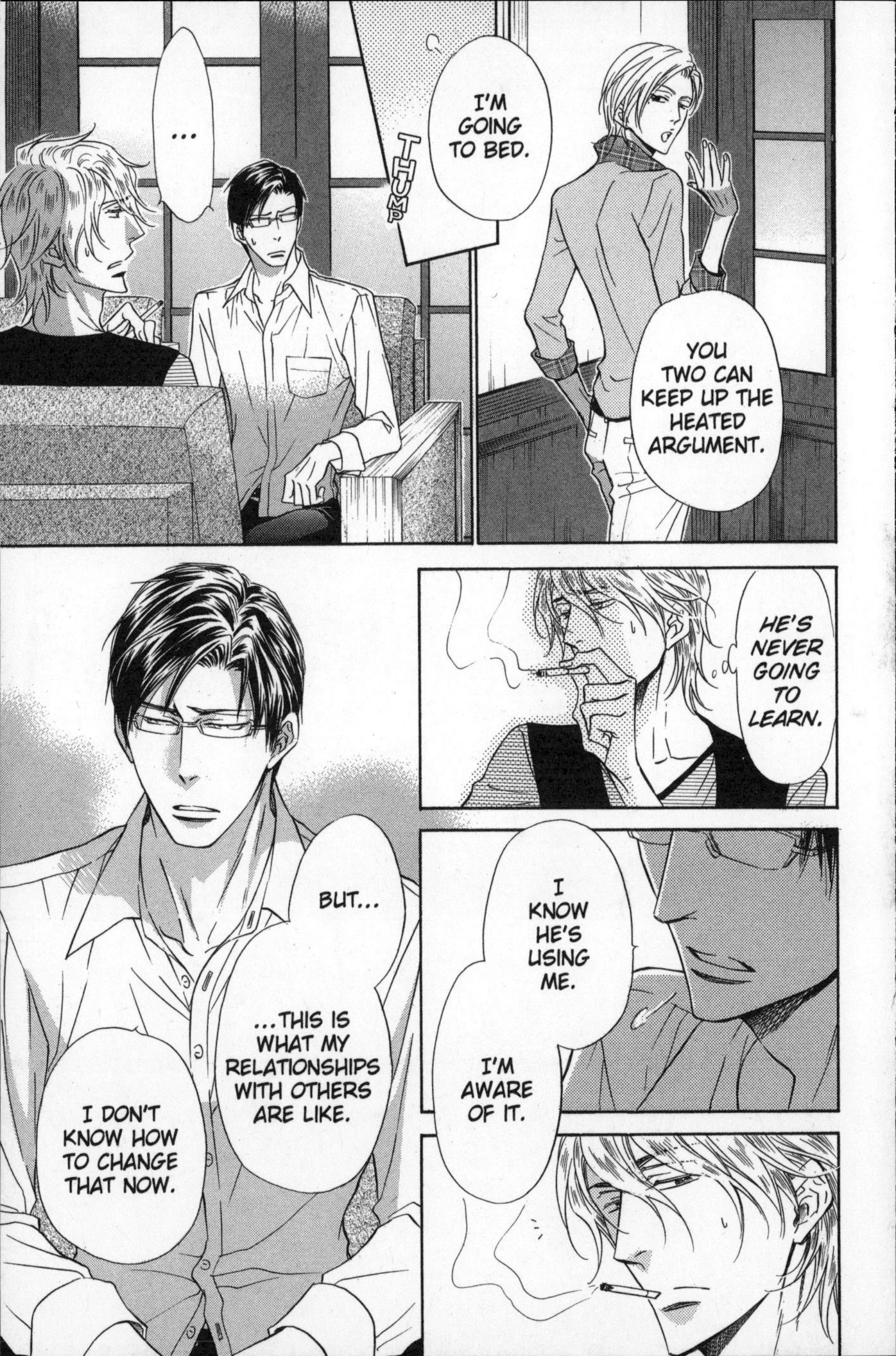
I'M GOING TO BED.
YOU TWO CAN KEEP UP THE HEATED ARGUMENT.
THUMP
...
HE'S NEVER GOING TO LEARN.
I KNOW HE'S USING ME.
I'M AWARE OF IT.
BUT...
...THIS IS WHAT MY RELATIONSHIPS WITH OTHERS ARE LIKE.
I DON'T KNOW HOW TO CHANGE THAT NOW.

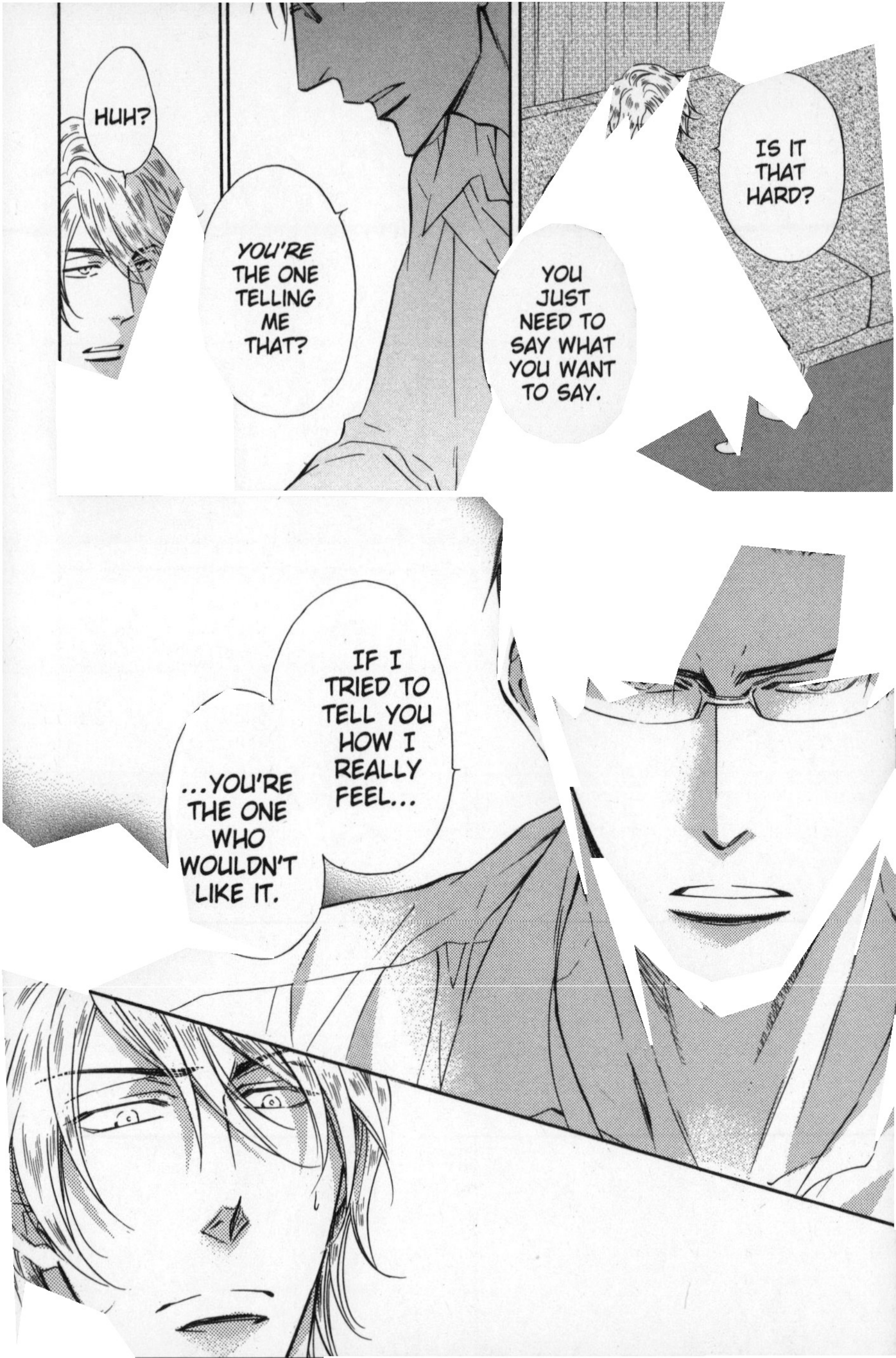
IS IT THAT HARD?
YOU JUST NEED TO SAY WHAT YOU WANT TO SAY.
YOU'RE THE ONE TELLING ME THAT?
HUH?
IF I TRIED TO TELL YOU HOW I REALLY FEEL...
...YOU'RE THE ONE WHO WOULDN'T LIKE IT.

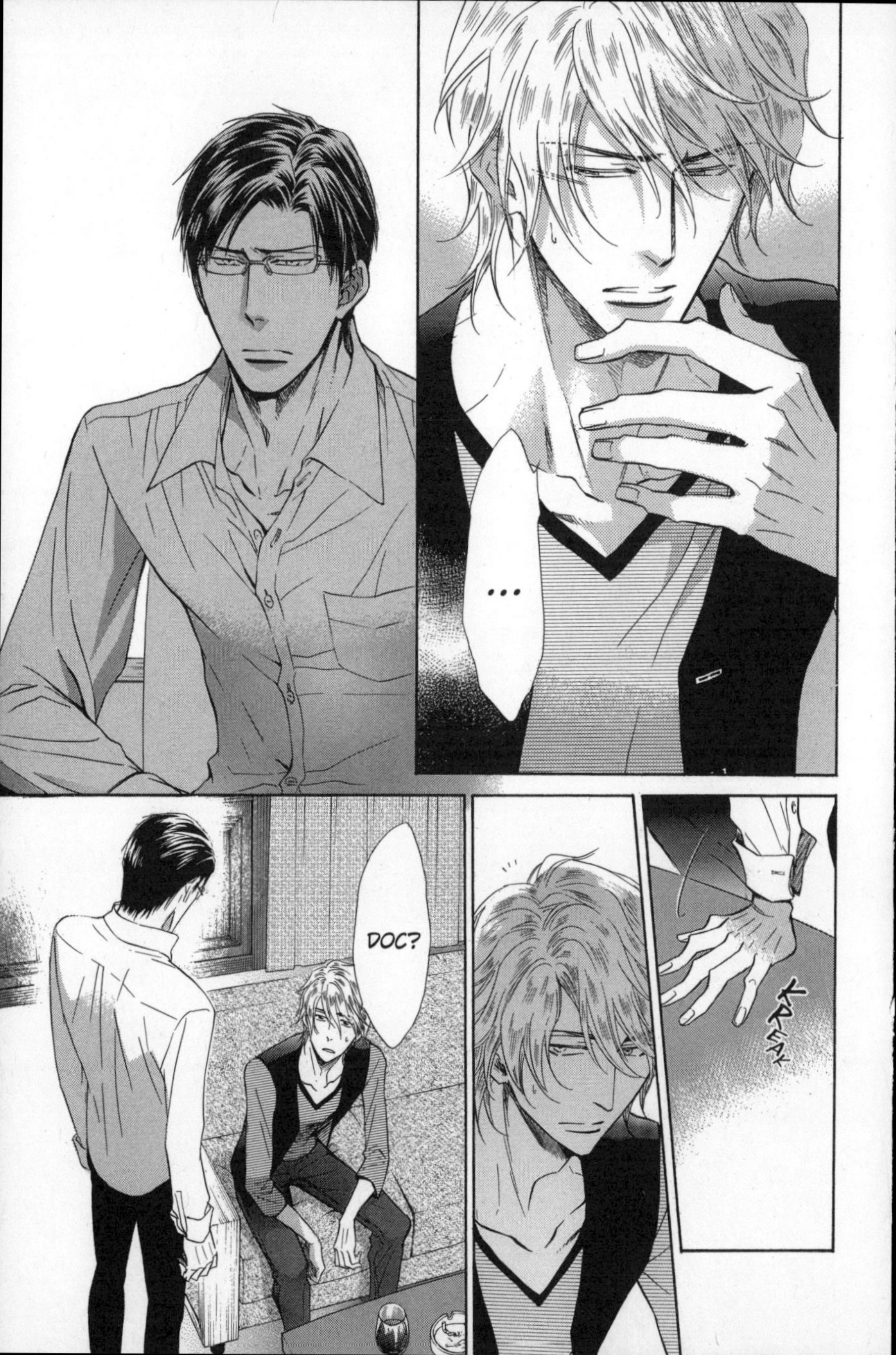
...
KREAK
DOC?

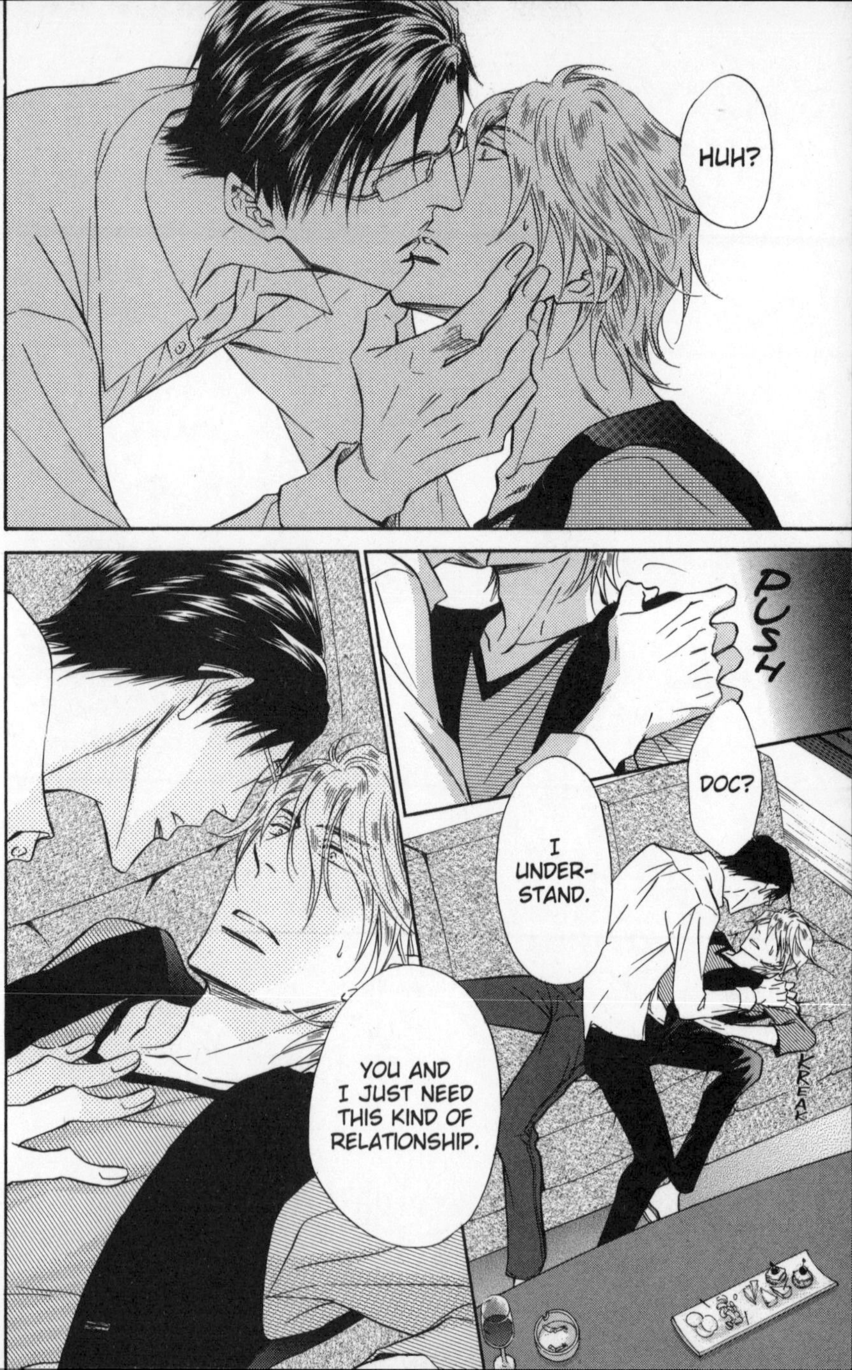
HUH?
PUSH
DOC?
I UNDER-STAND.
KREAK
YOU AND I JUST NEED THIS KIND OF RELATIONSHIP.

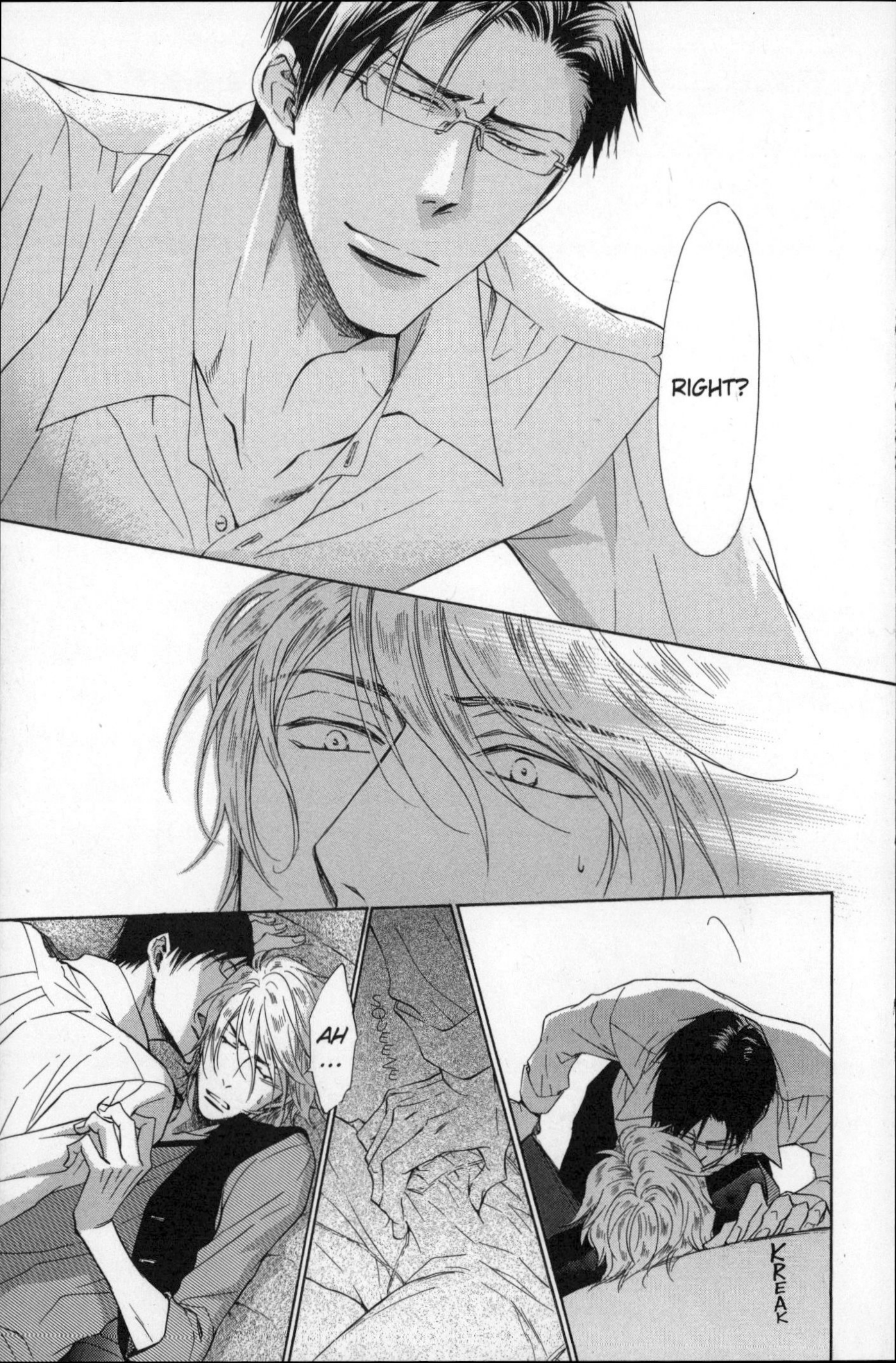
RIGHT?
KREAK
SQUEEZE
AH ...

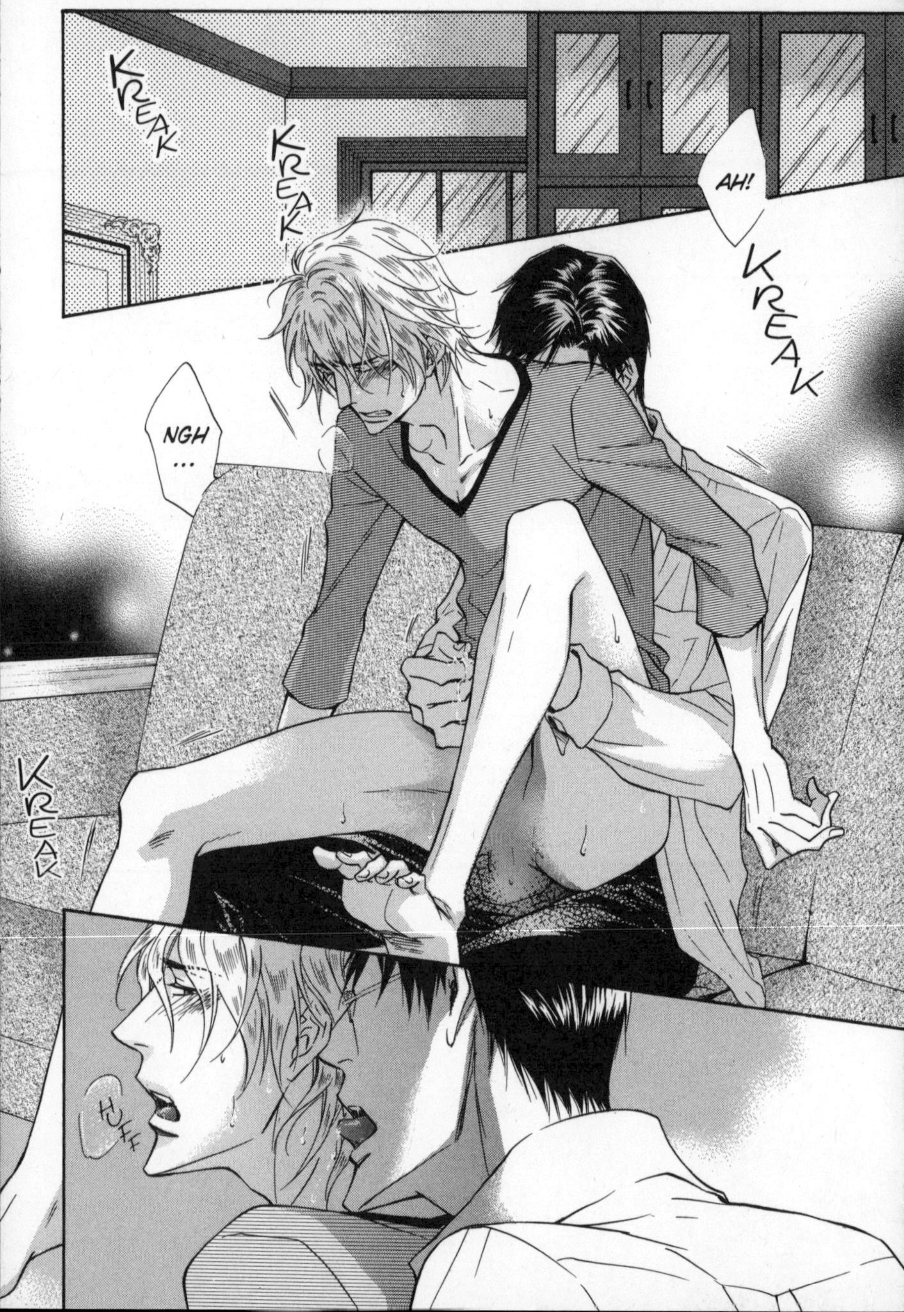

AH!
KREAK
KREAK
KREAK
NGH ...
KREAK
HUFF

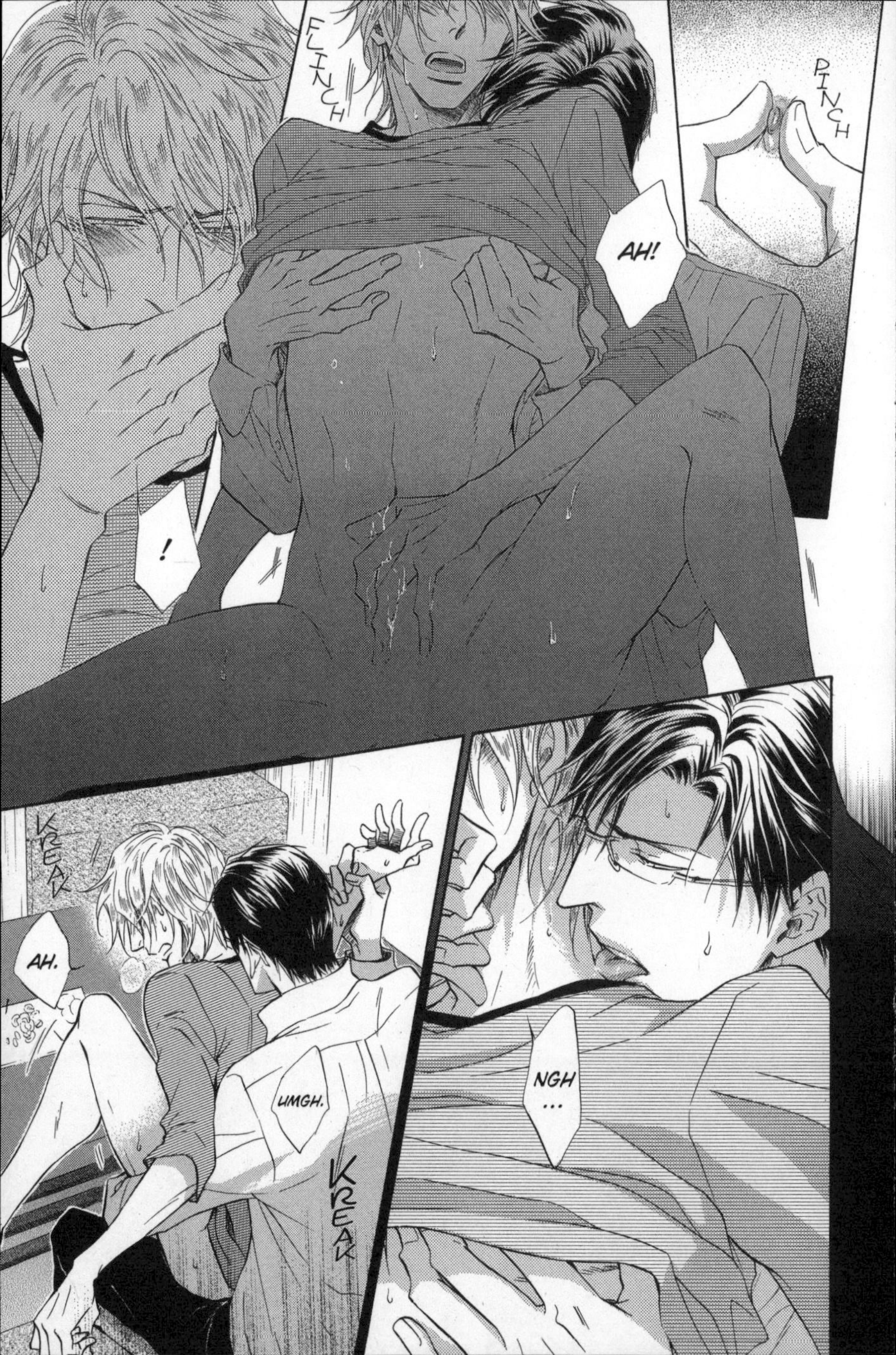
PINCH
FLINCH
AH!
!
NGH ...
KREAK
AH.
UMGH.
KREAK

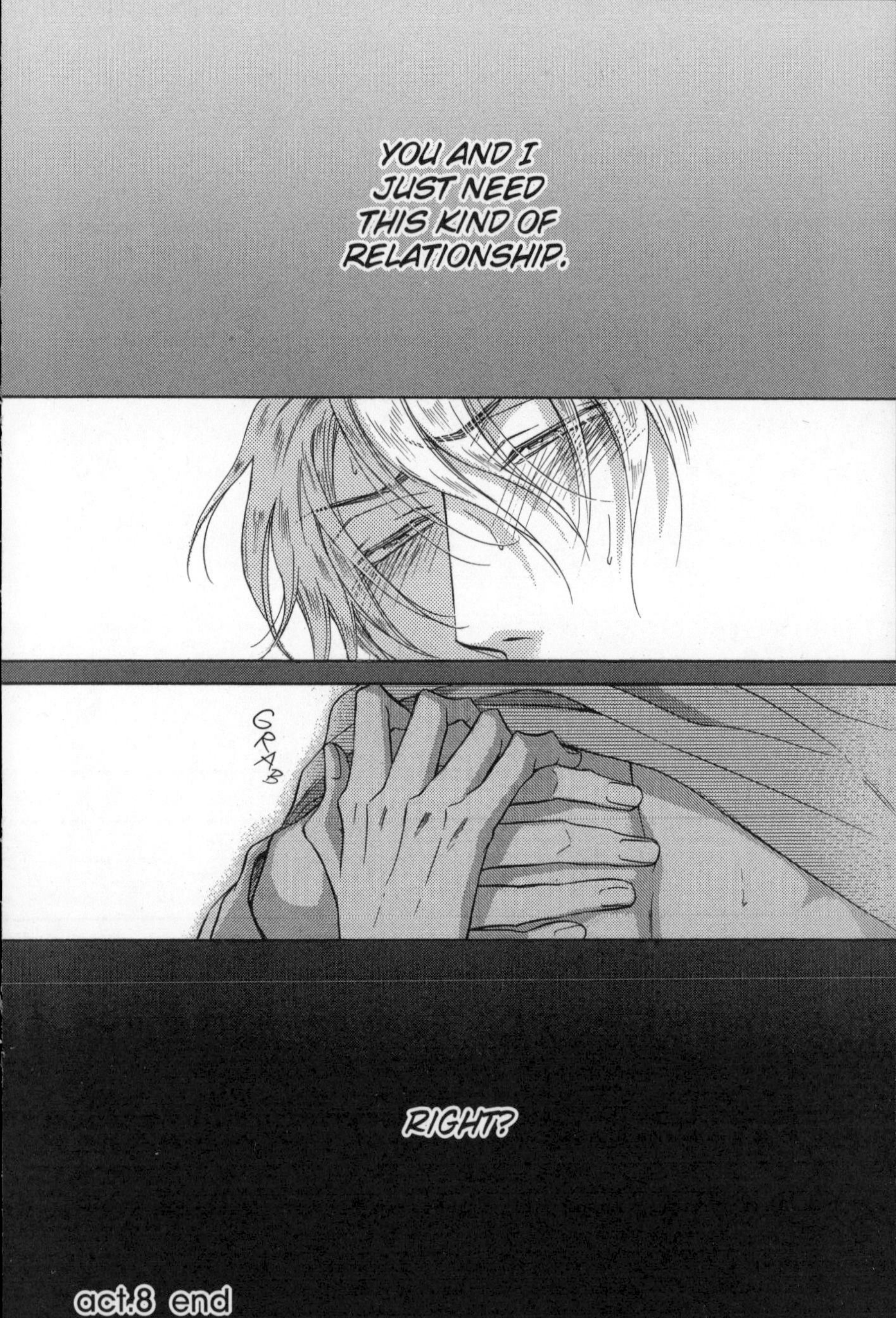
YOU AND I JUST NEED THIS KIND OF RELATIONSHIP.
GRAB
RIGHT?
act.8 end

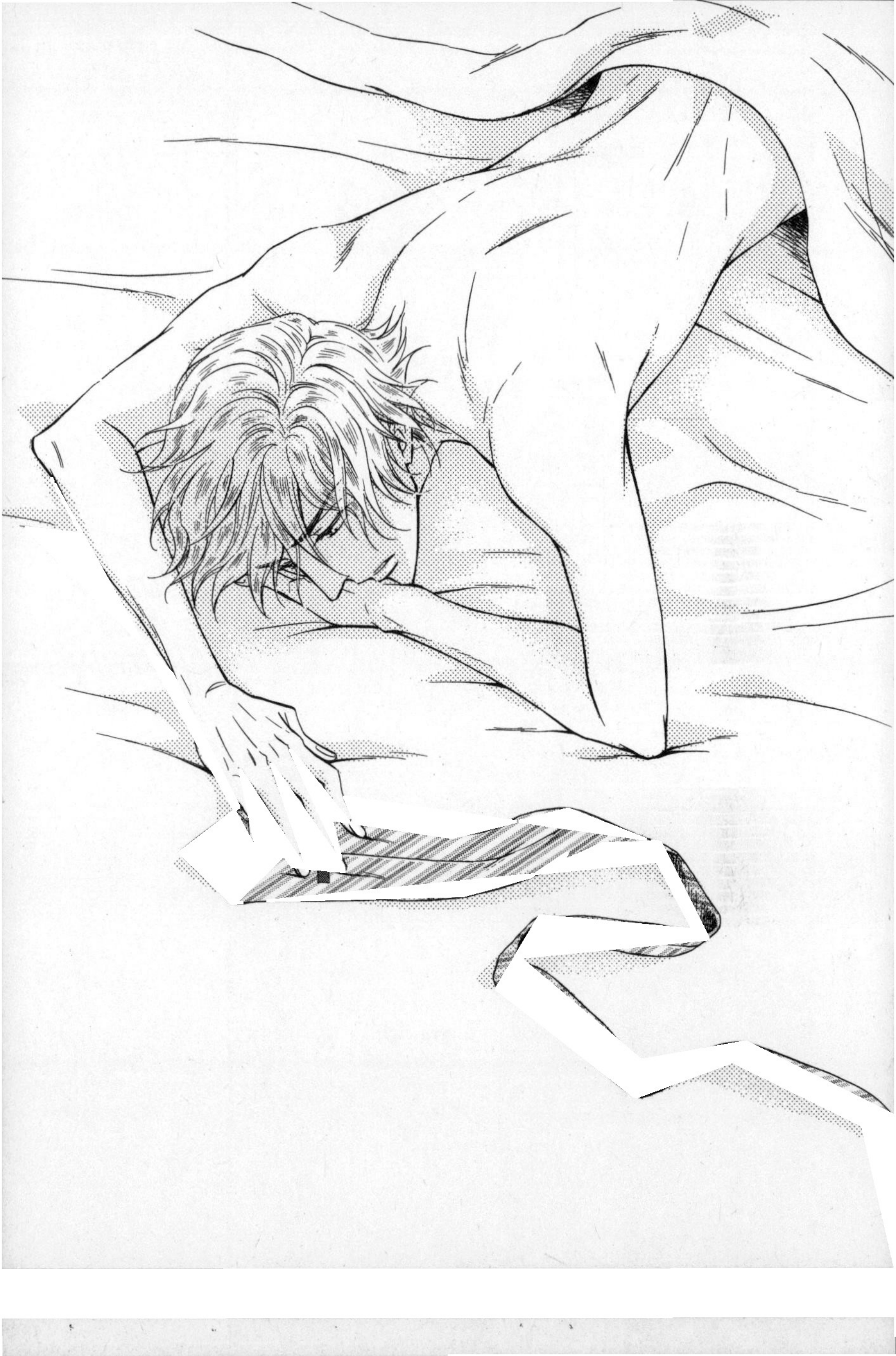

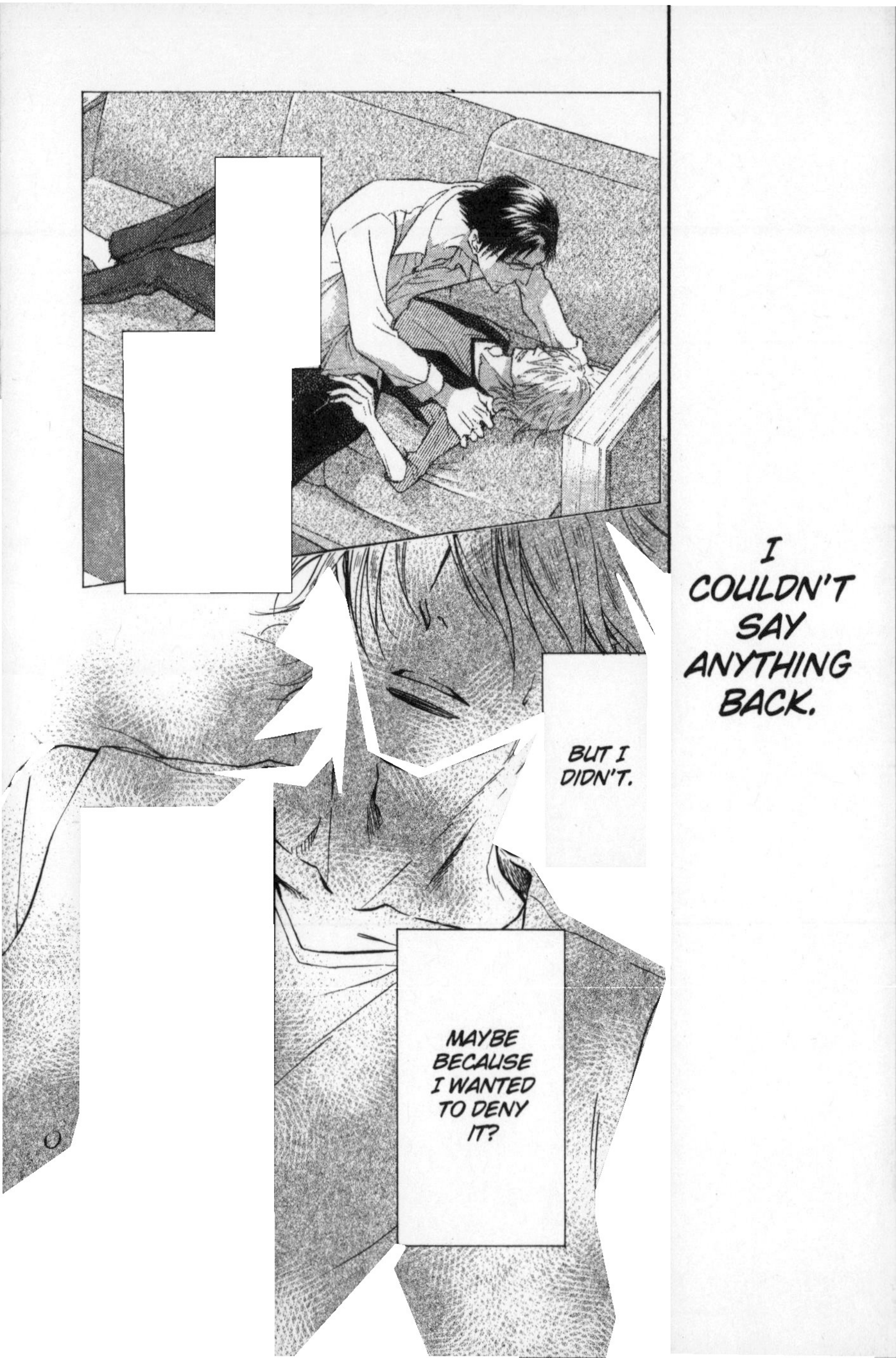
I COULDN'T SAY ANYTHING BACK.
BUT I DIDN'T.
MAYBE BECAUSE I WANTED TO DENY IT?

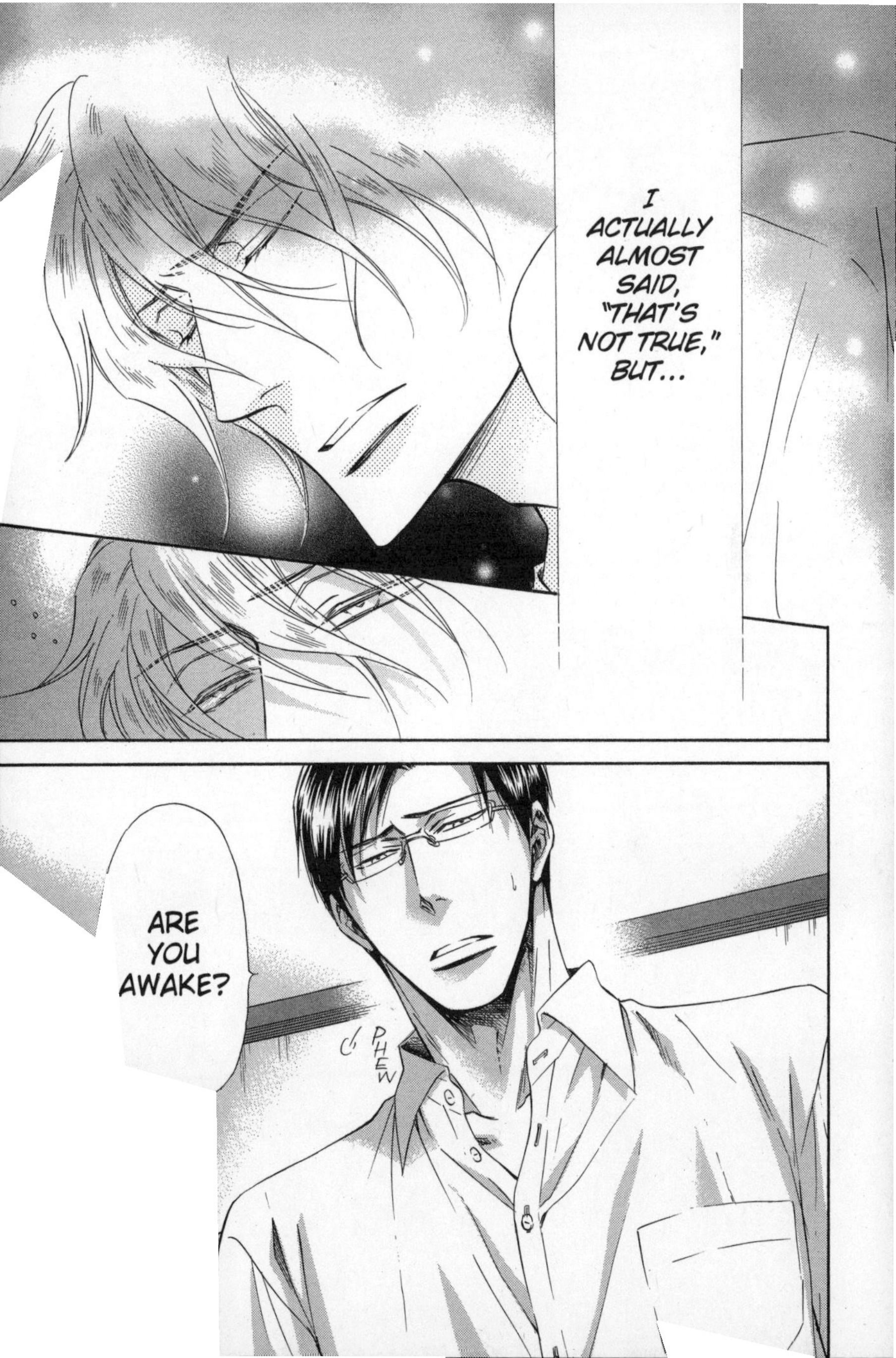
I ACTUALLY ALMOST SAID, "THAT'S NOT TRUE," BUT...
ARE YOU AWAKE?
PHEW

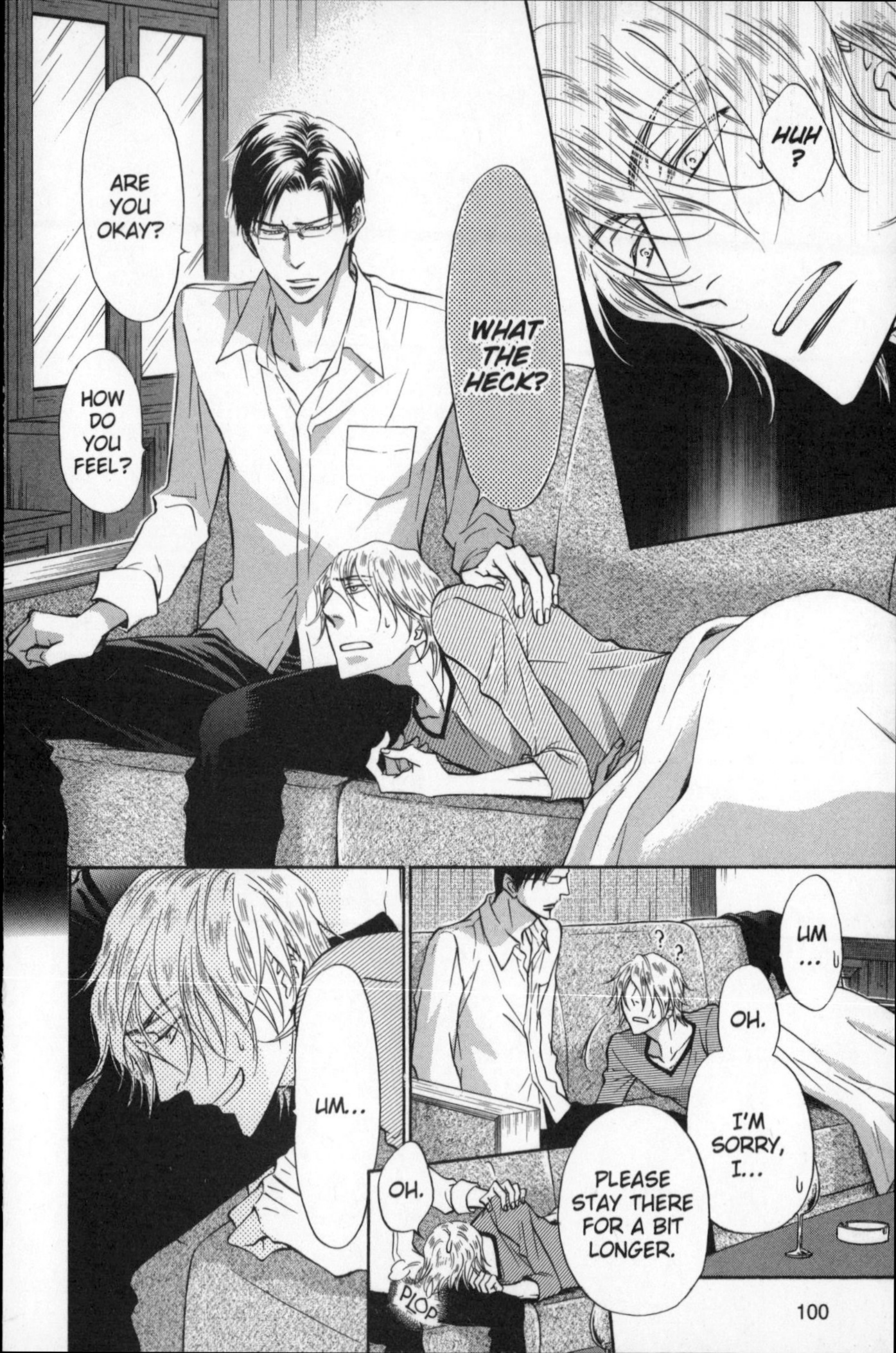
HUH ?
WHAT THE HECK?
ARE YOU OKAY?
HOW DO YOU FEEL?
UM ...
OH.
I'M SORRY, I...
PLEASE STAY THERE FOR A BIT LONGER.
OH.
PLOP
UM...

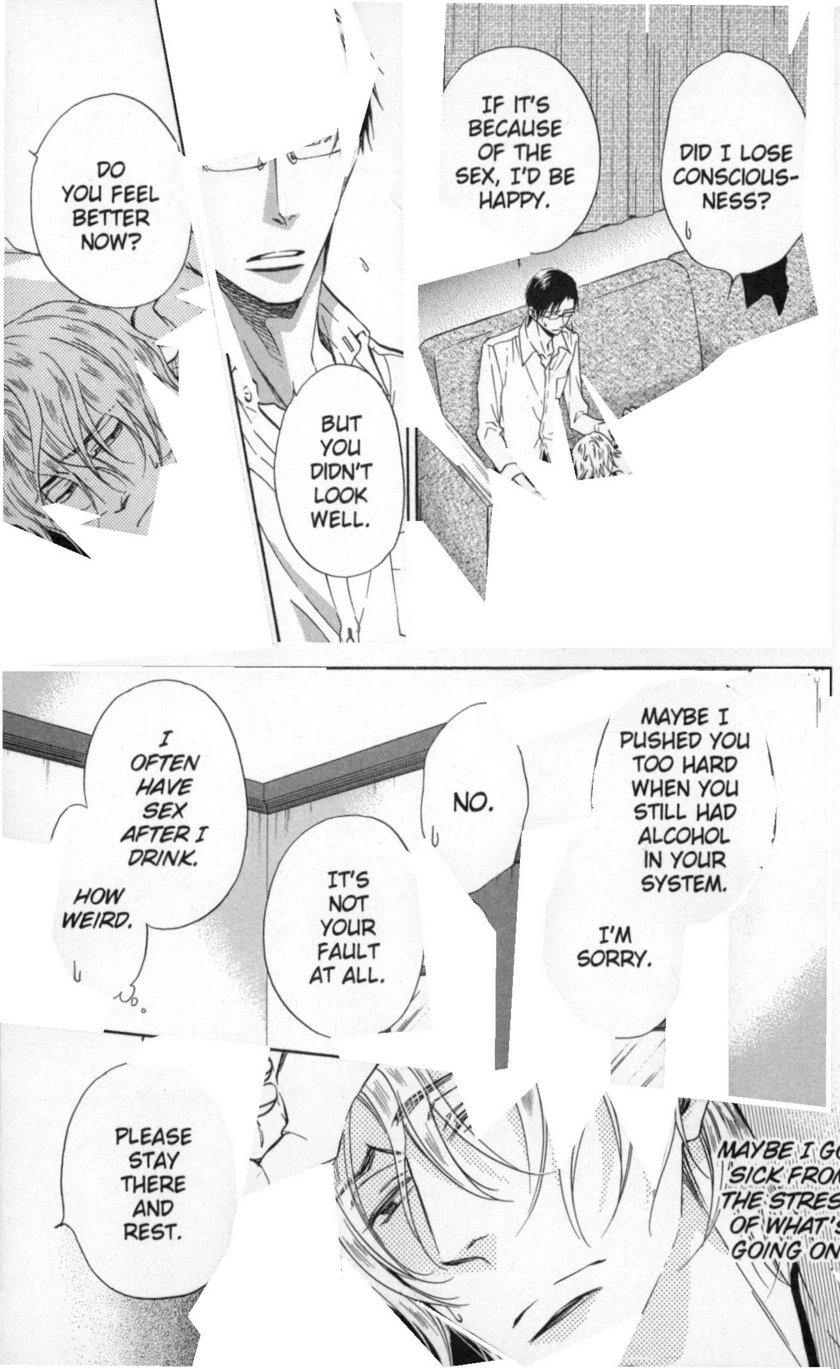
DID I LOSE CONSCIOUSNESS?
IF IT'S BECAUSE OF THE SEX, I'D BE HAPPY.
BUT YOU DIDN'T LOOK WELL.
DO YOU FEEL BETTER NOW?
MAYBE I PUSHED YOU TOO HARD WHEN YOU STILL HAD ALCOHOL IN YOUR SYSTEM.
I'M SORRY.
NO.
IT'S NOT YOUR FAULT AT ALL.
I OFTEN HAVE SEX AFTER I DRINK.
HOW WEIRD.
MAYBE I GOT SICK FROM THE STRESS OF WHAT'S GOING ON.
PLEASE STAY THERE AND REST.

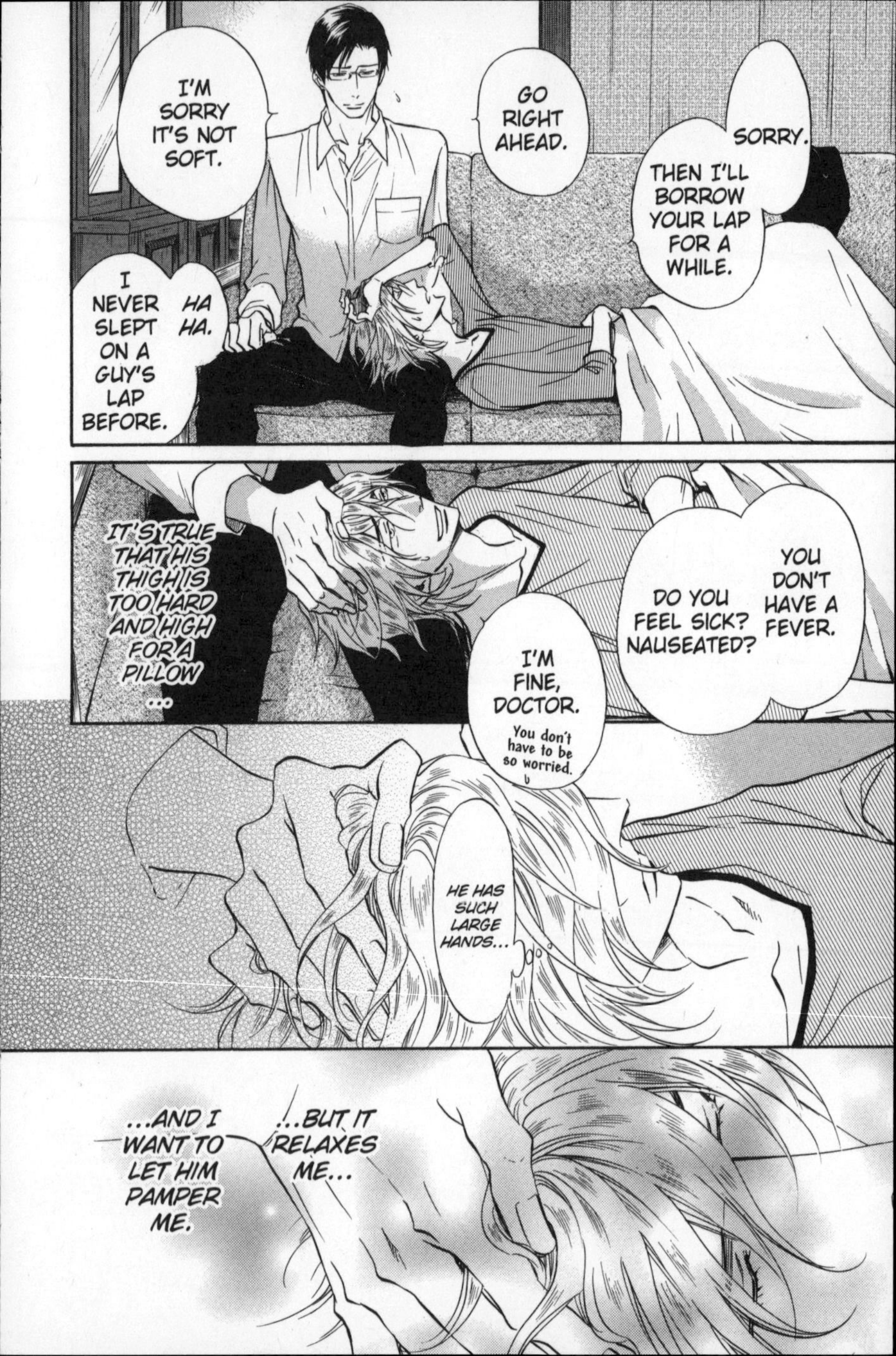
SORRY.
THEN I'LL BORROW YOUR LAP FOR A WHILE.
GO RIGHT AHEAD.
I'M SORRY IT'S NOT SOFT.
HA HA.
I NEVER SLEPT ON A GUY'S LAP BEFORE.
YOU DON'T HAVE A FEVER.
DO YOU FEEL SICK? NAUSEATED?
I'M FINE, DOCTOR.
You don't have to be so worried.
IT'S TRUE THAT HIS THIGH IS TOO HARD AND HIGH FOR A PILLOW...
HE HAS SUCH LARGE HANDS...
...BUT IT RELAXES ME...
...AND I WANT TO LET HIM PAMPER ME.

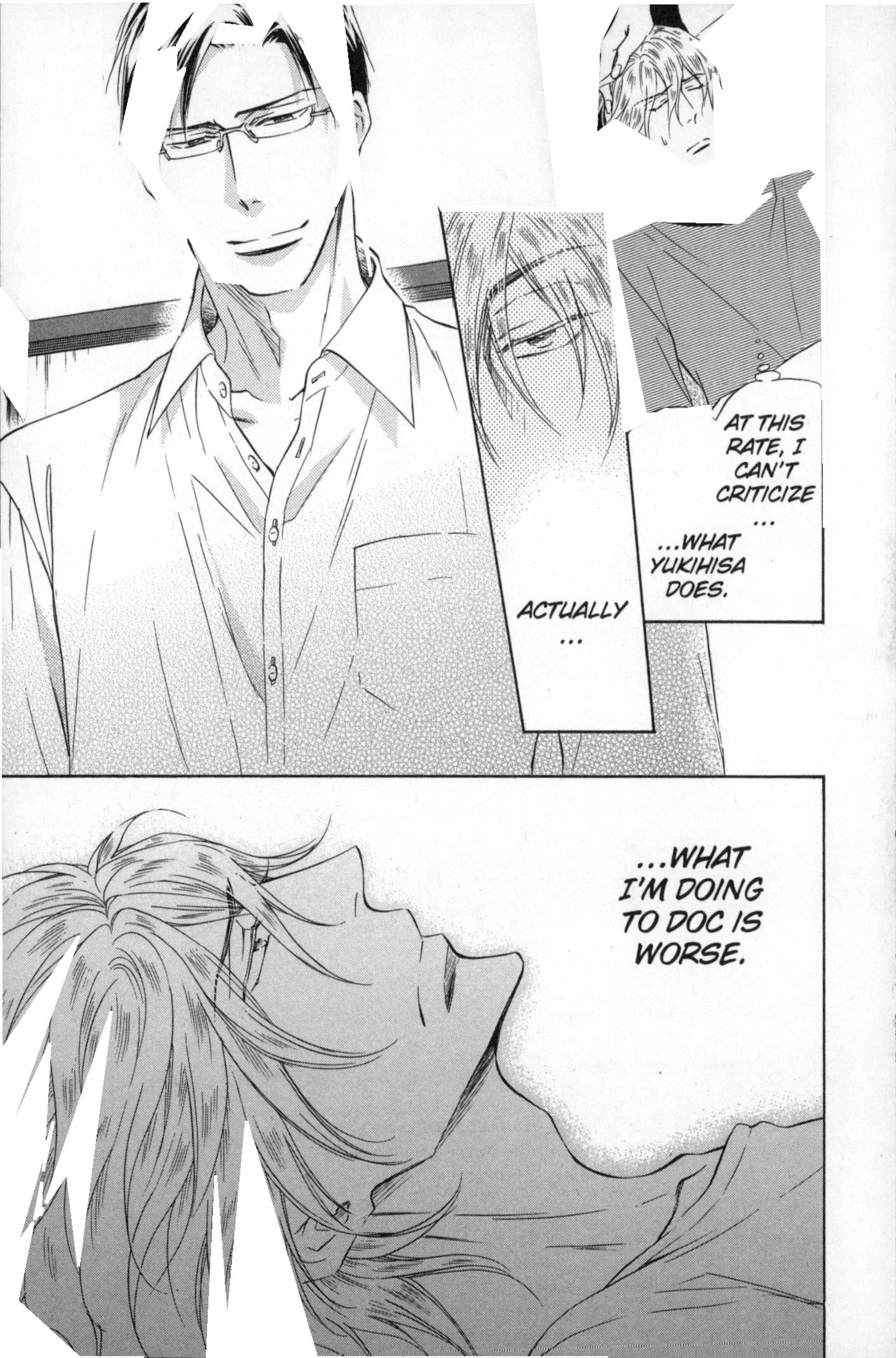
AT THIS RATE, I CAN'T CRITICIZE ...
...WHAT YUKIHISA DOES.
ACTUALLY ...
...WHAT I'M DOING TO DOC IS WORSE.

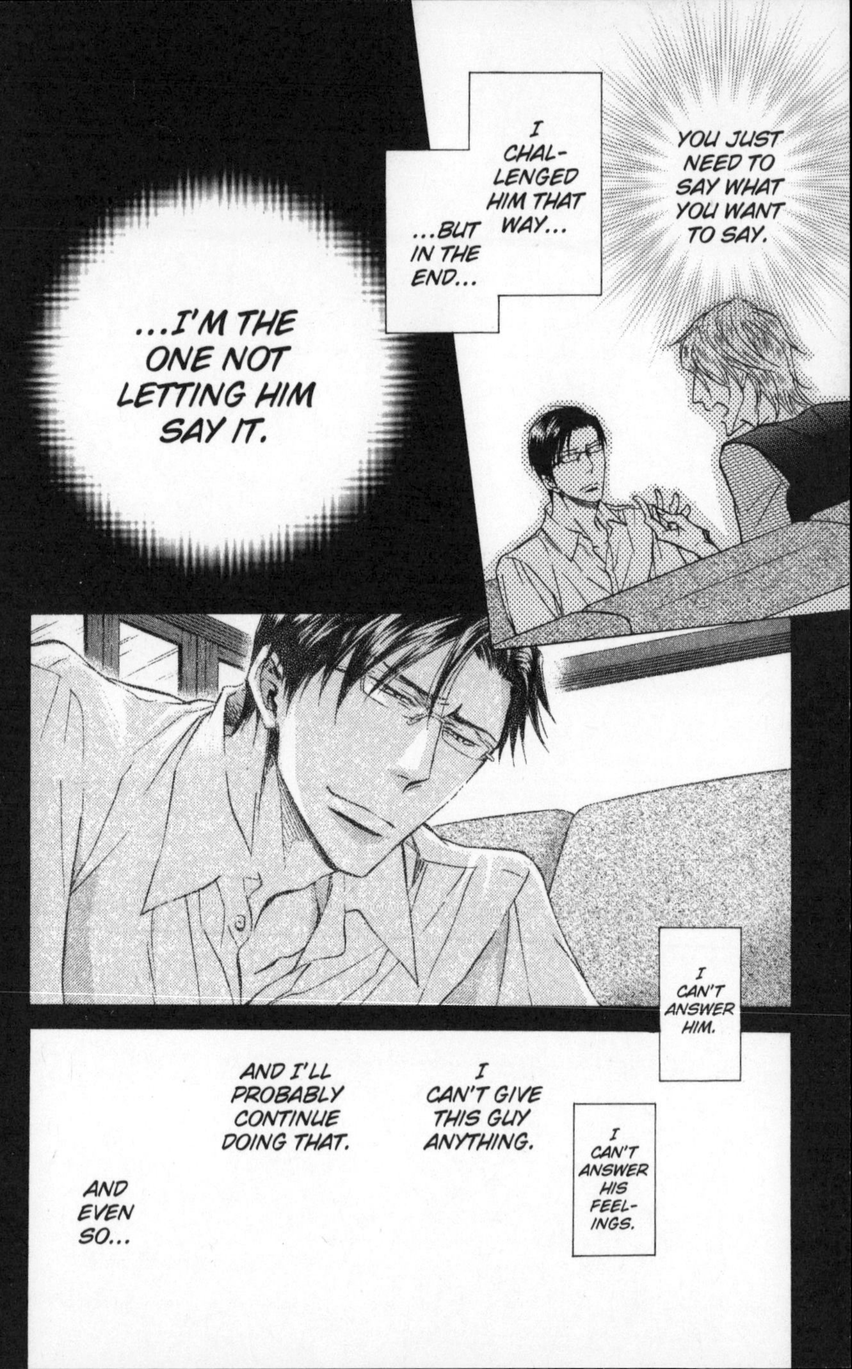
YOU JUST NEED TO SAY WHAT YOU WANT TO SAY.
I CHALLENGED HIM THAT WAY...
...BUT IN THE END...
...I'M THE ONE NOT LETTING HIM SAY IT.
I CAN'T ANSWER HIM.
I CAN'T ANSWER HIS FEELINGS.
I CAN'T GIVE THIS GUY ANYTHING.
AND I'LL PROBABLY CONTINUE DOING THAT.
AND EVEN SO...

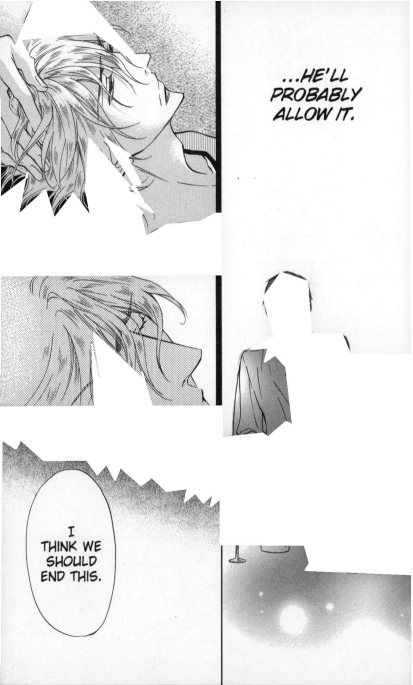

...HE'LL PROBABLY ALLOW IT.

I THINK WE SHOULD END THIS.

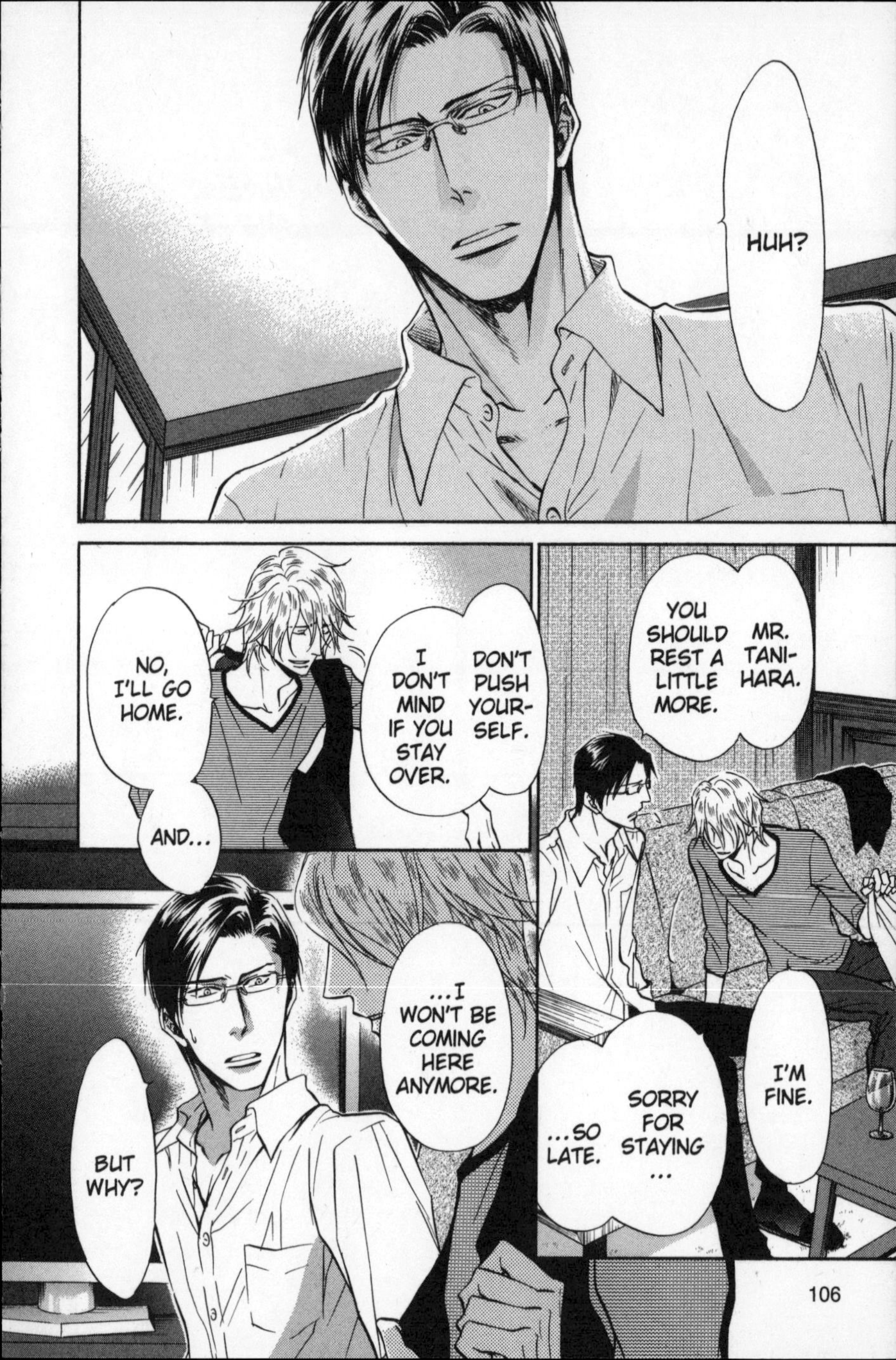
HUH?
MR. TANI-HARA.
YOU SHOULD REST A LITTLE MORE.
I'M FINE.
SORRY FOR STAYING ...
...SO LATE.
DON'T PUSH YOURSELF.
I DON'T MIND IF YOU STAY OVER.
NO, I'LL GO HOME.
AND...
...I WON'T BE COMING HERE ANYMORE.
BUT WHY?

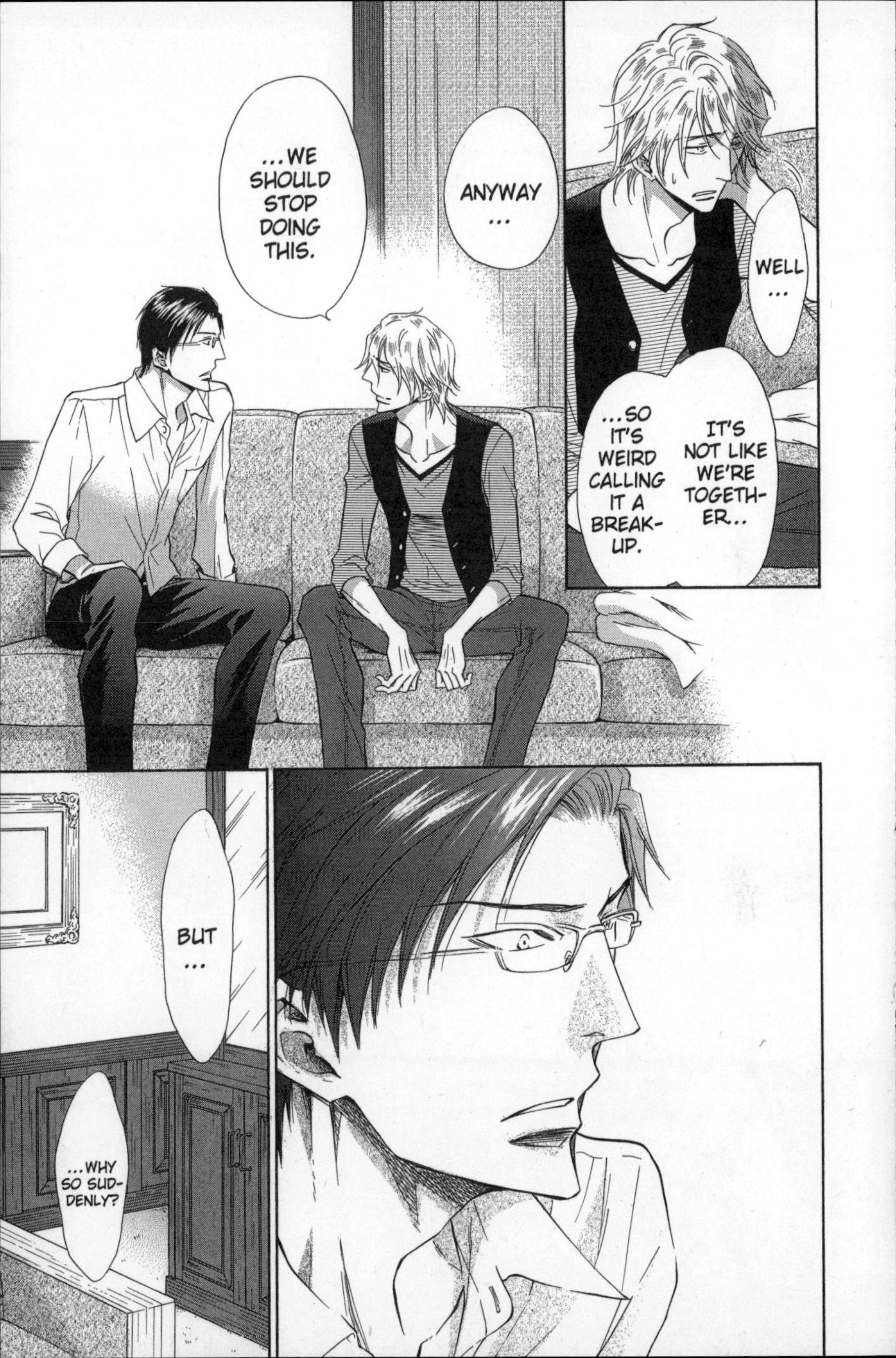
WELL ...
IT'S NOT LIKE WE'RE TOGETH-ER...
...SO IT'S WEIRD CALLING IT A BREAK-UP.
ANYWAY ...
...WE SHOULD STOP DOING THIS.
BUT ...
...WHY SO SUD-DENLY?

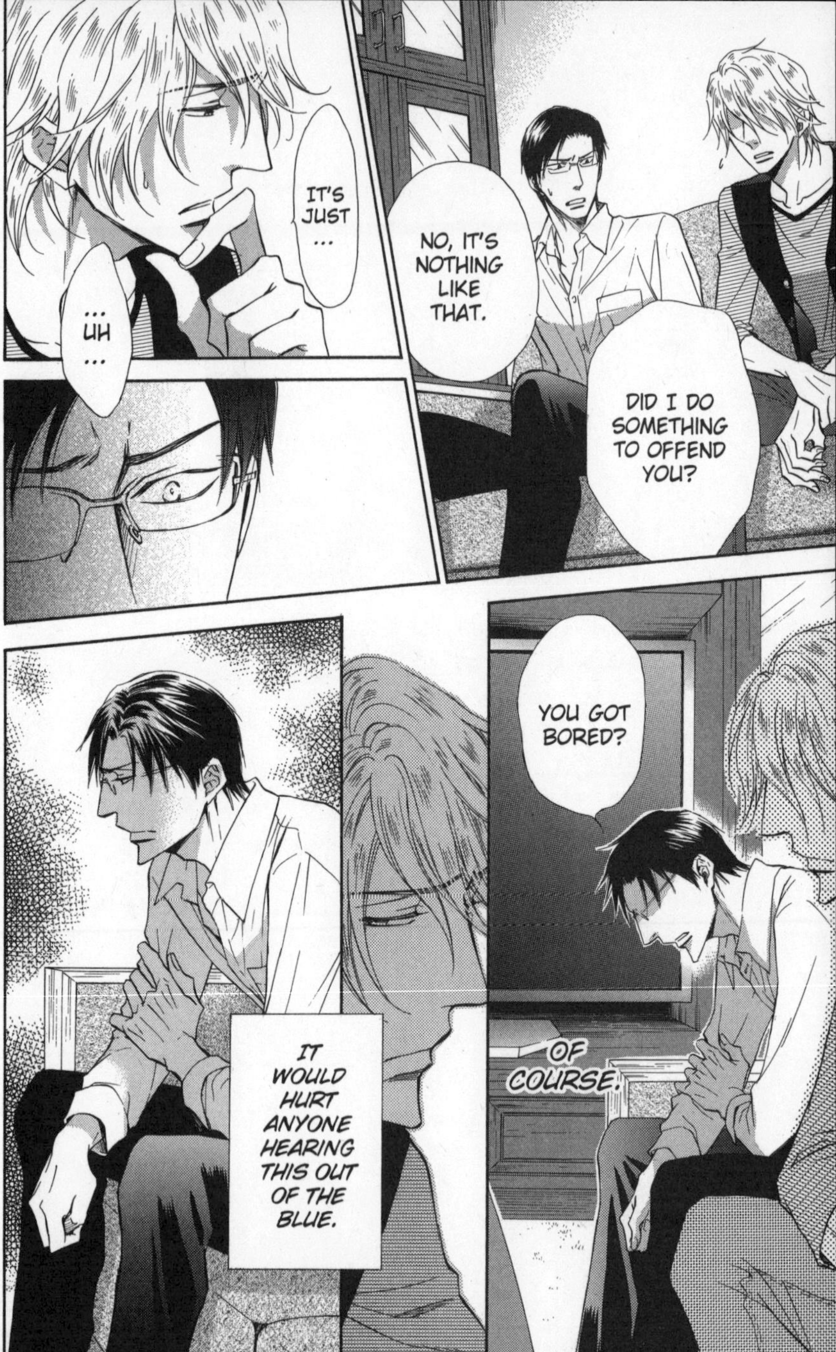
DID I DO SOMETHING TO OFFEND YOU?
NO, IT'S NOTHING LIKE THAT.
IT'S JUST ...
... UH ...
YOU GOT BORED?
OF COURSE.
IT WOULD HURT ANYONE HEARING THIS OUT OF THE BLUE.

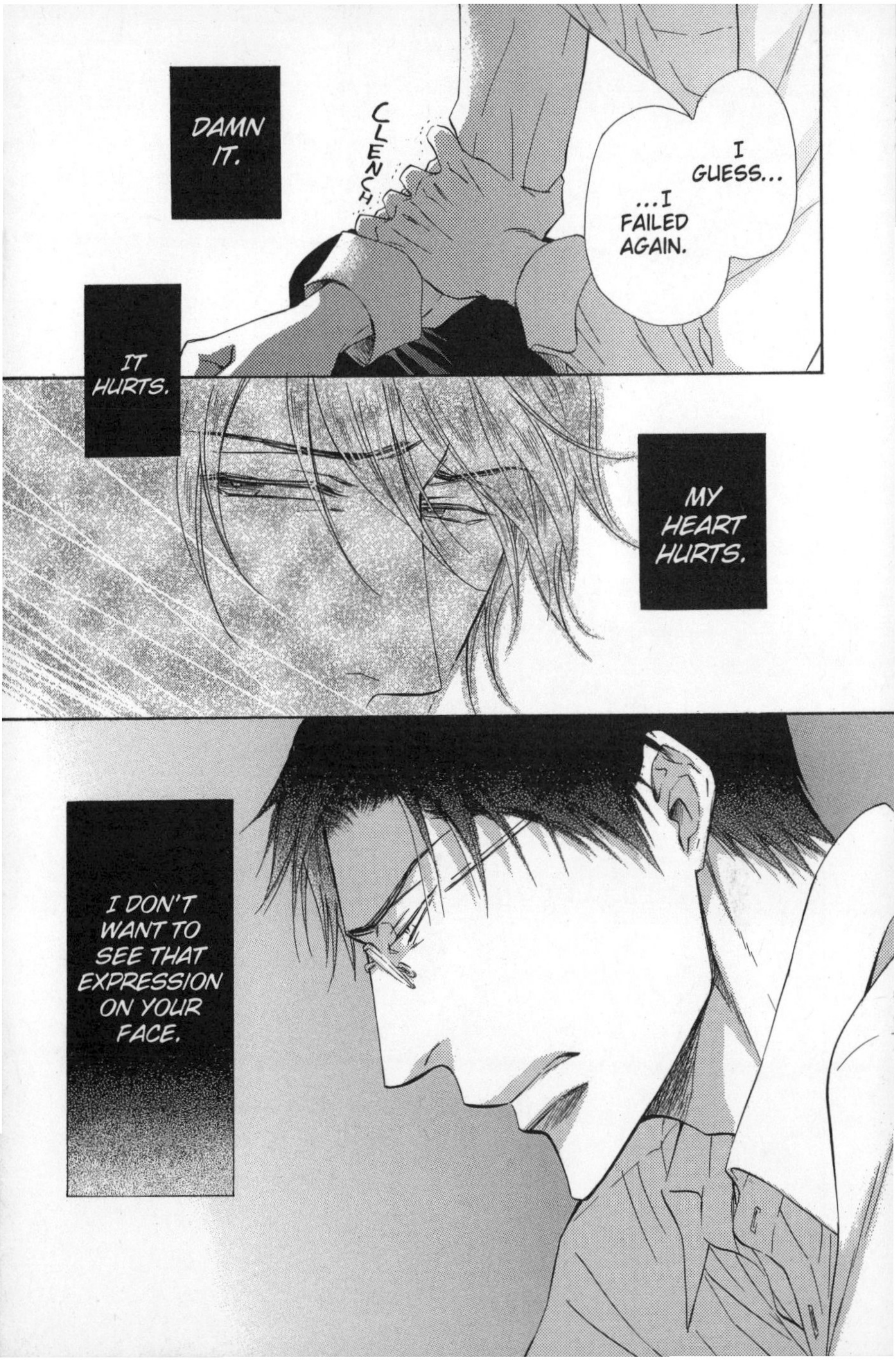
I GUESS...
...I FAILED AGAIN.
CLENCH
DAMN IT.
IT HURTS.
MY HEART HURTS.
I DON'T WANT TO SEE THAT EXPRESSION ON YOUR FACE.

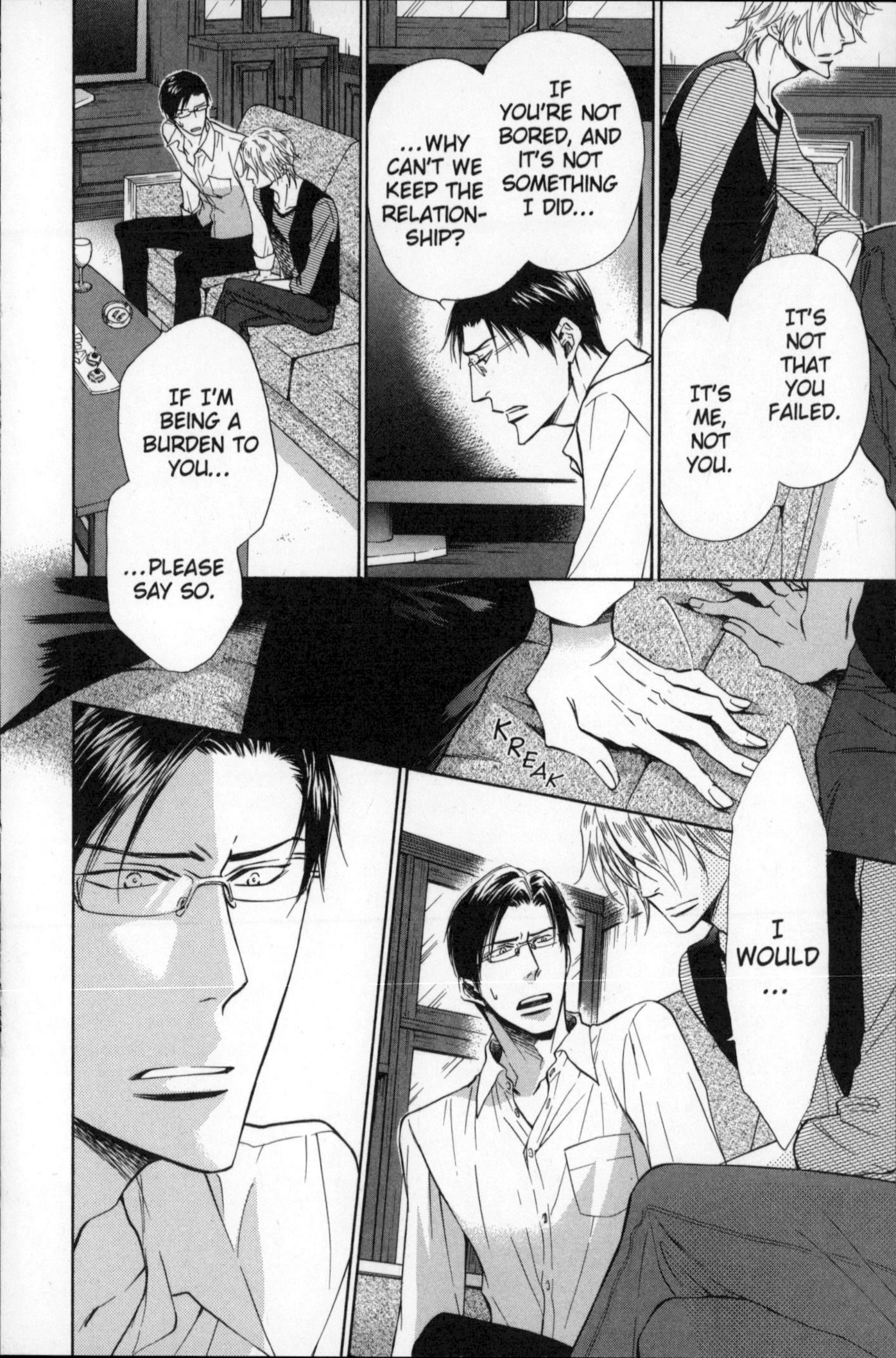
IT'S NOT THAT YOU FAILED.
IT'S ME, NOT YOU.
IF YOU'RE NOT BORED, AND IT'S NOT SOMETHING I DID...
...WHY CAN'T WE KEEP THE RELATIONSHIP?
IF I'M BEING A BURDEN TO YOU...
...PLEASE SAY SO.
KREAK
I WOULD ...

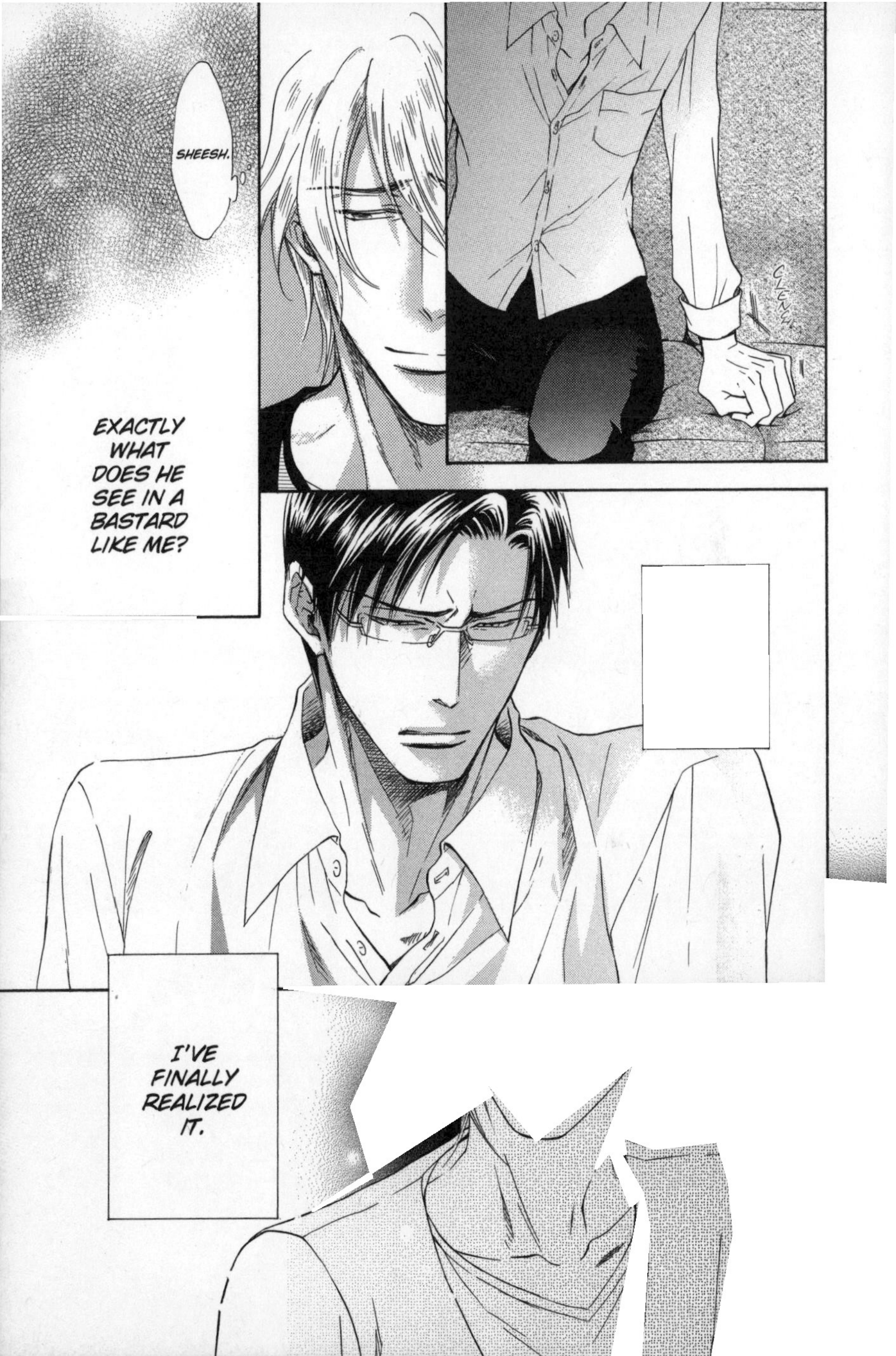
CLENCH
SHEESH.
EXACTLY WHAT DOES HE SEE IN A BASTARD LIKE ME?
I'VE FINALLY REALIZED IT.

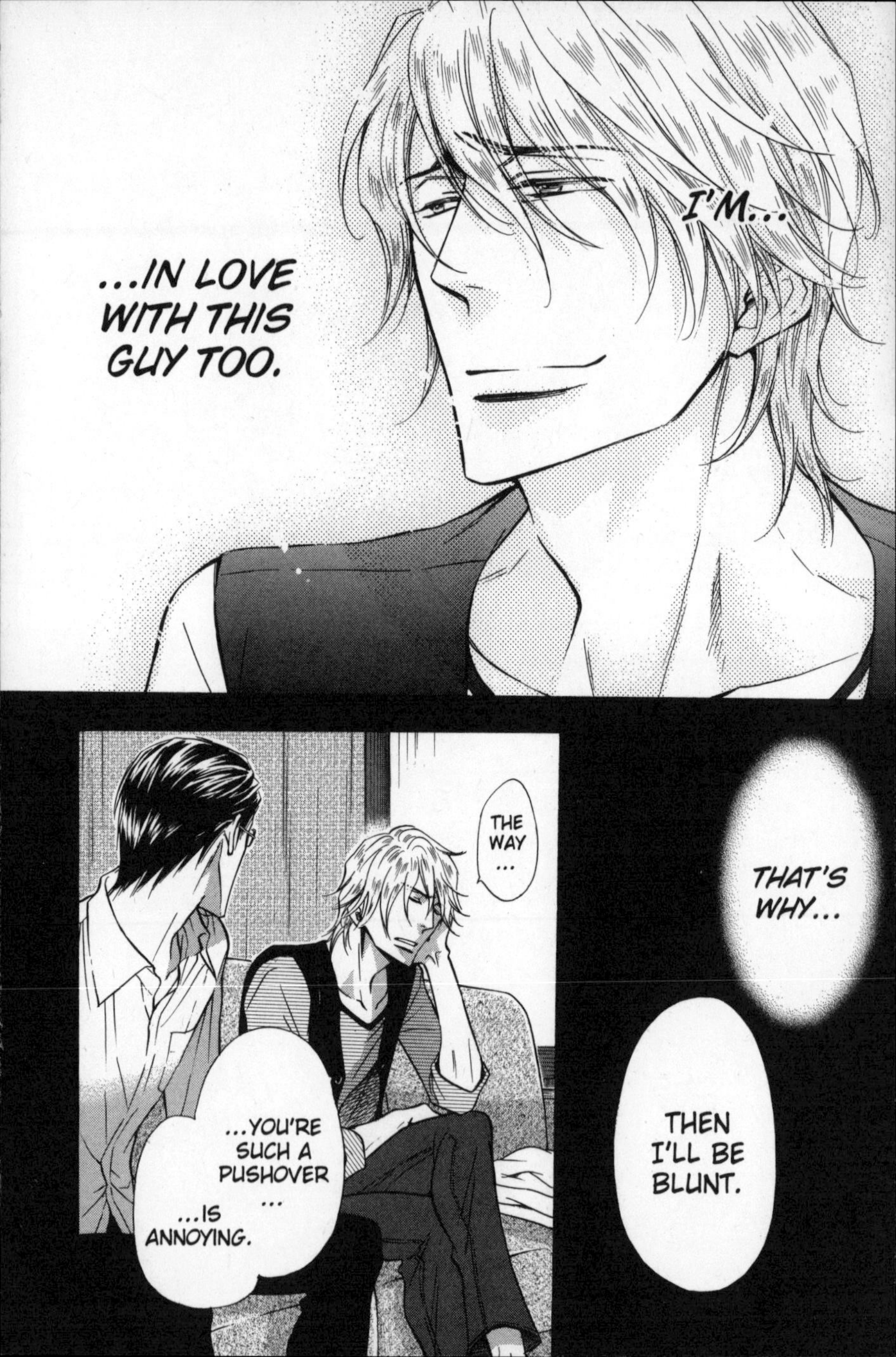
I'M...
...IN LOVE WITH THIS GUY TOO.
THAT'S WHY...
THEN I'LL BE BLUNT.
THE WAY...
...YOU'RE SUCH A PUSHOVER...
...IS ANNOYING.

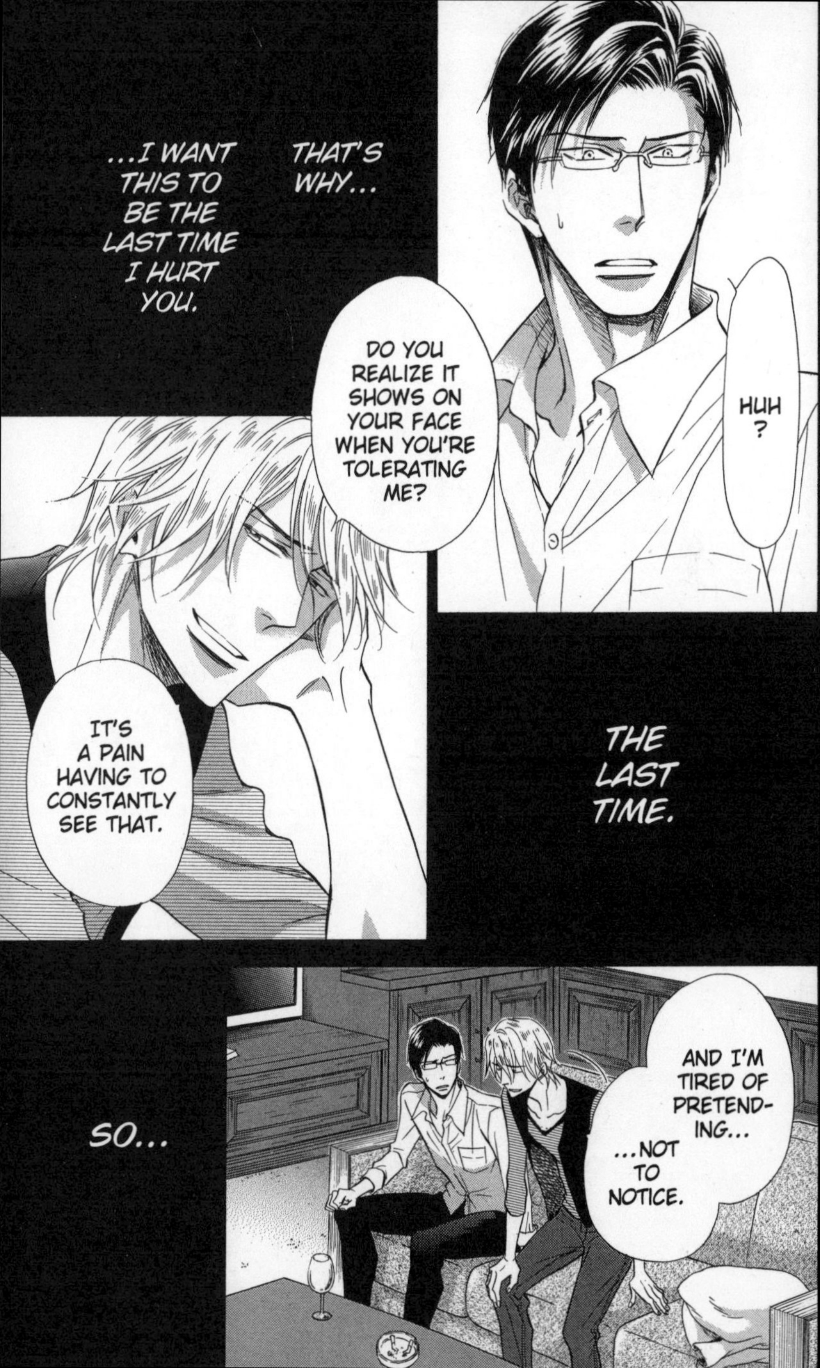
HUH?
THAT'S WHY...
...I WANT THIS TO BE THE LAST TIME I HURT YOU.
DO YOU REALIZE IT SHOWS ON YOUR FACE WHEN YOU'RE TOLERATING ME?
IT'S A PAIN HAVING TO CONSTANTLY SEE THAT.
THE LAST TIME.
AND I'M TIRED OF PRETEND-ING...
...NOT TO NOTICE.
SO...

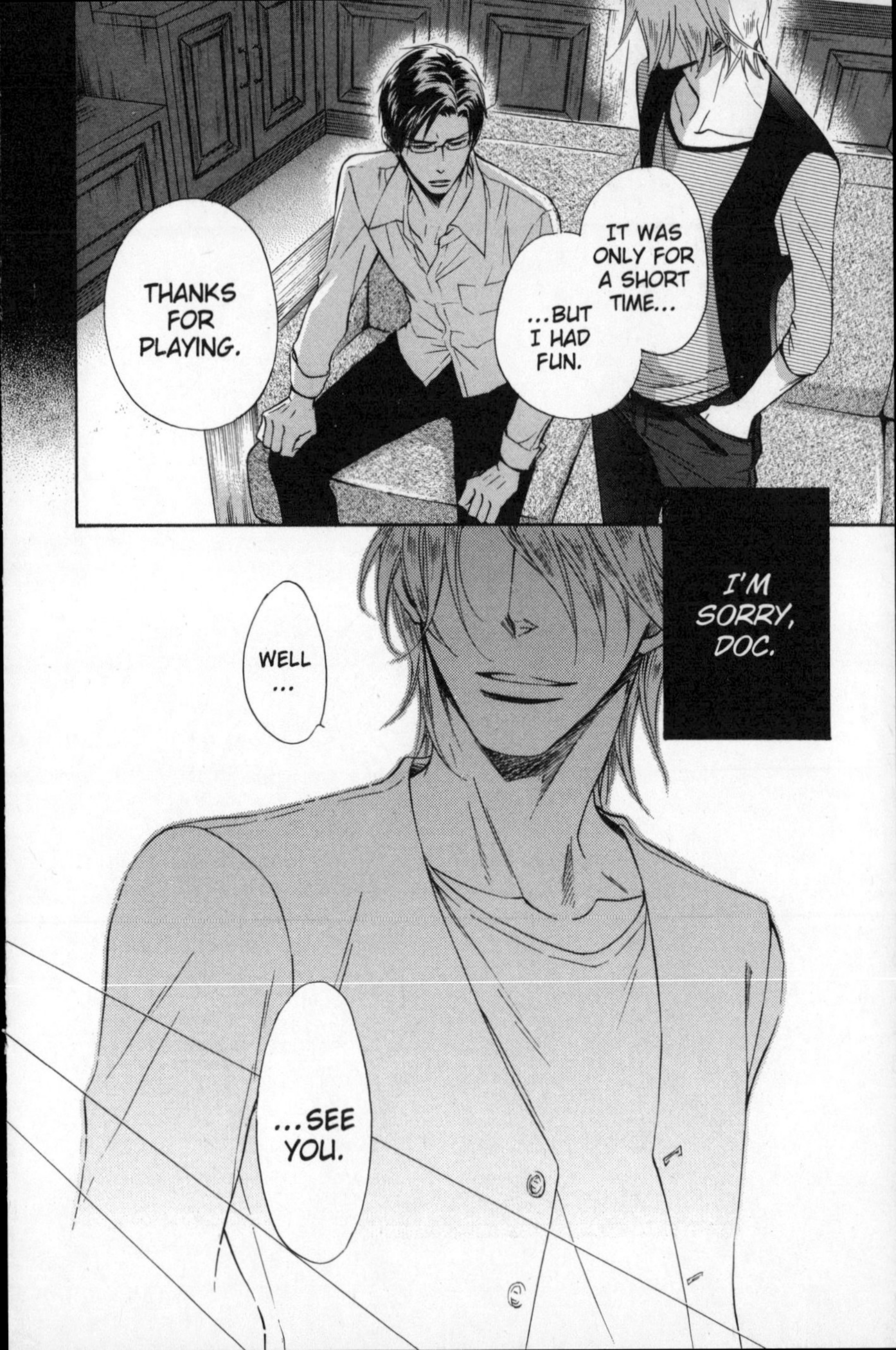
IT WAS ONLY FOR A SHORT TIME...
...BUT I HAD FUN.
THANKS FOR PLAYING.
I'M SORRY, DOC.
WELL ...
...SEE YOU.

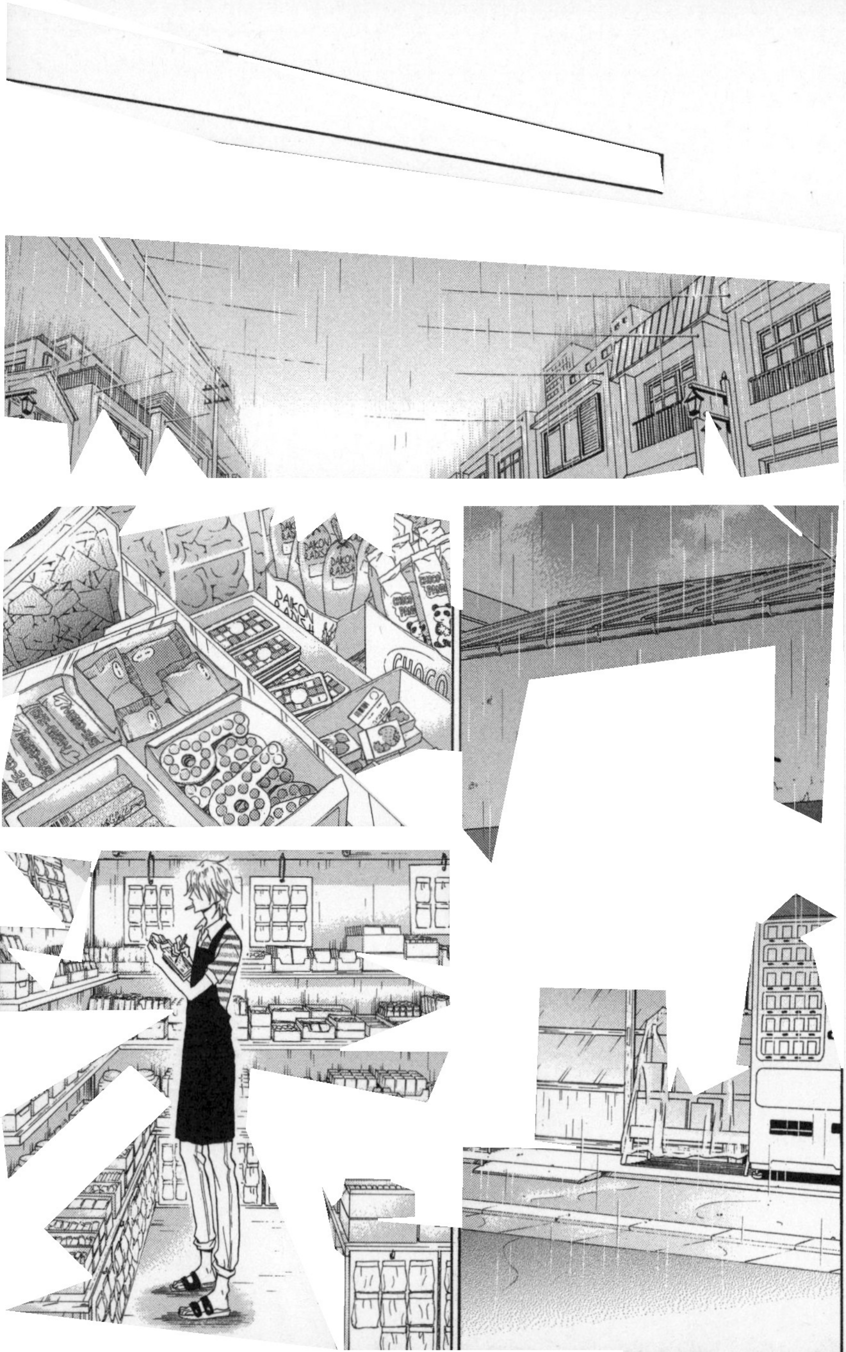
DAIKON RADISH
CHOCO

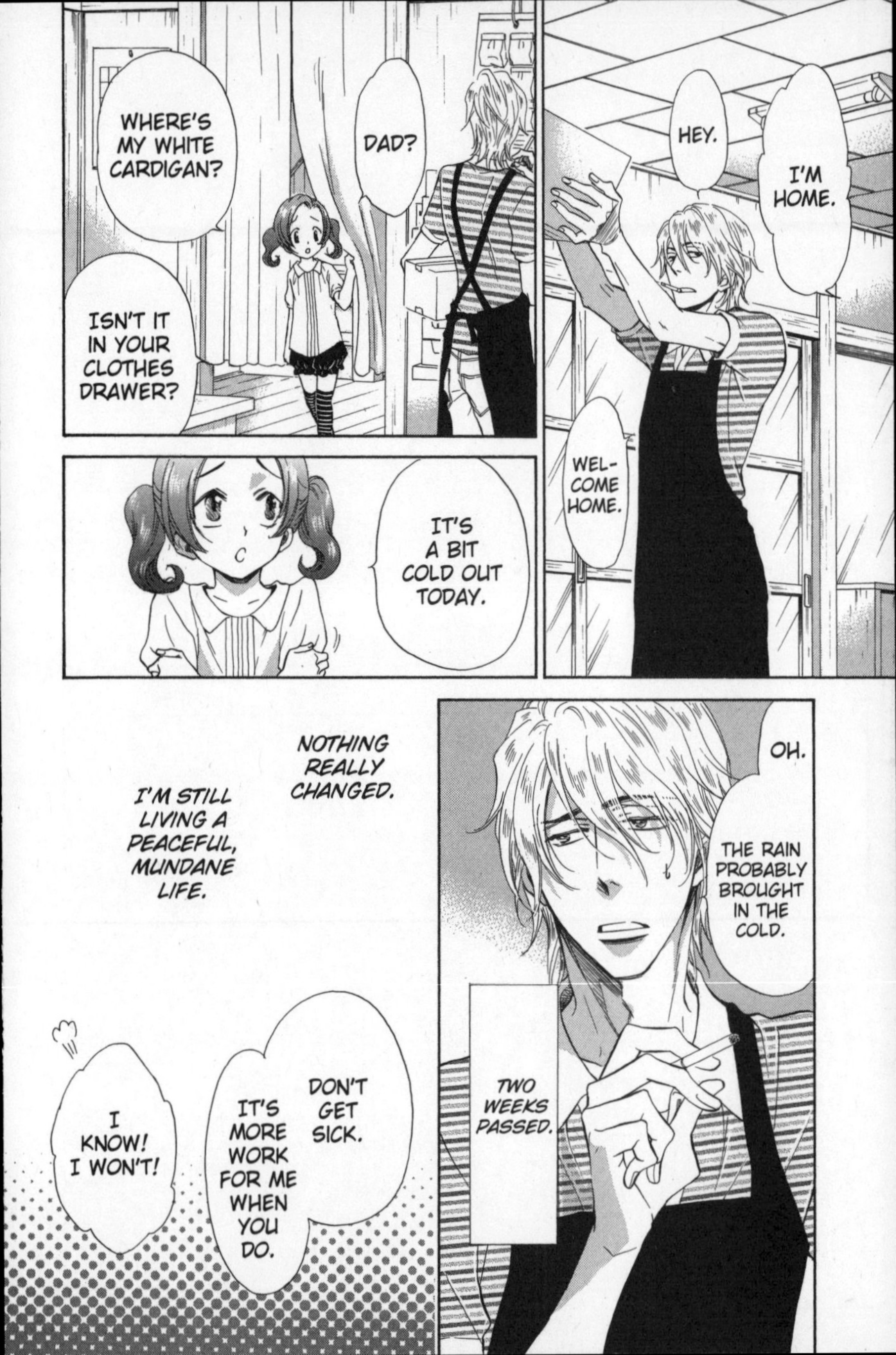

I'M HOME.
HEY.
WELCOME HOME.
DAD?
WHERE'S MY WHITE CARDIGAN?
ISN'T IT IN YOUR CLOTHES DRAWER?
IT'S A BIT COLD OUT TODAY.
OH.
THE RAIN PROBABLY BROUGHT IN THE COLD.
TWO WEEKS PASSED.
NOTHING REALLY CHANGED.
I'M STILL LIVING A PEACEFUL, MUNDANE LIFE.
DON'T GET SICK.
IT'S MORE WORK FOR ME WHEN YOU DO.
I KNOW! I WON'T!

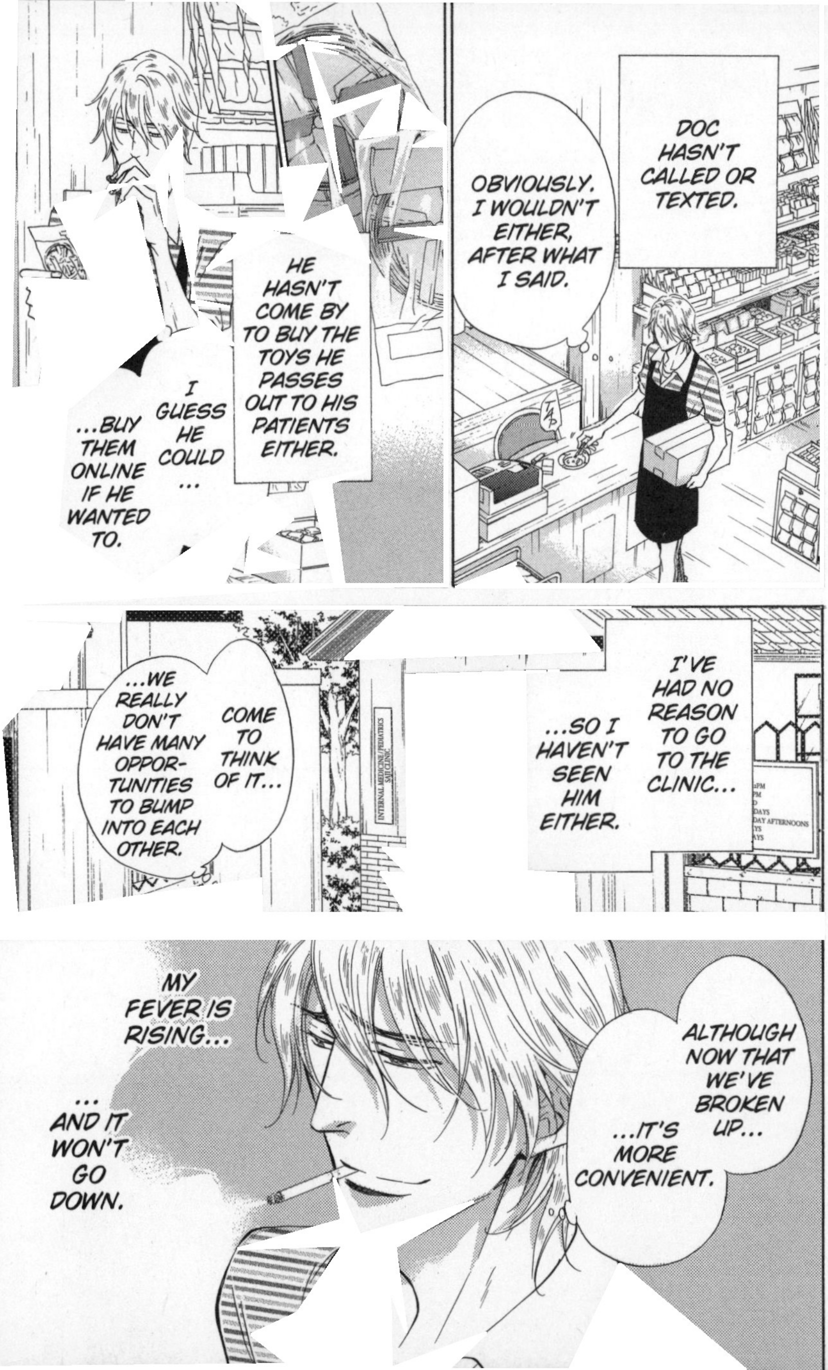
DOC HASN'T CALLED OR TEXTED.
OBVIOUSLY. I WOULDN'T EITHER, AFTER WHAT I SAID.
HE HASN'T COME BY TO BUY THE TOYS HE PASSES OUT TO HIS PATIENTS EITHER.
I GUESS HE COULD...
...BUY THEM ONLINE IF HE WANTED TO.
I'VE HAD NO REASON TO GO TO THE CLINIC...
...SO I HAVEN'T SEEN HIM EITHER.
INTERNAL MEDICINE/PEDIATRICS SAJI CLINIC
COME TO THINK OF IT...
...WE REALLY DON'T HAVE MANY OPPORTUNITIES TO BUMP INTO EACH OTHER.
ALTHOUGH NOW THAT WE'VE BROKEN UP...
...IT'S MORE CONVENIENT.
MY FEVER IS RISING...
...AND IT WON'T GO DOWN.

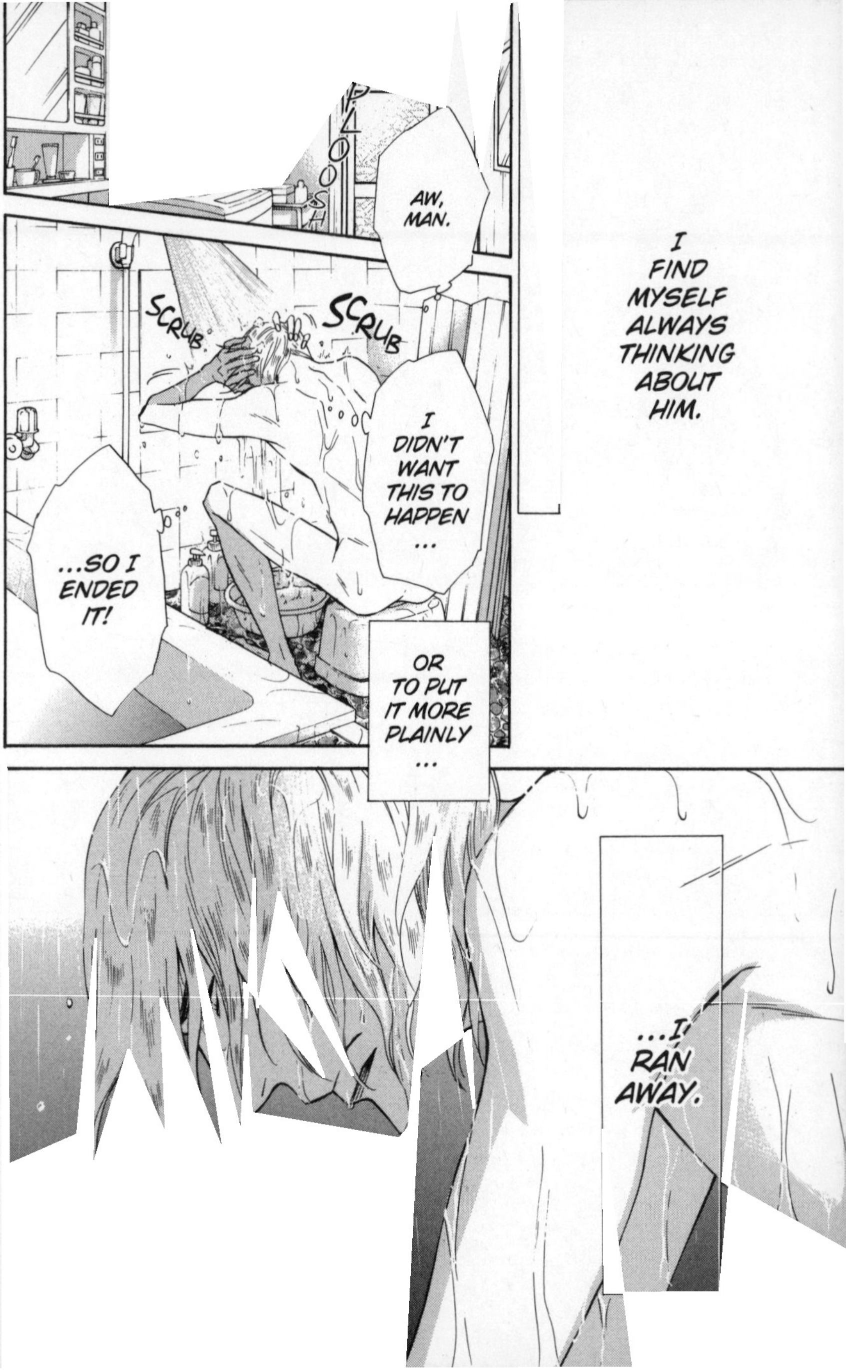
I FIND MYSELF ALWAYS THINKING ABOUT HIM.
PLOOSH
AW, MAN.
SCRUB
SCRUB
I DIDN'T WANT THIS TO HAPPEN...
...SO I ENDED IT!
OR TO PUT IT MORE PLAINLY...
...I RAN AWAY.

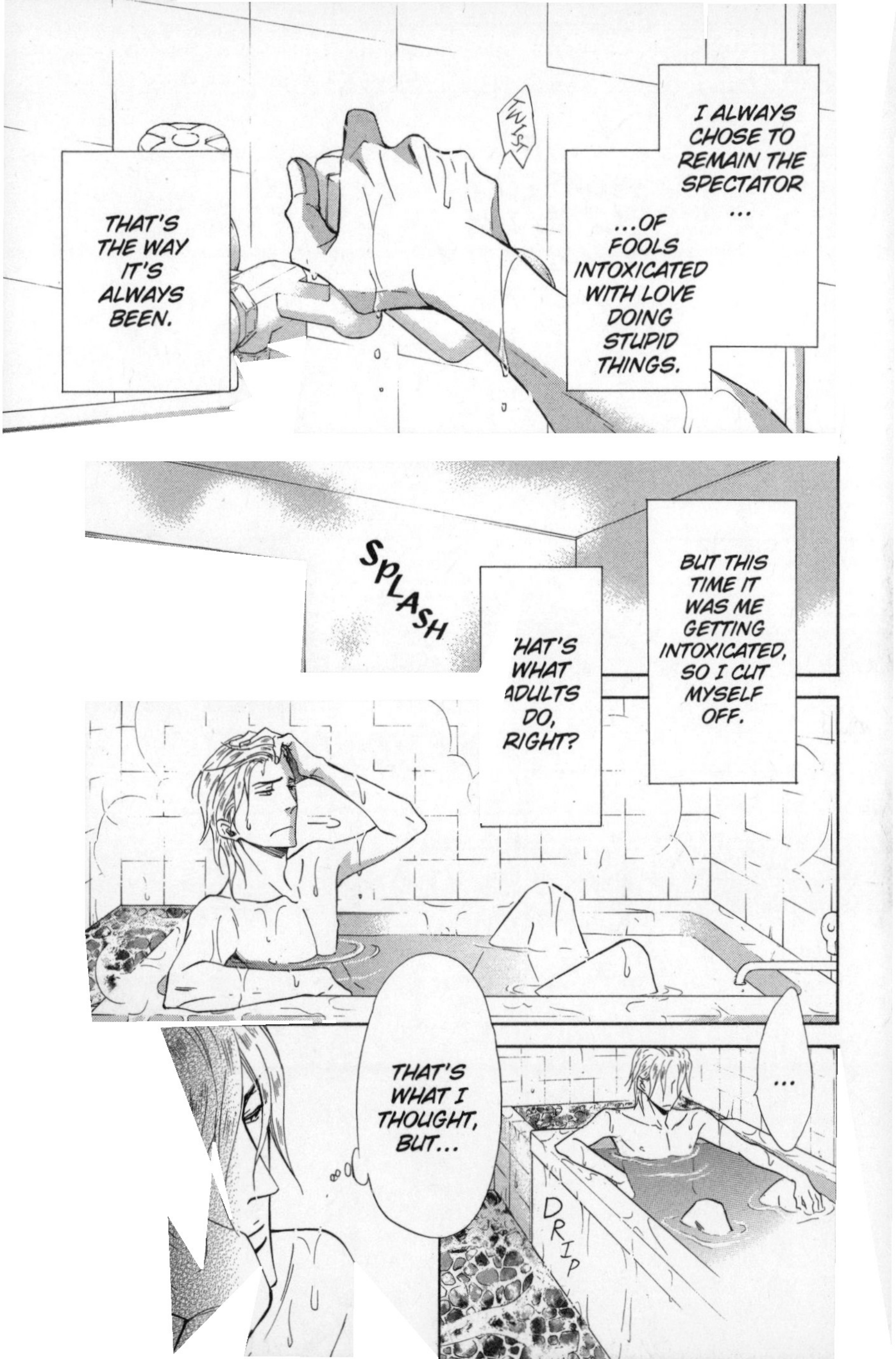
I ALWAYS CHOSE TO REMAIN THE SPECTATOR ...
...OF FOOLS INTOXICATED WITH LOVE DOING STUPID THINGS.
TWIST
THAT'S THE WAY IT'S ALWAYS BEEN.
SPLASH
BUT THIS TIME IT WAS ME GETTING INTOXICATED, SO I CUT MYSELF OFF.
THAT'S WHAT ADULTS DO, RIGHT?
...
THAT'S WHAT I THOUGHT, BUT...
DRIP

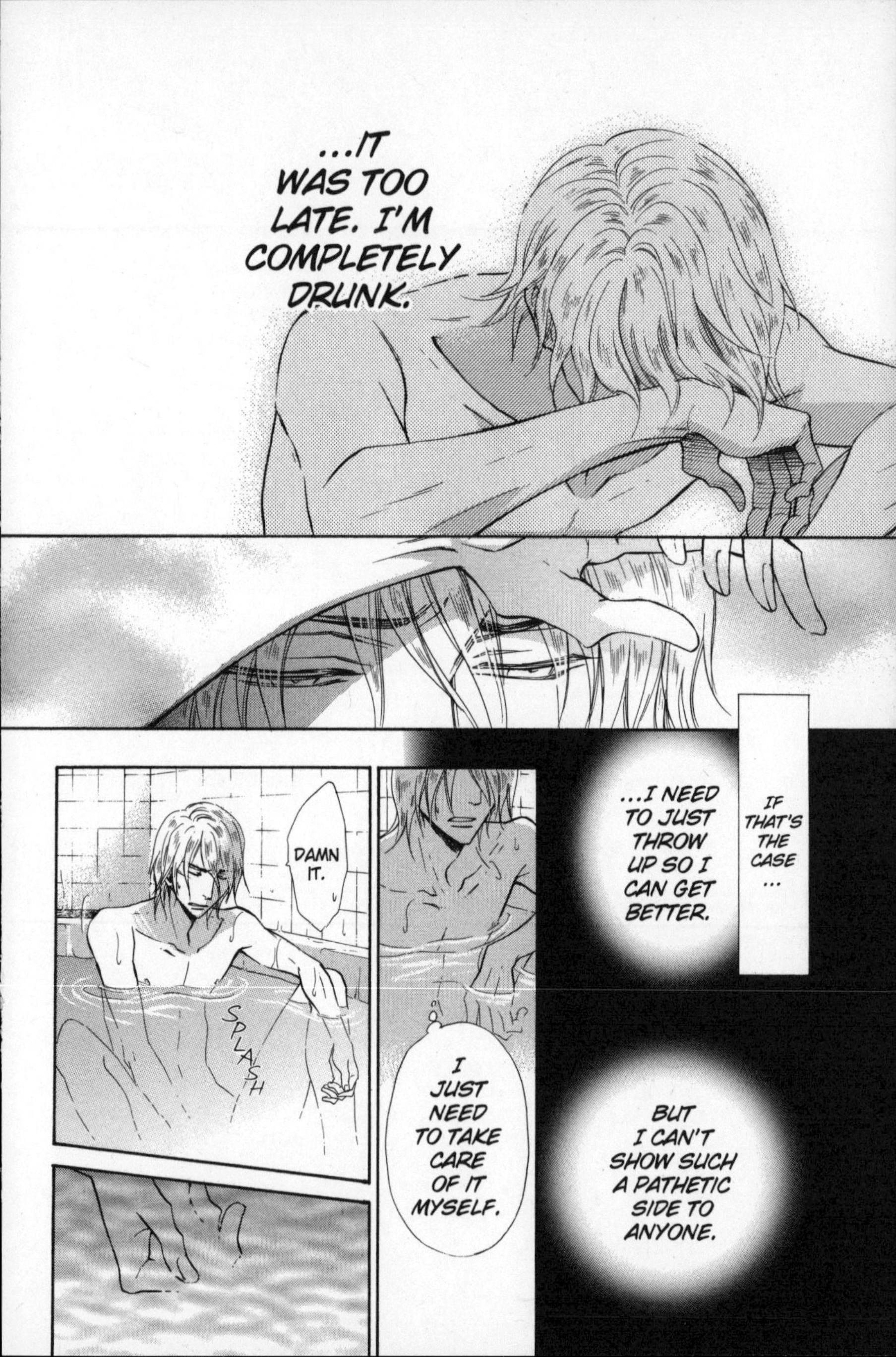
...IT WAS TOO LATE. I'M COMPLETELY DRUNK.
IF THAT'S THE CASE...
...I NEED TO JUST THROW UP SO I CAN GET BETTER.
BUT I CAN'T SHOW SUCH A PATHETIC SIDE TO ANYONE.
I JUST NEED TO TAKE CARE OF IT MYSELF.
DAMN IT.
SPLASH

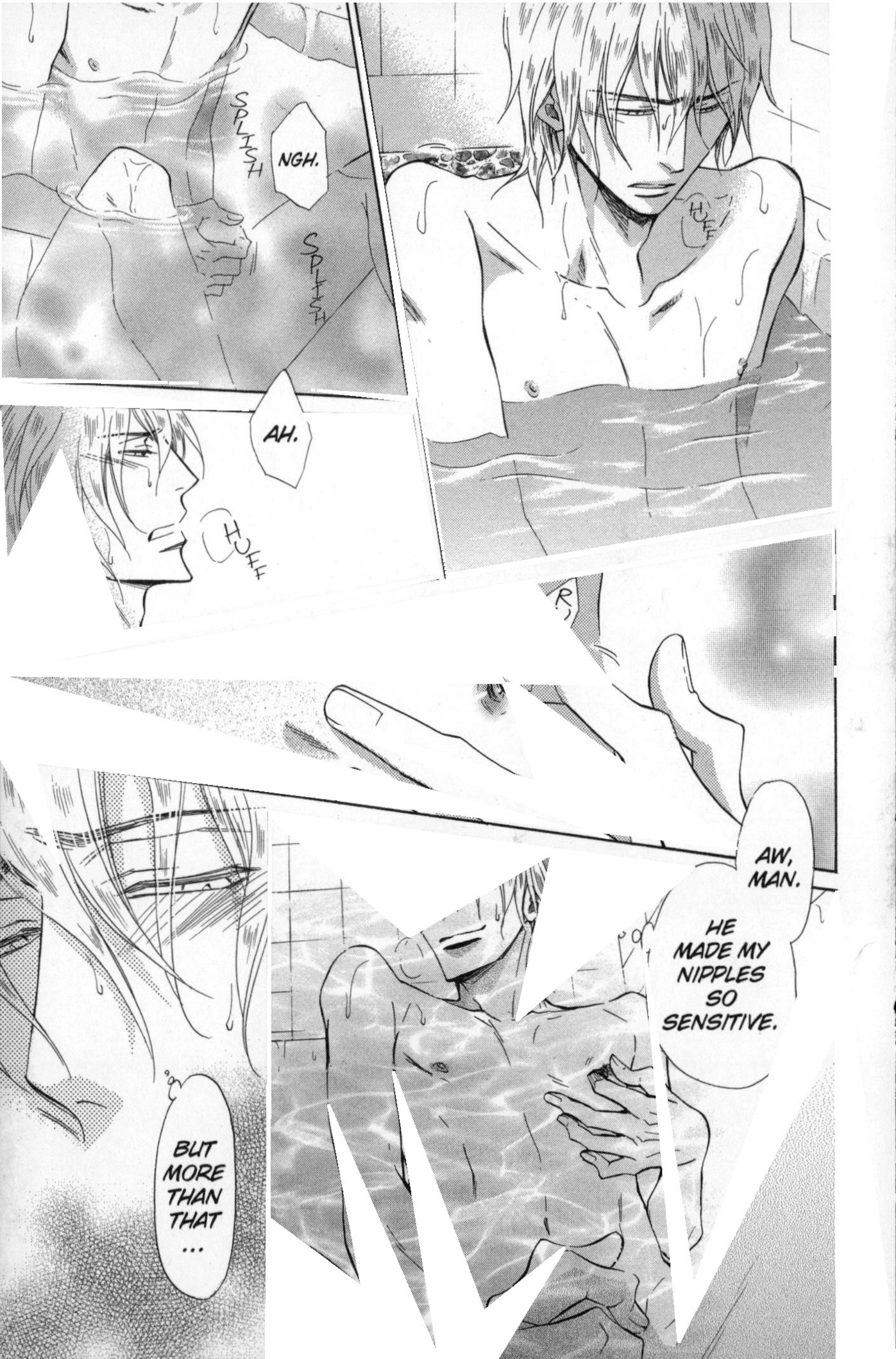
HUFF
SPLISH
NGH.
SPLISH
AH.
HUFF
AW, MAN.
HE MADE MY NIPPLES SO SENSITIVE.
BUT MORE THAN THAT ...

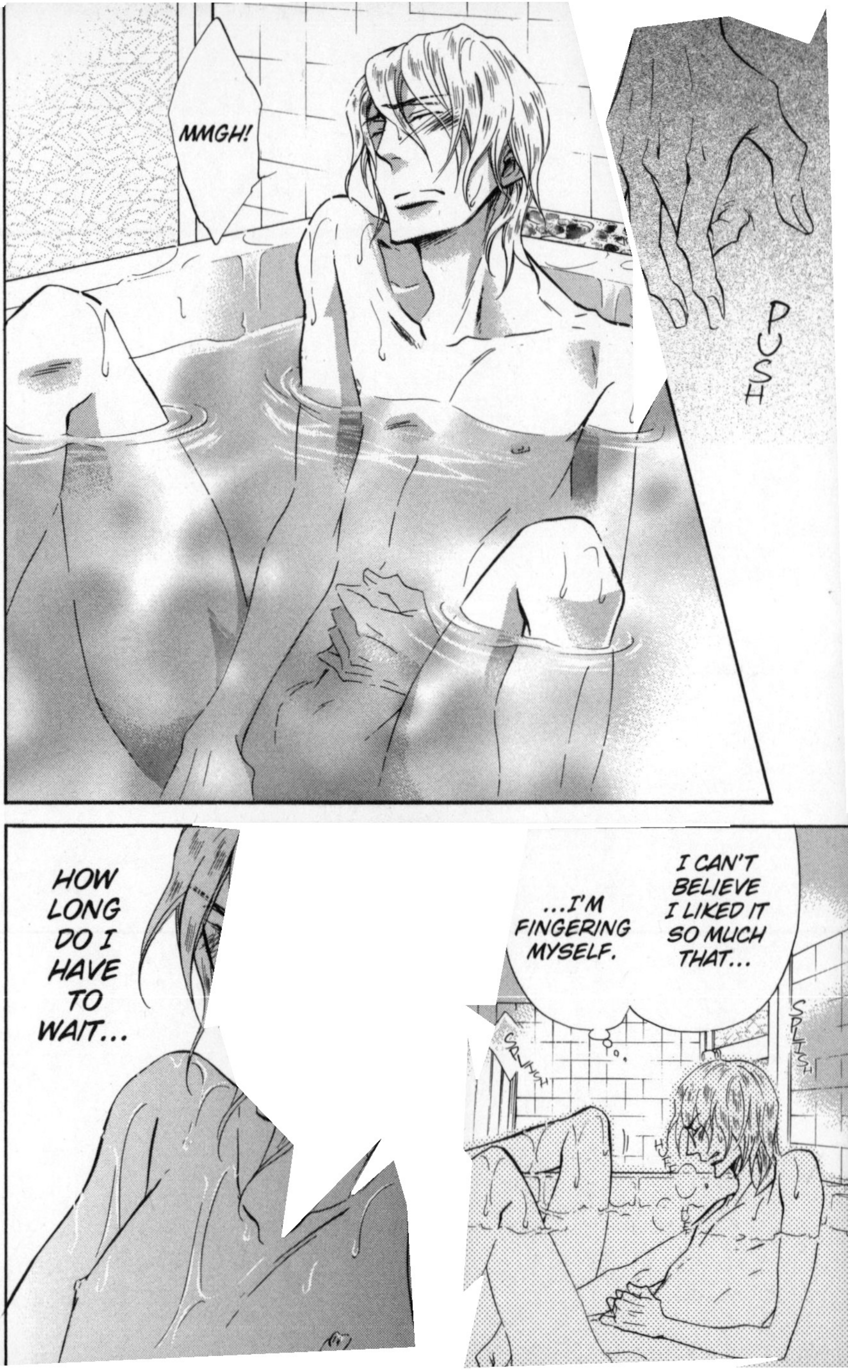
PUSH
MMGH!
I CAN'T BELIEVE I LIKED IT SO MUCH THAT...
...I'M FINGERING MYSELF.
SPLISH
SPLISH
HUFF
HOW LONG DO I HAVE TO WAIT...

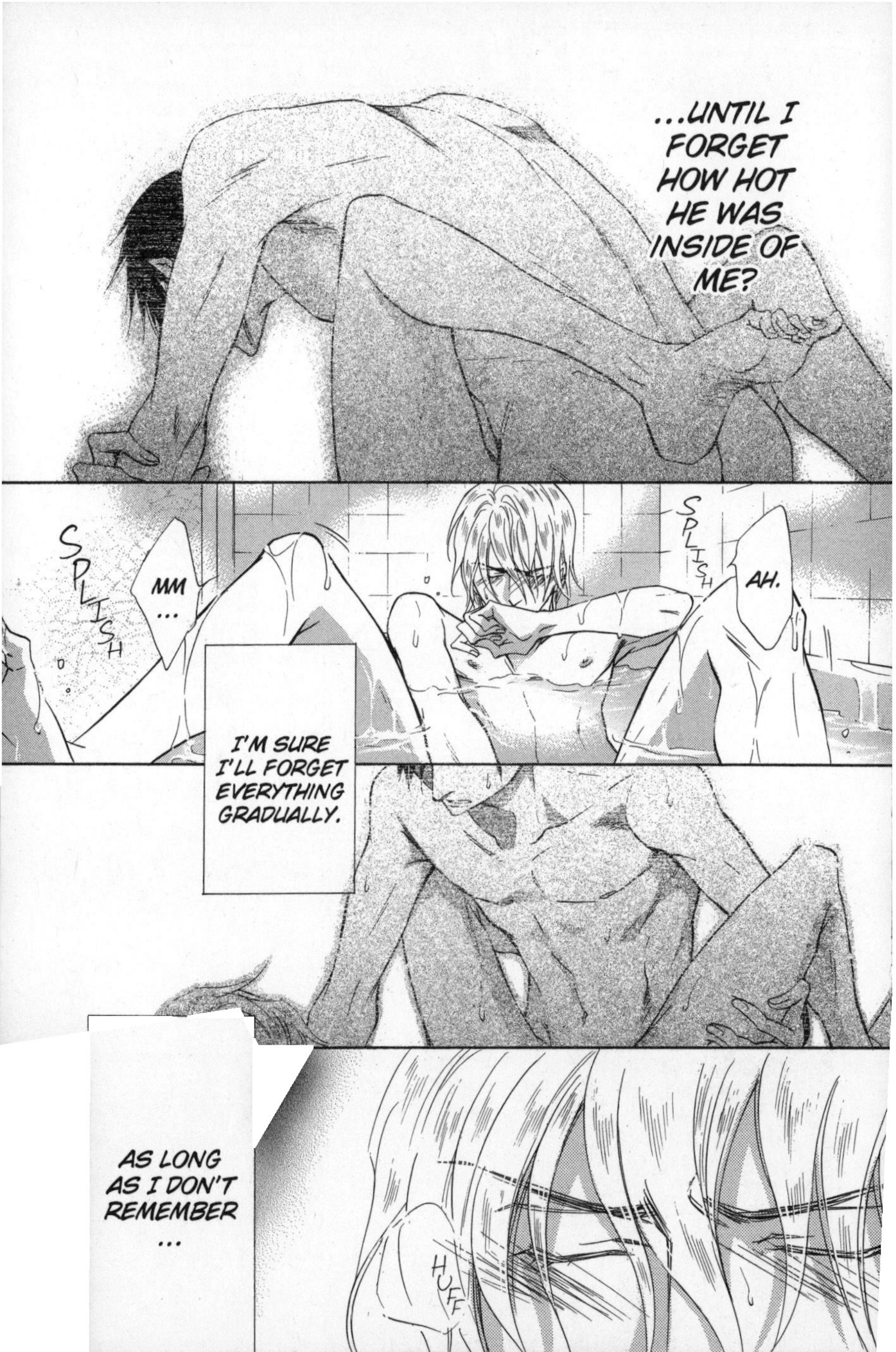
...UNTIL I FORGET HOW HOT HE WAS INSIDE OF ME?
SPLISH
AH.
SPLISH
MM ...
I'M SURE I'LL FORGET EVERYTHING GRADUALLY.
HUFF
AS LONG AS I DON'T REMEMBER ...

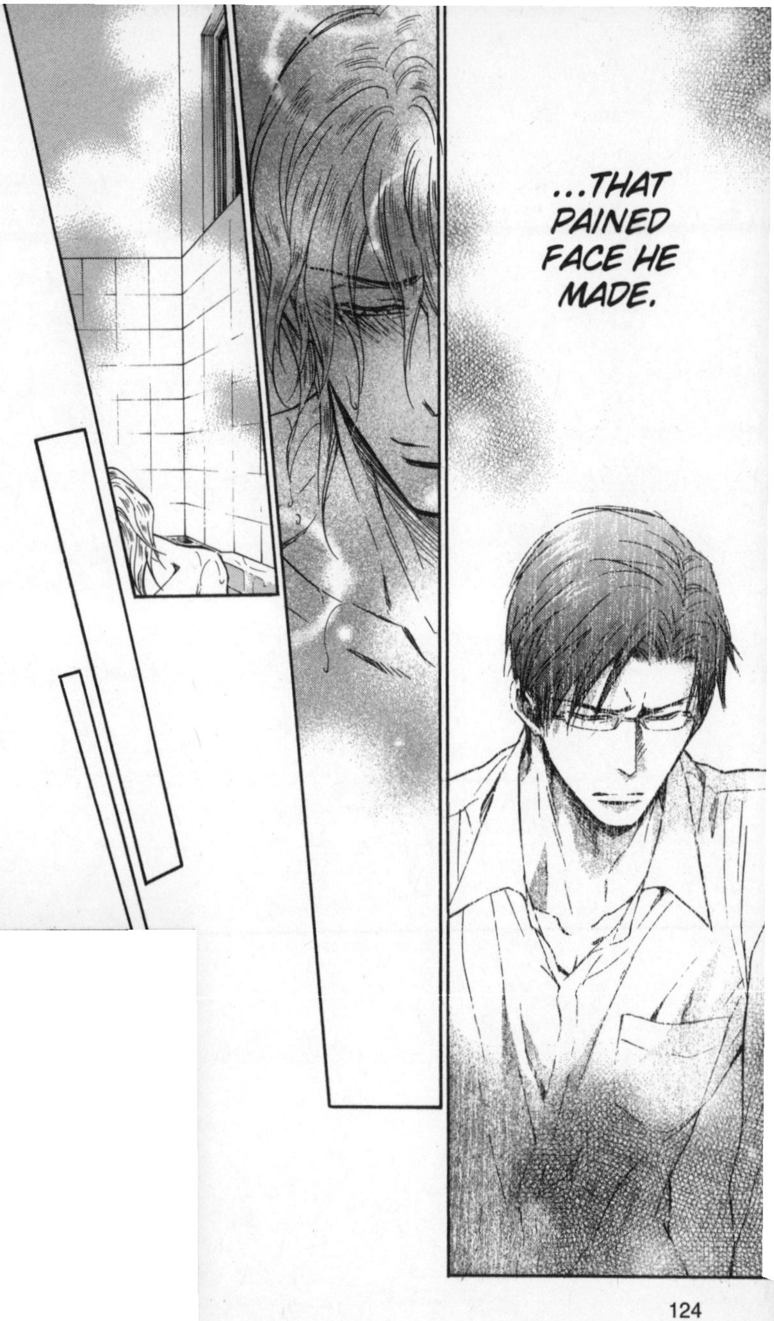
...THAT
PAINED
FACE HE
MADE.

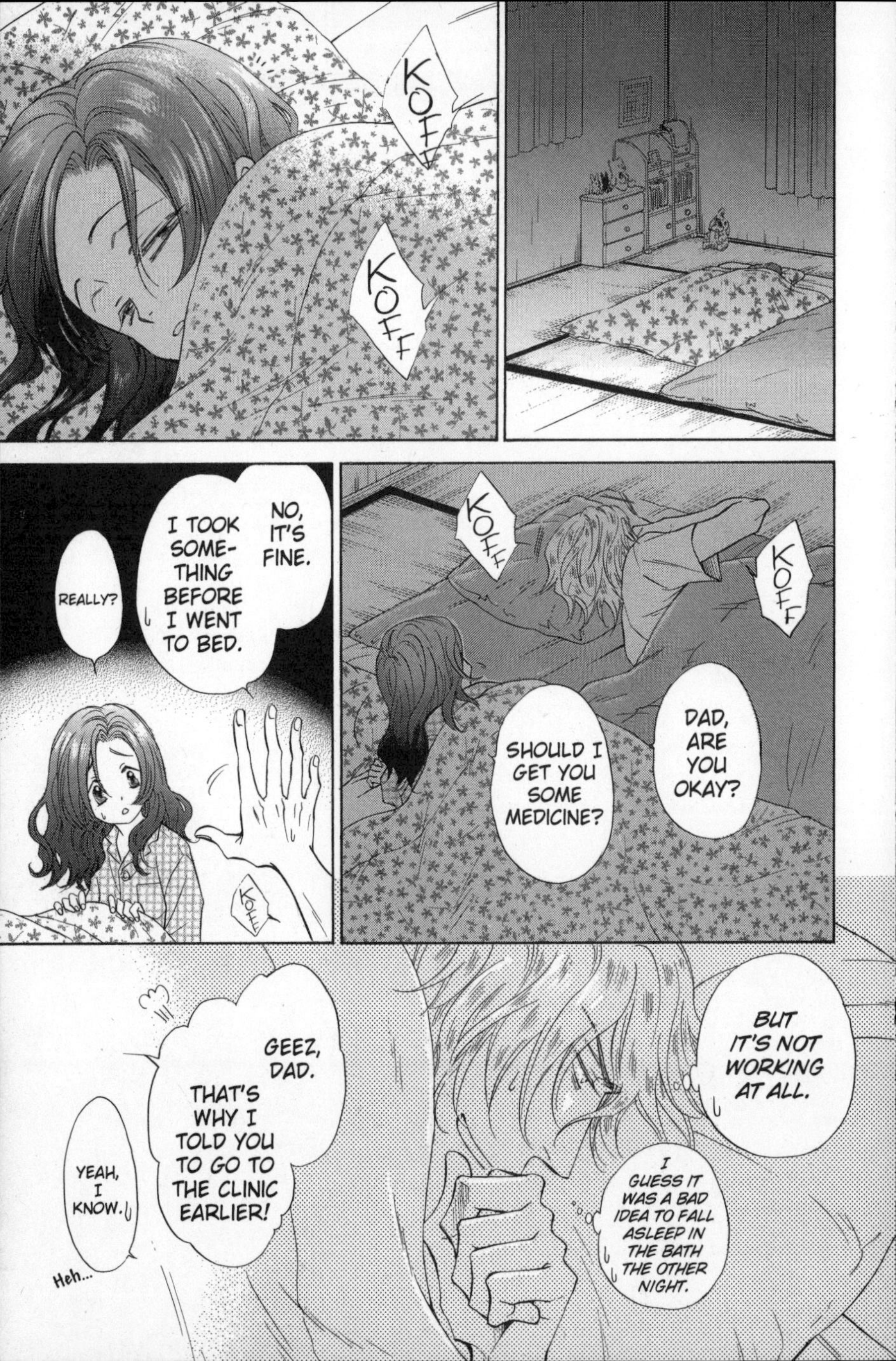
KOFF
KOFF
KOFF
KOFF
DAD, ARE YOU OKAY?
SHOULD I GET YOU SOME MEDICINE?
NO, IT'S FINE.
I TOOK SOME-THING BEFORE I WENT TO BED.
REALLY?
KOFF
BUT IT'S NOT WORKING AT ALL.
I GUESS IT WAS A BAD IDEA TO FALL ASLEEP IN THE BATH THE OTHER NIGHT.
GEEZ, DAD.
THAT'S WHY I TOLD YOU TO GO TO THE CLINIC EARLIER!
YEAH, I KNOW.
Heh...

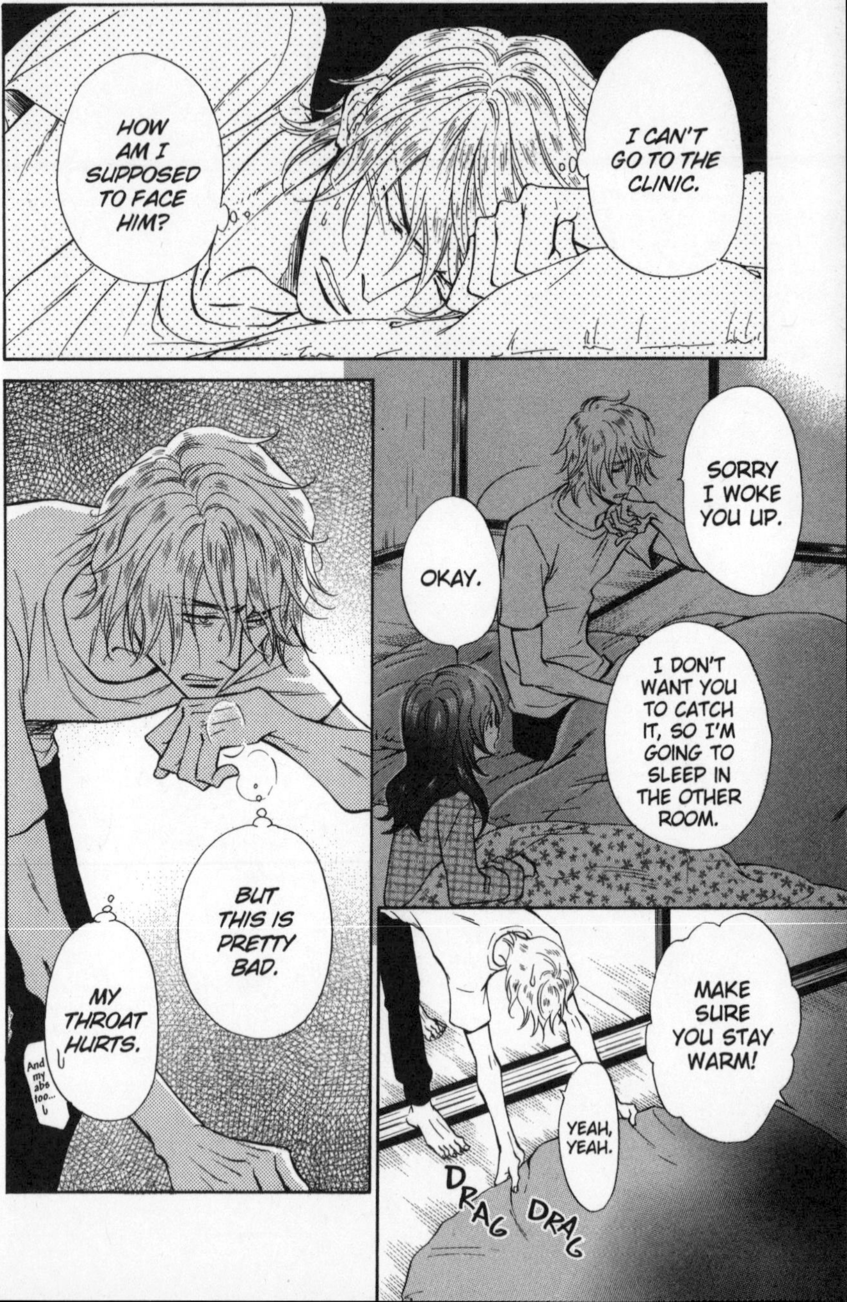
I CAN'T GO TO THE CLINIC.
HOW AM I SUPPOSED TO FACE HIM?
SORRY I WOKE YOU UP.
OKAY.
I DON'T WANT YOU TO CATCH IT, SO I'M GOING TO SLEEP IN THE OTHER ROOM.
MAKE SURE YOU STAY WARM!
YEAH, YEAH.
DRAG DRAG
BUT THIS IS PRETTY BAD.
MY THROAT HURTS.
And my abs too...

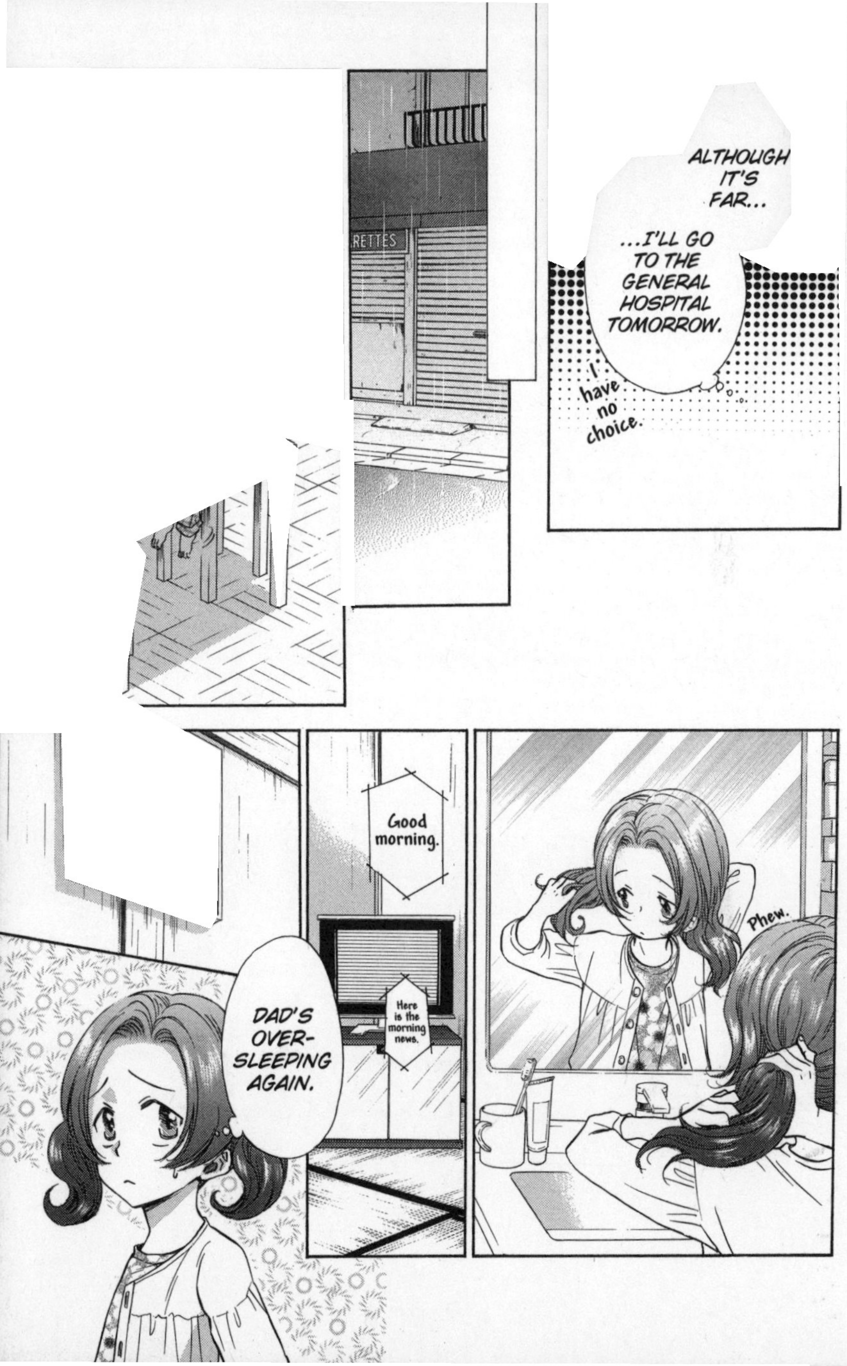
ALTHOUGH IT'S FAR...
...I'LL GO TO THE GENERAL HOSPITAL TOMORROW.
I have no choice.
RETTES
Phew.
Good morning.
Here is the morning news.
DAD'S OVER-SLEEPING AGAIN.

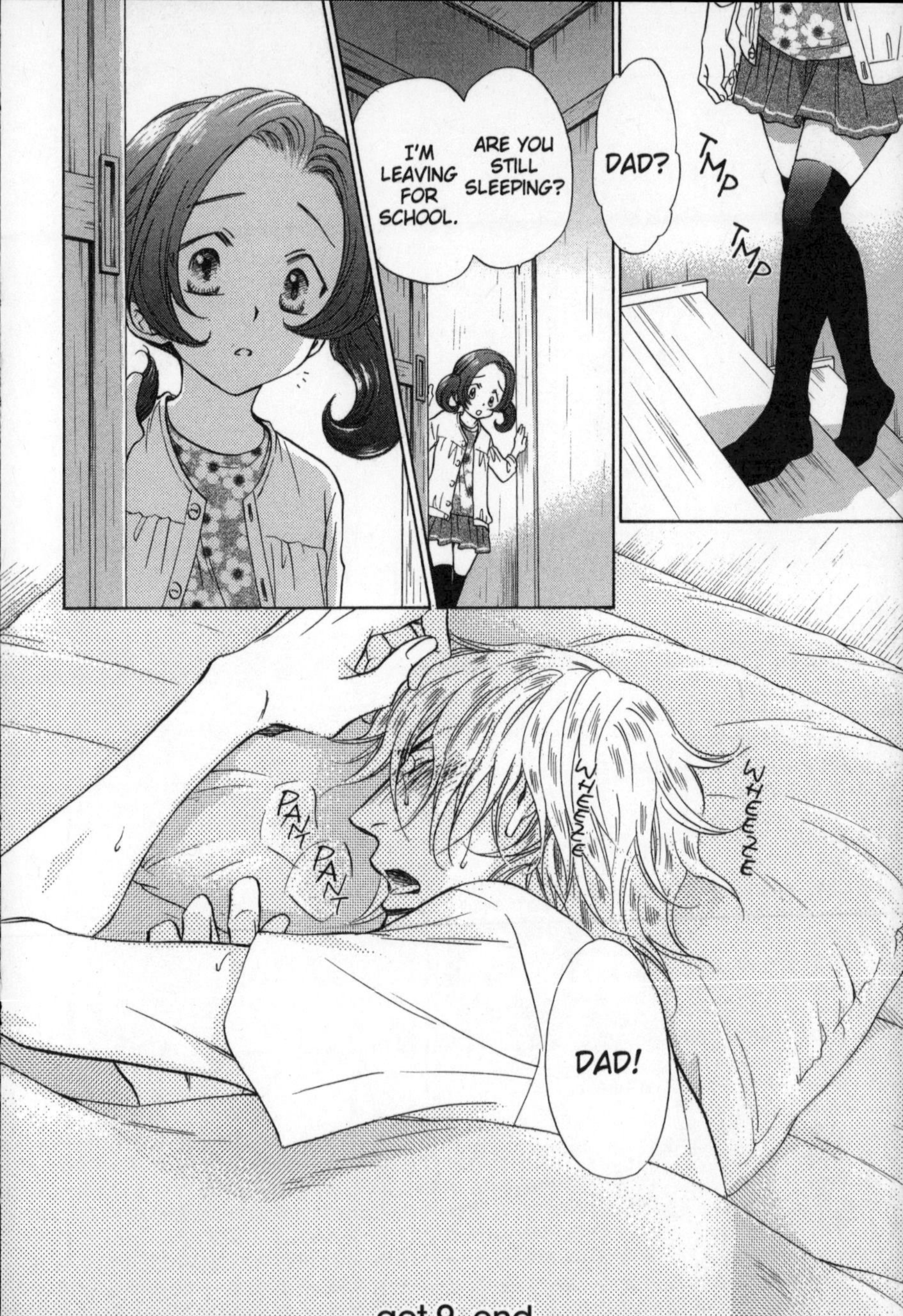
TMP
TMP
DAD?
ARE YOU STILL SLEEPING?
I'M LEAVING FOR SCHOOL.
WHEEZE
WHEEZE
PANT PANT
DAD!

act.9 end

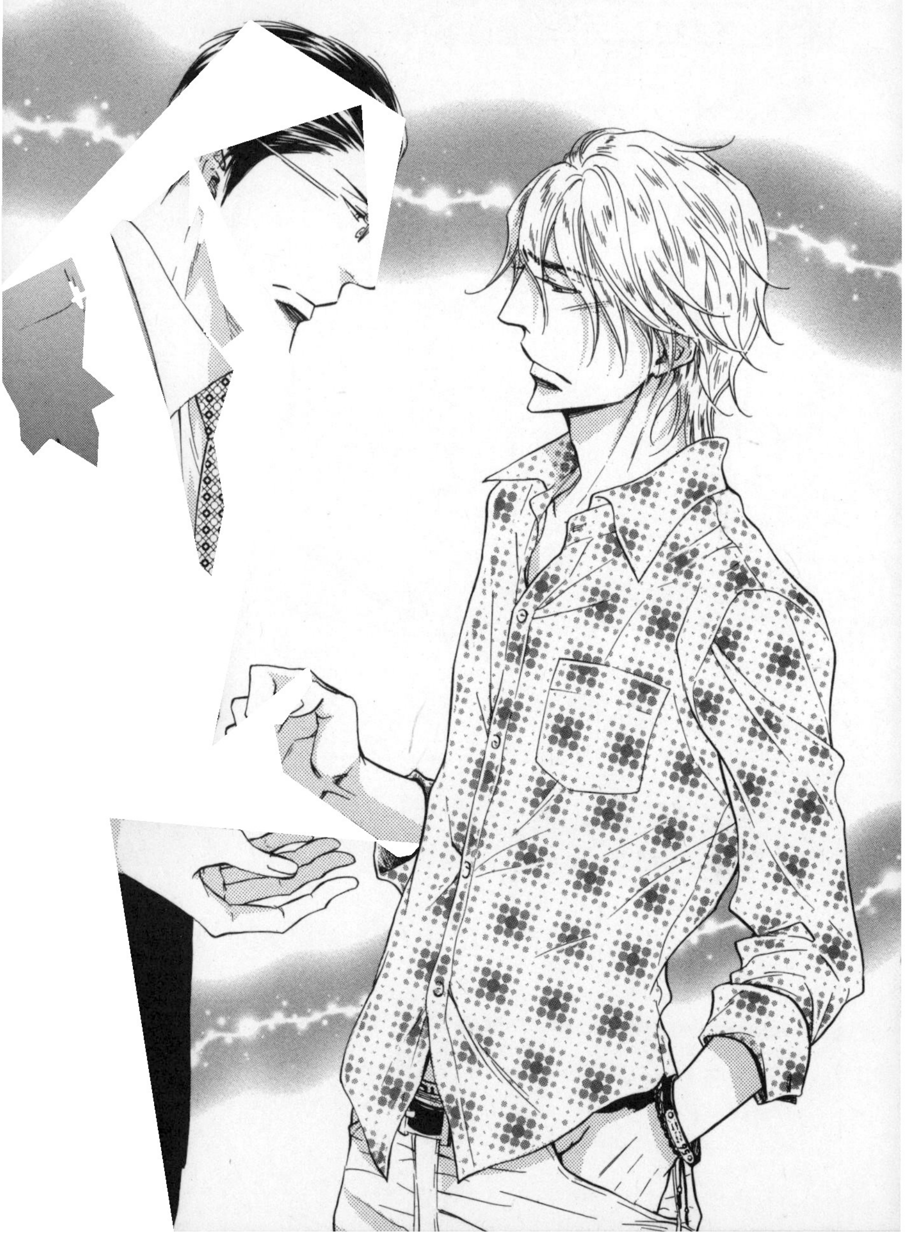

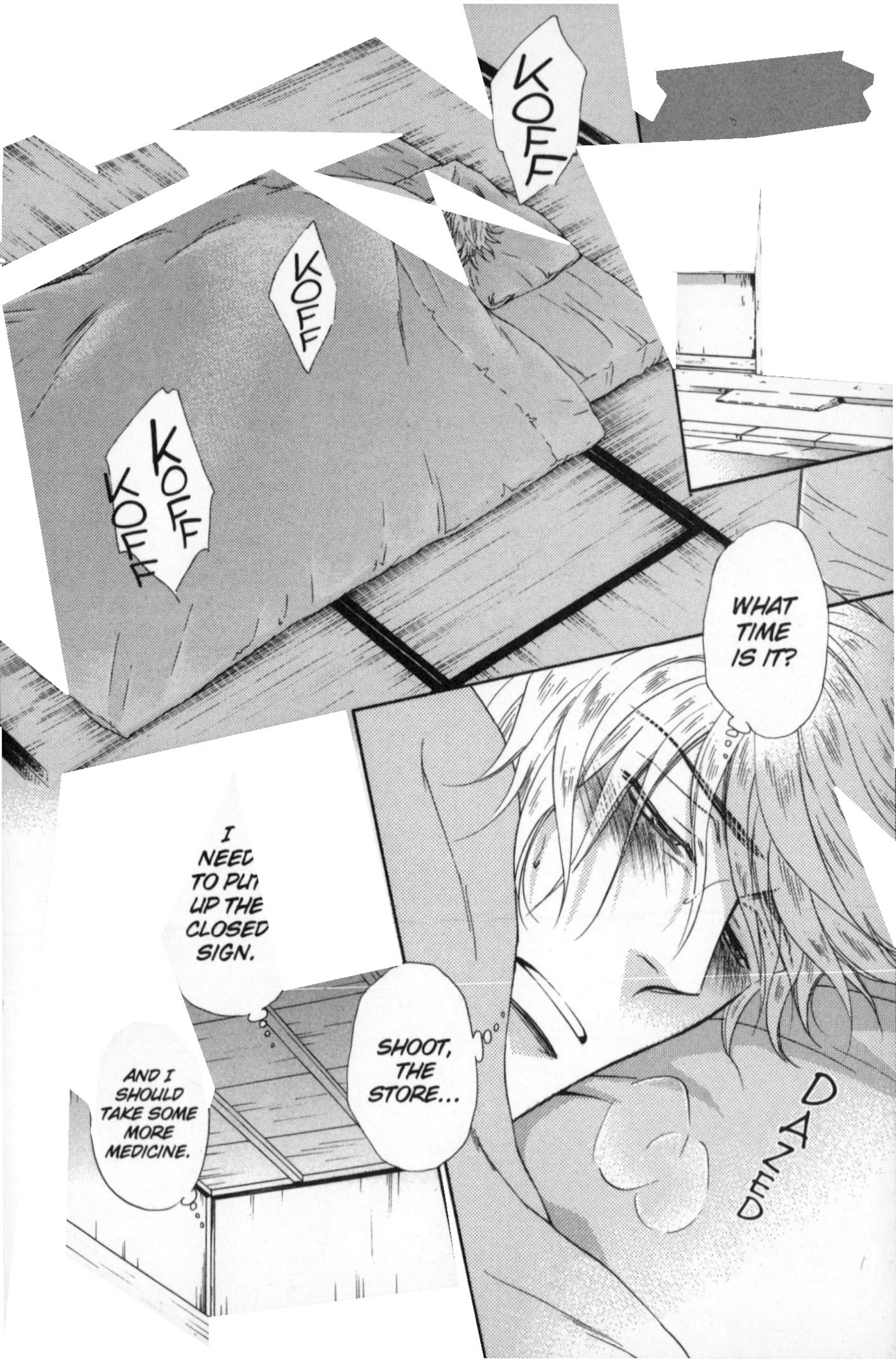
KOFF
KOFF
KOFF KOFF
WHAT TIME IS IT?
DAZED
SHOOT, THE STORE...
I NEED TO PUT UP THE CLOSED SIGN.
AND I SHOULD TAKE SOME MORE MEDICINE.

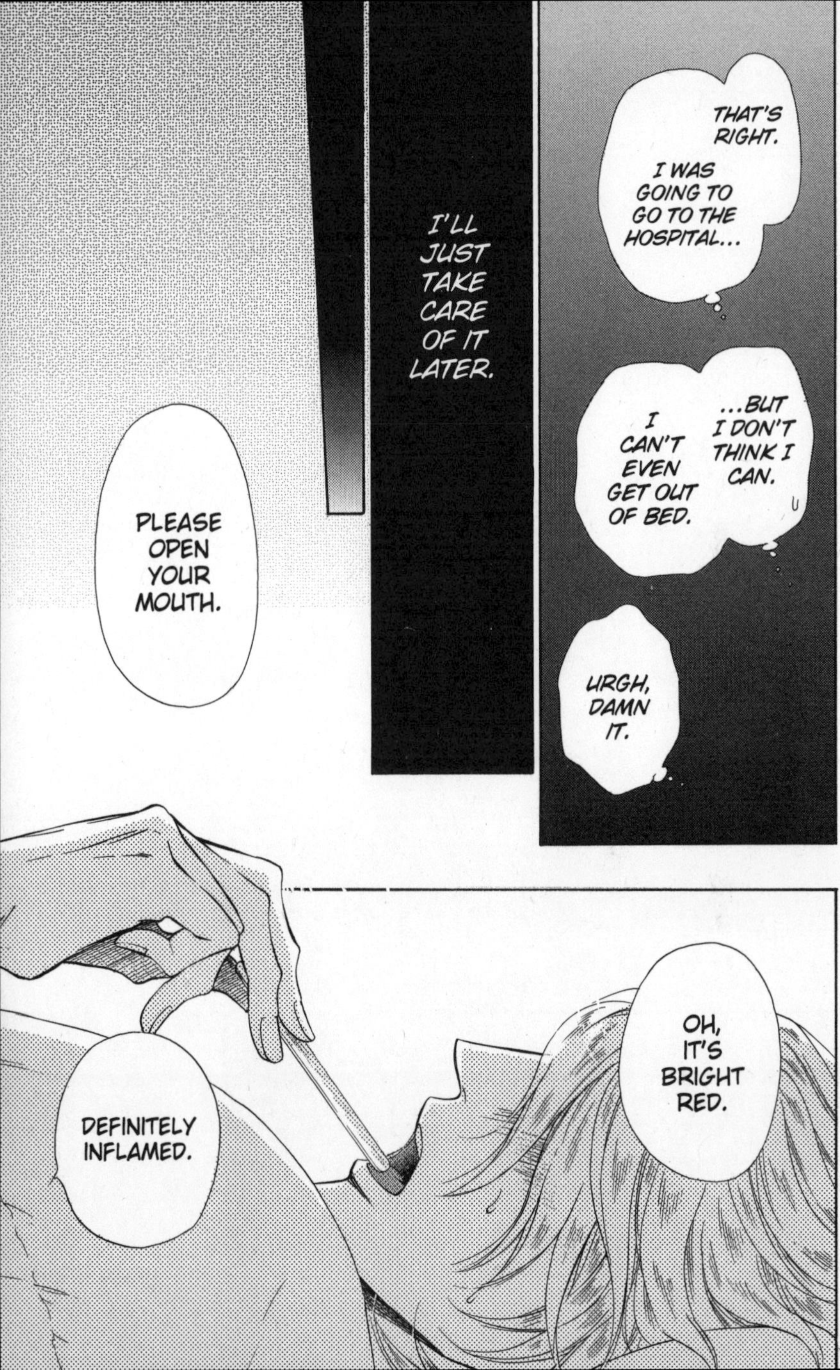
THAT'S RIGHT. I WAS GOING TO GO TO THE HOSPITAL...
...BUT I DON'T THINK I CAN.
I CAN'T EVEN GET OUT OF BED.
URGH, DAMN IT.
I'LL JUST TAKE CARE OF IT LATER.
PLEASE OPEN YOUR MOUTH.
OH, IT'S BRIGHT RED.
DEFINITELY INFLAMED.

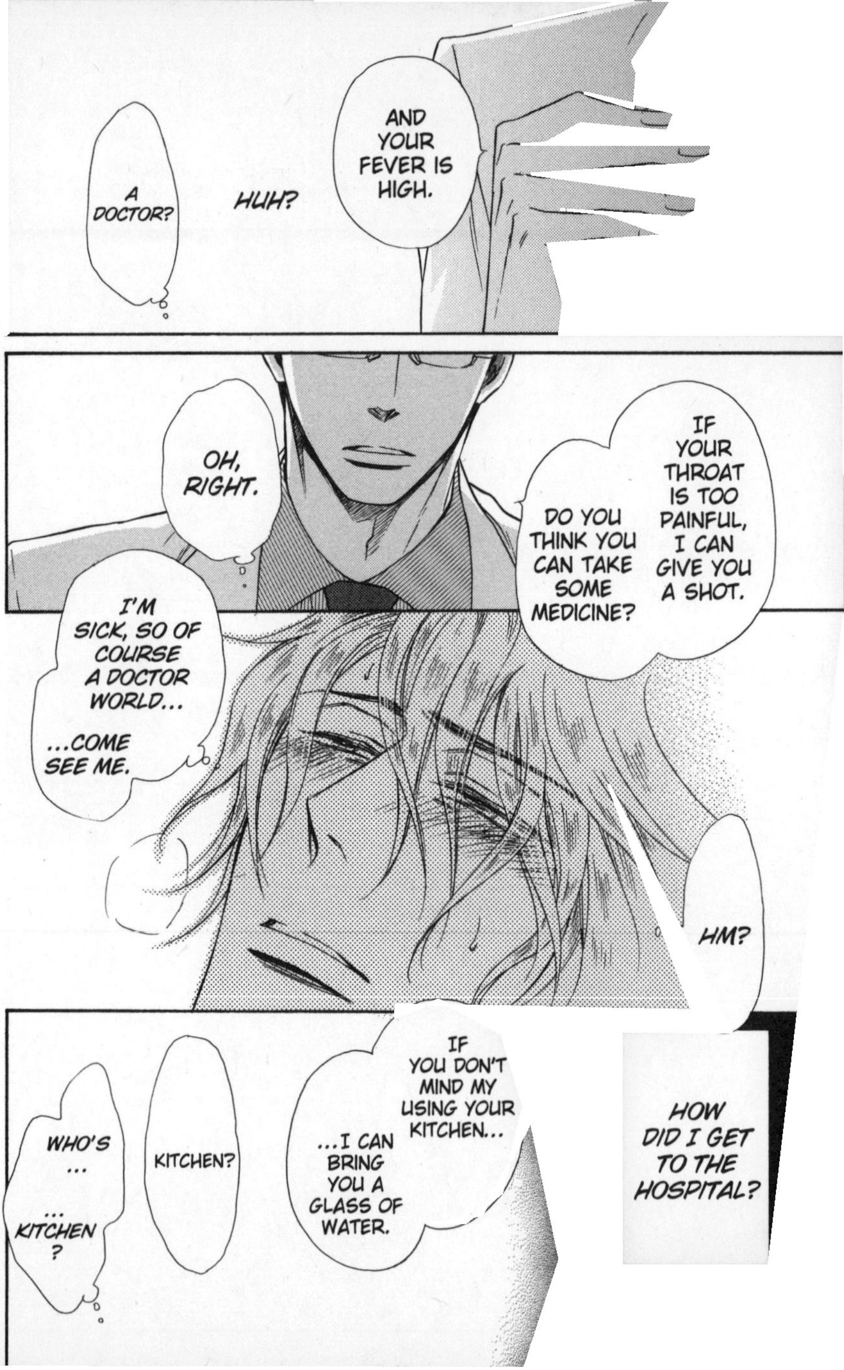
AND YOUR FEVER IS HIGH.
HUH?
A DOCTOR?
IF YOUR THROAT IS TOO PAINFUL, I CAN GIVE YOU A SHOT.
DO YOU THINK YOU CAN TAKE SOME MEDICINE?
OH, RIGHT.
I'M SICK, SO OF COURSE A DOCTOR WORLD...
...COME SEE ME.
HM?
HOW DID I GET TO THE HOSPITAL?
IF YOU DON'T MIND MY USING YOUR KITCHEN...
...I CAN BRING YOU A GLASS OF WATER.
KITCHEN?
WHO'S ... ... KITCHEN ?

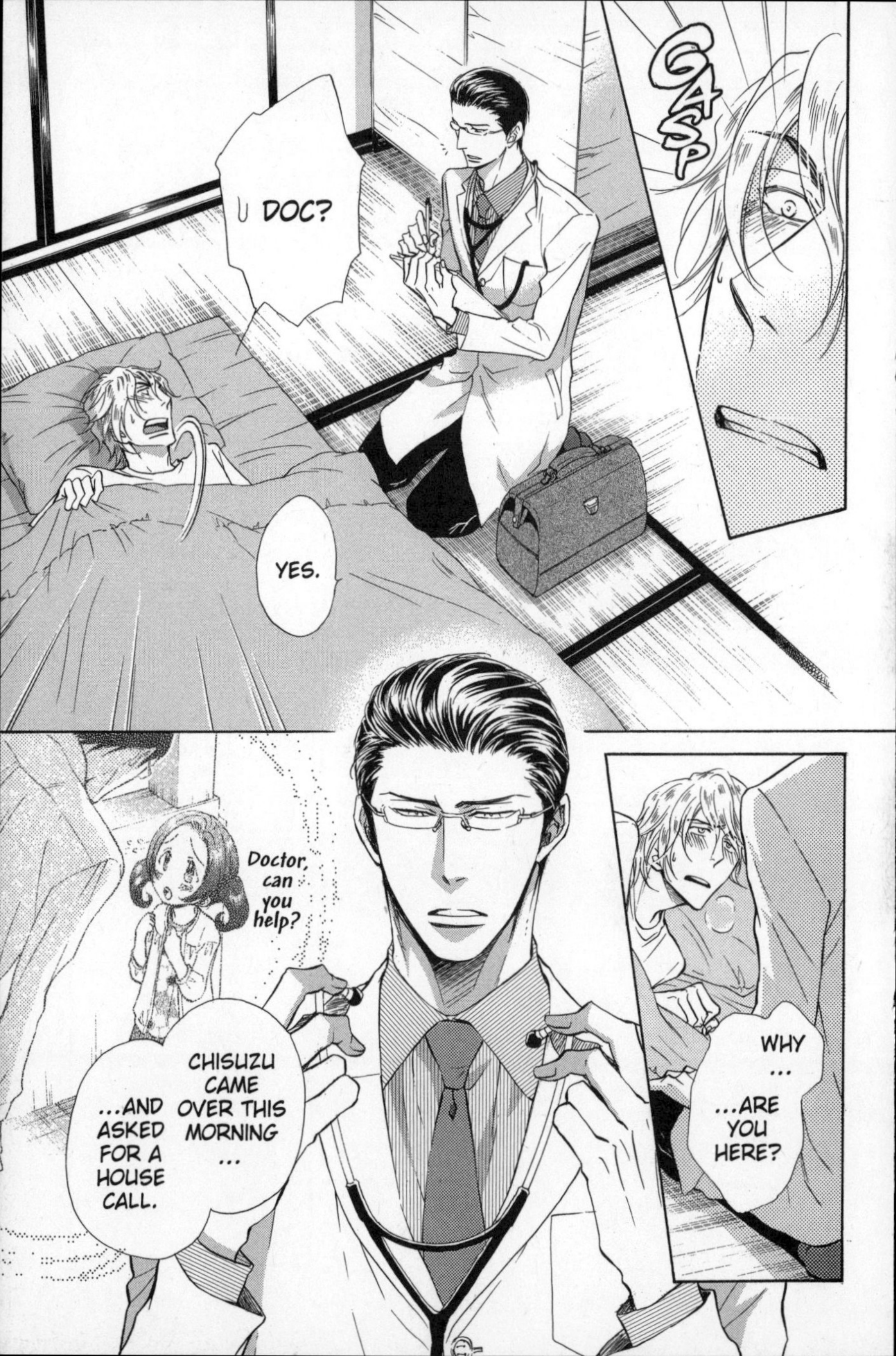
GASP
DOC?
YES.
WHY ... ...ARE YOU HERE?
Doctor, can you help?
CHISUZU CAME OVER THIS MORNING ...
...AND ASKED FOR A HOUSE CALL.

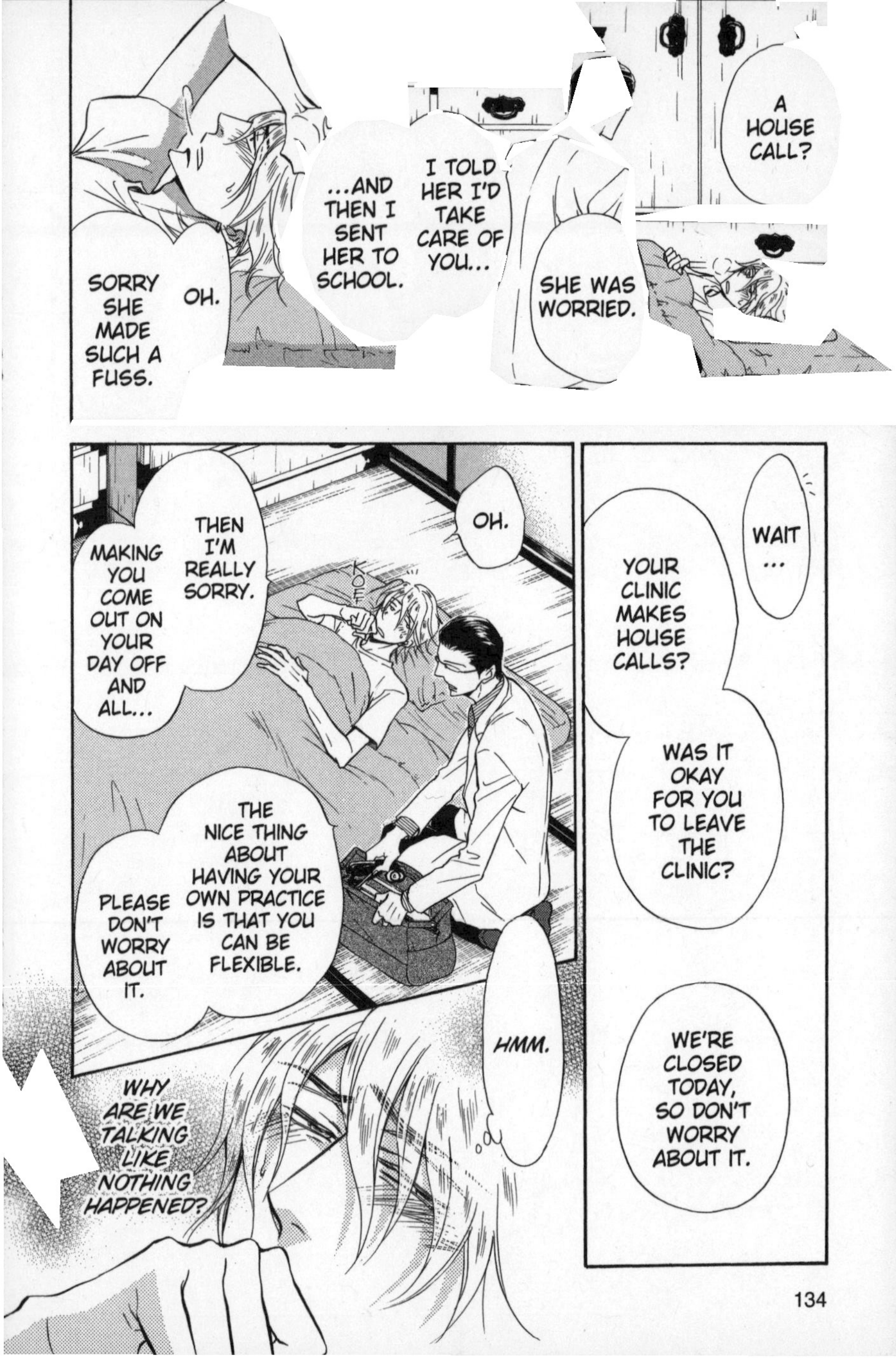
A HOUSE CALL?
SHE WAS WORRIED.
I TOLD HER I'D TAKE CARE OF YOU...
...AND THEN I SENT HER TO SCHOOL.
OH.
SORRY SHE MADE SUCH A FUSS.
WAIT...
YOUR CLINIC MAKES HOUSE CALLS?
WAS IT OKAY FOR YOU TO LEAVE THE CLINIC?
OH.
KOF
THEN I'M REALLY SORRY.
MAKING YOU COME OUT ON YOUR DAY OFF AND ALL...
THE NICE THING ABOUT HAVING YOUR OWN PRACTICE IS THAT YOU CAN BE FLEXIBLE.
PLEASE DON'T WORRY ABOUT IT.
WE'RE CLOSED TODAY, SO DON'T WORRY ABOUT IT.
HMM.
WHY ARE WE TALKING LIKE NOTHING HAPPENED?

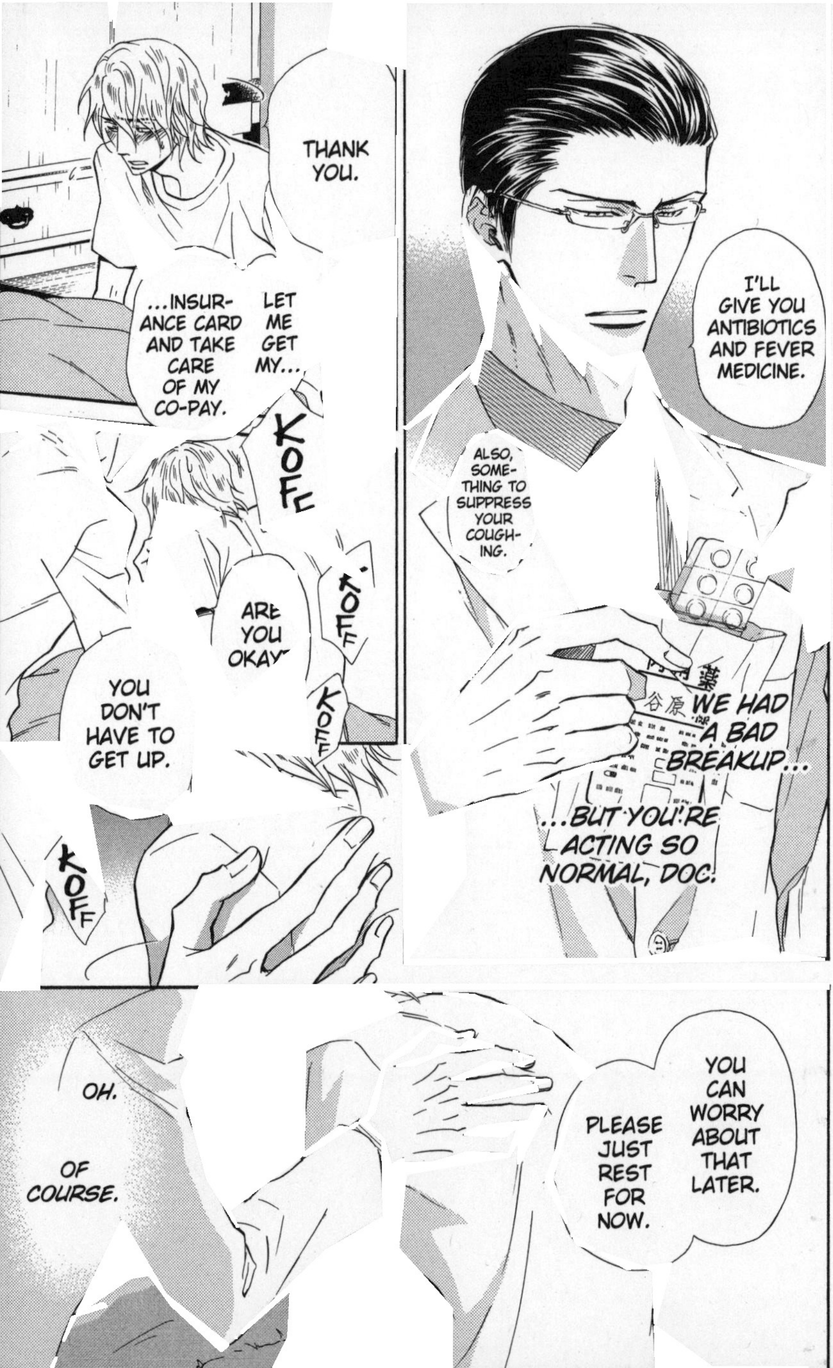
I'LL GIVE YOU ANTIBIOTICS AND FEVER MEDICINE.
ALSO, SOMETHING TO SUPPRESS YOUR COUGHING.
WE HAD A BAD BREAKUP...
...BUT YOU'RE ACTING SO NORMAL, DOC.
THANK YOU.
LET ME GET MY...
...INSURANCE CARD AND TAKE CARE OF MY CO-PAY.
KOFF
ARE YOU OKAY
KOFF
KOFF
YOU DON'T HAVE TO GET UP.
KOFF
YOU CAN WORRY ABOUT THAT LATER.
PLEASE JUST REST FOR NOW.
OH.
OF COURSE.

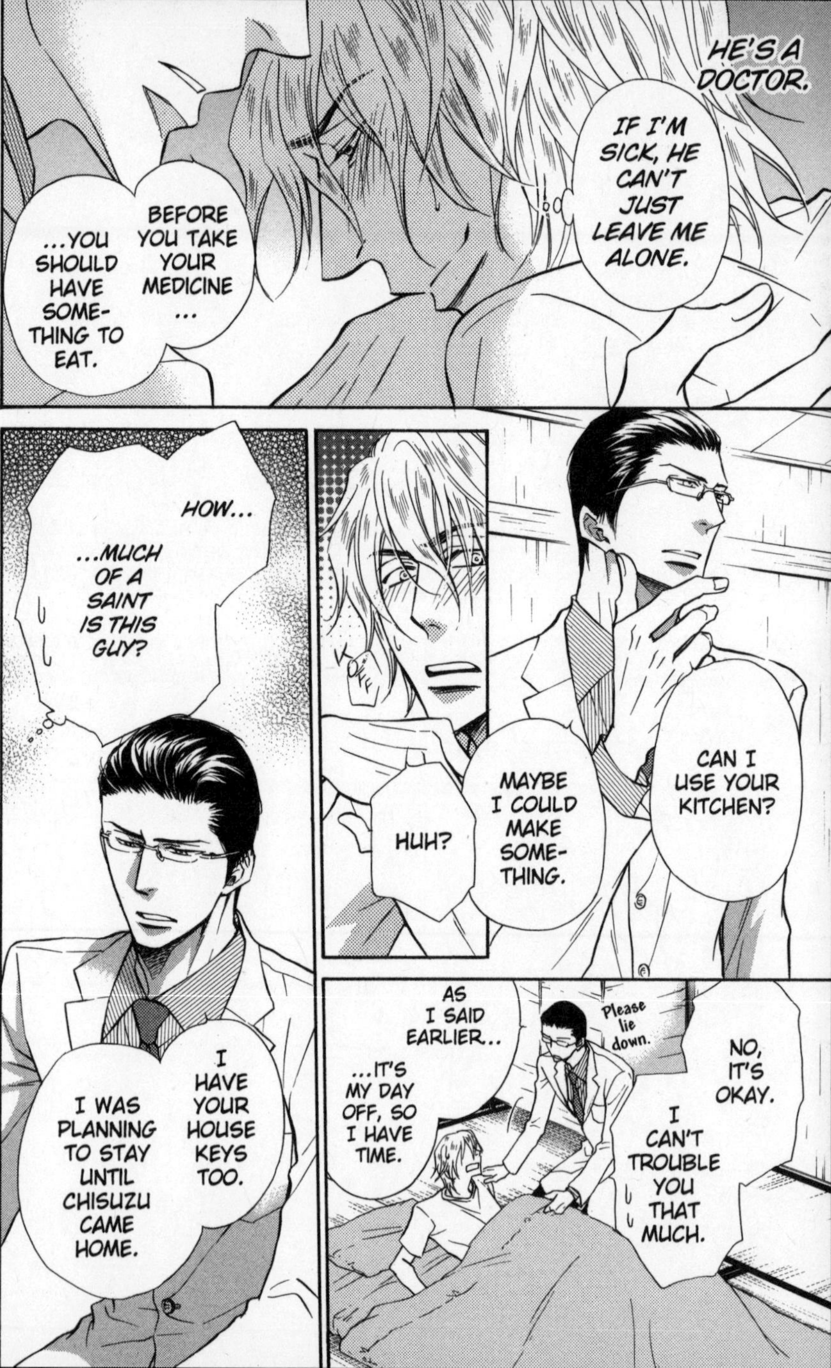
HE'S A DOCTOR.
IF I'M SICK, HE CAN'T JUST LEAVE ME ALONE.
BEFORE YOU TAKE YOUR MEDICINE...
...YOU SHOULD HAVE SOME-THING TO EAT.
CAN I USE YOUR KITCHEN?
MAYBE I COULD MAKE SOME-THING.
HUH?
NO, IT'S OKAY.
I CAN'T TROUBLE YOU THAT MUCH.
Please lie down.
AS I SAID EARLIER...
...IT'S MY DAY OFF, SO I HAVE TIME.
HOW...
...MUCH OF A SAINT IS THIS GUY?
I HAVE YOUR HOUSE KEYS TOO.
I WAS PLANNING TO STAY UNTIL CHISUZU CAME HOME.

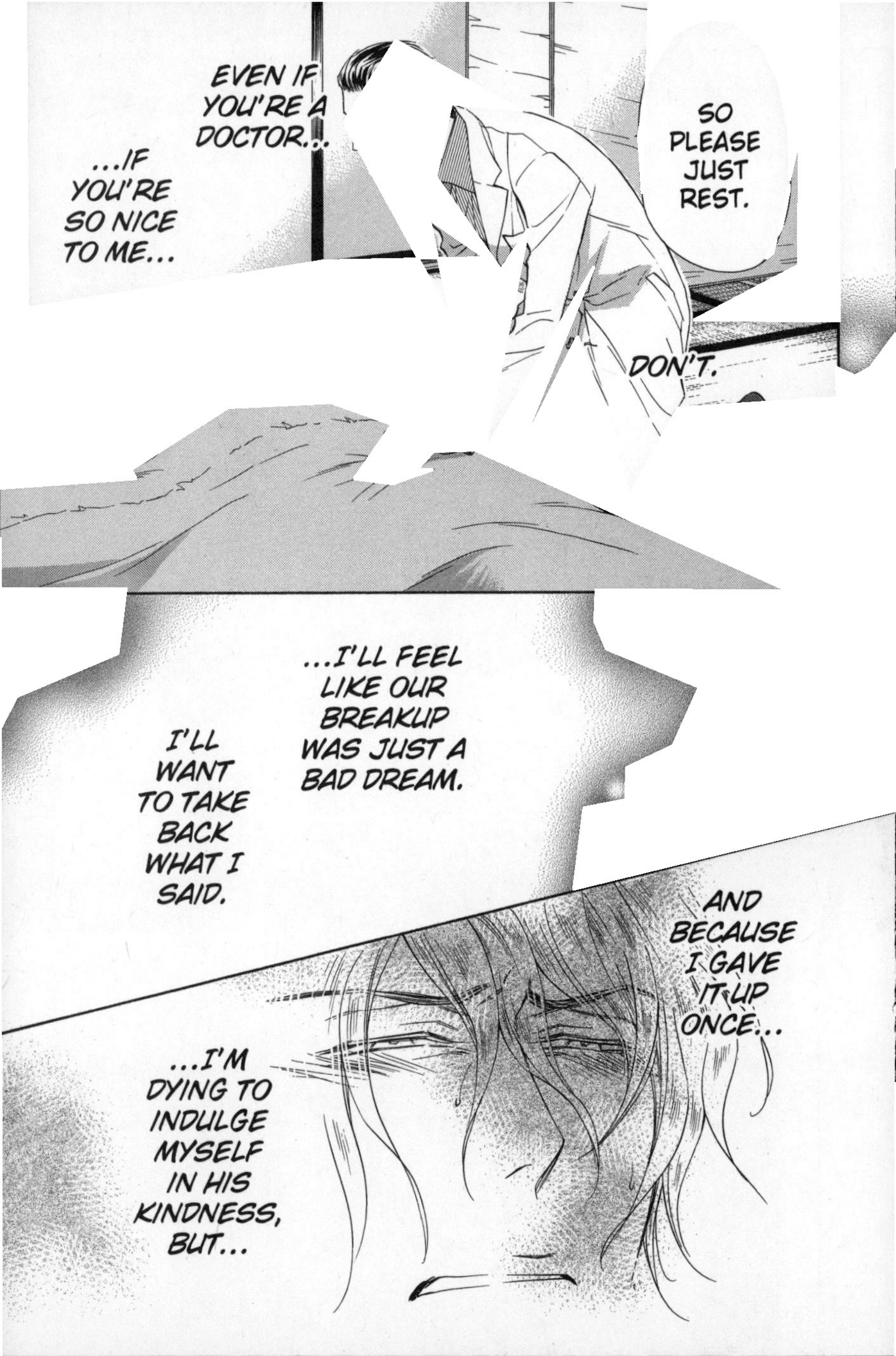
SO PLEASE JUST REST.
DON'T.
EVEN IF YOU'RE A DOCTOR...
...IF YOU'RE SO NICE TO ME...
...I'LL FEEL LIKE OUR BREAKUP WAS JUST A BAD DREAM.
I'LL WANT TO TAKE BACK WHAT I SAID.
AND BECAUSE I GAVE IT UP ONCE...
...I'M DYING TO INDULGE MYSELF IN HIS KINDNESS, BUT...

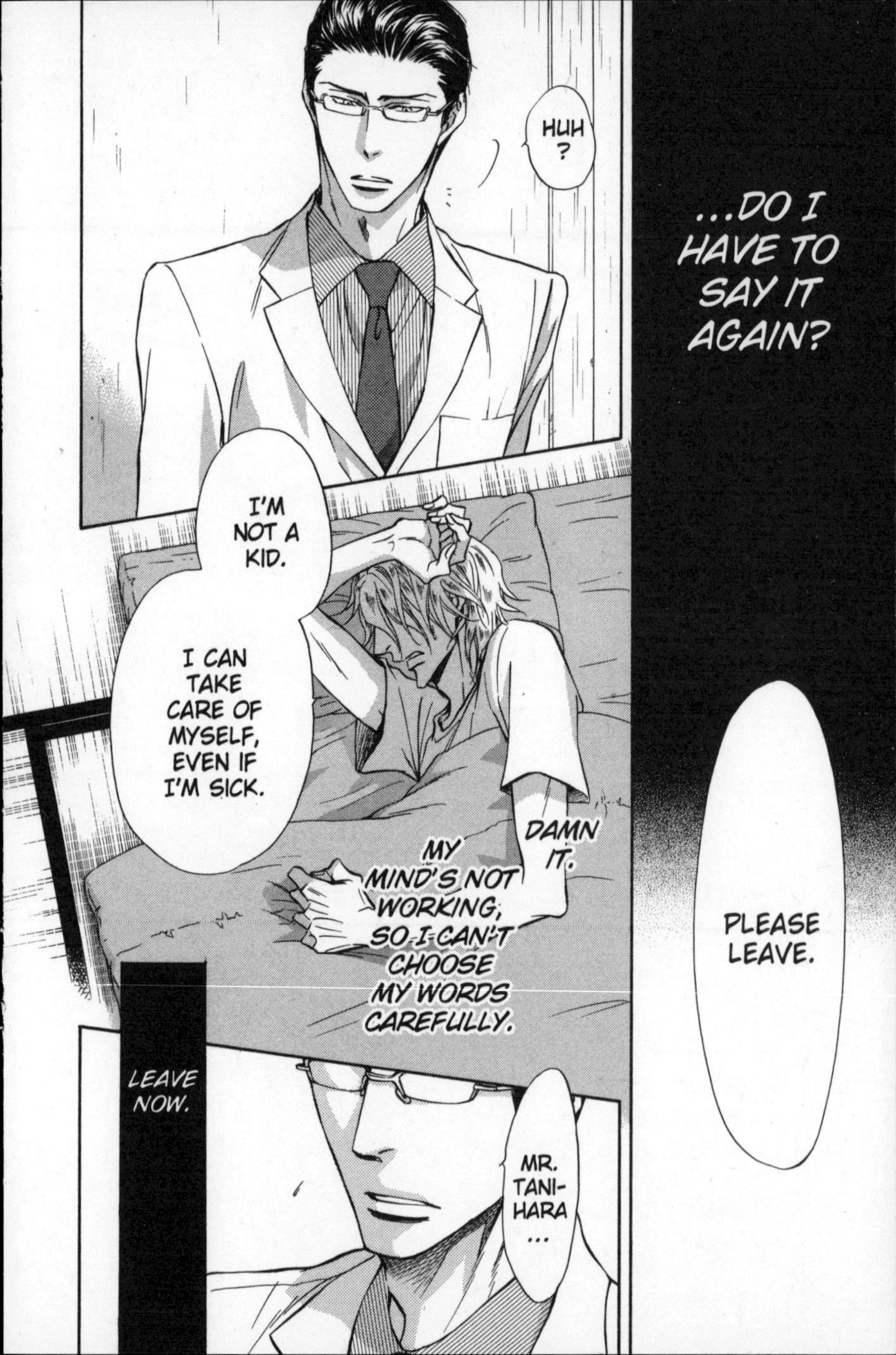
...DO I HAVE TO SAY IT AGAIN?
PLEASE LEAVE.
HUH?
I'M NOT A KID.
I CAN TAKE CARE OF MYSELF, EVEN IF I'M SICK.
DAMN IT.
MY MIND'S NOT WORKING, SO I CAN'T CHOOSE MY WORDS CAREFULLY.
MR. TANIHARA...
LEAVE NOW.

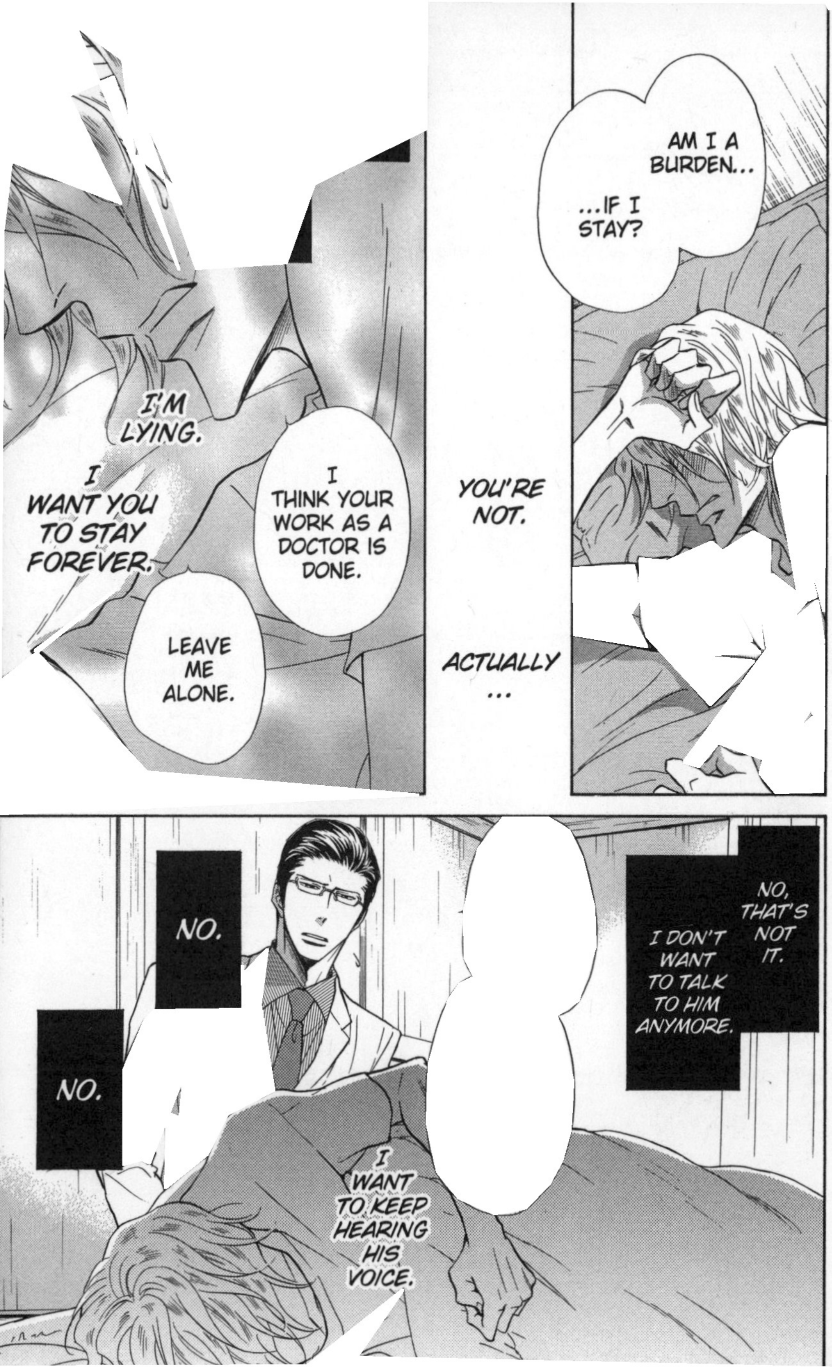
AM I A BURDEN...
...IF I STAY?
YOU'RE NOT.
ACTUALLY ...
I THINK YOUR WORK AS A DOCTOR IS DONE.
LEAVE ME ALONE.
I'M LYING.
I WANT YOU TO STAY FOREVER.
NO, THAT'S NOT IT.
I DON'T WANT TO TALK TO HIM ANYMORE.
I WANT TO KEEP HEARING HIS VOICE.
NO.
NO.

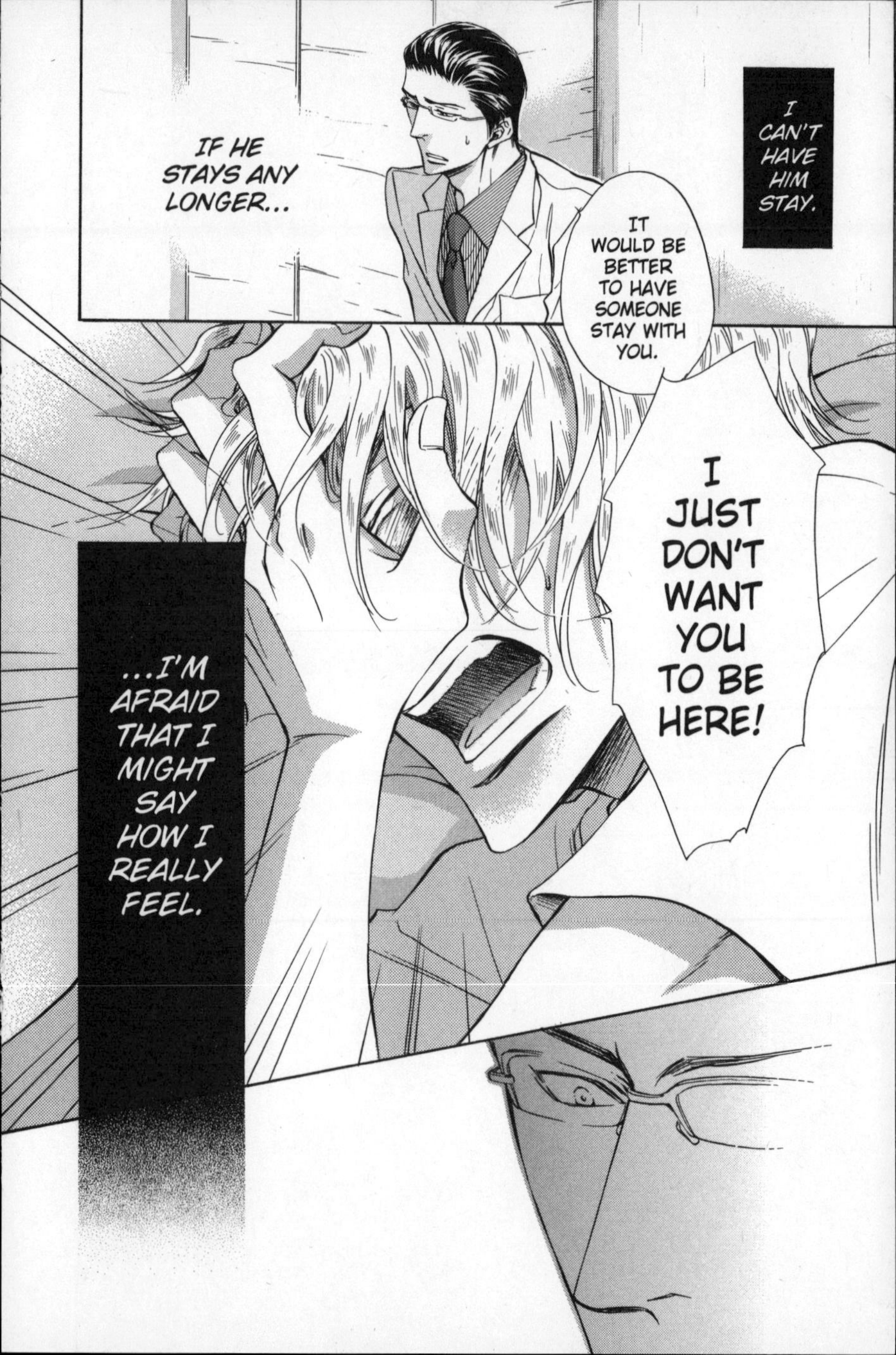
I CAN'T HAVE HIM STAY.
IT WOULD BE BETTER TO HAVE SOMEONE STAY WITH YOU.
IF HE STAYS ANY LONGER...
I JUST DON'T WANT YOU TO BE HERE!
...I'M AFRAID THAT I MIGHT SAY HOW I REALLY FEEL.

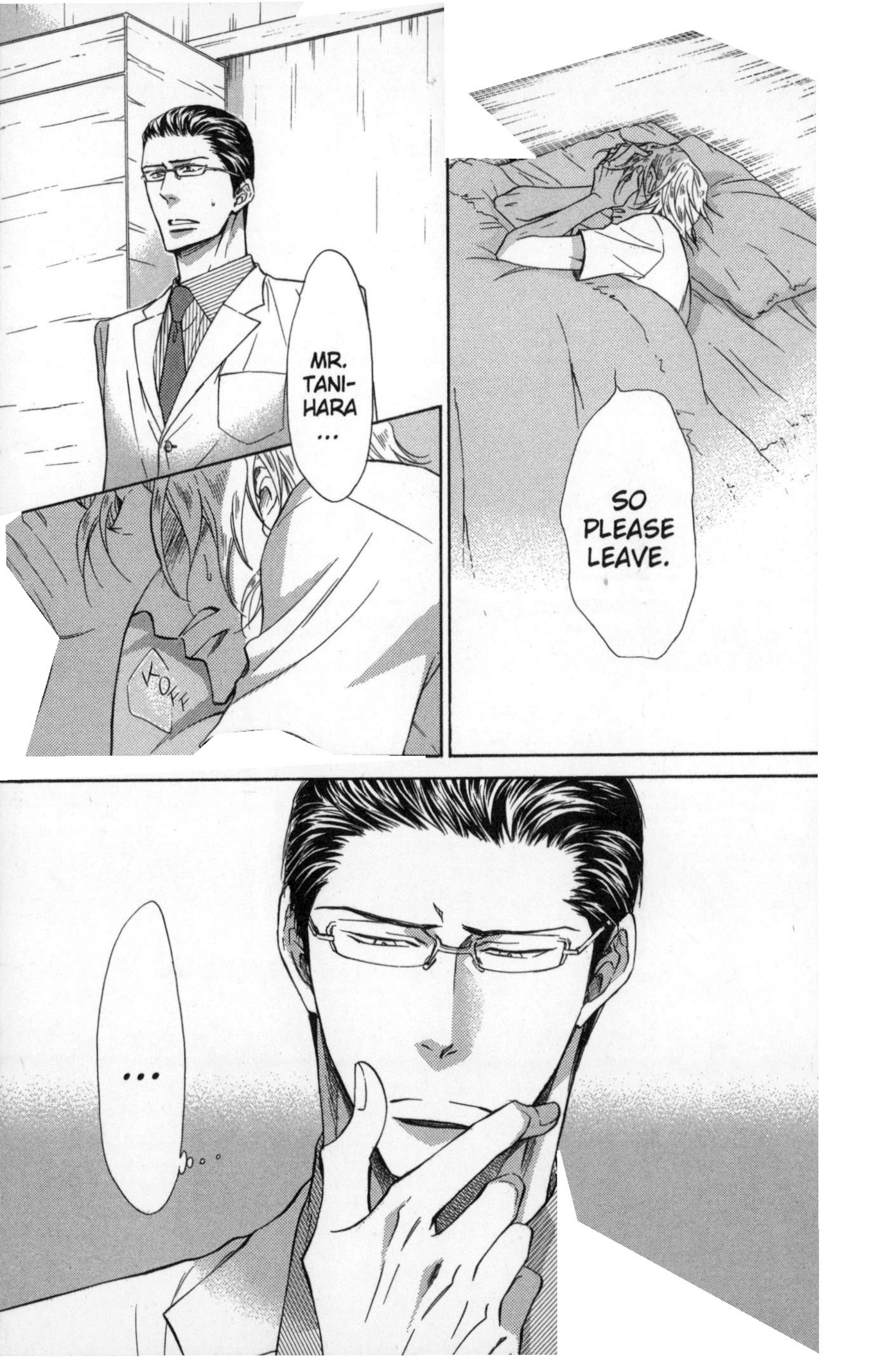
SO PLEASE LEAVE.
MR. TANI-HARA ...
...

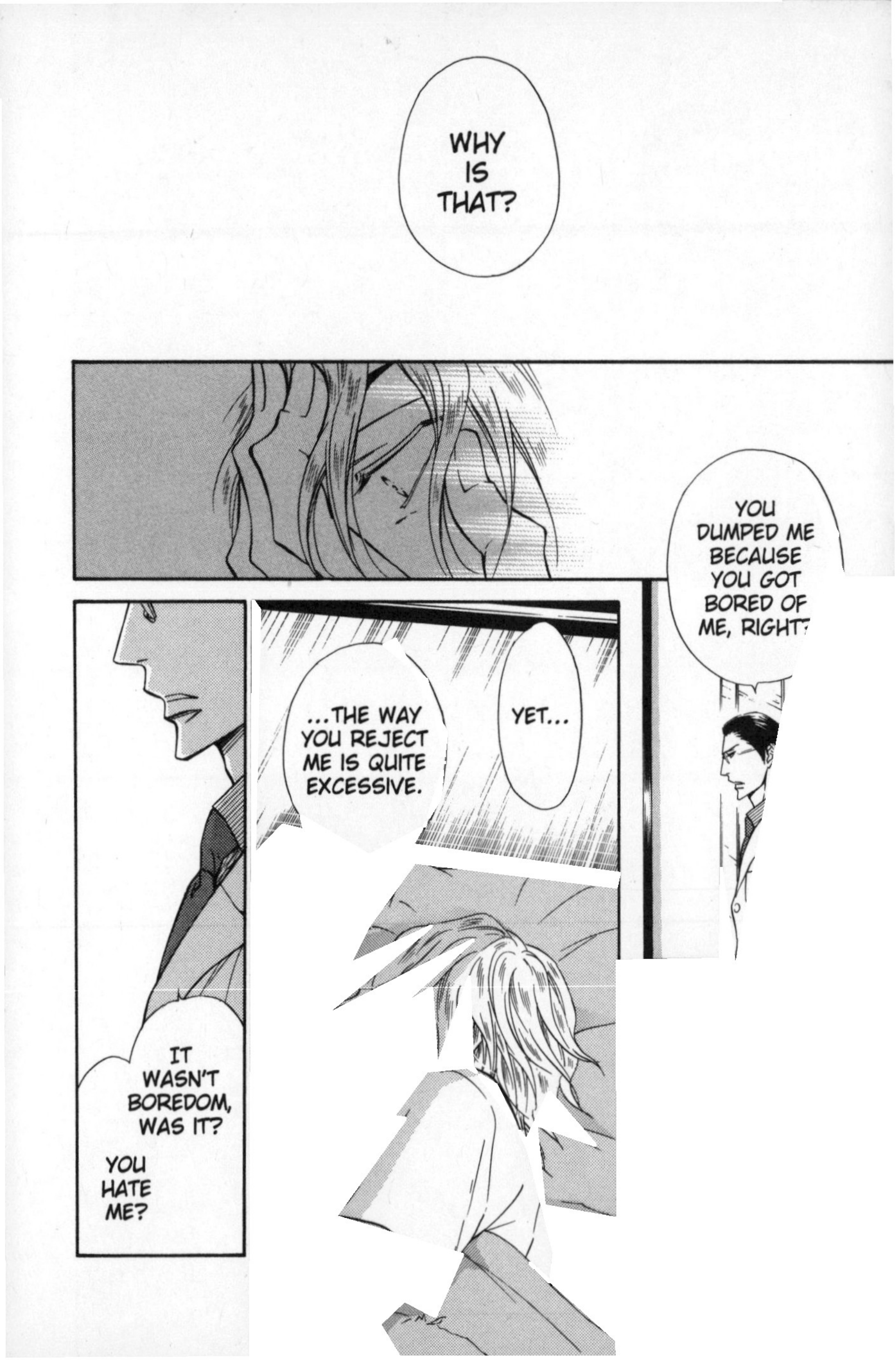
WHY IS THAT?
YOU DUMPED ME BECAUSE YOU GOT BORED OF ME, RIGHT?
YET...
...THE WAY YOU REJECT ME IS QUITE EXCESSIVE.
IT WASN'T BOREDOM, WAS IT?
YOU HATE ME?

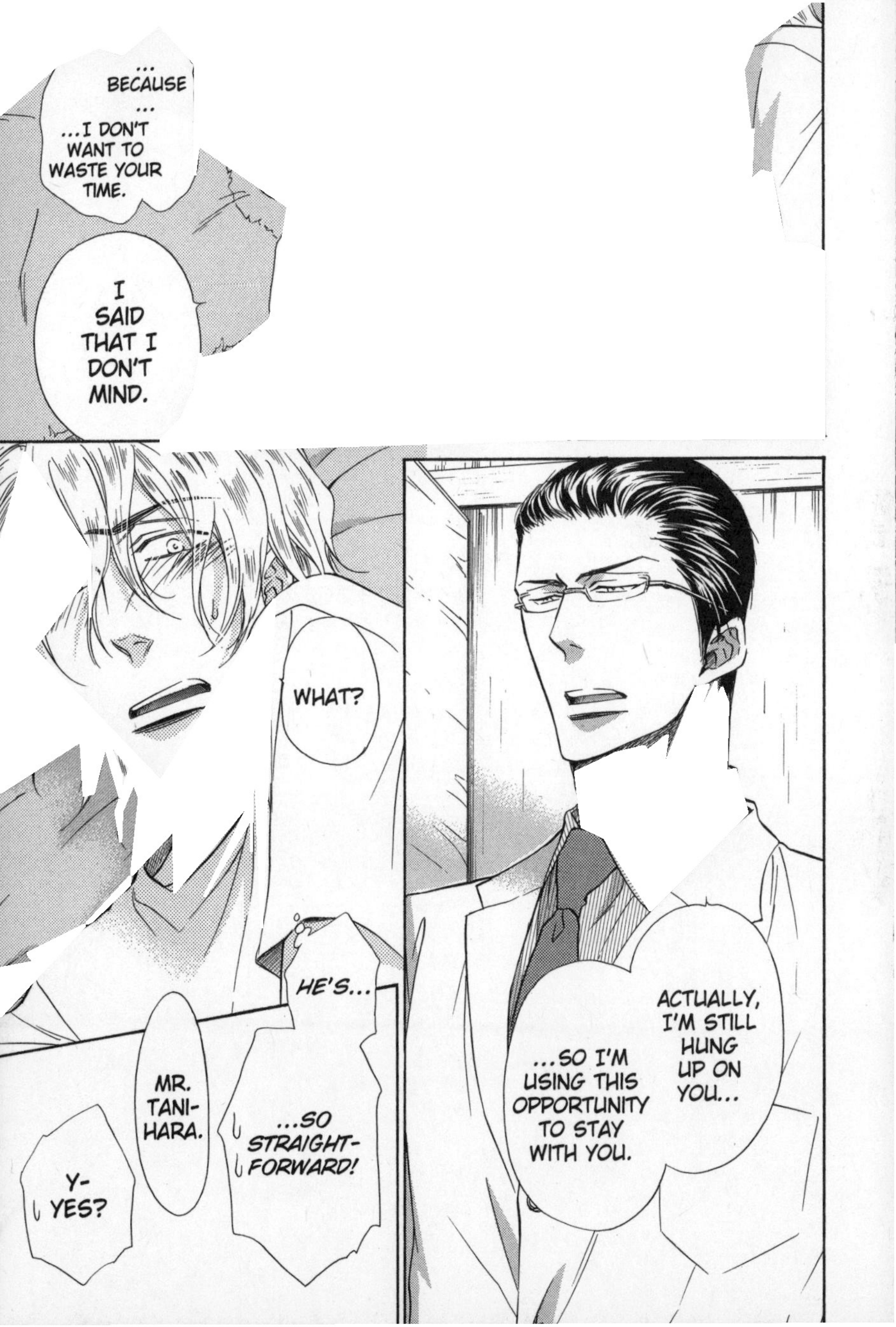
...BECAUSE ... ...I DON'T WANT TO WASTE YOUR TIME.
I SAID THAT I DON'T MIND.
ACTUALLY, I'M STILL HUNG UP ON YOU...
...SO I'M USING THIS OPPORTUNITY TO STAY WITH YOU.
WHAT?
HE'S...
...SO STRAIGHT-FORWARD!
MR. TANI-HARA.
Y-YES?

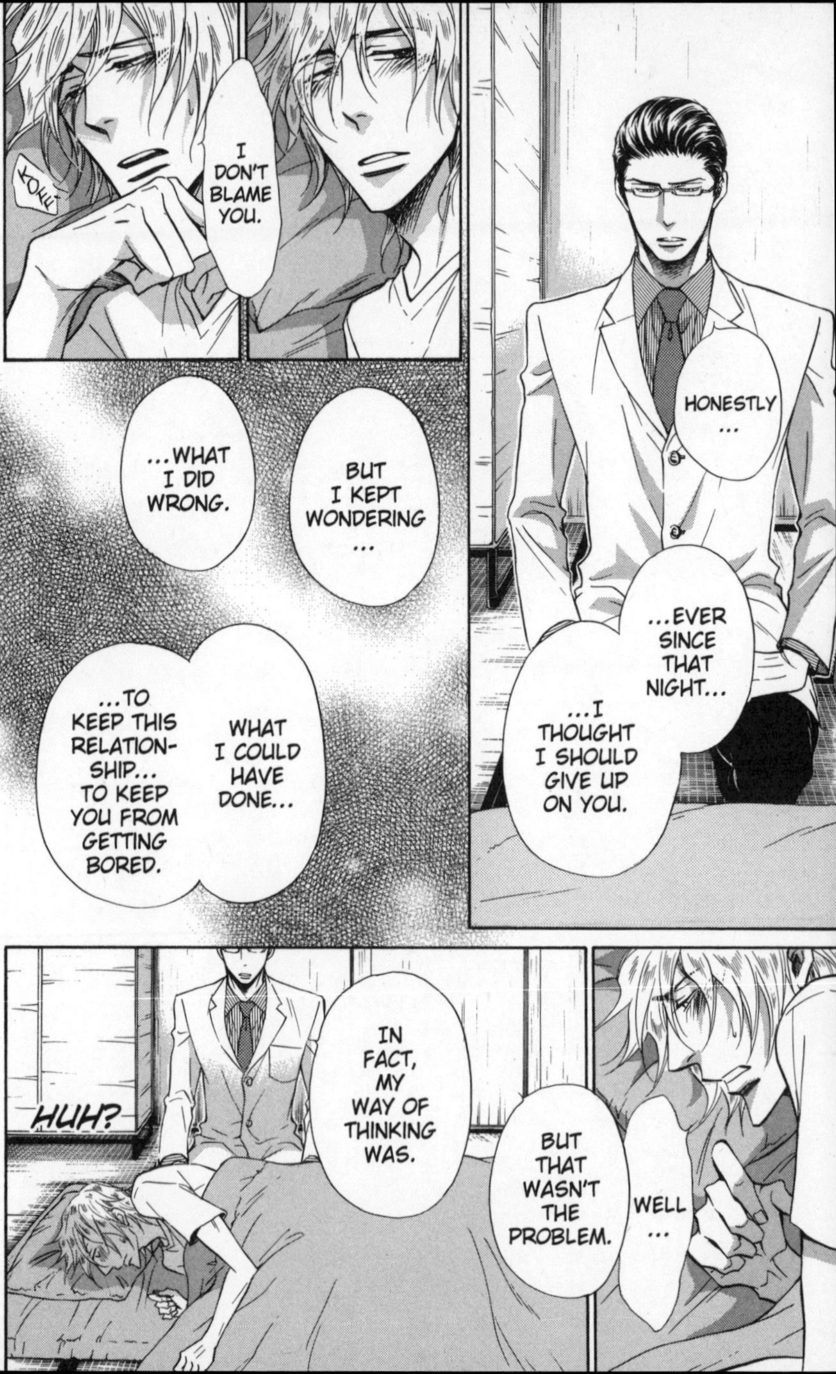
HONESTLY...
...EVER SINCE THAT NIGHT...
...I THOUGHT I SHOULD GIVE UP ON YOU.
I DON'T BLAME YOU.
KOHH
BUT I KEPT WONDERING...
...WHAT I DID WRONG.
WHAT I COULD HAVE DONE...
...TO KEEP THIS RELATION-SHIP... TO KEEP YOU FROM GETTING BORED.
WELL...
BUT THAT WASN'T THE PROBLEM.
IN FACT, MY WAY OF THINKING WAS.
HUH?

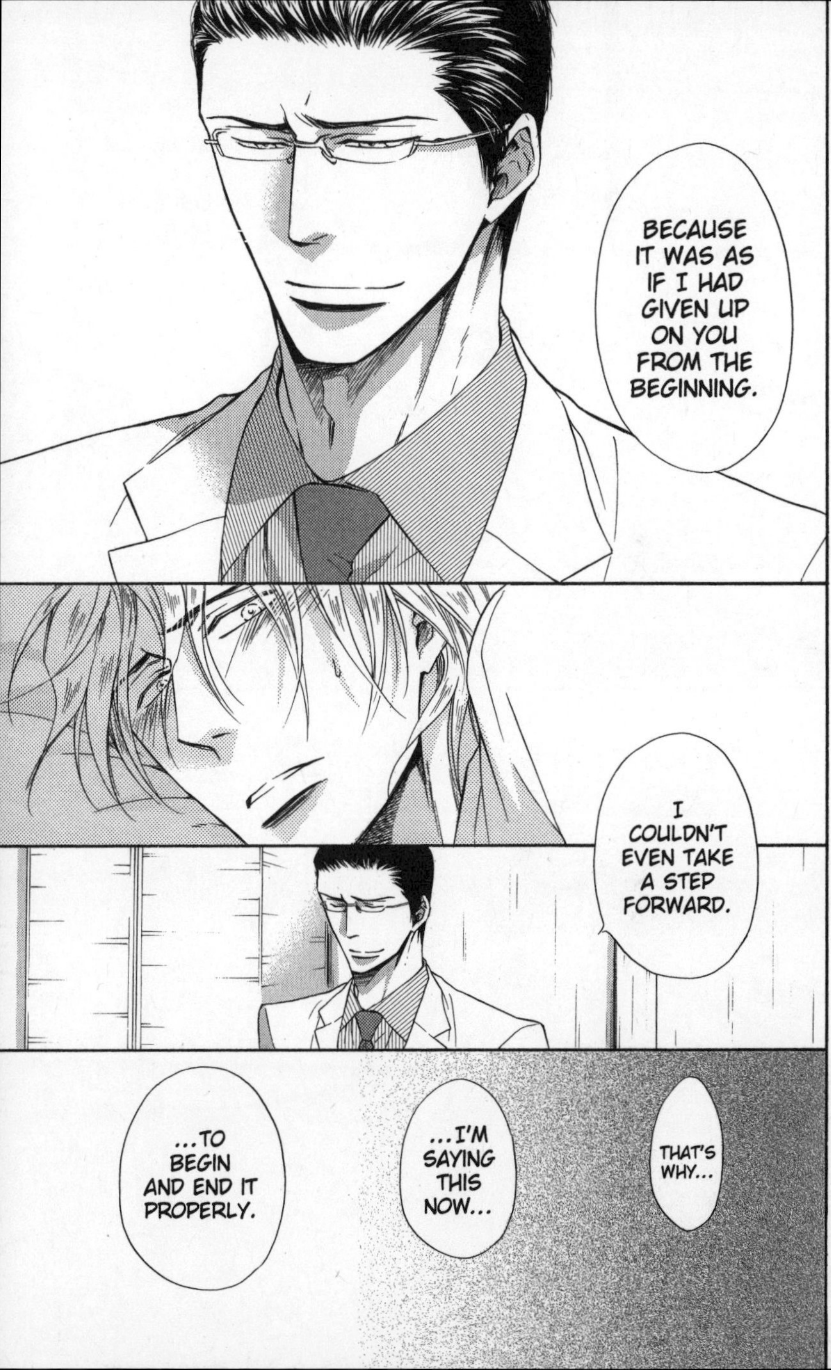
BECAUSE IT WAS AS IF I HAD GIVEN UP ON YOU FROM THE BEGINNING.
I COULDN'T EVEN TAKE A STEP FORWARD.
THAT'S WHY...
...I'M SAYING THIS NOW...
...TO BEGIN AND END IT PROPERLY.

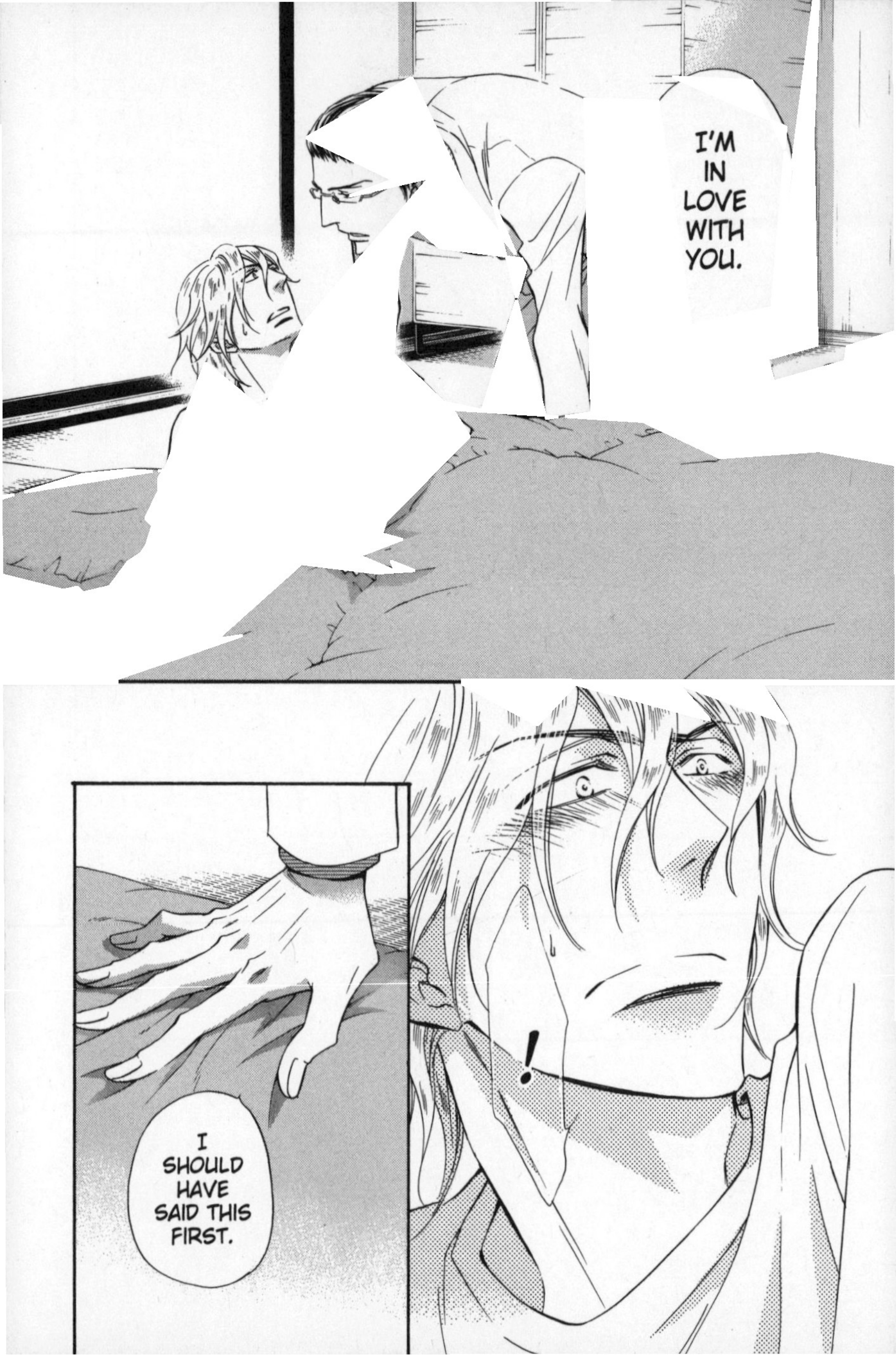
I'M IN LOVE WITH YOU.
!
I SHOULD HAVE SAID THIS FIRST.

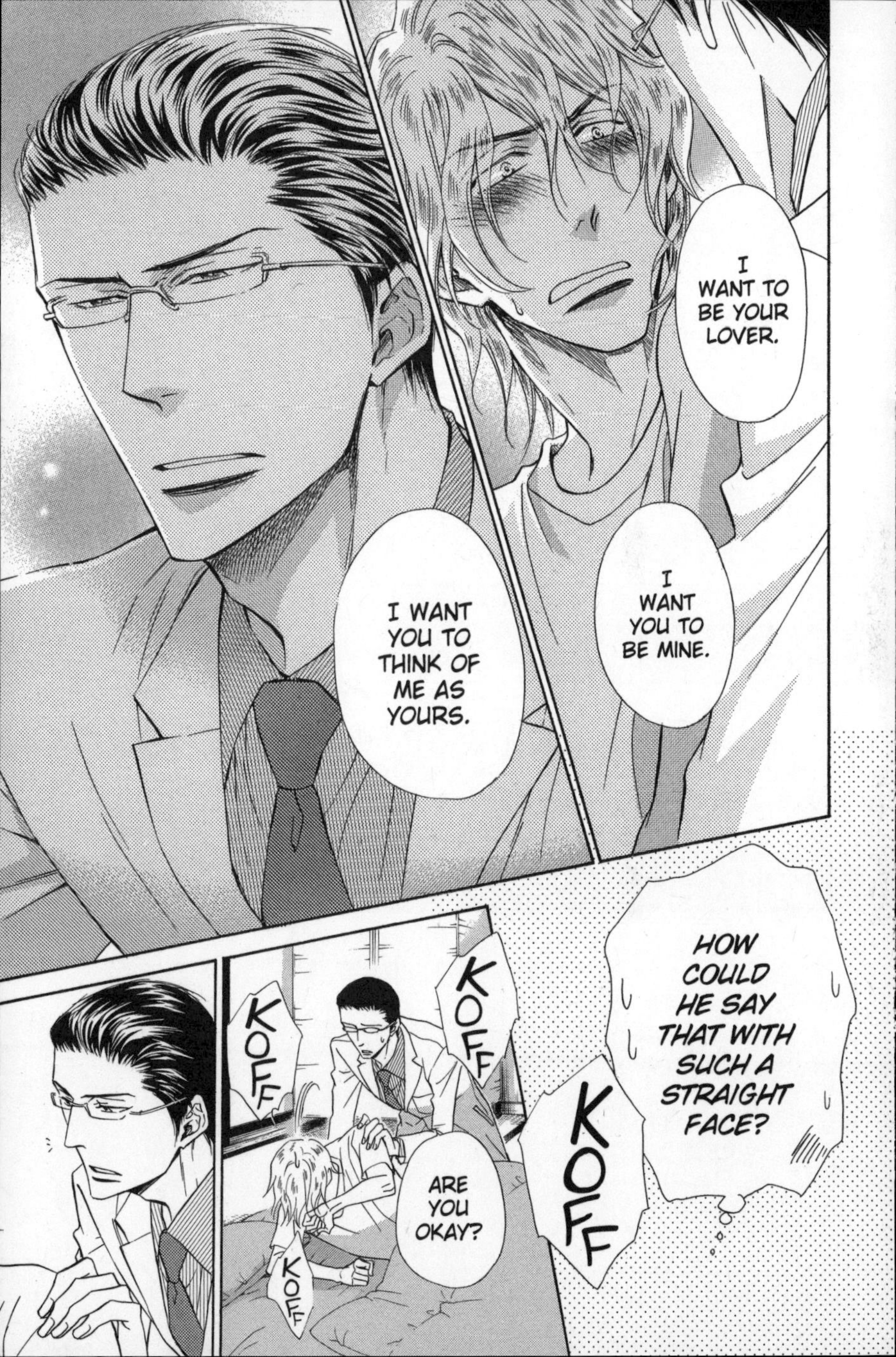

I WANT TO BE YOUR LOVER.
I WANT YOU TO BE MINE.
I WANT YOU TO THINK OF ME AS YOURS.
HOW COULD HE SAY THAT WITH SUCH A STRAIGHT FACE?
KOFF
KOFF
KOFF
ARE YOU OKAY?
KOFF
KOFF

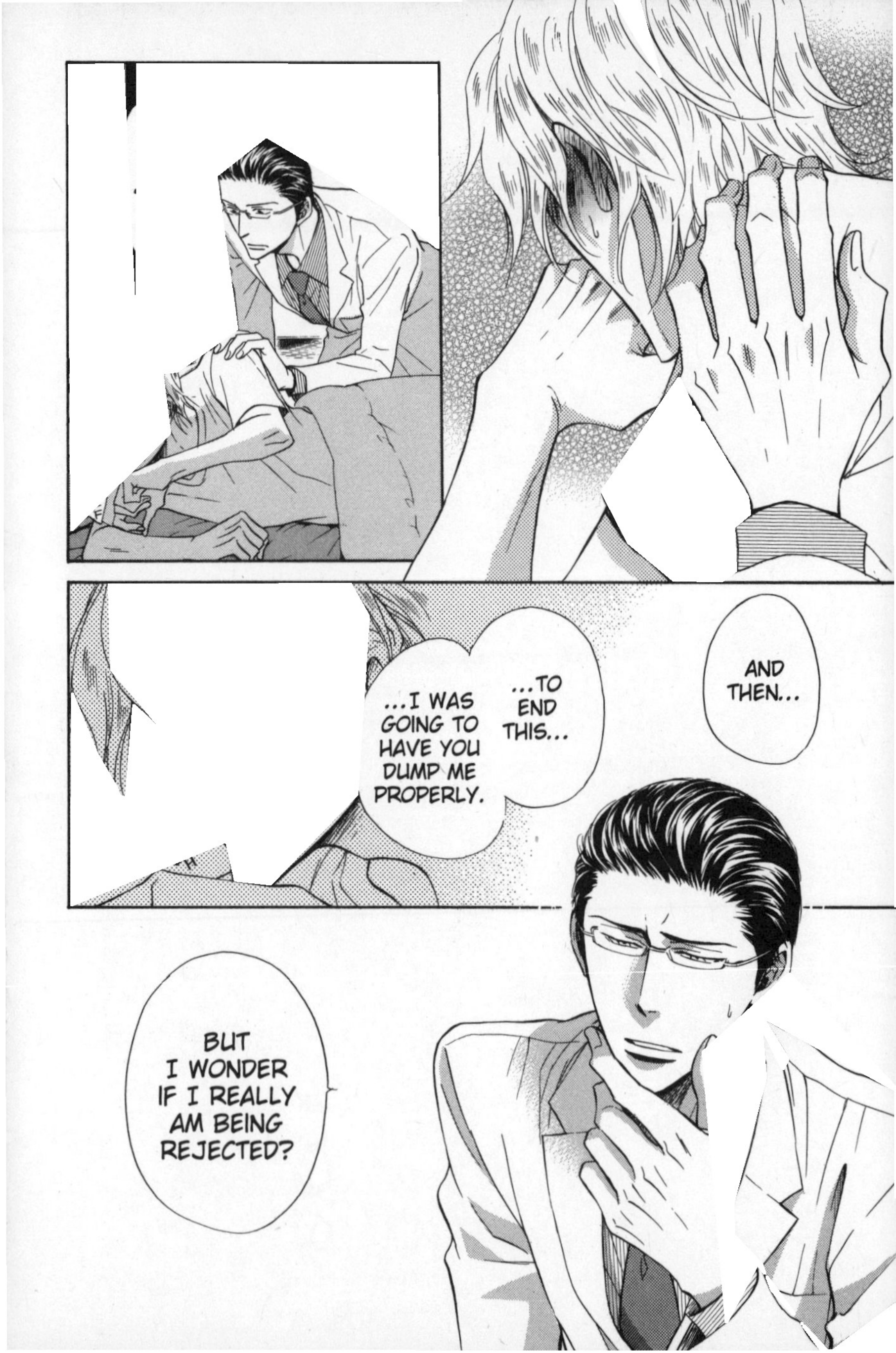
AND THEN...
...TO END THIS...
...I WAS GOING TO HAVE YOU DUMP ME PROPERLY.
BUT I WONDER IF I REALLY AM BEING REJECTED?

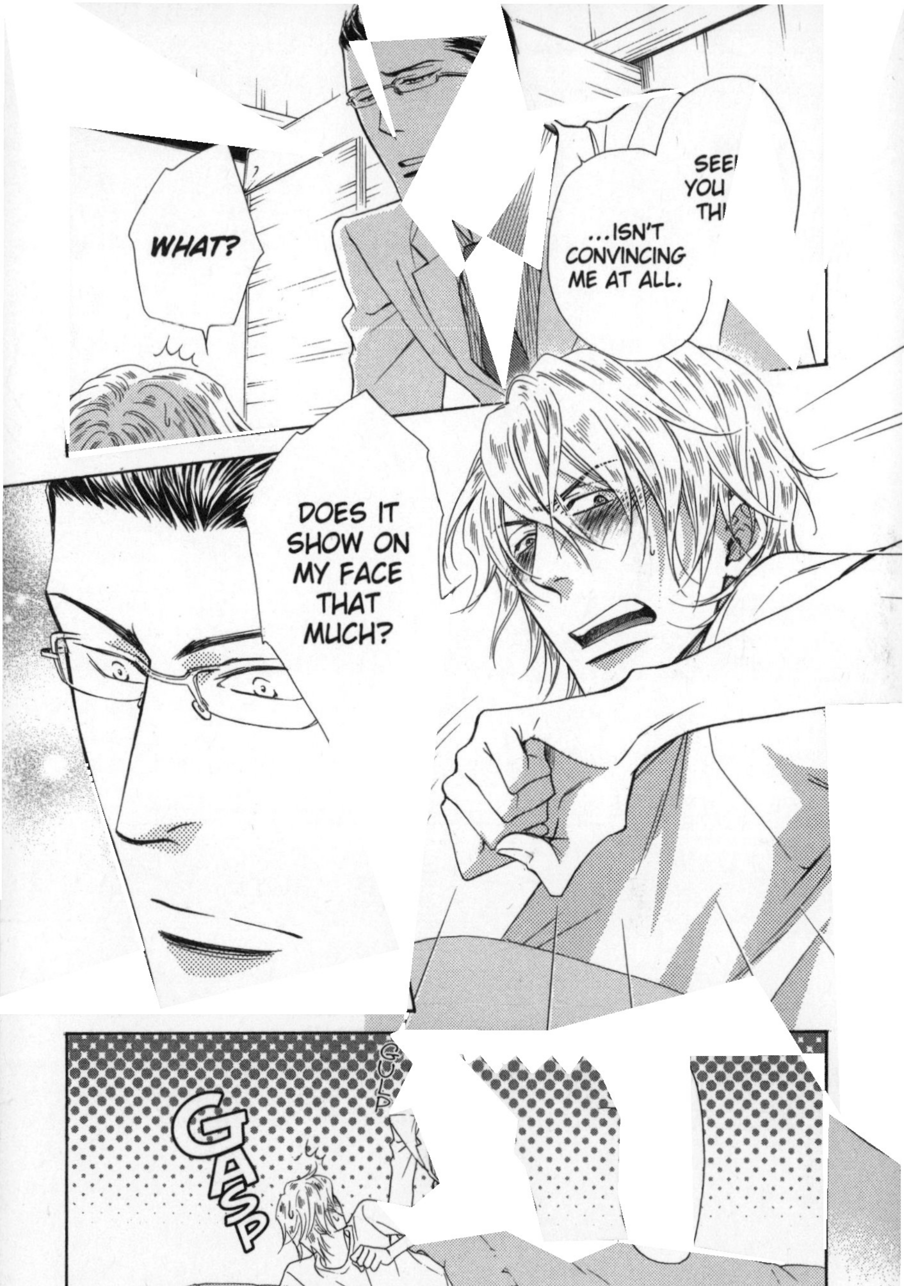
...ISN'T CONVINCING ME AT ALL.
WHAT?
DOES IT SHOW ON MY FACE THAT MUCH?
GULP
GASP

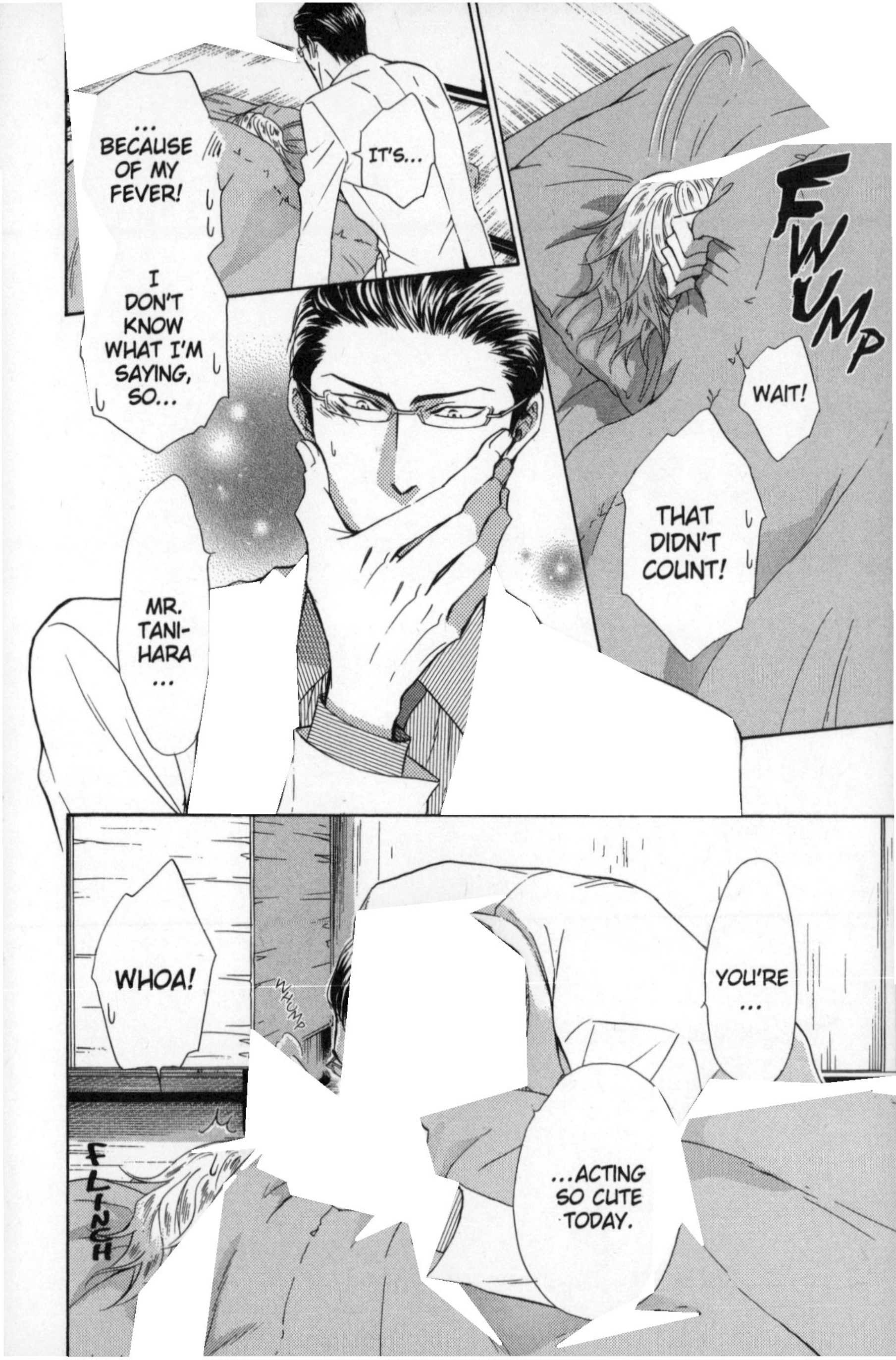
FWUMP
WAIT!
THAT DIDN'T COUNT!
IT'S...
...BECAUSE OF MY FEVER!
I DON'T KNOW WHAT I'M SAYING, SO...
MR. TANI-HARA...
YOU'RE...
...ACTING SO CUTE TODAY.
WHUMP
WHOA!
FLINCH

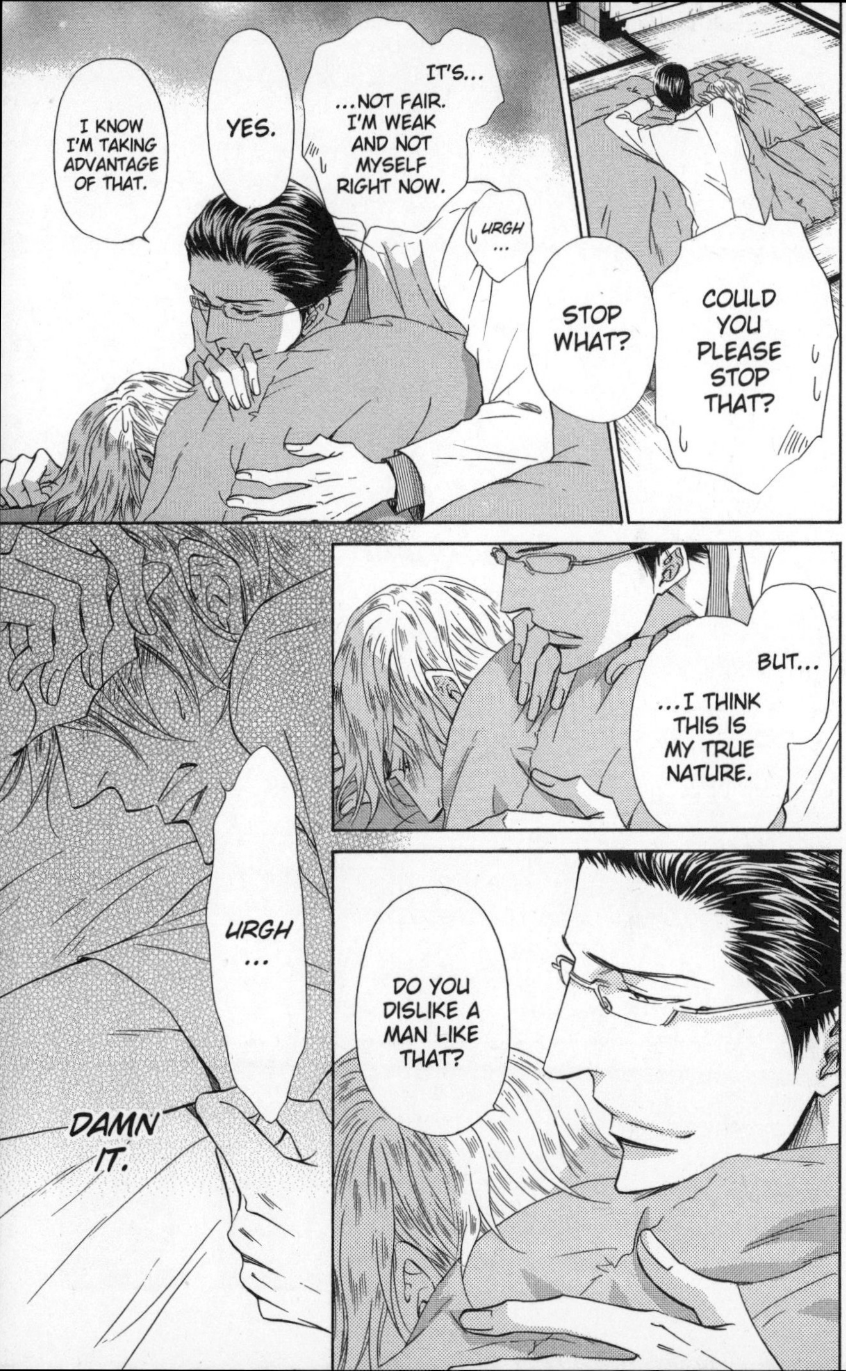
COULD YOU PLEASE STOP THAT?
STOP WHAT?
IT'S...
...NOT FAIR. I'M WEAK AND NOT MYSELF RIGHT NOW.
URGH ...
YES.
I KNOW I'M TAKING ADVANTAGE OF THAT.
BUT...
...I THINK THIS IS MY TRUE NATURE.
DO YOU DISLIKE A MAN LIKE THAT?
URGH ...
DAMN IT.

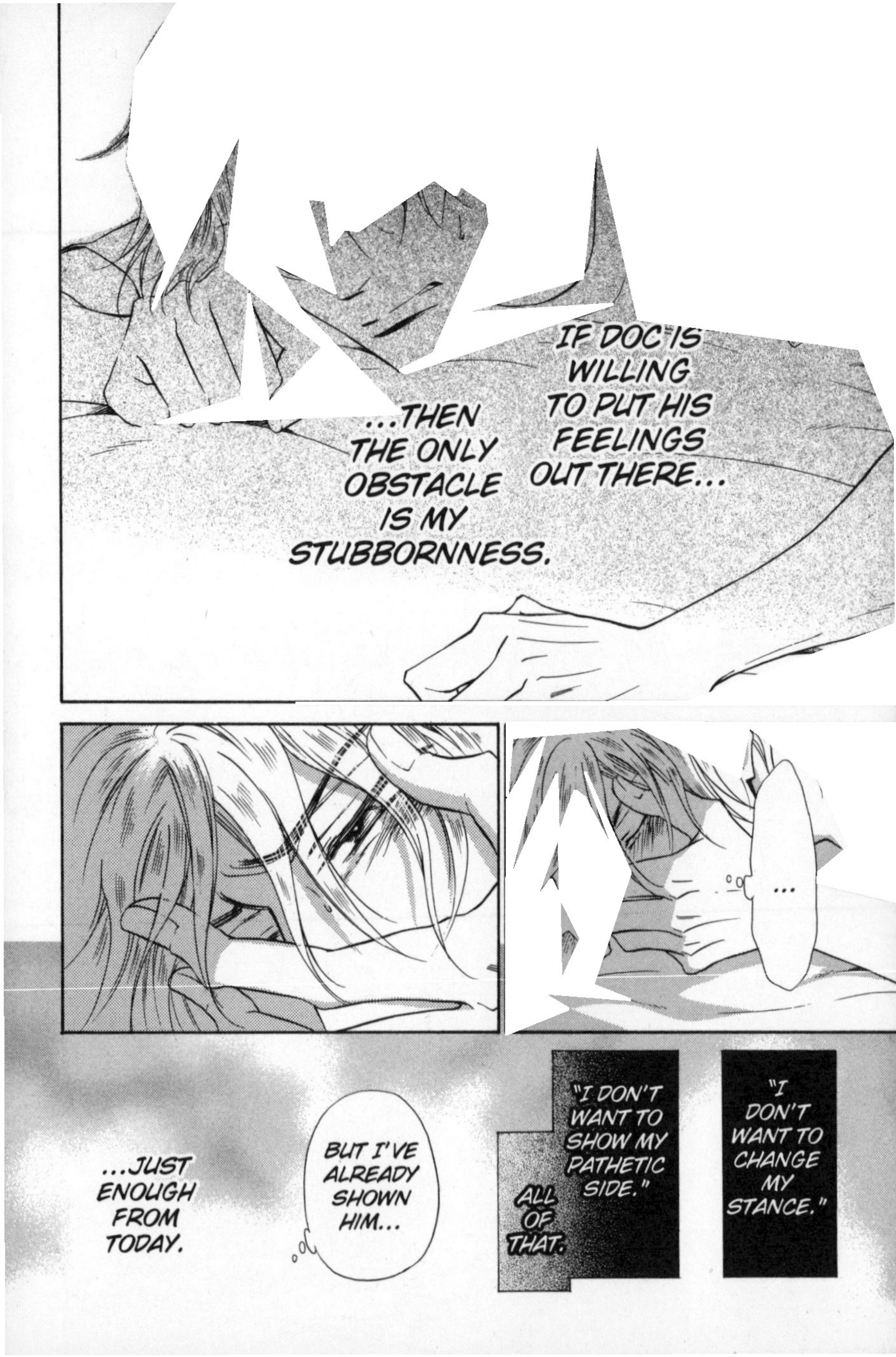
IF DOC IS WILLING TO PUT HIS FEELINGS OUT THERE...
...THEN THE ONLY OBSTACLE IS MY STUBBORNNESS.
...
"I DON'T WANT TO CHANGE MY STANCE."
"I DON'T WANT TO SHOW MY PATHETIC SIDE."
ALL OF THAT.
BUT I'VE ALREADY SHOWN HIM...
...JUST ENOUGH FROM TODAY.

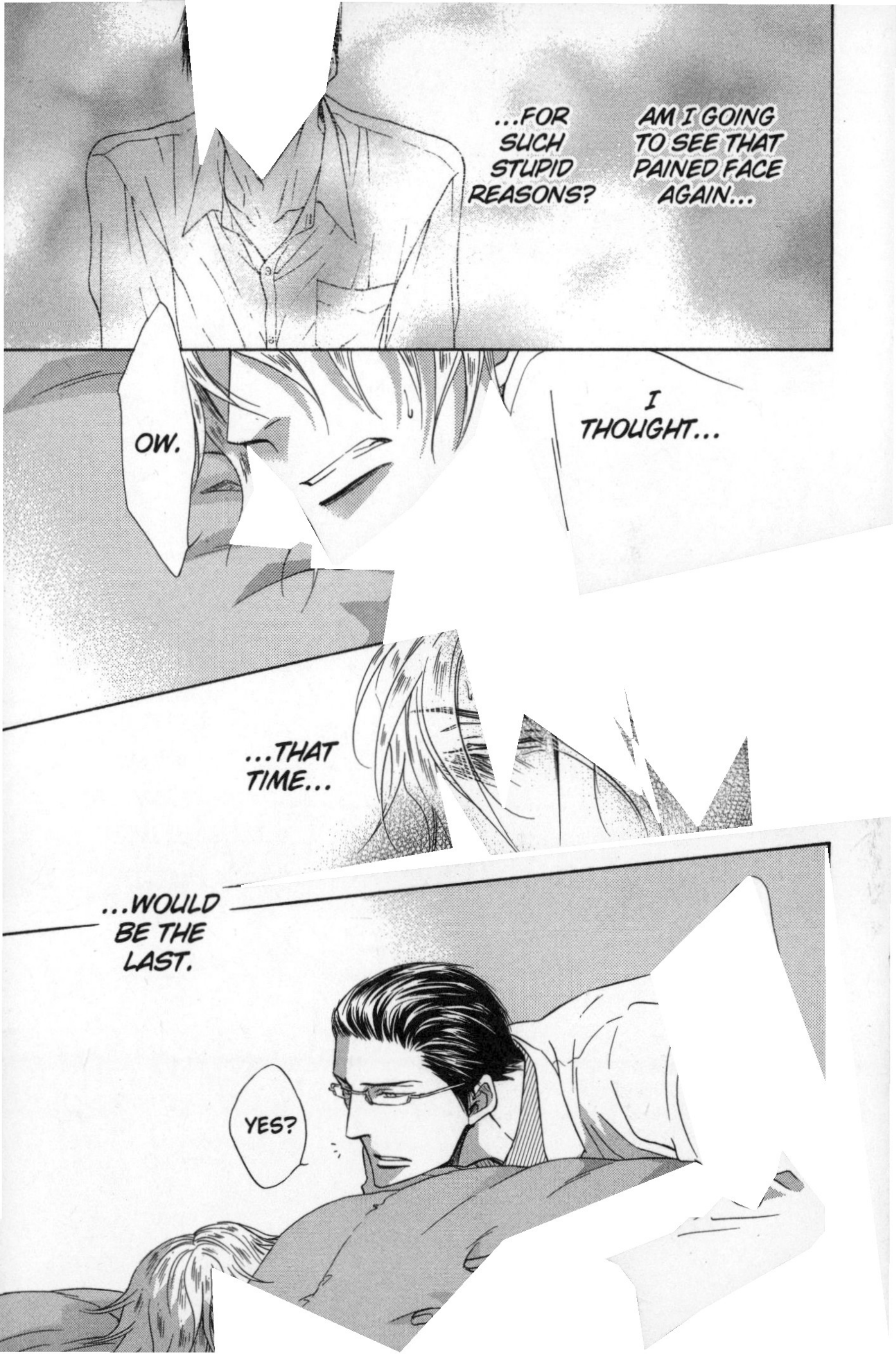
AM I GOING TO SEE THAT PAINED FACE AGAIN...
...FOR SUCH STUPID REASONS?
I THOUGHT...
OW.
...THAT TIME...
...WOULD BE THE LAST.
YES?

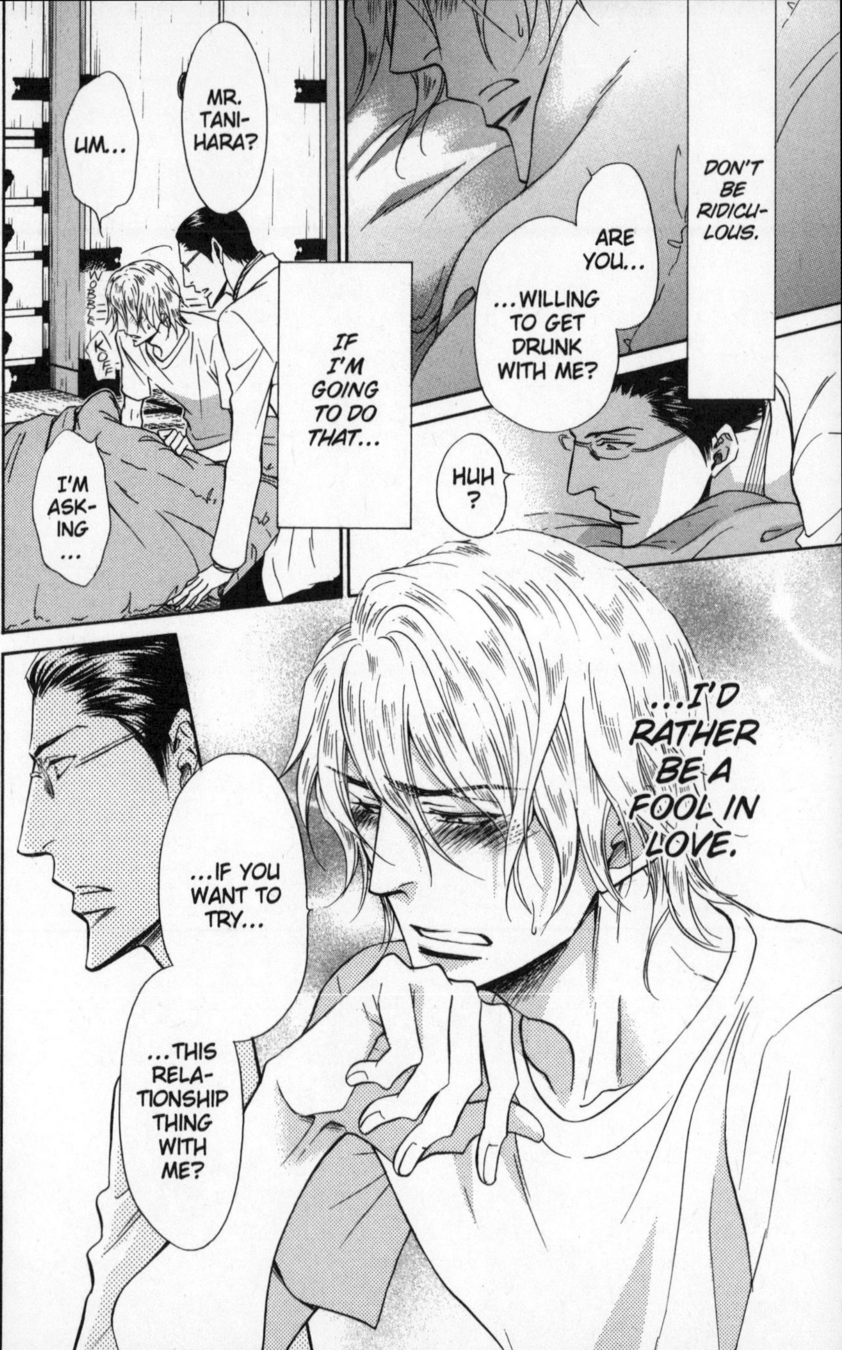
DON'T BE RIDICULOUS.
ARE YOU...
...WILLING TO GET DRUNK WITH ME?
HUH?
MR. TANIHARA?
UM...
WOBBLE
KOFF
I'M ASKING...
IF I'M GOING TO DO THAT...
...I'D RATHER BE A FOOL IN LOVE.
...IF YOU WANT TO TRY...
...THIS RELATIONSHIP THING WITH ME?

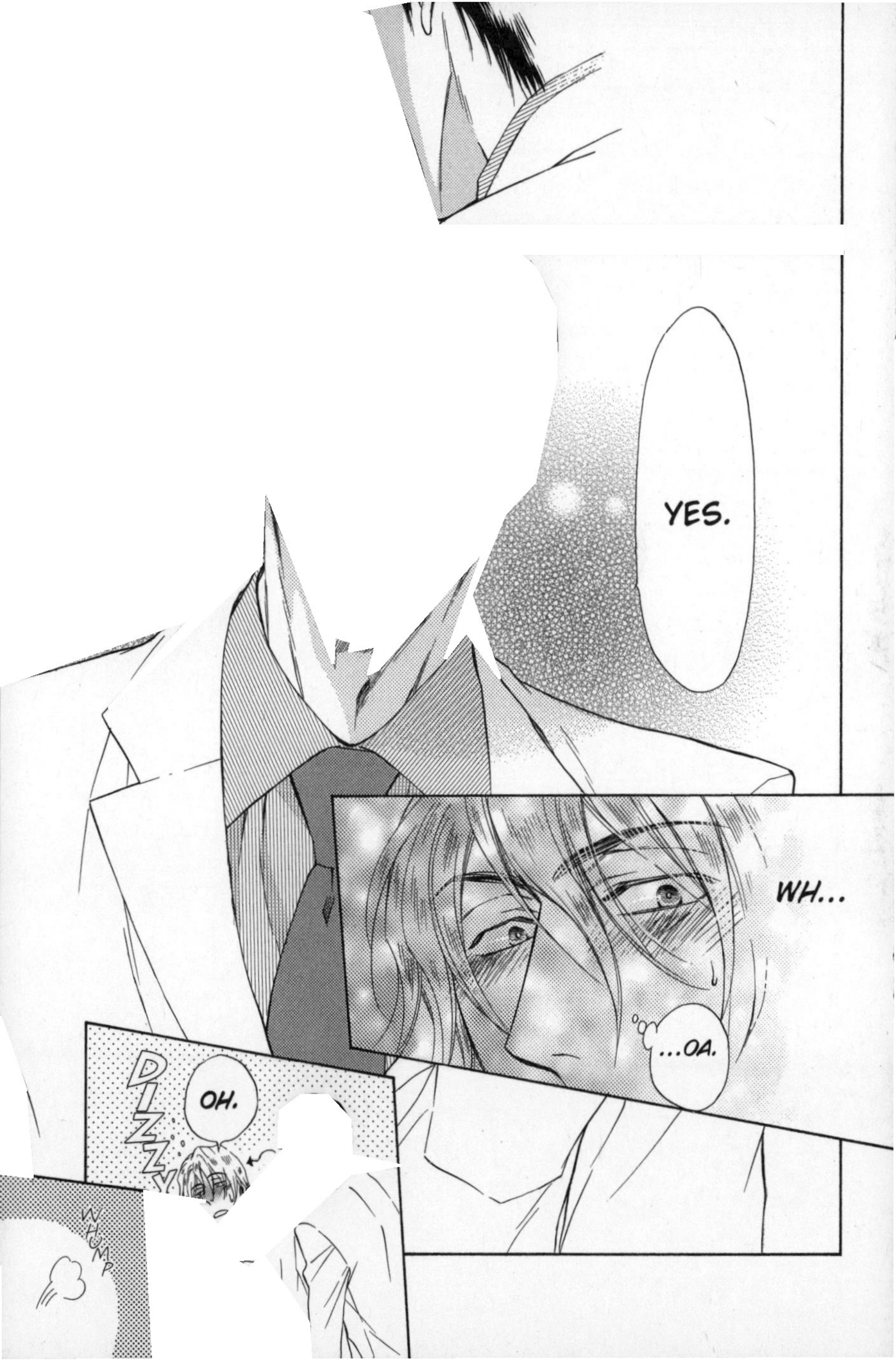
YES.
WH...
...OA.
OH.
DIZZY
WHUMP

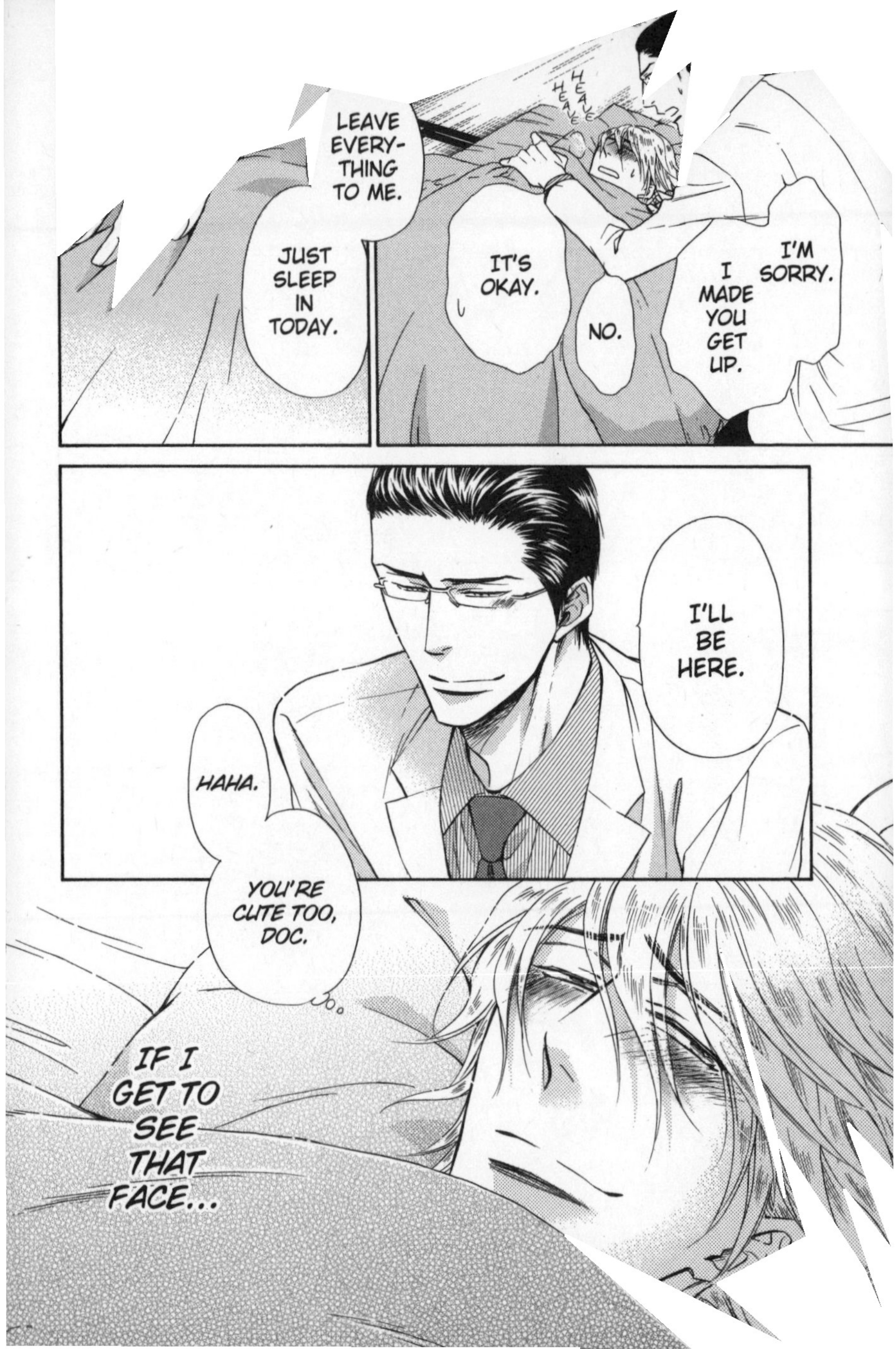
HEAVE HEAVE
I'M SORRY.
I MADE YOU GET UP.
NO.
IT'S OKAY.
LEAVE EVERY-THING TO ME.
JUST SLEEP IN TODAY.
I'LL BE HERE.
HAHA.
YOU'RE CUTE TOO, DOC.
IF I GET TO SEE THAT FACE...

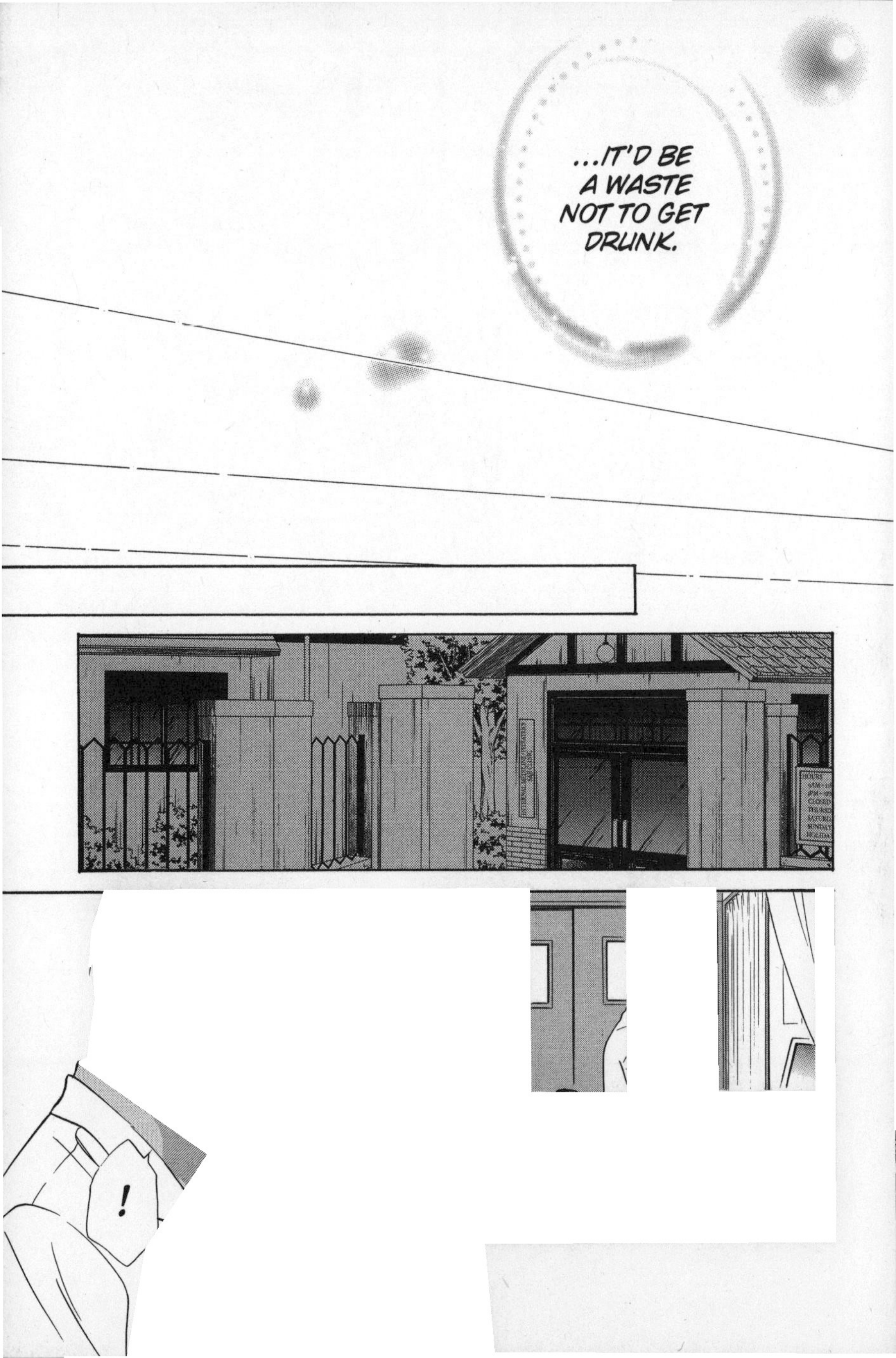
...IT'D BE A WASTE NOT TO GET DRUNK.
!

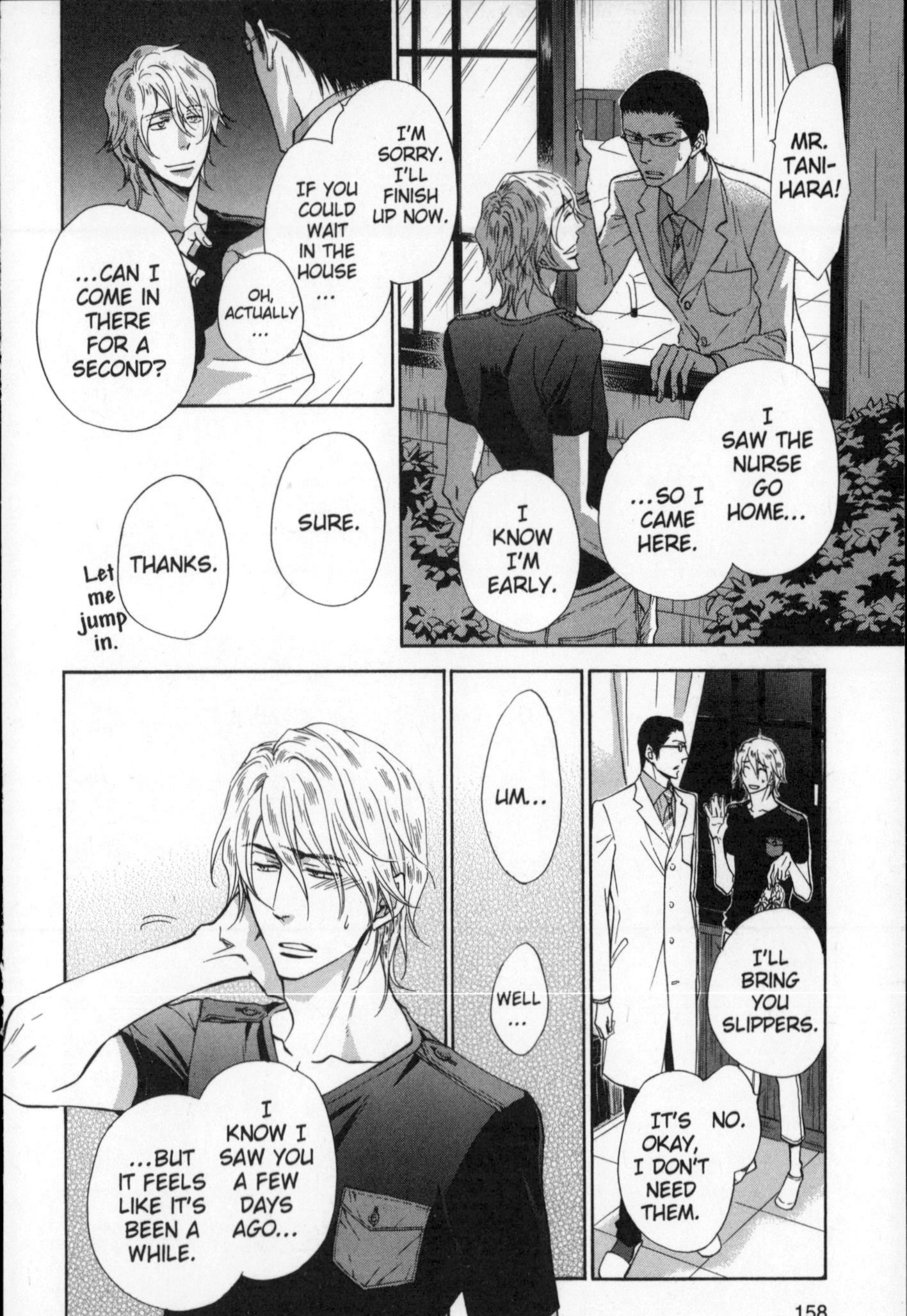
MR. TANI-HARA!
I SAW THE NURSE GO HOME...
...SO I CAME HERE.
I KNOW I'M EARLY.
I'M SORRY. I'LL FINISH UP NOW.
IF YOU COULD WAIT IN THE HOUSE...
OH, ACTUALLY...
...CAN I COME IN THERE FOR A SECOND?
SURE.
THANKS.
Let me jump in.
I'LL BRING YOU SLIPPERS.
NO.
IT'S OKAY, I DON'T NEED THEM.
UM...
WELL...
I KNOW I SAW YOU A FEW DAYS AGO...
...BUT IT FEELS LIKE IT'S BEEN A WHILE.

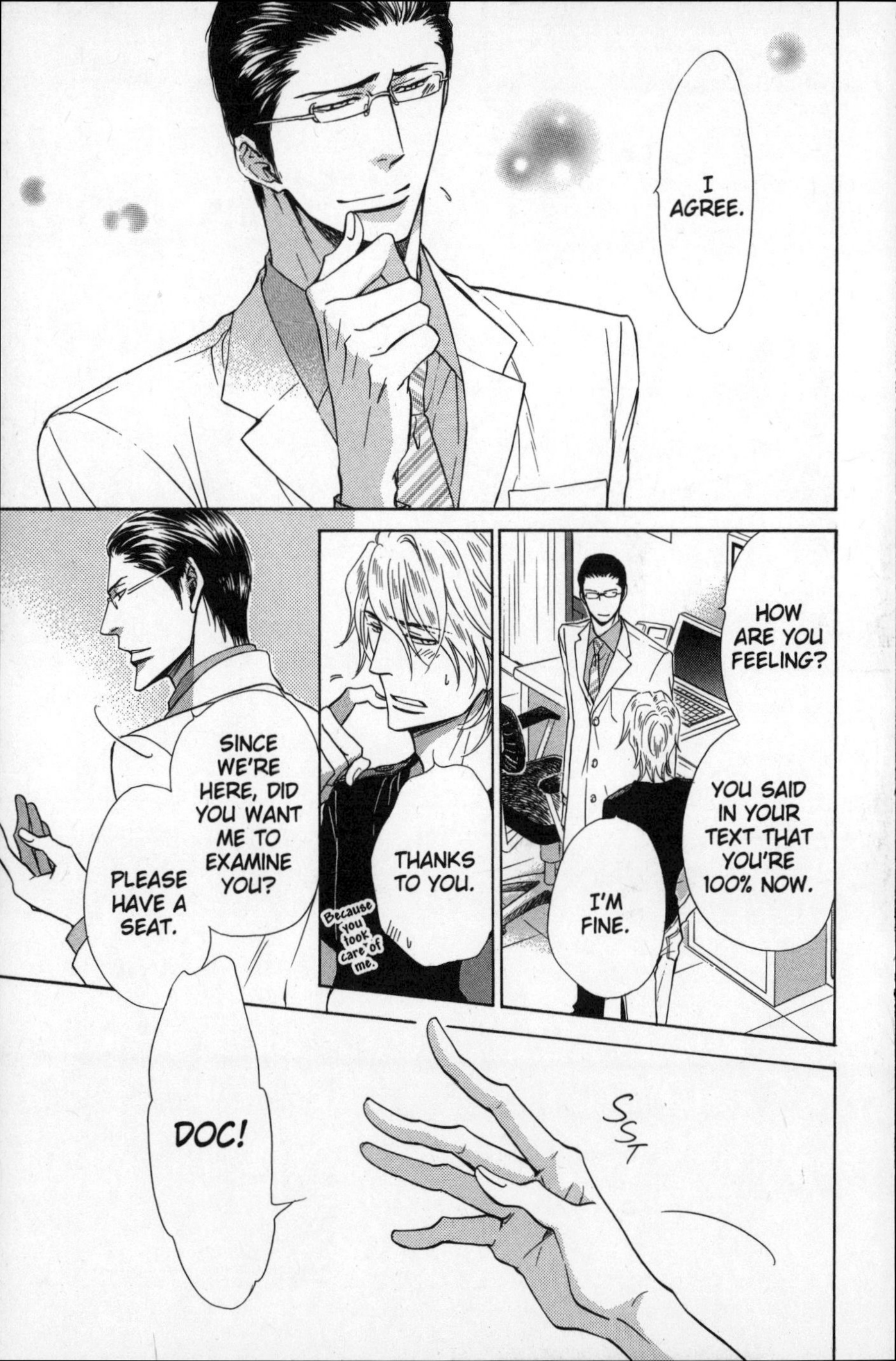

I AGREE.
HOW ARE YOU FEELING?
YOU SAID IN YOUR TEXT THAT YOU'RE 100% NOW.
I'M FINE.
THANKS TO YOU.
Because you took care of me.
SINCE WE'RE HERE, DID YOU WANT ME TO EXAMINE YOU?
PLEASE HAVE A SEAT.
DOC!
SST

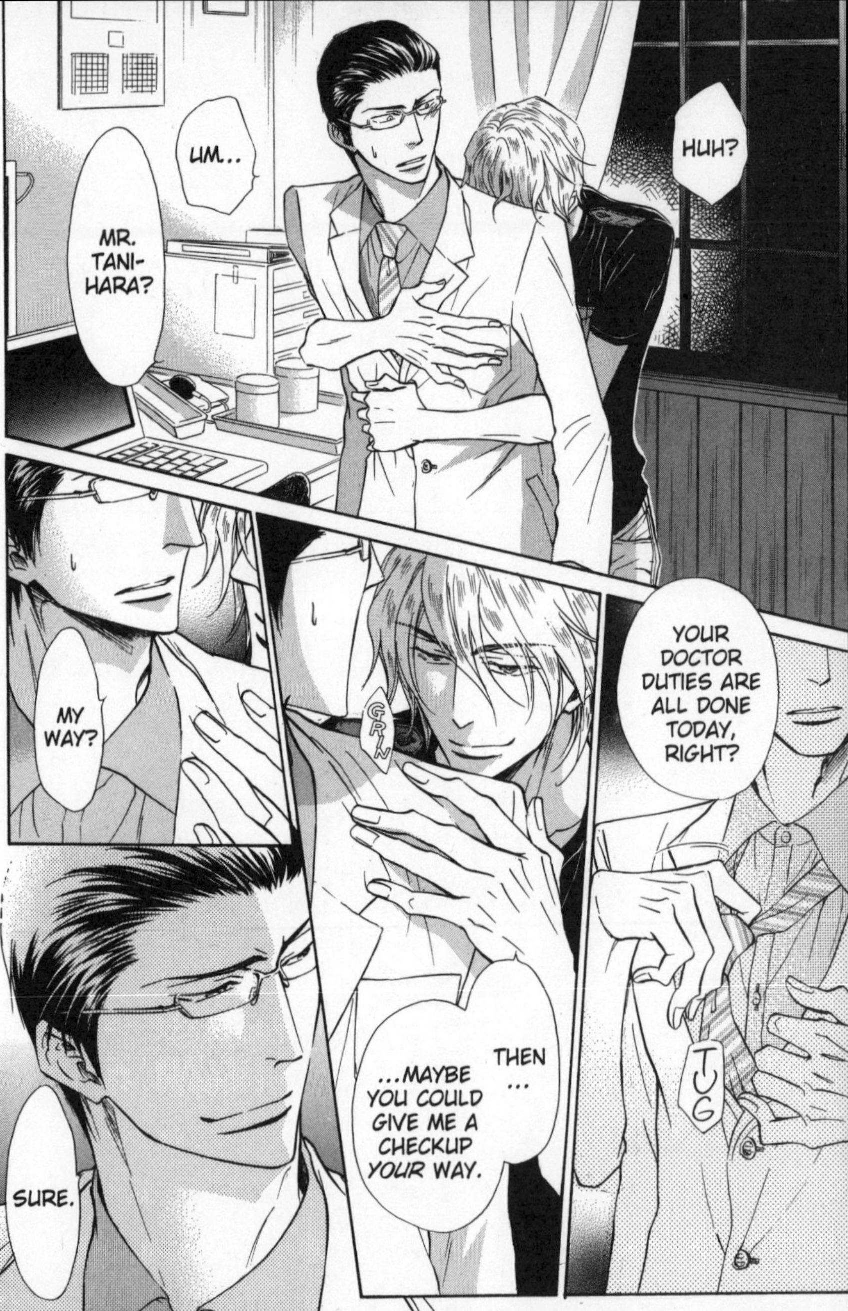
HUH?
UM...
MR. TANI-HARA?
YOUR DOCTOR DUTIES ARE ALL DONE TODAY, RIGHT?
TUG
GRIN
THEN ...
...MAYBE YOU COULD GIVE ME A CHECKUP *YOUR* WAY.
MY WAY?
SURE.

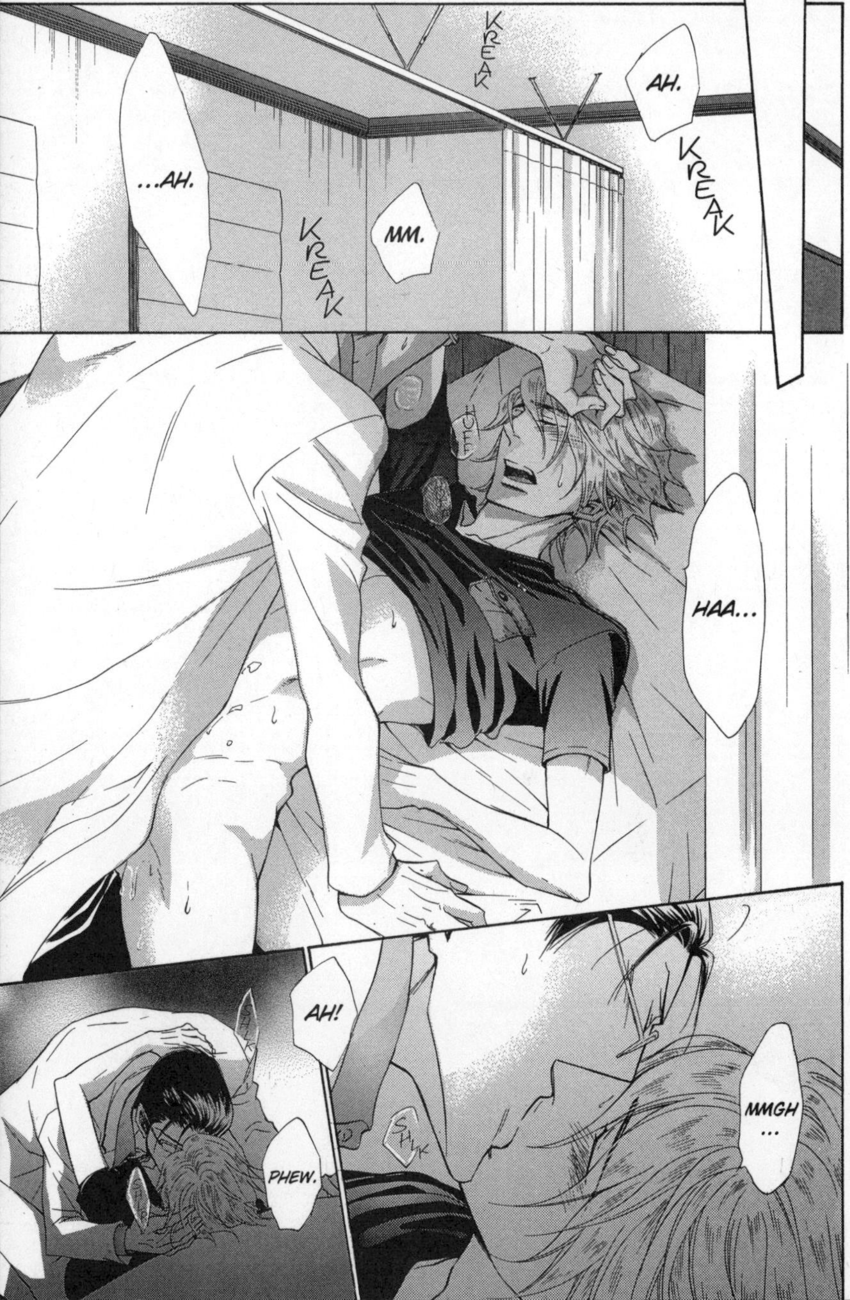
AH.
KREAK
KREAK
MM.
KREAK
...AH.
HUFF
HAA...
MMGH ...
AH!
SHK
SHK
PHEW.

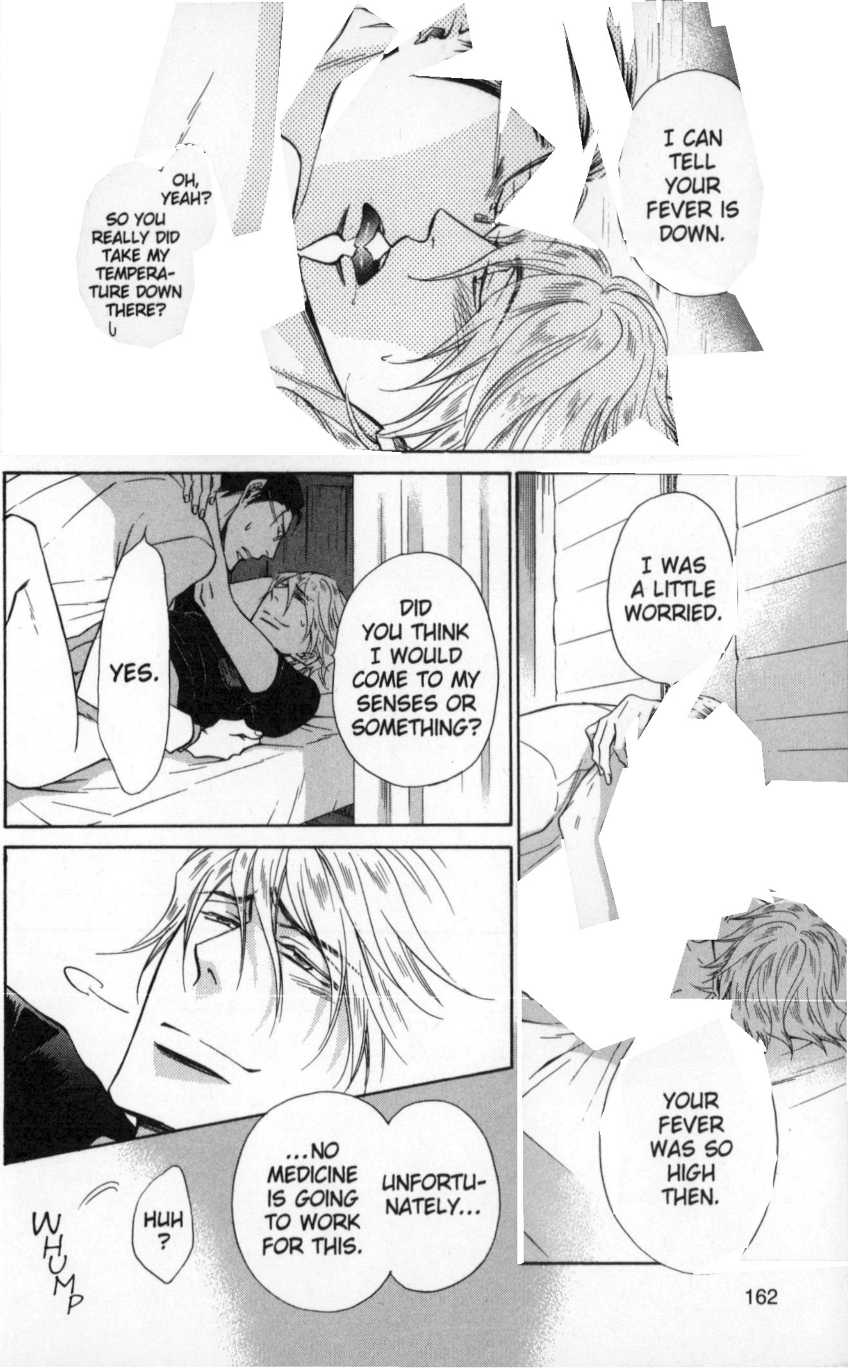
I CAN TELL YOUR FEVER IS DOWN.
OH, YEAH? SO YOU REALLY DID TAKE MY TEMPERATURE DOWN THERE?
I WAS A LITTLE WORRIED.
YOUR FEVER WAS SO HIGH THEN.
DID YOU THINK I WOULD COME TO MY SENSES OR SOMETHING?
YES.
UNFORTUNATELY...
...NO MEDICINE IS GOING TO WORK FOR THIS.
HUH?
WHUMP

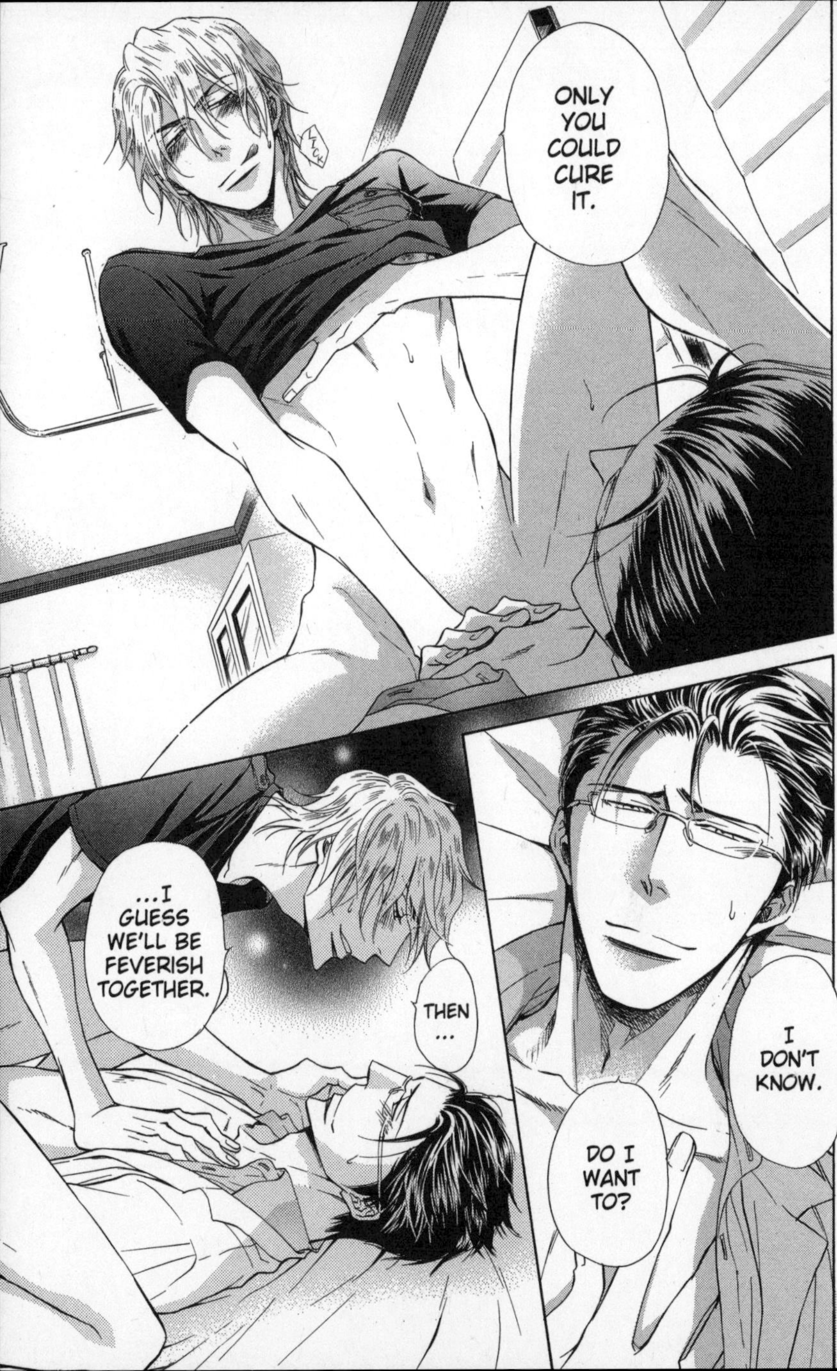
ONLY YOU COULD CURE IT.
LICK
I DON'T KNOW.
DO I WANT TO?
THEN...
...I GUESS WE'LL BE FEVERISH TOGETHER.

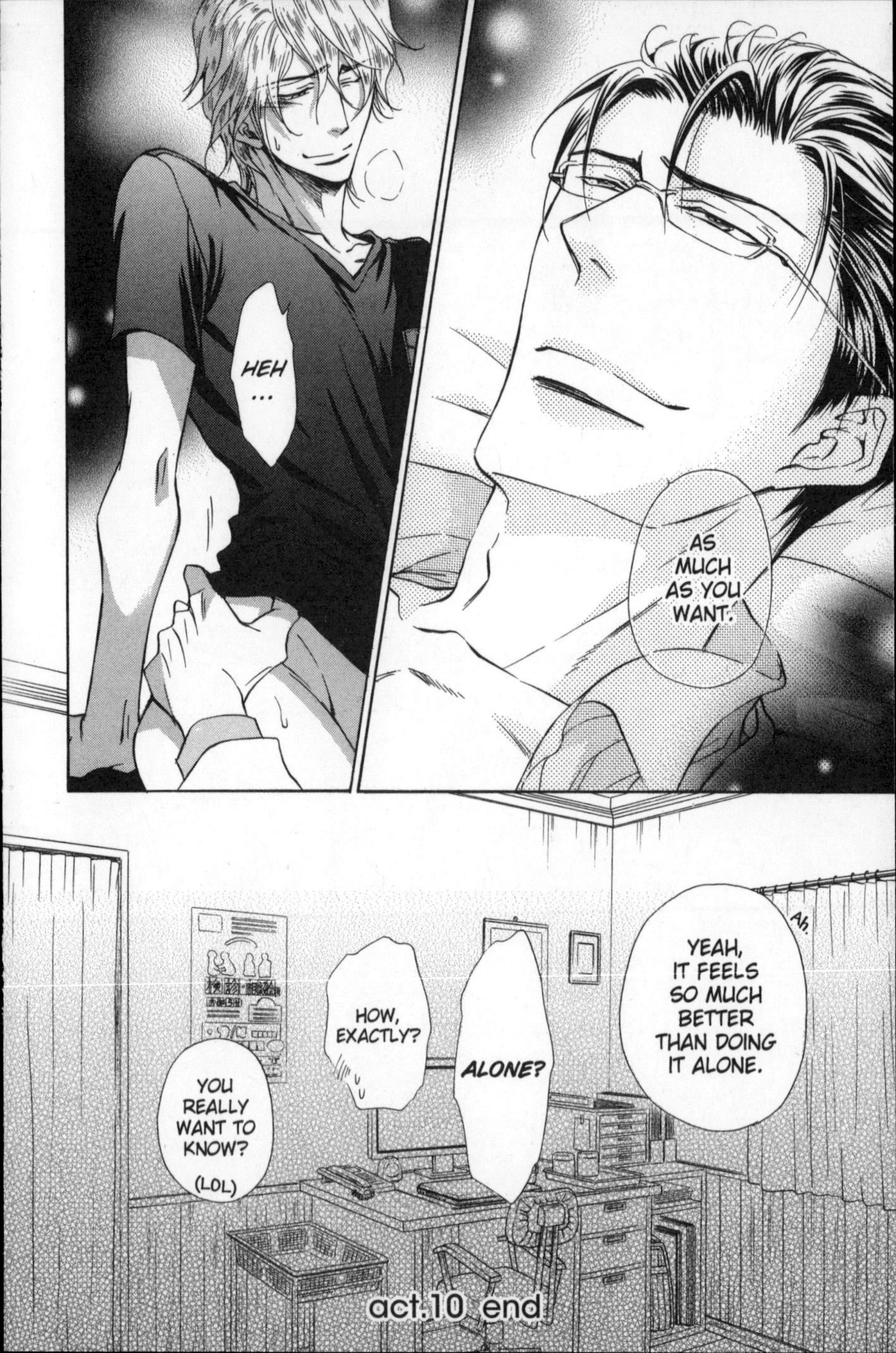
AS MUCH AS YOU WANT.
HEH ...
Ah.
YEAH, IT FEELS SO MUCH BETTER THAN DOING IT ALONE.
ALONE?
HOW, EXACTLY?
YOU REALLY WANT TO KNOW? (LOL)
act.10 end

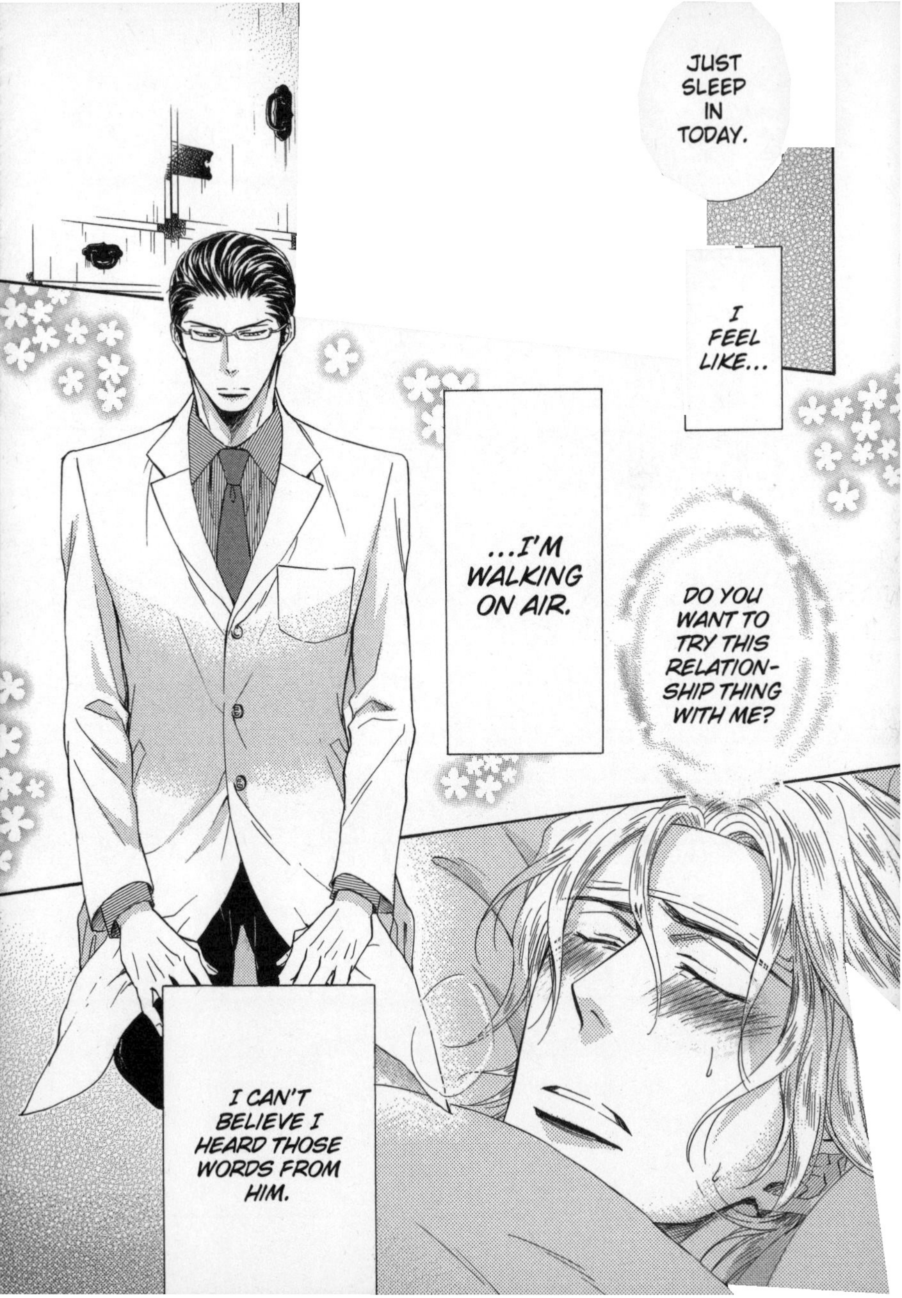
JUST SLEEP IN TODAY.
I FEEL LIKE...
...I'M WALKING ON AIR.
DO YOU WANT TO TRY THIS RELATION-SHIP THING WITH ME?
I CAN'T BELIEVE I HEARD THOSE WORDS FROM HIM.

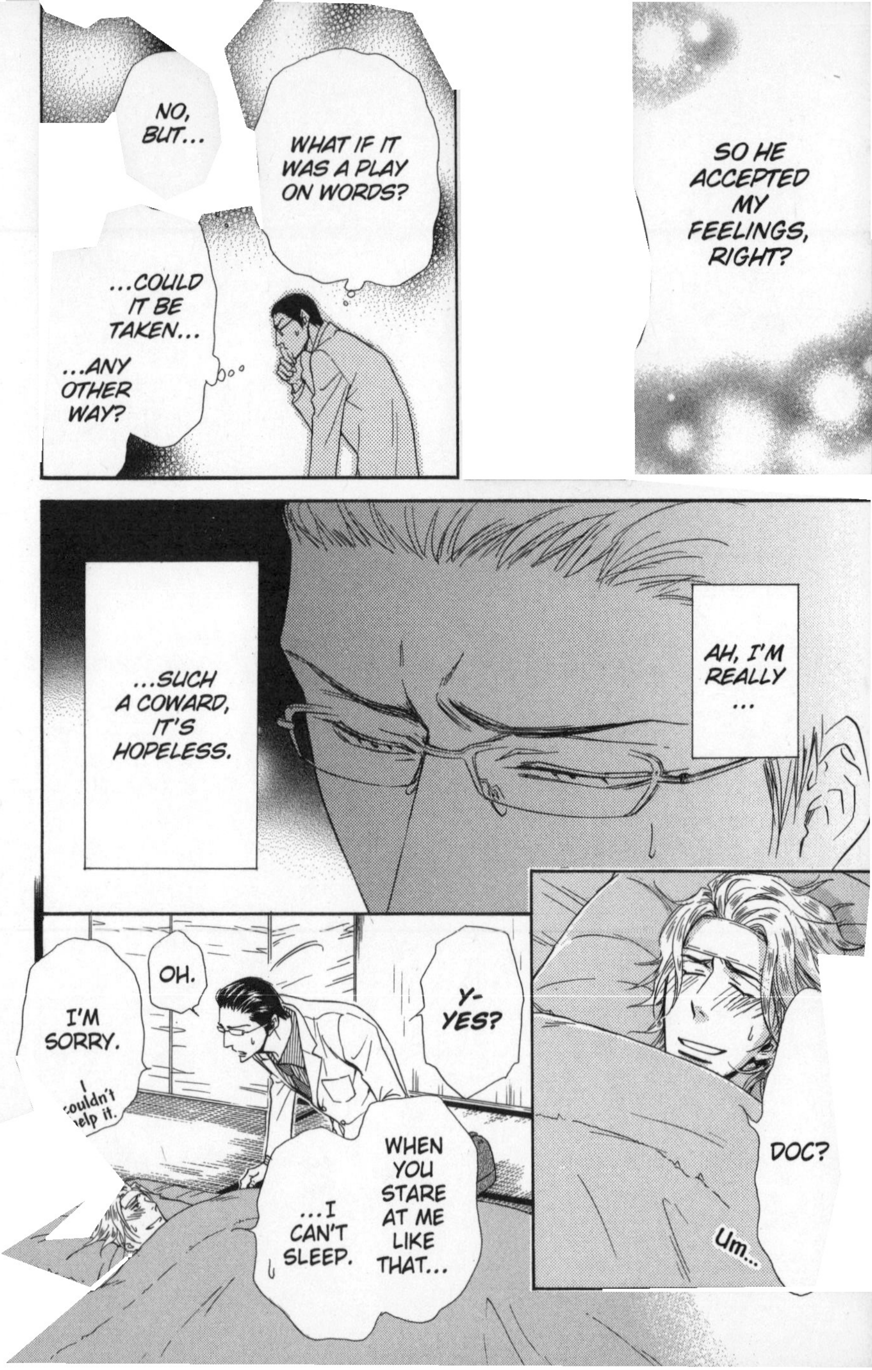
SO HE ACCEPTED MY FEELINGS, RIGHT?
WHAT IF IT WAS A PLAY ON WORDS?
NO, BUT...
...COULD IT BE TAKEN...
...ANY OTHER WAY?
AH, I'M REALLY ...
...SUCH A COWARD, IT'S HOPELESS.
DOC?
Um...
Y-YES?
WHEN YOU STARE AT ME LIKE THAT...
...I CAN'T SLEEP.
OH.
I'M SORRY.
I couldn't help it.

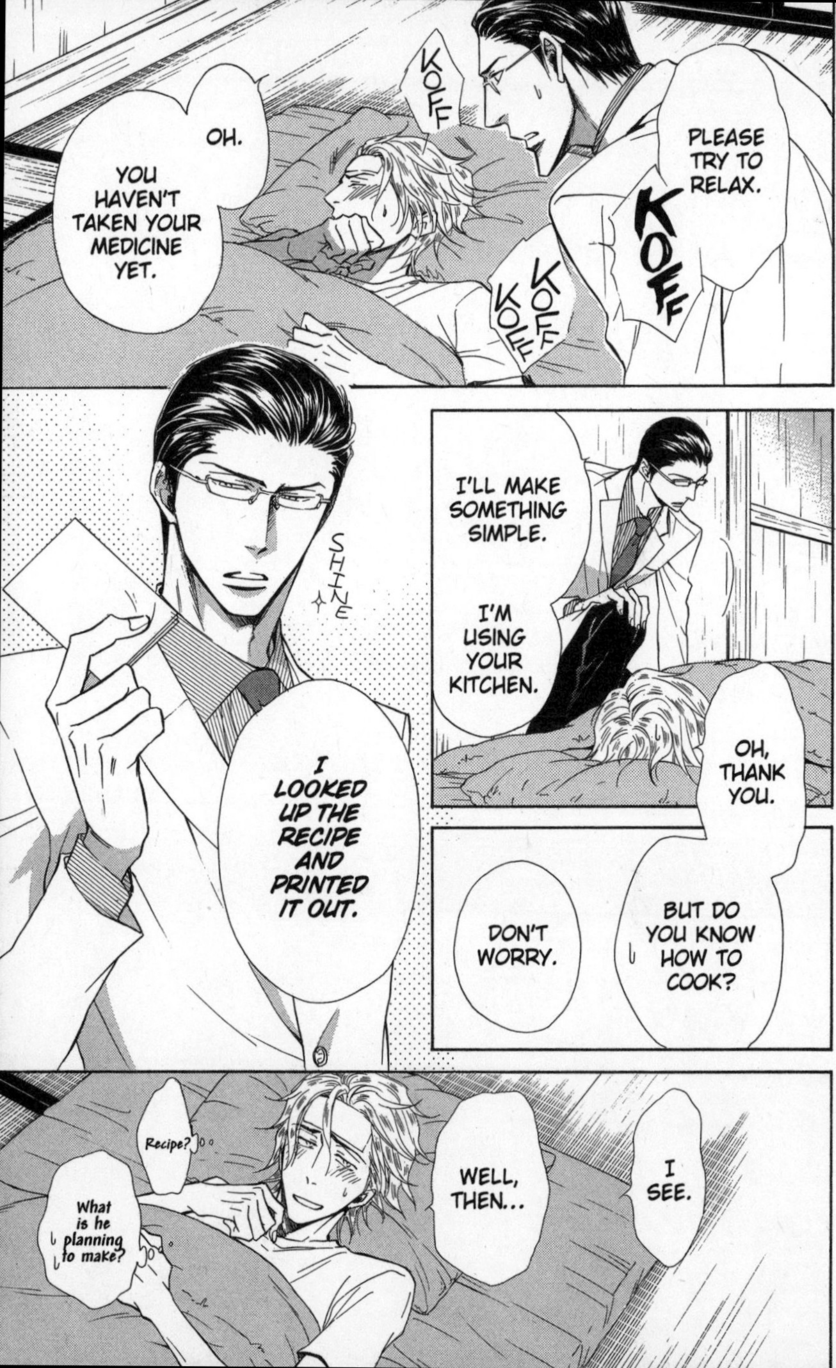
PLEASE TRY TO RELAX.
KOFF
KOFF
KOFF KOFF
OH.
YOU HAVEN'T TAKEN YOUR MEDICINE YET.
I'LL MAKE SOMETHING SIMPLE.
I'M USING YOUR KITCHEN.
OH, THANK YOU.
BUT DO YOU KNOW HOW TO COOK?
DON'T WORRY.
SHINE
I LOOKED UP THE RECIPE AND PRINTED IT OUT.
I SEE.
WELL, THEN...
Recipe?
What is he planning to make?

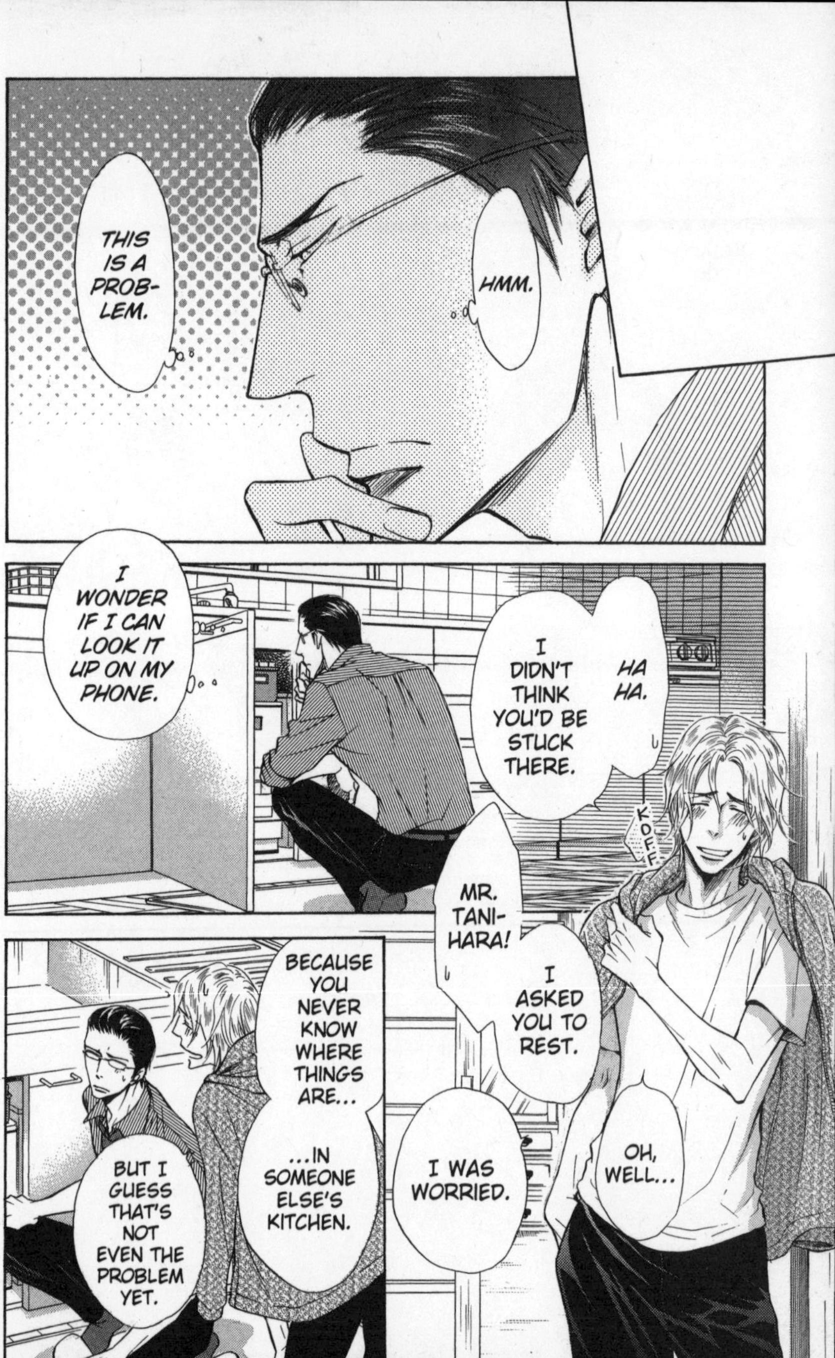
HMM.
THIS IS A PROB-LEM.
I WONDER IF I CAN LOOK IT UP ON MY PHONE.
HA HA.
I DIDN'T THINK YOU'D BE STUCK THERE.
KOFF
MR. TANI-HARA!
I ASKED YOU TO REST.
OH, WELL...
I WAS WORRIED.
BECAUSE YOU NEVER KNOW WHERE THINGS ARE...
...IN SOMEONE ELSE'S KITCHEN.
BUT I GUESS THAT'S NOT EVEN THE PROBLEM YET.

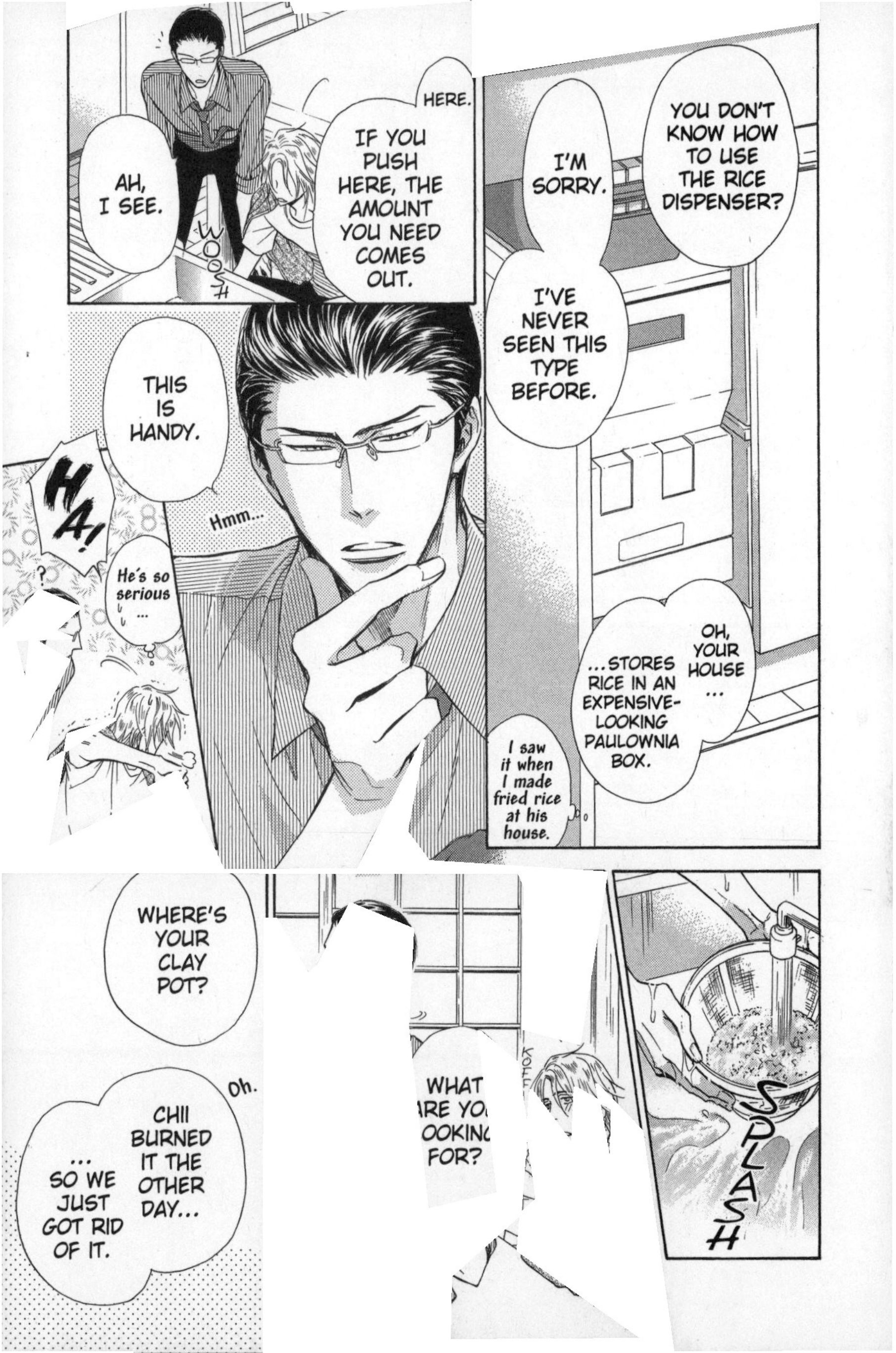
YOU DON'T KNOW HOW TO USE THE RICE DISPENSER?
I'M SORRY.
I'VE NEVER SEEN THIS TYPE BEFORE.
OH, YOUR HOUSE ...
...STORES RICE IN AN EXPENSIVE-LOOKING PAULOWNIA BOX.
I saw it when I made fried rice at his house.
HERE.
IF YOU PUSH HERE, THE AMOUNT YOU NEED COMES OUT.
WOOSH
AH, I SEE.
THIS IS HANDY.
Hmm...
HA!
He's so serious ...
SPLASH
KOFF
WHAT ARE YOU LOOKING FOR?
WHERE'S YOUR CLAY POT?
Oh.
CHII BURNED IT THE OTHER DAY...
... SO WE JUST GOT RID OF IT.

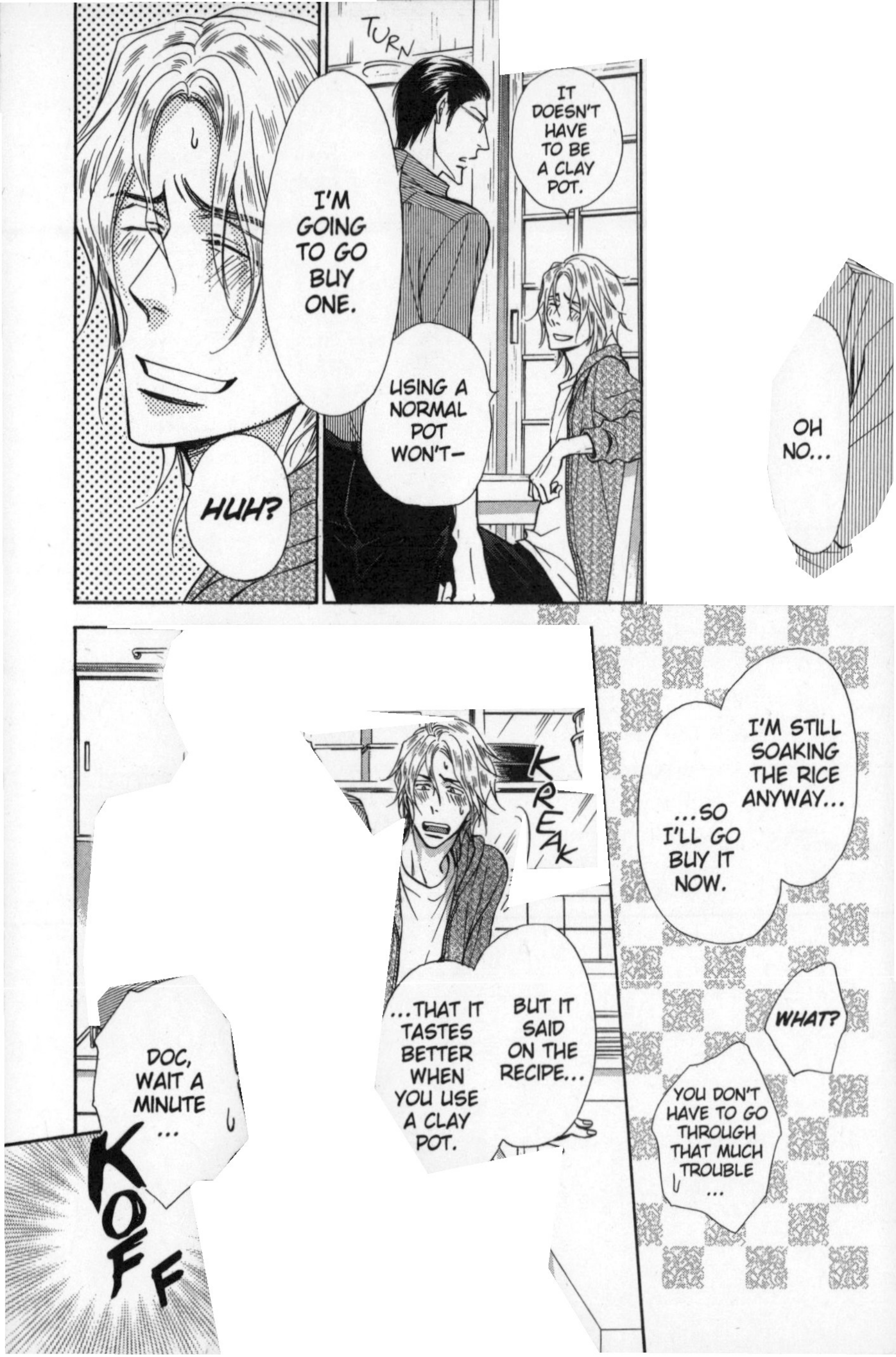
OH NO...
IT DOESN'T HAVE TO BE A CLAY POT.
TURN
I'M GOING TO GO BUY ONE.
USING A NORMAL POT WON'T—
HUH?
I'M STILL SOAKING THE RICE ANYWAY...
...SO I'LL GO BUY IT NOW.
WHAT?
YOU DON'T HAVE TO GO THROUGH THAT MUCH TROUBLE...
KREAK
BUT IT SAID ON THE RECIPE...
...THAT IT TASTES BETTER WHEN YOU USE A CLAY POT.
DOC, WAIT A MINUTE...
KOFF

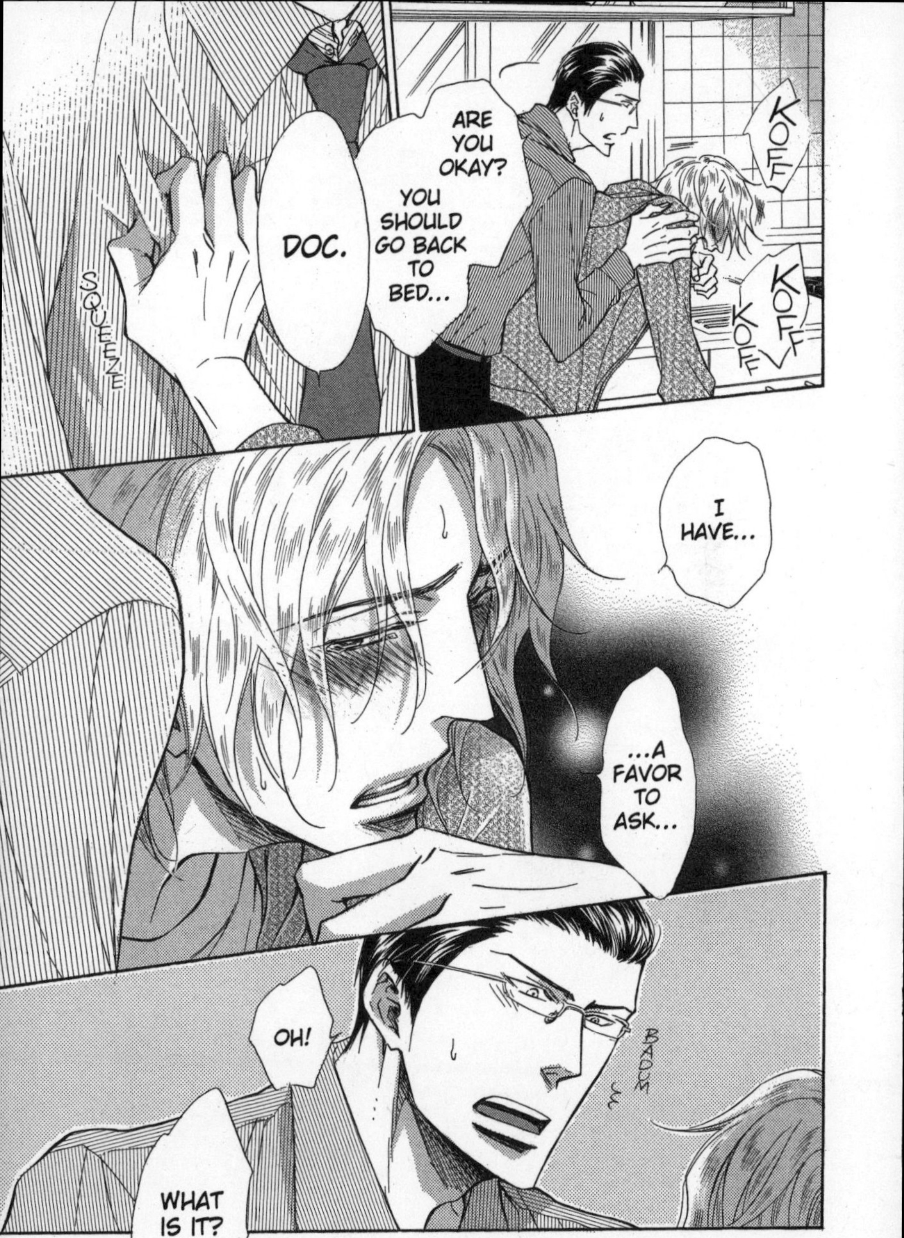
KOFF
KOFF
KOFF
ARE YOU OKAY?
YOU SHOULD GO BACK TO BED...
DOC.
SQUEEZE
I HAVE...
...A FAVOR TO ASK...
BADUM
OH!
WHAT IS IT?

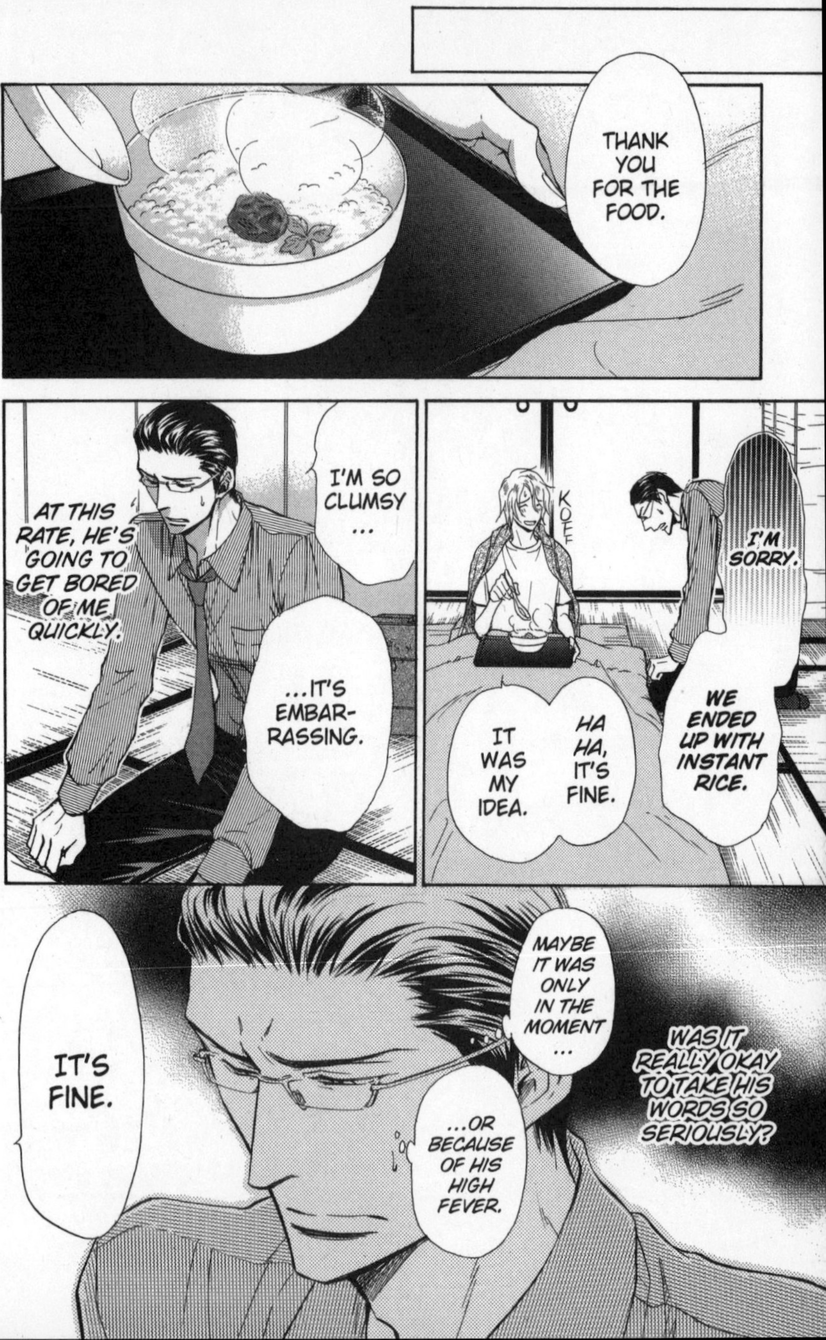
THANK YOU FOR THE FOOD.
I'M SORRY.
WE ENDED UP WITH INSTANT RICE.
KOFF
HA HA, IT'S FINE.
IT WAS MY IDEA.
I'M SO CLUMSY ...
AT THIS RATE, HE'S GOING TO GET BORED OF ME QUICKLY.
...IT'S EMBARRASSING.
WAS IT REALLY OKAY TO TAKE HIS WORDS SO SERIOUSLY?
MAYBE IT WAS ONLY IN THE MOMENT ...
...OR BECAUSE OF HIS HIGH FEVER.
IT'S FINE.

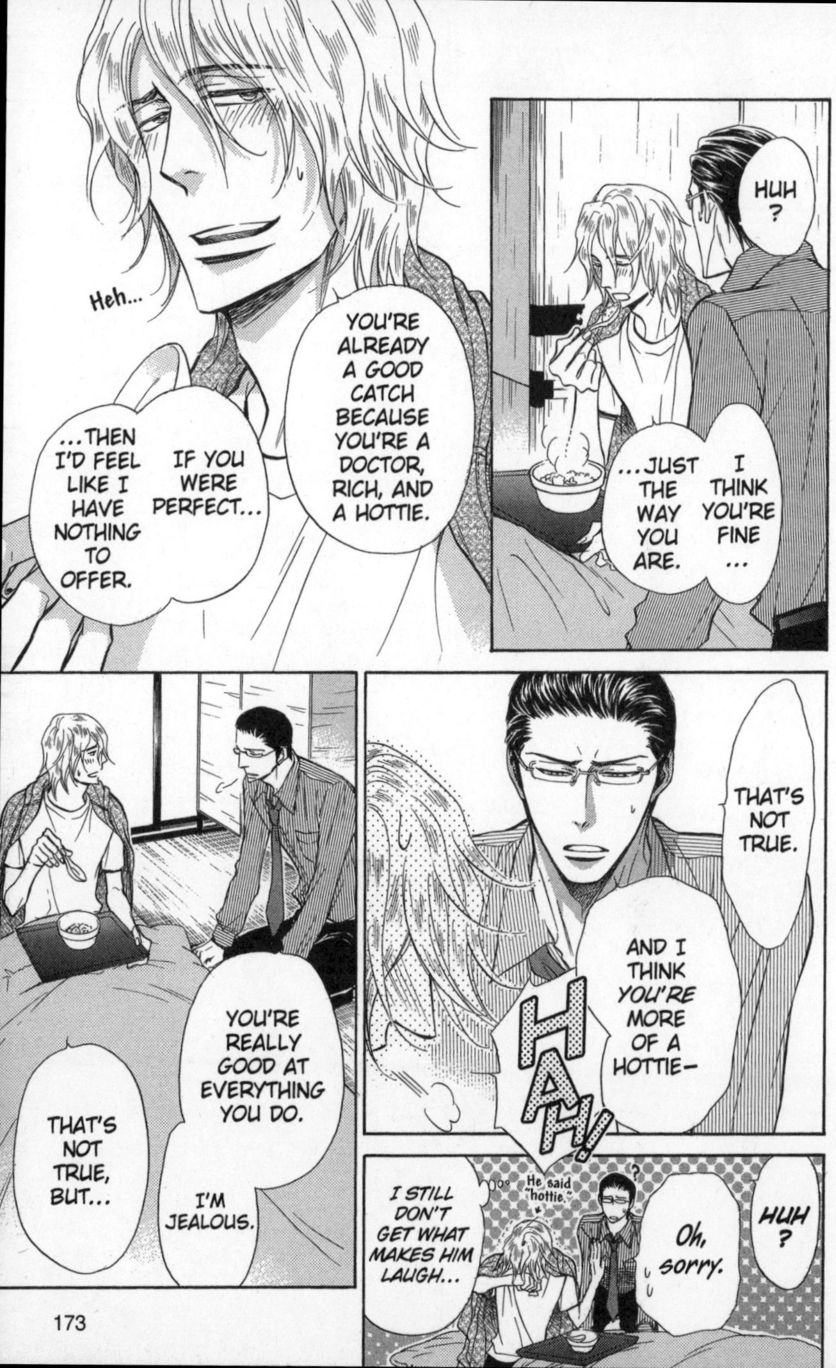
HUH?
I THINK YOU'RE FINE...
...JUST THE WAY YOU ARE.
Heh...
YOU'RE ALREADY A GOOD CATCH BECAUSE YOU'RE A DOCTOR, RICH, AND A HOTTIE.
IF YOU WERE PERFECT...
...THEN I'D FEEL LIKE I HAVE NOTHING TO OFFER.
THAT'S NOT TRUE.
AND I THINK YOU'RE MORE OF A HOTTIE—
HAH!
HUH?
Oh, sorry.
He said "hottie."
I STILL DON'T GET WHAT MAKES HIM LAUGH...
YOU'RE REALLY GOOD AT EVERYTHING YOU DO.
THAT'S NOT TRUE, BUT...
I'M JEALOUS.

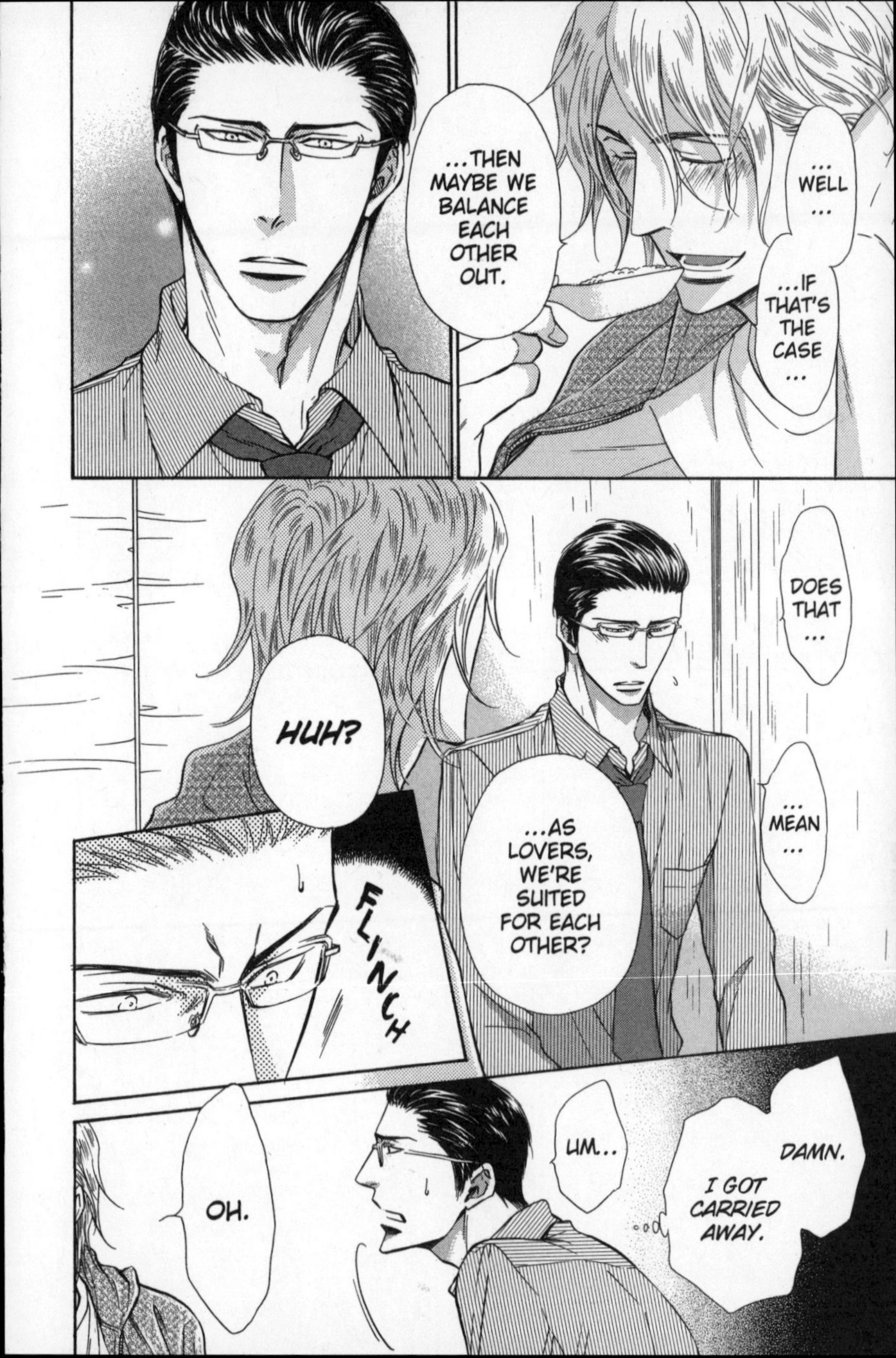
...WELL...
...IF THAT'S THE CASE...
...THEN MAYBE WE BALANCE EACH OTHER OUT.
DOES THAT...
...MEAN...
...AS LOVERS, WE'RE SUITED FOR EACH OTHER?
HUH?
FLINCH
DAMN.
I GOT CARRIED AWAY.
UM...
OH.

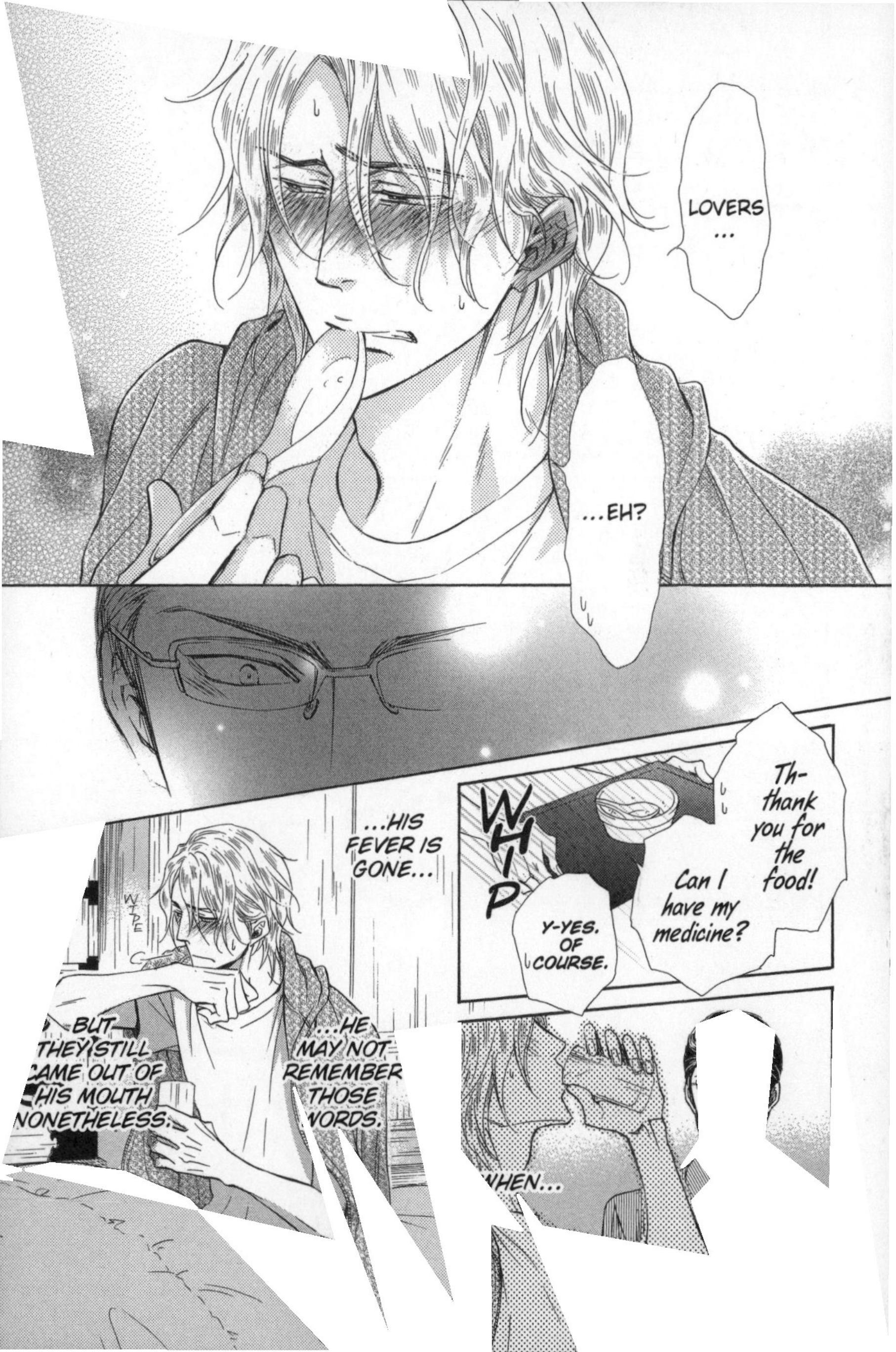
LOVERS ...
...EH?
WHIP
Th-thank you for the food!
Can I have my medicine?
Y-YES. OF COURSE.
WHEN...
...HIS FEVER IS GONE...
WIPE
...HE MAY NOT REMEMBER THOSE WORDS.
BUT THEY STILL CAME OUT OF HIS MOUTH NONETHELESS.

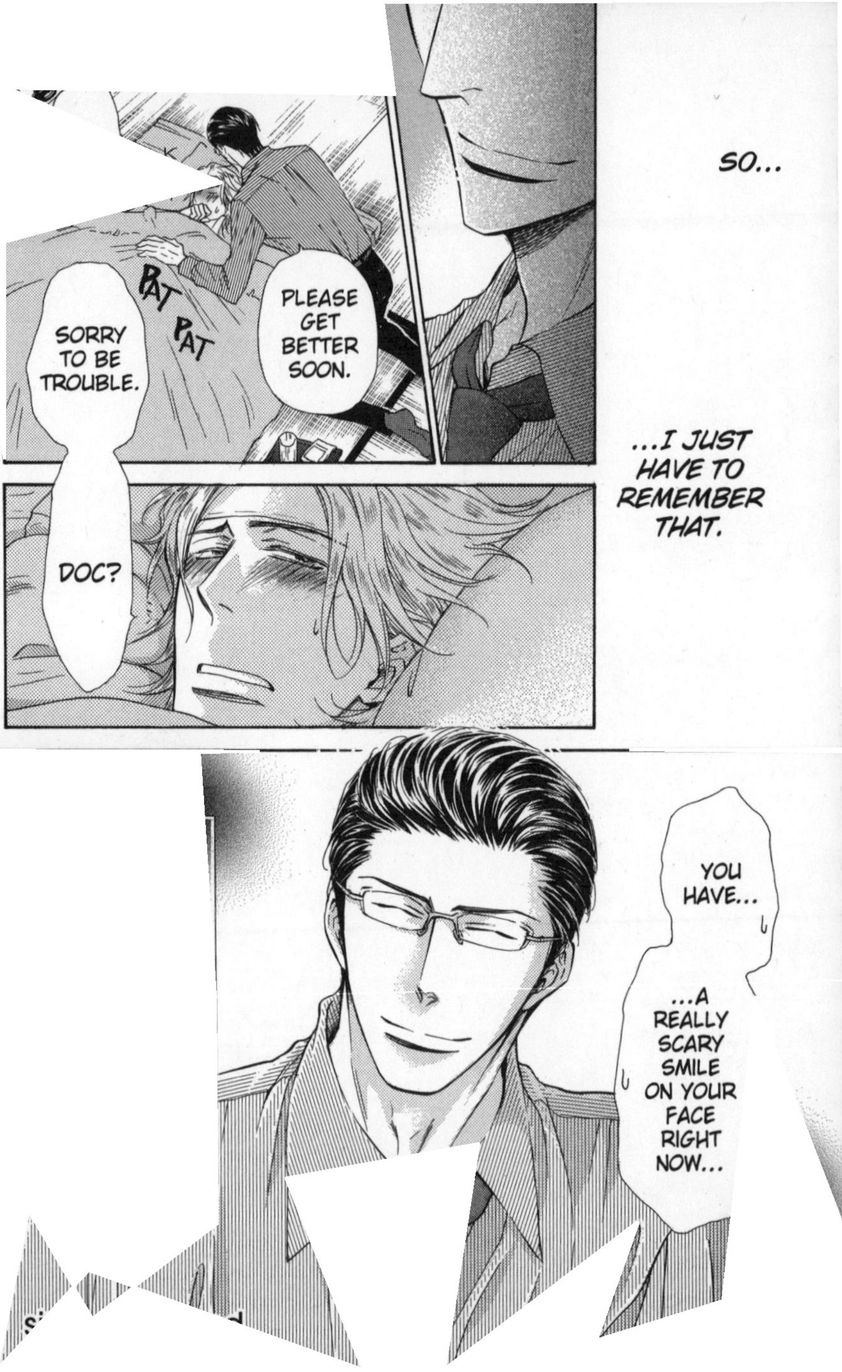
SO...
PLEASE GET BETTER SOON.
PAT PAT
SORRY TO BE TROUBLE.
...I JUST HAVE TO REMEMBER THAT.
DOC?
YOU HAVE...
...A REALLY SCARY SMILE ON YOUR FACE RIGHT NOW...

秘めごとあそび

“Among the candy store toys, my favorite was the balloon you blew up using a straw. But when I looked up the name of it, it sounded like a pharmaceutical product! Like something that would be bad for you! If you're interested, please look it up on the internet!”

About the Author

Yaya Sakuragi's previous English-language releases include *Tea For Two, Hey, Sensei?, Stay Close to Me,* and *Bond of Dreams, Bond of Love.* Also a prolific novel illustrator, she was born July 6th and is a Cancer with an A blood type.

Hide and Seek
Volume 2
SuBLime Manga Edition

Story and Art by **Yaya Sakuragi**

Translation—**Satsuki Yamashita**
Touch-up Art and Lettering—**Annaliese Christman**
Cover and Graphic Design—**Courtney Utt**
Editor—**Jennifer LeBlanc**

HIMEGOTO ASOBI Volume 2
© Yaya SAKURAGI 2013
Edited by KADOKAWA SHOTEN
First published in Japan in 2013 by KADOKAWA CORPORATION, Tokyo.
English translation rights arranged with KADOKAWA CORPORATION, Tokyo.

**ASUKA
COMICS
CL^D_X**

Printed in the U.S.A.

Published by SuBLime Manga
P.O. Box 77010
San Francisco, CA 94107

10 9 8 7 6 5 4 3 2
First printing, March 2014
Second printing, January 2017

www.SuBLimeManga.com

For more information

on all our products, along with the most up-to-date news on releases, series announcements, and contests, please visit us at:

SuBLimeManga.com

twitter.com/**SuBLimeManga**

facebook.com/**SuBLimeManga**

SUBLIME
MANGA

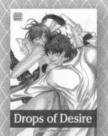

Downloading is as easy as:

1

Login/Email
Password

LOGIN
REGISTER NOW
Forgot Password

2

PAY with **PayPal**

— OR —

Pay Now with **amazon**
The Simple, Trusted Way to Pay

Digital Edition includes **BOTH**
Download-to-own PDF and
online viewing option.

3

View your purchase as:

DOWNLOAD-TO-OWN **PDF**

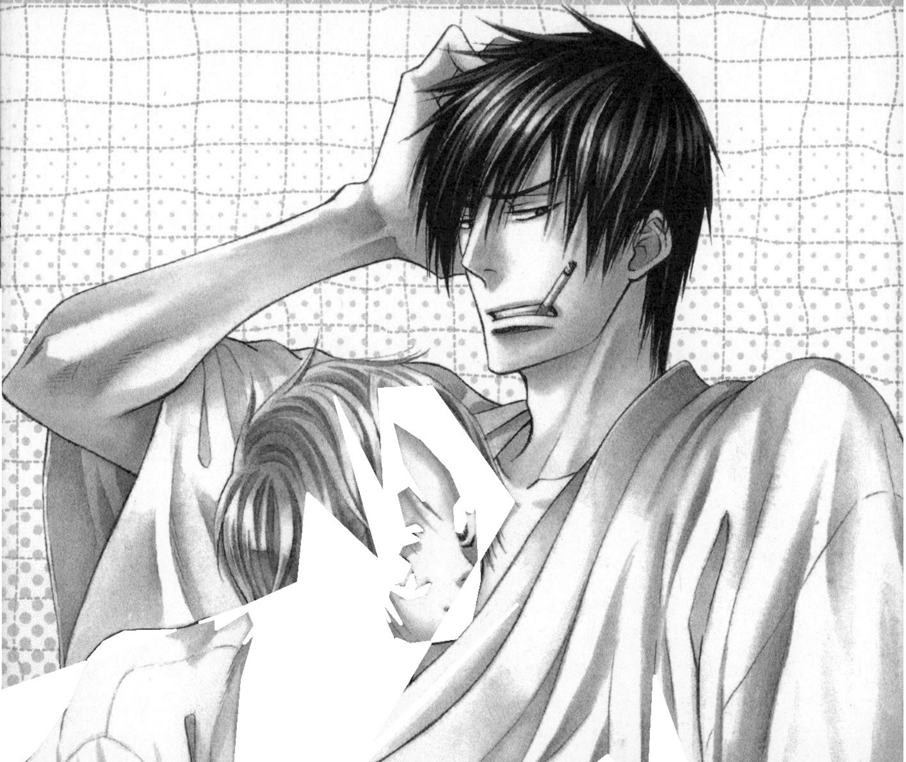

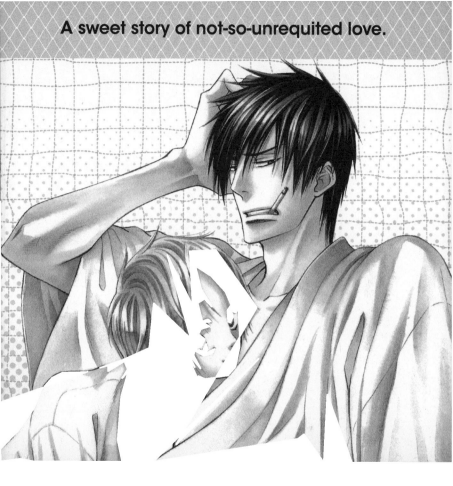

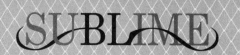

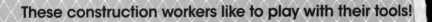